More praise for *Meister Eckhart* by Matthew Fox

"Matthew Fox is among the great theologians, mystics, and intellectuals of our time, and I have long held that he is at his best when teaching and writing about Meister Eckhart. This book is unlike anything I've ever read on Eckhart in that it skillfully and honestly engages Eckhart's work as it can be applied to the great struggles of our day, through the work of some of the great thinkers and activists of modern times. Eckhart is vastly underappreciated, but I think this creative and dialogical approach can lead to a new recognition of his incredible work. Moreover, Meister Eckhart's work is the perfect way to get to know Creation Spirituality, the movement in Western spirituality that Fox has synthesized. And perhaps most importantly, this book, in its masterful weaving of Eckhart's timeless spirituality with the most timely of contemporary movements, radicals, and rebels, can help us to begin to reimagine ourselves at this pivotal moment in human history."

— Theodore Richards, author of *Creatively Maladjusted:*
The Wisdom Education Movement Manifesto and
Cosmosophia: Cosmology, Mysticism, and the Birth of a New Myth

"Matthew Fox's prophetic voice lights up our landscape, which is darkened by unchecked corporate greed, militarism, and intolerance that manifest in the massive destruction of all life-forms on our planet. Using the profound teachings of Meister Eckhart, Fox encourages, inspires, and guides us to take action to realize our own inner power and to make each of our days count. The wisdom contained in this book will help us to meet our responsibility in this critical time of human history. It is a must-read."

— Lily Yeh, Barefoot Artist

"Matthew Fox, like Meister Eckhart, is a prophet whose message transcends his, or any, religion. He reveals a thrilling potential for a kind of cosmic wholeness in us that we may never have imagined but that is actually supported by modern cosmology and could help heal our world. With both empathic understanding and extraordinary intellectual command, Fox lets a wide range of important thinkers, religious and secular, male and female, Eastern and Western, speak for themselves, echoing in many ways Eckhart's far earlier discoveries. Fox makes the mystical practical. He quotes Heschel — 'Wonder rather than doubt is the root of knowledge' — and adds that not seeing this is the reason our education system bores kids and fails to inspire them.

The diametric opposite of religious writers who ignore or even deny science that appears to conflict with their dogma, Fox thirsts to understand modern science and regrets only that Eckhart did not have the chance. One of Eckhart's deepest insights, centuries ahead of his time, was that "we are all interdependent." Fox illustrates this with the recent discovery that we humans are almost entirely made of the rarest material in the universe — stardust, which is a mere 0.01 percent of cosmic density — but that stardust came into existence only because of the behavior of the other

99.99 percent of the content of the universe over billions of years. This is truly a vast amplification of Eckhart's fundamental idea.

For Fox, mysticism is a human, not a religious, path, and through Christianity, Buddhism, Judaism, Islam, or any other tradition (perhaps even science), 'we come to a common underground river of wisdom.' And he doesn't want anyone's metaphor system to get in the way of their seeing it. If, as one of the mystics (Baal Shem Tov) that Fox quotes taught, we can experience a trace of heaven on Earth, and joy, love, and even ecstasy in daily life, many people would trade their wealth for this. Fox asks only that we trade our superficiality."

— Nancy Ellen Abrams and Joel Primack, authors of
The View from the Center of the Universe

"Along with Matthew Fox's ever-engaging scholarship and style, I am moved by his generosity. He not only gives us his beloved spiritual father as a living presence for our lives but also brings us a whole rainbow of mystic-warriors as companions on the way. From Carl Jung to Karl Marx to Adrienne Rich and Lily Yeh, they each serve as a lens through which we see more vividly Meister Eckhart's meaning for this moment of our journey."

— Joanna Macy, coauthor of
Active Hope: How to Face the Mess We're in without Going Crazy

"Matthew Fox is perhaps the greatest writer on Meister Eckhart that has ever existed. No one paints as broad a portrait of the master as Fox does in this book. He has walked with Eckhart, as a living presence, for over forty years. From modern feminism to archaic shamanism, C. G. Jung to Otto Rank, Ananda Coomaraswamy to Bill Everson, Fox has successfully bridged a gap between Eckhart as a shamanistic personality and Eckhart as a postmodern mentor to the interfaith movement, revealing just how cosmic Eckhart really is and how remarkably relevant to today's religious crisis! This book is a must for anyone who wants to know Eckhart intimately, in the now."

— Steven Herrmann, author of *Spiritual Democracy:
The Wisdom of Early American Visionaries for the Journey Forward*

"Whether our species has a future on Earth does not depend on the development of more gee-whiz technologies, but on whether we are willing to move into the psycho-spiritual dimension proclaimed by Meister Eckhart and elucidated by Matthew Fox in this important book. *Now* is our moment to awaken to the God-consciousness that Eckhart knew, and that many in our own time have already claimed, as Fox shows. This intrinsic aspect of who we are does not have to be acquired, for it already exists as part of our original equipment. In this endeavor, however, time is not on our side. Urgency is afoot. On this crucial journey, let Meister Eckhart and Matthew Fox be your guides."

— Larry Dossey, MD, author of *One Mind:
How Our Individual Mind Is Part of a Greater Consciousness and Why It Matters*

MEISTER ECKHART

Books by Matthew Fox

Letters to Pope Francis: Rebuilding a Church with Justice and Compassion

Occupy Spirituality: A Radical Vision for a New Generation (with Adam Bucko)

Hildegard of Bingen: A Saint for Our Times:
Unleashing Her Power in the 21st Century

The Pope's War: Why Ratzinger's Secret Crusade Has Imperiled
the Church and What Can Be Saved

Christian Mystics: 365 Readings and Meditations

The Hidden Spirituality of Men: Ten Metaphors to Awaken the Sacred Masculine

The A.W.E. Project: Reinventing Education, Reinventing the Human

A New Reformation: Creation Spirituality & the Transformation of Christianity

Creativity: Where the Divine and the Human Meet

Prayer: A Radical Response to Life
(formerly *On Becoming a Musical, Mystical Bear*)

One River, Many Wells: Wisdom Springing from Global Faiths

Sins of the Spirit, Blessings of the Flesh:
Lessons for Transforming Evil in Soul and Society

The Physics of Angels (with biologist Rupert Sheldrake)

Natural Grace (with biologist Rupert Sheldrake)

Wrestling with the Prophets: Essays on Creation Spirituality and Everyday Life

The Reinvention of Work: A New Vision of Livelihood for Our Time

Sheer Joy: Conversations with Thomas Aquinas on Creation Spirituality

Creation Spirituality: Liberating Gifts for the Peoples of the Earth

The Coming of the Cosmic Christ:
The Healing of Mother Earth and the Birth of a Global Renaissance

Illuminations of Hildegard of Bingen

Original Blessing: A Primer in Creation Spirituality

Meditations with Meister Eckhart

A Spirituality Named Compassion

Confessions: The Making of a Post-denominational Priest

Hildegard of Bingen's Book of Divine Works, Songs & Letters

Whee! We, Wee All the Way Home: A Guide to Sensual, Prophetic Spirituality

Religion USA: Religion and Culture by Way of Time Magazine

Manifesto for a Global Civilization (with Brian Swimme)

Passion for Creation: Meister Eckhart's Creation Spirituality
(formerly *Breakthrough: Meister Eckhart's Creation Spirituality in New Translation*)

In the Beginning There Was Joy (children's book)

Western Spirituality: Historical Roots, Ecumenical Routes, editor

MEISTER ECKHART

A Mystic-Warrior for Our Times

Matthew Fox

New World Library
Novato, California

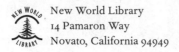 New World Library
14 Pamaron Way
Novato, California 94949

Text design by Tona Pearce Myers

Library of Congress Cataloging-in-Publication Data
Fox, Matthew, 1940–
Meister Eckhart : a mystic-warrior for our times / Matthew Fox.
    pages   cm
Includes bibliographical references.
ISBN 978-1-60868-265-2 (pbk. : alk. paper) — ISBN (invalid) 978-1-60868-266-9 (ebook : alk. paper)
1. Eckhart, Meister, –1327. I. Title.
B765.E34F67 2014
230'.2092—dc23   2014008787

First printing, July 2014
ISBN 978-1-60868-265-2
Printed in Canada on 100% postconsumer-waste recycled paper

 New World Library is proud to be a Gold Certified Environmentally Responsible Publisher. Publisher certification awarded by Green Press Initiative. www.greenpressinitiative.org

10   9   8   7   6   5   4   3

To all those today, young and old, East and West, male and female,
gay and straight, being called before time runs out on our species
to be spiritual warriors on behalf of Mother Earth...and leaders
in the next and crucial stage of human evolution and expansion of consciousness.
May Meister Eckhart challenge and inspire us all.

"What is life? God's being is my life."
— MEISTER ECKHART

CONTENTS

INTRODUCTION

It is a great privilege to be presenting Meister Eckhart. Eckhart is a man for our times, a mystic-warrior for our age, and I am eager to see him better known and more deeply understood. I hope this book brings him to an ever-expanding audience. Meister Eckhart deserves to be present in all our conversations about interfaith, in all our interspiritual dialogues and actions.

Meister Eckhart was a late-thirteenth- and early-fourteenth-century preacher and mystic, yet like Rumi and Hafiz, he remains relevant today. He speaks to so many and touches people's hearts. Postmodern times are well served by premodern thinkers, especially when it comes to caring about cosmos and psyche. It was modern consciousness, not our ancient ancestors, who split psyche from cosmos. Today's new cosmology offers an opportunity to remarry the two, and Eckhart can be a leader in such an effort, as are the wisdom teachers of indigenous traditions.

Carl Jung says that "it is to the mystics that we owe what is best in humanity," and "only the mystic brings what is creative to religion itself." In this time, humanity is on a death spiral and none of our modern institutions are working. This includes religion, which is embarrassing itself profoundly with papal corruption and Protestant ennui in the West and with fundamentalist aggression in portions of Islam, Judaism, and Christianity. Clearly, religion needs re-creating. This is the kind of thing Eckhart and other deep mystics can inspire.

Jung warned Westerners: "What it has taken China thousands of years to build cannot be grasped by theft.... Of what use to us is the wisdom of the Upanishads or the insight of Chinese yoga, if we desert the foundations of our own culture as though they were errors outlived and, like homeless pirates, settle with thievish intent on foreign shores?" With Eckhart, we touch the depths of Western culture's wisdom, which connects to the depths of Eastern wisdom. We can reach these depths as we begin to know the truth of the Western tradition as Eckhart lays it out for us.

Today's seekers want less religion and more experience or spirituality. Eckhart is the best of the best from the Western tradition. He is not only about deep contemplation but about deep action — otherwise he would not have been put on trial by a corrupt papacy and condemned by the same. In his day, he took on the vested power interests of patriarchy and of economic privilege and of religiosity — and he paid a steep price for it. After his papal condemnation, his work was buried deep in the Western consciousness for centuries. Now is the time to resurrect it. This book is both introductory and substantive. Eckhart is far too important a historic figure and too profound a teacher to be merely introduced. He holds secrets to many of today's most pressing problems of conscience, consciousness, and culture.

His own Deep Ecumenism, his ecology and green thinking, his shamanism, his extolling of creativity and the artist, his warriorhood on behalf of economic and gender justice, his sense of humor, his courage to speak truth to power and to undergo the price for it, his naming of both an Apophatic and a Cataphatic Divinity — all speak to today's deepest spiritual and cultural needs. Young people especially ought to be as awakened by his message as were his contemporaries, who made him the most popular preacher of his time.

Why This Book?

This is my third book on Meister Eckhart. My two previous books, written over thirty years ago, were quite different from each other. One, *Meditations with Meister Eckhart*, was a right-brain book — a book intended for meditation purposes with just a simple sentence or two from him on each page. It was a way to get Eckhart into the world and into our hearts. The second,

Passion for Creation: The Earth-Honoring Spirituality of Meister Eckhart, was a 580-page tome containing thirty-eight of his sermons (including treatises and biblical commentaries), each with a commentary by myself that also presented other of his writings. Originally called *Breakthrough: Meister Eckhart's Creation Spirituality in New Translation,* the book contained translations rendered by a professional translator with over forty-five years of experience translating German philosophy into English. Mine was the first translation into English from the critical editions of Josef Quint.

My introduction to Eckhart, to his times and his work, in *Passion for Creation* still holds (except for a few minor historical findings since) as a solid and substantive background. I have also published three in-depth articles on Meister Eckhart, including "Meister Eckhart on the Fourfold Path of a Creation-Centered Spiritual Journey," for it was in studying Eckhart that I discovered the four paths of Creation Spirituality. In addition, I published "Meister Eckhart and Karl Marx: The Mystic as Political Theologian" and "Creation-Centered Spirituality from Hildegard of Bingen to Julian of Norwich: 300 Years of an Ecological Spirituality in the West."

In addition, I have taught Eckhart countless times in master's and doctoral programs in a number of institutions, but especially at my own Institute for Culture and Creation Spirituality (since closed) and my University of Creation Spirituality. I have seen so many students come alive, become healed, become juiced, and get to the heart of the Christian message by interacting with Eckhart. I see so much in today's New Testament scholarship that corresponds to Eckhart's biblical perspective, including a critical understanding of the difference between Jesus and Christ; panentheism, that is, God in us and us in God; an understanding of the Christ that each of us is meant to be; and much more. I have found many who do not identify as Christian — Buddhists and Jews and Hindus and Sufis and Goddess worshippers and indigenous peoples — turned on by Eckhart's language and perspective.

It is time to put Meister Eckhart into the world anew as all of us, no matter what our faith path or lack thereof, face our tumultuous times, which include planetary devastation, reptilian-brain-driven wars and rumors of wars, religious strife, patriarchal aggression, and ecclesial malfeasance. Eckhart speaks to the deepest in the human condition. He calls forth the mystic and prophet, the contemplative and the activist in all of us.

The Method of This Book

In this book I follow the basic methodology I created to bring Hildegard of Bingen into today's world in *Hildegard of Bingen, a Saint for Our Times: Unleashing Her Power for the Twenty-First Century.* That is to say, I put Eckhart in the room with twentieth-century thinkers and activists — from Rabbi Heschel to David Korten, from Black Elk to Lily Yeh, from Adrienne Rich to Teilhard de Chardin, from Thich Nhat Hanh to Anita Roddick, from Marcus Borg and John Dominic Crossan to Carl Jung and Father Bede Griffiths, and more. I think this is the surest, and most fun, way to see Eckhart at work in our time. His teachings are deep and universal. They touch us profoundly and have the potential to move us to the next level of human evolution. Readers will be deeply immersed in his thoughts and ideas as they read his words in a modern context.

One caveat: Any one of these dialogues with Eckhart could easily fill a book by itself (in fact, a friend of mine is working on a book on Jung and Eckhart). Thus, the dialogues by no means exhaust the connections between Eckhart and these other thinkers. They are suggestive and open the door, I hope, to further interactions. The chapters are not discrete or separate, either — rather, the themes gradually build. Sometimes they spiral on into other chapters and other thinkers, with the deliberate intention to keep the dialogue going ever deeper in the heart and mind of the reader as the book progresses.

Many of today's problematic challenges are addressed by Eckhart's genius and within the wide breadth of his interests. Whether we are talking about the lost God of joy and wonder, or today's cosmology and ecology, or the gifts from Buddhism or Hinduism or Sufism or indigenous wisdom, or depth psychology, or the blessings from the return of the Divine Feminine and women's empowerment, or a healthy direction for our economics and education, Eckhart offers wisdom for our journey as individuals and as communities.

Eckhart's Life in a Glance

Eckhart was born near Hocheim, Germany, in 1260. It appears his ancestors had been knights and horsemen. At about the age of seventeen, he left for Cologne to join the Dominican Order, where he studied briefly with the scientist-philosopher Albert the Great (who had been Thomas Aquinas's professor in the order) before Albert died. Just about the time of Eckhart's entrance into the order, Aquinas died. Almost immediately three bishops condemned Aquinas's work for being too willing to integrate body and soul, spirit and matter, and essentially for preferring Aristotle over Plato. All his life as a Dominican, Eckhart lived under the shadow of this suspect Dominican theologian, his brother Thomas Aquinas. It was only near the time of Eckhart's own death that Aquinas emerged from the shadows and was canonized a saint.

Eckhart studied at the University of Paris (where Aquinas had taught), and he taught there on three occasions. The last was in 1311, just a year after theologian Marguerite Porete was burned at the stake (for more on this, see chapter five). Eckhart held positions of considerable administrative responsibility as provincial in Germany and Bohemia and as prior in Erfurt, Germany. We have about one hundred of his German sermons, three of his treatises, and a number of his exegetical works (written in Latin). He was the most visible and popular preacher of his day, and this drew scrutiny as well as political attacks from powers that be in the financial as well as political and ecclesial worlds. Toward the end of his life he was put on trial in Cologne, a trial that he did not lose. But shortly afterward, he was called to Avignon, France, where Pope John XXII resided. There, Eckhart underwent another trial, and twenty-nine of his statements, a number taken out of context, were condemned. The latest historical scholarship has concluded that he died while still in Avignon and a week before the papal bull condemning him was promulgated. The year was 1329.   *AGE 69*

Eckhart's condemnation was tragic for Christianity, as it raised doubts about his spirituality of engaged and prophetic mysticism. Other spiritual movements to follow, such as that led by Thomas à Kempis, were excessively introspective and not at all oriented toward the spirituality of creation and toward social justice. One wonders if the Reformation could have been averted had Eckhart's theology been promulgated instead of condemned. While Luther was influenced indirectly through Eckhart's disciple John Tauler and also the work called *Theological Germanica,* it was the radical Protestants (such as Hans Hutt, Sebastian Franck, and Hans Denck) who most employed Eckhart's teachings, especially those about every creature as a word of God.

Eckhart's influence has extended to many more, however. Eckhart's ideas have affected thinkers and activists of all kinds through the centuries. Here is a short list: Carl Jung, Karl Marx, Thomas Merton, Bill Everson, David Suzuki, Dorothee Soelle, Rufus Jones, Martin Luther, Julian of Norwich, John of the Cross, Teresa of Avila, Rudolf Otto, Erich Fromm, Ernst Bloch, Josiah Royce, Martin Heidegger, Friedrich Schelling, Hegel, Angelus Silesius, Ignatius of Loyola, Howard Thurman, Saint Paul of the Cross, Thomas Munzer, Jacob Boehme, John Tauler, Nicholas of Cusa, Walter Hilton, Jan van Ruysbroeck, Saul Bellow, John Updike, Annie Dillard, Anne Morrow Lindbergh, Ira Progoff, Eckhart Tolle, Martin Buber, Martin Luther King Jr., Dag Hammerskjold, and Robert Mueller.

Modern Translations of Eckhart

We can be happy that all of Eckhart's German sermons now exist in a critical English translation, done by M. O'C. Walshe, a practicing Buddhist. Unfortunately, however, I feel that Walshe makes several serious mistakes in his translations. The most important is rendering the word "mercy" in place of "compassion." These words are not interchangeable, especially from a biblical and Jewish perspective. I tackled this distinction thirty-five years ago in *A Spirituality Named Compassion,* which was strongly influenced by Meister Eckhart. "Mercy" in English has come to mean a sort of "buffer" between judgment and the person judged. But in fact, true compassion is about justice and about being with the oppressed in solidarity — Eckhart himself teaches this in his brilliant exegesis of Luke 6:26, which I translated in my major work *Passion for Creation.* There he says: "Compassion means justice."

As I note in *A Spirituality Named Compassion,* citing biblical scholar Jose Miranda:

> *"The path of which I speak is beautiful and pleasant, joyful and familiar."*

"Biblical compassion is not condescension; it is unreserved commitment to the weak, the poor, and the oppressed. It acknowledges their rights; it is identical to an absolute sense of justice."....The Christian empire distorted the Jewish words for justice, namely *saphat* and *mispat*, translating them as "judgment," when in fact they meant "justice." Jose Miranda says that "the true meaning of *saphat* is not 'to judge' but rather 'to do justice to the weak and oppressed.'"

Nor am I alone in this assessment. Contemporary biblical scholar Marcus Borg makes a similar point when he writes: "Compassion is quite different from mercy, and being compassionate quite different from being merciful. In English *mercy* and *merciful* most commonly imply a superior in relationship to a subordinate, and also a situation of wrongdoing: one is merciful toward somebody to whom one has the right (or power) to act otherwise. *Compassion* suggests something else." It is a pity that Walshe ignored my work and that historian Bernard McGinn, when he reissued these translations in 2010, continued to ignore the biblical basis of Eckhart's treatment of compassion and acquiesced to Walshe's mistranslation of a term so important to Eckhart's theology.

Another mistake in Walshe's translation is equating "spark of the soul" with "synderesis," when in fact synderesis is the threshold to conscience, not conscience itself. I also decry his translating "Holy Spirit" as "Holy Ghost." I thought we moved beyond ghostliness in our theological language many years ago. Walshe also translates "person" as "man" exclusively, which is the opposite of Eckhart's gender justice consciousness. Finally, one wonders why, on several occasions, Walshe attacks quite mercilessly the work of Ms. Evans, who translated Eckhart from the Pfeiffer editions in 1924 and 1931. Nevertheless, taking these caveats into account, it is a good thing to have all the German corpus of Eckhart in English. However, rather than relying on Walshe, I will offer my own translations here for the most part — those from my critical translation of *Breakthrough* (later called *Passion for Creation*) and translations from other sermons appearing here for the first time. For that I was assisted most ably by Katherine L. Ziegler, PhD, whose mystical sensitivity as well as linguistic acumen in middle German was most appreciated. Note that each of the block quotes in the book is a citation from Meister Eckhart.

Where Might Eckhart Lead Us?

Once we grasp the heart of Eckhart's teachings, we find that they take us away from sterile and external religion to a deep spirituality, one that imbues every dimension of our conscience and consciousness. His teachings put Christ back into Christianity and offer a "Christ Path" that is far deeper than institutional Christianity has put forward for centuries. They also offer a living bridge between all world spiritual traditions, without which the human species cannot, it seems to me, survive.

By the end of this book, where is Eckhart leading us? He leads us to the land of the mystic-warrior, to the land where our action flows from being or nonaction, from contemplation, from love — from the Cataphatic Divinity. And, yes, also from our brokenness, our wounds, our grief, as well as our silence — from the Apophatic Divinity. This is one reason today that so many feel a calling to go deeper, travel deeper, take on spirituality as distinct from mere religion. We all feel the call, consciously or unconsciously, from Gaia, from Mother Earth, from our children and grandchildren and ancestors to come, from Spirit, to change our ways. To undergo metanoia — or conversion, rebirth, waking up, or all of the above.

To do this we need to be lovers again who are more in love with the world than ever. More grateful for existence, for the nourishing and beautiful Earth, for her marvelous creatures, for her suffering, than ever before. More struck by reverence and respect for the miracle of our being here, the gift of existence in this amazing universe with its 13.8-billion-year history — "isness is God," says Eckhart. Eckhart takes us there, for he is a lover and a traveler into the deep. He is both mystic and warrior.

What distinguishes a warrior from a soldier is that a warrior is a mystic, a lover, one possessed by beauty, one alive with radical amazement, one seized by the Cataphatic Divinity, the God of Light and Creation. It takes a warrior to become a mystic, for the mystic cannot survive in denial; the mystic hunts everywhere in search of his or her beloved. "Where have you hid my beloved?" asks the lover in the Song of Songs. This lamentation also begins "Spiritual Canticle," the love poem by John of the Cross: "Where have you hidden, Beloved, and left me moaning?" We search the highways and the byways, as John of the Cross did, and we eventually come to this holy aware-ness. "My Beloved is the mountains, / and lonely wooded valleys...."

Like the historical Jesus who derives from the wisdom tradition of Israel (a fact that Eckhart knew well and today's New Testament scholarship is finally rediscovering), Eckhart, too, is steeped in the wisdom or creation-centered tradition of the scriptures wherein all of nature is revelatory, a "book about God," as Eckhart puts it.

So it is with us at this precarious moment. Are we sustainable? Only if we "become sweet lovers," says Hafiz. Only if we become mystic-warriors. Only if we not only fall in love but develop the astuteness to defend our beloved, the Earth, with all of our resources at hand. Our left brains of analy-sis and rationality are essential; as Eckhart says, "We are compassionate like the Father when we are compassionate, not from passion, not from impulse, but from deliberate choice and reasonable decision.... The passion does not take the lead but follows, does not rule but serves." Our right brains of intu-ition, imagination, creativity, and mysticism are essential, too. We need to create learning centers and wisdom schools where both are honored. We need to resurrect common values — which is not that hard, since atheist and Buddhist, Jew and Muslim, Christian and Goddess worshipper, indigenous and Taoist, can recognize four things: 1) the Earth is sacred, and 2) the Earth is in trouble, and 3) we humans are greatly responsible for the latter, and 4) we can, with imagination and work and strength, do something to posi-tively change that.

Eckhart helps to carry us to this new level of evolution, this deeper expression of what it means to be human at this time in history. He asks that we live in depth, not superficially, whether we are talking about reli-gion or education, economics or ecology. "Deep Ecology" is a phrase coined decades ago to name an ecological movement that was not merely about switching the hats of power but of going deeper into the land of the sacred, the place where in our deepest intuition (Eckhart would say, in the "spark of the soul" from which conscience is born) dwells the Divine and all the angels and spirit helpers who can assist us in this shamanistic vocation to heal so that the people may live. We need all the resources we possess as a species — sci-ence and technology along with our varied spiritual traditions.

We need what I call in the conclusion the four Es: we must awaken Deep

Ecumenism, Deep Ecology, Deep Economics, and Deep Education. Deep Ecumenism is in many ways the starting point, since without a spiritual depth and practice it is unimaginable that we will have the energy or the vision for the letting go and the birthing that survival will require. Eckhart is a leader like none other in Deep Ecumenism. I think this book demonstrates that. Who else has worked out of the depth of his own tradition (his Christianity) and has been named a Hindu by Hindus; a Buddhist by Buddhists; a Sufi by Sufis; a depth psychologist who discovered the self by a depth psychologist; a shaman by students of shamanism?

Not ecology as we know it; not education as we know it; not economics as we know it; not religion as we know it — none of these things is currently up to the task at hand. We need to go deeper. Just as Adrienne Rich and Meister Eckhart tell us, diving deep and also surfacing. Moving inward and outward, but always deeply. Deep where the joy resides (via positiva); where the darkness, pain, and grief cry to us (via negativa); where creativity is unearthed (via creativa); where the passion for justice and compassion return again (via transformativa).

We need ecological mystic-warriors, ecumenical mystic-warriors, educational mystic-warriors, and economic mystic-warriors. *There* is where Eckhart is leading us. Down and deep and dirty, in the sense that we are on new terrain, that there will be trial and error, but it is better to be in the dark than overly confident in a diminishing and damaging light. Eckhart leads us to a new and deeper marriage of Divine Feminine and Sacred Masculine. We can no longer put off the need to balance our masculine and feminine natures — personally, collectively, and in all of our institutions. These are common values we can all hold dear and act from. Eckhart takes us there.

Poet Bill Everson makes the point that for the East the mandala is the principal archetype, but for Westerners it is vocation, since for us action is the way to salvation. He views the East as "essentially a contemplative society," and therefore its controlling symbol is the mandala, "while the controlling symbol in the West, which lays its accent on action, is vocation. I think vocation is to us what the mandala is to them. It's vocation that integrates us, gives us our wholeness, and takes our acts from the linear world to the cyclical, collective world." As East and West come together, we need to marry compassion with action, the mandala with vocation or holy work. Service and compassion and justice are actions. Eckhart brings them together. So do the four paths that are, in fact, a mandala. East and West are today awakening to this common truth. Eckhart invokes both.

Along the way Meister Eckhart is a very special guide — he challenges us all. His leadership calls us to a new level of evolution and consciousness. He calls us to leave old wineskins behind. Such a leap is not an option. We are talking about our survival as a species. Nor is Eckhart's call a burden. As he said, "The path of which I speak is beautiful and pleasant, joyful and familiar." My hope in offering this book is that, on reading it and praying it, the reader will grow in appreciation of Eckhart, but above all the reader will grow in appreciating the mystic-warrior within, which requires nurturing and educating to come to ripeness and maturity. Eckhart is a superb gardener for your mystic-warrior, a planter of seeds and waterer of the same. May your path be beautiful and pleasant, joyful and familiar, and may it develop a strong and courageous heart.

CHAPTER ONE

THE GOD OF AWE, WONDER, RADICAL AMAZEMENT, AND JUSTICE

Meister Eckhart Meets Rabbi Heschel

Awareness of the divine begins with wonder.

— RABBI HESCHEL

All that exists rejoices in its existence.

— MEISTER ECKHART

This chapter puts Rabbi Abraham Joshua Heschel and Meister Eckhart in the room together and asks: What did they preach in common, this early-fourteenth-century Dominican of the Christian lineage and this twentieth-century rabbi of the Jewish Hasidic tradition? To begin at the beginning, we will look at the principal themes of wonder, awe, radical amazement, reverence, gratitude, and the divine presence as Shekinah. All these are responses to the God of Light and the God of creation, which is called classically the "Cataphatic Divinity."

Heschel wrote many books, and he called his work "depth theology," meaning a theology that digs "beneath the dogmas and traditional formulations of the Judeo-Christian traditions which so often have served as substitute for the root experiences of biblical faith." He has been called "the outstanding Jewish thinker of his generation" and "the most productive and by far the best theological mind in modern and contemporary Judaism." Protestant Reinhold Niebuhr called him "the most authentic prophet of religious life in our culture."

If Heschel and Eckhart were in a room together, what would they say to each other, and what do they both say to us today?

Rabbi Heschel: A Brand Plucked from the Fire

Born in Warsaw, Poland, on January 11, 1907, Abraham Joshua Heschel was a descendant in a long line of rabbis that can be traced back to the late fifteenth century. Over seven prior generations, all his male ancestors were Hasidic rabbis. His mother's side also contained historically significant rabbis. Thus, one person commented that Heschel was related "to almost every important Hasidic 'dynasty' in Europe." Understandably, Heschel grew up in a rich milieu of Jewish spiritual piety and practice, and all his life he managed to balance the experiential side of religion with the intellectual side, or in my language, spirituality with theology. As a child he was introduced to two very different Jewish thinkers. One was the eighteenth-century rabbi Reb Baal Shem Tov, who very much preached a God of the via positiva: He found God everywhere and rejoiced in God's presence. He taught people to find a trace of heaven on Earth and inspired joy and ecstasy with an emphasis on love.

The second influence on Heschel from an early age was the nineteenth-century Hasidic master Menahem Mendl of Kotzk, also known as Kotzker. He was very much a preacher of the via negativa who "stormed the heavens" and was, Heschel says, "dreadfully aware of God's absence. Instead of a heaven on earth, he talked about our living in a chamber of hell; instead of joy and ecstasy, he warned of fear and trembling. Instead of love, he taught truth." As Heschel tells us, these two thinkers played out in his soul and work his entire life:

> Years later I realized that, in being guided by both the Baal Shem Tov and the Kotzker, I had allowed two forces to carry on a struggle within me....In a very strange way, I found my soul at home with the Baal Shem but driven by the Kotzker. Was it good to live with one's heart torn between the joy of Mezbizh [the home of the Baal Shem] and the

anxiety of Kotzk? To live in both awe and consternation, in fervor and horror, with my conscience on mercy and my eyes on Auschwitz, wavering between exaltation and dismay? Was this a life a man would choose to live? I had no choice: My heart was in Mezbizh, my mind in Kotzk. I was taught about inexhaustible mines of meaning by the Baal Shem; from the Kotzker I learned to detect immense mountains of absurdity standing in the way. The one taught me song, the other — silence. The one reminded me that there could be a Heaven on earth, the other shocked me into discovering Hell in the alleged Heavenly places in our world.

One senses in the poetry of Heschel's telling the deep dialectic or polarity we all feel between the joy of living and the pain of living. His was an authentic dance between the via positiva and the via negativa experiences of divinity, which Heschel never abandoned his entire lifetime.

As a young man Heschel left his home in Poland to attend the University of Berlin. The year was 1927, and he astutely enrolled *both* at the university and at a Jewish school, the Hochschule für die Wissenschaft des Judentums. Here was another polarity that Heschel wrestled with all his life: how to engage modern non-Jewish society with his rich Jewish heritage. He was critical of his training in philosophy, as he wrote: "In the academic environment in which I spent my student years philosophy had become an isolated, self-subsisting, self-indulgent entity, a *Ding an sich* [thing in itself], encouraging suspicion instead of love of wisdom." After all, "love of wisdom" is the etymological meaning of the word "philosophy." He bemoaned the lack of "human solidarity," how "speculative prosperity is no answer to spiritual bankruptcy," and the "tragic failure of the modern mind, incapable of preventing its own destruction." He chose for his dissertation a study on the prophets, which allowed him to explore "how to think in a Jewish way of thinking." His thesis, published in 1936, became the basis of his classic work *The Prophets*, published in English in 1962 at the height of the civil rights movement in America.

The period between 1936 and 1962 was, of course, a significant chapter in world history. Appointed by Martin Buber to head Jewish Adult Education in Frankfurt, Germany, in 1937, Heschel was deported by the Nazi regime in October 1938. He taught in Warsaw for eight months at a rabbinical seminary, and just six weeks before the Nazis invaded Poland, he left to accept an invitation at the Hebrew Union College in Cincinnati, Ohio. He was thirty-three years old, and he lived in the United States until his death in 1972, five years in Cincinnati and twenty-seven years in New York.

As a professor at Union Theological Seminary in New York, Heschel gave this testimony of his journey and that of his people:

> I speak as a person who was able to leave Warsaw, the city in which I was born, just six weeks before the disaster began. My destination was New York, it would have been Auschwitz or Treblinka. I am a brand plucked from the fire, in which my people was burned to death. I am a brand plucked from the fire of an altar of Satan on which millions of human lives were exterminated to evil's greater glory, and on which so much else was consumed: the divine image of so many human beings, many people's faith in the God of justice and compassion, and much of the secret and power of attachment to the Bible bred and cherished in the heart of men for nearly two thousand years.

Heschel joined the civil rights movement and marched with Dr. Martin Luther King Jr. at Selma and elsewhere. He was not content to theologize about the prophets from the comfort of academic protection but joined the struggle for justice in the streets — and he endured much abuse even from his own Jewish circles for showing such leadership. Like Eckhart, who also fought against educational and religious stagnation as well as against the social injustices of his day, Heschel insisted on renewing religion by putting experience first. "Faith is not a stagnant pool," he said. "It is rather a fountain that rises with the influx of personal experience. Personal faith flows out of an experience and a pledge." He insisted that antecedents of faith, or sources of faith, are needed "because it is useless to offer conclusions of faith to those who do not possess the prerequisites of faith." In other words, one renews religion by way of spirituality. In doing so, as Jewish scholar Fritz Rothschild put it, "Heschel has propounded a truly revolutionary doctrine challenging the whole venerable tradition of Jewish and Christian metaphysical theology."

When Heschel and Eckhart get together, do they both challenge the whole venerable tradition of Jewish and Christian theology still?

Awe, Wonder, and Radical Amazement

"Everything praises God," says Meister Eckhart, and Heschel declares that "what we lack is not a will to believe but a will to wonder." Rabbi Heschel says we ought to "stand still and behold!" Why? "Behold not only in order to explain, to fit what we see into our notions; behold in order to stand face to face with the beauty and grandeur of the universe." He calls us not to take for granted the beauty of our cosmos, the miracle of our existence.

Eckhart also calls us to behold, and he even defines what is behind our power of beholding: "The word 'behold' implies three things: something great, something marvelous, or something rare." What is great and marvelous and rare calls out to us. It is God's word, God's communication to us to pay attention and open our hearts up. The great, the marvelous, and the rare is something Heschel senses, too, when he speaks of "radical amazement" and our need to cultivate a sense of the sublime. For him, the sublime is "the silent allusion of things to a meaning greater than themselves." We are carried to an encounter with transcendence and meaning, an awareness that "the world in its grandeur is full of a spiritual radiance."

Heschel calls for "standing still" as a requisite in order to behold, and Eckhart calls for us to be empty in order to be fully present and fully mindful to the glory of existence. Being still brings with it a deep listening, which is required, according to Eckhart, if we are to receive the revelation that glory intends for us. A kind of unknowing precedes the knowing. Eckhart writes, "Wherever this word is to be heard, it must occur in stillness and in silence. We cannot be of greater service to this Word than through stillness and silence. *There* we can hear it and understand it correctly, in that state of unknowing. Where we know nothing, it becomes apparent and reveals itself." And again, we journey deep into the very ground of hearing to hear the Divine Word, which "lies hidden in the soul in such a way that one does not know it or hear it. Unless room is made in the ground of hearing, it cannot be heard; indeed, all voices and sounds must go out, and there must be absolute silence there and stillness."

We have to develop a "sense for the inexpedient," Heschel teaches, if we are to stand still to be touched by beauty and grandeur. Eckhart says the same thing when he talks about living and working "without a why or wherefore." Eckhart repeats this theme of inexpediency often:

Whoever dwells in the goodness of God's nature dwells in God's love. Love, however, has no why. If I had a friend and loved him because all the good I wished came to me through him, I would not love my friend but myself. I ought to love my friend for his own goodness and for his own virtue and for everything that he is in himself.... This is exactly the way it is with people who are in God's love and who do not seek their own interest either in God or in themselves or in things of any kind. They must love God alone for his goodness and for the goodness of his nature and all the things he has in himself. This is the right kind of love.

Eckhart contrasts that inexpedient love to expedient love this way: Some people "want to love God in the same way as they love a cow. You love it for the milk and the cheese and for your own profit. So do all people who love God for the sake of outward riches or inward consolation. But they do not love God correctly, for they merely love their own advantage." Eckhart criticizes such "expediency" when he says: "Every single person who seeks anything or even something with his or her works is working for a why and is a servant and a mercenary. Therefore, if you wish to be conformed and transformed into justice, do not intend anything in your work and strive for no why, either in time or in eternity. Do not aim at reward or blessedness, neither this nor that. For such works are truly fully dead."

In reflecting on Psalm 8, Eckhart celebrates our sacred response to sublimity and grandeur. The psalm reads:

Yahweh, our Lord,
how great your name throughout the earth!...
I look up at your heavens, made by your fingers,
at the moon and stars you set in place —
Ah, what is man that you should spare a thought for him,
the son of man that you should care for him?
Yet you have made him little less than a god.
You have crowned him with glory and splendor,
made him lord over the work of your hands....
Yahweh, our Lord,
how great your name throughout the earth!

Eckhart comments on this psalm:

> The prophet [or psalmist] marveled at two things — first, what God
> did with the stars, the moon and the sun. The second marvel concerns
> the soul, that God has done and does such great things with it and for
> its sake:...He has made it...like his essence...and like the ground
> wherein he subsists in himself, where he is always bearing his only-
> begotten Son, there where the Holy Spirit blossoms forth. This work
> [of forming the soul] is a pouring out yet a staying within.

Exegeting the wisdom literature that the Psalms represent, Eckhart calls
our attention first to nature and the cosmos as a source of marveling but also
to the human person. He himself marvels in amazement at the wonders of
creation and creativity when he says: "It is an amazing thing that something
flows forth and nonetheless remains within. Words flow forth and yet remain
within — that is certainly amazing! All creatures flow outward and nonetheless remain within — that is extremely amazing. What God has given and
what God promises to give — that is amazing, inconceivable, and unbelievable. And that is as it should be, for if it were comprehensible and believ-
able, things would not be right." Notice his gradations of amazement: First,
things are "amazing," then "certainly amazing," then "extremely amazing,"
and finally "amazing, inconceivable, and unbelievable." Yes, Eckhart tasted
amazement.

So did Rabbi Heschel. He says that "the world is not just here. It shocks
us into amazement." It certainly shocks — and rocks — Meister Eckhart.
John Merkle, a Roman Catholic lay theologian, wrote a brilliant book summarizing Heschel's work called *The Genesis of Faith: The Depth Theology
of Abraham Joshua Heschel.* He writes: "Heschel begins his depth theology
or philosophy of religion where religion itself begins — with the sense of
the sublime or with what he also calls the awareness of grandeur." Heschel
teaches that "grandeur fills him [humans] with awe," but that modern society, with its emphasis on exploiting nature, barely gives time or notice to
appreciating the sublimity and grandeur of our world. Heschel writes:

> The obsession with power has completely transformed the life of man
> and dangerously stunted his concern for beauty and grandeur. We
> have achieved plenty, but lost quality; we have easy access to pleasure,

we forget the meaning of joy. But what is more serious is the fact that man's worship of power has resurrected the demon of power.... When man looks only at that which is useful, he eventually becomes useless to himself.

Tasting God

One experiences the sublime, one tastes it, as in the psalmist's song, "Taste and see the goodness of God." The word "taste" in both Hebrew and Latin comes from the word for wisdom. Eckhart tells this story: "I was once asked why good people feel so happy with God and are so eager to serve Him. I replied by saying it was because they had tasted God, and it would be strange indeed if the soul that had once tasted and tried God could taste anything else." We begin the spiritual life with tasting, which is where wisdom begins also. Thus we can say that "awe is the beginning of wisdom," and a life of wisdom is predicated on a tasting of awe and a celebrating of awe as our primary spiritual experience. A culture of wisdom would hold awe up as a primary value. Knowledge alone does not suffice, and inherited knowledge (yes, dogmas) can be especially dangerous. Heschel warns us: "It is impossible to be at ease and to repose on ideas which have turned into habits, on 'canned' theories in which our own or other people's insights are preserved. We can never leave behind our concerns in the safe-deposit of opinions, nor delegate its force to others and so attain vicarious insights. We must keep our own amazement, our own eagerness alive." We do not want to reduce our alive minds to a mere "series of cliches."

Heschel cautions that in our day and age, when knowledge is king, we need to be on guard, for "the immense preciousness of being...is not an object of analysis but a cause of wonder." Indeed, he says, "Just to be is a blessing, just to live is holy." Eckhart, too, waxes eloquent about beingness itself — indeed, he says being belongs properly to God alone and all creatures are participants in that Divine gift, for God is "isness" and "creation is the giving of being." Furthermore, "God is like nothing so much as being. To the extent that anything has being it resembles God." Every creature loves its own being; even when "caterpillars fall from trees, they crawl high on a wall in order to preserve their being. So noble is being." Even a soul being tortured in hell, Eckhart maintains, is so in love with its being, "which it has received directly from God," that it "would still not wish not to be." So precious is being.

All creatures have being in common, and from the perspective of being, no beings are superior or inferior. We are all one at that level. And we are all interconnected. Being allows life to happen. Eckhart writes, "God's isness is my life. If my life is God's isness, then God's isness is my isness and God's mode is my mode, neither more nor less." Furthermore, joy follows, for "all that exists rejoices in its existence."

There is an equality of being for "God loves all creatures equally and fills them with his being," Eckhart writes. "And we should lovingly meet all creatures in the same way." Here we have a foundation for a truly ecological view of the world. Heschel makes the same point when he observes that "within our wonder we become alive to our living in the great *fellowship of all beings*, we cease to regard things as opportunities to exploit." To move into wonder and awe is to move beyond exploitation. It is to start life and culture all over again.

Doubt vs. Wonder

We need wonder to restart culture because the modern agenda started philosophy not with awe and wonder but with doubt. Heschel claims this is destructive because "wonder rather than doubt is the root of knowledge." Merkle comments that a philosophy "that begins in doubt will find it difficult, if not impossible, to include wonder." This explains why we live in a society that is less and less wonder oriented, and why our educational systems are failing — and boring — our young people. Heschel makes the point that there is no word in biblical Hebrew for doubt — but there are many words for wonder.

Human dignity derives from our capacity for the sublime — which alone lies at "the root of man's creative activities in art, thought and noble living," suggests Heschel. Indeed, he argues that the presence of sublimity and grandeur in human consciousness is proof of their reality, for "to assert that the most sensitive minds of all ages were victims of an illusion; that religion, poetry, art, philosophy were the outcome of a self-deception is too sophisticated to be reasonable." Indeed, even science depends on the "original abyss of radical amazement," according to Heschel. Human consciousness elicits its own wonder and awe — think of music and architecture and poetry and painting — and awakens grandeur and sublimity.

This is God's handiwork. Eckhart, like Heschel, takes seriously the biblical teaching that humans are made in God's image and likeness:

> God has formed and created the soul very like himself, for we read that our Lord said: "Let us make human beings in our own image" (Gn. 1:26). And this is what he did. So like to himself did he make the soul of a person that neither in the kingdom of heaven or on earth among all the splendid creatures that God created in such a wonderful way is there any creature that resembles him as much as does the soul of a human being alone.

In depth and breadth, human consciousness seems almost unique, Eckhart writes, for "when God made creatures, they were so small and narrow that he could not operate in any of them. He made the soul, however, so like and similar in appearance to himself that he could give himself to the soul." Both Eckhart and Heschel marvel at humanity's existence. Says Eckhart: "I often say, and think even more often, how marvelous the intellect is that God has poured into the soul."

Heschel puts it this way: "Human life is holy, holier even than the scrolls of the Torah.... Reverence for God is shown in reverence for man.... An act of violence is an act of desecration. To be arrogant toward man is to be blasphemous toward God." The responsibility humans are called to — the biblical command to "do justice, to love mercy, and to walk humbly with thy God" (Micah 6:8) — cannot happen without a deep sense of reverence that comes from an awareness of the sublime. "There is no sense of responsibility without reverence for the sublime in human existence," Heschel writes. Humans are a unique symbol of God. "The symbol of God is man, every man. God created man in His image (*Tselem*), in His likeness (*Demuth*)."

Sublime Mystery, Ever New and Everlasting

As important as the sublime and awe are as starting points for our spiritual journey, Heschel stresses that they are only the finger pointing toward the moon, not the moon itself. In his words, "the grandeur of nature is only the beginning. Beyond the grandeur is God." As full of grandeur as the world and humans are, the sublime is powerful because it reveals "the presence of God. It is never an ultimate aspect of reality, a quality meaningful in itself. It stands for something greater." Heschel says: "Sublime, magnificent is the world. Yet if it were not for His word, there would be no world, no sublimity and no magnificence." The sublime "is not a thing, a quality but rather a happening, an act of God, a marvel.... There are no sublime facts; there are only divine *acts*." A "marvel" is, of course, the root meaning of the word "miracle."

Heschel talks about mystery when he talks about being. "The roots of existence are never plain, never flat; existence is anchored in *depth*.... What *is*, is more than what you see; what *is*, is 'far off and deep, exceedingly deep.' *Being is mysterious*." Because "the self did not originate in the self," we have to say that "existence is not a property but a trust." Eckhart concurs, saying we should consider everything in life, from parents to property to halls to time, as "on loan." As Heschel puts it, "we are witnesses rather than authors of birth and death." Neither the human nor the world can account for its own existence. In Heschel's words, "Man is neither the lord

> [*"Everything praises God."*]

of the universe nor even the master of his own destiny. Our life is not our own property but a possession of God. And it is this divine ownership that makes life a sacred thing." Eckhart elaborates: "God gives nothing good to creatures but only lends it. The sun gives air heat, but the light is loaned, and so, as soon as the sun sets, the air loses the light, but retains the heat, for this is given to the air as its own." Heschel also sees life as "on loan," writing: "I am endowed with a will, but the will is not mine; I am endowed with freedom but it is a freedom imposed on the will. Life is something that visits my body, a transcendent loan; I have neither initiated nor conceived its worth and meaning. The essence of what I am is not mine. I am what is not mine." God is the giver of being: "I have not brought my being into being. Nor was I thrown into being. My being is obeying the saying 'Let there be!'"

Heschel speaks of "the sublime, the marvel, the mystery and the

Presence." The Presence is revealed by glory for "the glory is the presence of God." The Presence has a name in Judaism, Shekinah, which brings the glory and presence home, one might say. Heschel explains, "'The whole earth is full of His glory' (Isaiah 6:3). Yet, although the Shekinah, the Presence is everywhere, the experience of the Shekinah is always somewhere." We intuit the omnipresent divine presence, according to Heschel. And we taste it in our being.

For both Heschel and Eckhart, creation is continually happening. Heschel makes the following point: "Whereas ontology asks about being as being, theology asks about *being as creation*, about being as a divine act. From the perspective of *continuous creation*, there is no being as being; there is only *continuous coming-into-being*." Eckhart, too, sees the world as a continuous coming into being: "God created the world in such a way that he is still continually creating it." There is an "eternal now" where God is at work — "whatever God gives...proceeds fully in an eternal now." But to appreciate this eternal now we have to leave behind everyday time (just as Heschel coached us to leave behind utilitarianism or expediency). Says Eckhart: "God so created all things that he nevertheless always creates in the present. The act of creation does not fade into the past but is always in the beginning and in process and new." And again, "God does not stop creating, but forever creates and begins to create....Every action of God is new and 'he makes all things new' (Ws 7.27)." Echoing Eckhart, Heschel writes: "God called the world into being, and that call goes on. There is a present moment because God is present. Every instant is an act of creation." Eckhart says, "There is no standing still for us in any path in this life, and there never has been for any person, no matter how advanced one might be."

Justice and Compassion

Part of the newness of the world is the prophetic imperative to do justice and show compassion, which is how, after all, we contribute to preserving creation and sustaining it. For God is "the transcendent care for being," Heschel says. "God is the source of goodness challenging us to share in the divine redemptive task of overcoming evil with good, falsehood with truth, hatred with love." Says Heschel: "We need feel no discomfort when God is called the ground of being. But those who insist that He is above the ground of being, that He is the source of qualms, conscience, and compassion, find very few ears." Rabbi Heschel teaches: "The Torah is primarily divine *ways* rather than divine laws. . . . His way, not only His demand. . . . Justice is an obligation to God."

Eckhart works deeply from Heschel's tradition when he declares that "the just person lives in God and God in him. Thus God will be born in this just person and the just person is born into God." Eckhart declares that "God is justice" and "compassion means justice," and Heschel says, "Justice is God's nature," and "being compassionate" is an expression of "His own nature." Justice must therefore be part of our nature, Eckhart proposes: "For the just person as such to act justly is to live; indeed, justice is his life, his being alive, his being, insofar as he is just." We will return to Eckhart's thoughts on spirituality and justice, especially in chapter twelve. Clearly, Eckhart has drunk deeply of the Jewish, prophetic tradition and its teaching of the "obligation to God," which is justice and compassion.

As we have seen, Heschel's understanding of awe, reverence, amazement, wonder, praise, inexpedience, and Shekinah, as well as his passion for justice and compassion, are profoundly allied with Eckhart's theology of the via positiva and the via transformativa. One would expect nothing less, since Eckhart's principal source is the teachings of the rabbi Jesus, who was steeped in the same wisdom and prophetic lineage of Israel that also fed Rabbi Heschel.

CHAPTER TWO

THE CHRIST OF THE COSMOS

Meister Eckhart Meets Teilhard de Chardin and Thomas Berry

*The cosmic sense must have been born as soon as humanity found itself
facing the frost, the sea and the stars. And since then we find evidence of it in all our
experience of the great and unbounded: in art, in poetry, and in religion.*

— TEILHARD DE CHARDIN

*Every being has its own voice. Every being declares itself to the entire universe.
Every being enters into communion with other beings.*

— THOMAS BERRY

All creatures are gladly doing the best they can to express God.

— MEISTER ECKHART

The first chapter held up awe and wonder as the starting point of our spiritual journey, but Rabbi Heschel reminds us: "Wonder is an act in which the mind confronts the universe." It is the universe itself that awakens our wonder. Without this cosmic reverence, we are lost, we are adrift, we are set up for detours and the worship of strange idols. Heschel warns us: "Forfeit your sense of awe and the universe becomes a market place for you." In other words, to abandon our capacity for awe and wonder is to set up a strange religion of marketplace cosmology. Consumerism replaces the universe. Who can deny that this happens in our world today, as the media, its chief preacher, shouts its wares with incessant advertising 24/7?

At the same time, we are blessed with new information about the universe, with whole new stories from evolution and from our starry ancestors. Like hungry souls invited to a lush banquet, we are amazed by the great news and marvelous stories of how we got here, where here is, and how long the gestation of the universe took in its unfolding. The universe in our time confronts us anew. Who can deny that such fresh marvels and wonders hold the power to awaken our species? To learn that the journey has lasted 13.8 billion years, as science now teaches us, and that the universe began smaller than a zygote and now contains hundreds of billions of galaxies, each with billions of stars and expanding still — who can hold back awe? Who can be indifferent to the wonder of our existence?

Could all this, could we ourselves, have occurred by chance? I and many others find that hard to swallow. After all, every building presumes an architect — buildings do not just happen. They require intelligence and planning. The universe is much more than a building — it *moves*. It is a literally organic construction, constantly growing and on the move. Any human structure is radically puny compared to the intricacy and immensity of the universe. I side with Arne Wyller, a Royal Swedish Academy professor in astrophysics, who calls God "the Planetary Mind" and writes that "my rational scientific mind stands in awe in front of the intellectual beauty of the Creation and the Creator." I side with physicist Erich Jantsch, who says, "God is the mind of the universe," and with Albert Einstein, who says, "There is no true science which does not emanate from the mysterious. Every thinking person must be filled with wonder and awe just by looking up at the stars....We need a cosmic religion....We must create a cosmic man, a man ruled by his conscience."

Eckhart's Cosmology

I also invoke Meister Eckhart. Like most premodern peoples, he was fascinated by cosmology. His brother Dominican Thomas Aquinas wrote that "every human being is *capax universi*," or capable of the universe. Time and again Eckhart invokes cosmology in his writings. Since he never heard the notion that the universe is a machine (the basic metaphor of the modern era), he never considered the universe to be anything but alive and fully connected to Mother Earth and humanity.

In one celebrated passage Eckhart writes that the human spirit "storms the firmament, and scales the heavens until it reaches the spirit that drives the heavens. As a result of heaven's revolution, everything in the world flourishes and bursts into leaf. The spirit, however, is never satisfied; it presses on ever further into the vortex (or whirlpool) and primary source in which the spirit has its origin." By speaking of the flourishing into leaf of everything in the world, Eckhart is praising what we now call photosynthesis, which is indeed a marriage of the sun and plants. But he is saying more in this amazing passage so filled with energy and verve: He declares, along with geologist Thomas Berry, that ecology is functional cosmology. To speak of the heavens is to speak of the life systems on earth. Earth is our hood in the universe, our local neighborhood. Ecological and cosmological awareness are in tandem. And the opposite is also true: to ignore the cosmos is to ignore ecology and Earth survival.

Eckhart agrees with Aquinas's observation that humans are capable of the universe: "If God had made a thousand heavens and a thousand earths the human soul could well grasp them by its power." Eckhart thinks cosmologically. He frequently addresses the "all" of creation: "With His love God gives *all creatures* their being and life, and maintains them with His love.... Should anyone ask what God is, this is what I would say now: that God is love, and in fact so lovable that *all creatures* seek to love His lovableness, whether they know it or not, or whether they wish to or not. So much is God love, and so lovable, that *everything* that *can* love *must* love Him, whether they will to do so or not." Eckhart is not anthropocentric. He thinks in terms of all being, and he invites us to do the same. He speaks about the universe this way: "Heaven is so immense and so wide that if I told you, you would not believe it. If you were to take a needle and prick the heavens with it then that part of heaven that the needle point pricked would be greater in comparison to heaven and the whole world, than heaven and the world are in comparison to God." Imagine how moved Eckhart would be to know what we know about the universe today — that it is billions of galaxies large, each with billions of stars! That is a lot of pinpricks!

Eckhart makes frequent connections between the work of the cosmos and the work of our psyches: "Humans are meant to be a heaven for God to dwell in. We should be fixed as the heavens are fixed." We have moral lessons to learn from the goings-on in the sky. "There are various things we should know about the heavens above: that they are firm, pure, all-embracing, and fruitful. These same qualities should be found in human beings, for each of us should be a heaven in which God dwells," he writes. If the heavens are firm, we should be firm. "The heavens...surround everything and contain everything in themselves. This too is something human beings can obtain in love, that they are able to contain everything in themselves — friends and foes alike.... The heavens are fruitful for they are helpful to every endeavor. The heavens work more than a carpenter when he builds a house."

Eckhart and his brother Aquinas were not suspicious of science. Quite the opposite — they were thrilled to learn from science, as was their elder, Hildegard of Bingen, who insisted that "all science comes from God." Aquinas says, "A mistake about creation results in a mistake about God." This both honors the scientist's vocation and cautions theologians, who should learn from science (not deny it) and be wary of any God teaching that derives from false science, or flight from science, as one finds in fundamentalism today. Aquinas spent his entire adult life bringing together the best science of his day — Aristotle who came to Europe via Islam — with his biblical-based and creation-based research. He insisted that revelation came in two volumes, one written in nature and one in the Bible. Eckhart learned from Aquinas and put it this way: "Our Lord does indeed open his mouth here below, teaching us through scripture and through creatures."

Heschel also held science in respect — but not scientism or the belief that science is the exclusive teacher of truth. He said, "Radical amazement is enhanced rather than reduced by the advancement of knowledge." Thus he, like Eckhart and Aquinas, realized the potential of scientific inquiry to advance, rather than diminish, our sense of awe and mysticism.

Both Eckhart and Aquinas, following the Jewish tradition and that of Dominican training, also teach that study is prayer. It feeds the soul's "inner work," provided, of course, that you bring your heart to it. Remember, in their understanding, as in the Jewish tradition, the intellect is *in the heart*. Eckhart calls the intellect "the temple of God. God dwells nowhere more truly than in his temple, in the intellect....He is there alone in his stillness." By teaching that the access to the intellect is through stillness, Eckhart is outrightly rejecting the modern notion that intellect or mind is exclusively rational. The door to the rational is words and quantity. The door to the right brain is awe, stillness, and grief. The premodern understanding of the intellect or mind is far, far broader than is the modern definition of truth as, to quote Descartes, "clear and distinct ideas." The intellect embraces both right-brain and left-brain thinking. Awe and wonder and wisdom are born not of rationality but of the right-brain experience. Heschel names this same reality when he observes, "Much of the wisdom inherent in our consciousness is the root, rather than the fruit, of reason. There are more songs in our souls than the tongue is able to utter." By referring to study as prayer, Eckhart is, of course, reflecting the *lectio divina* practice of the monastic tradition, which respects study — including study of nature — since it feeds heart work.

Today's Cosmologists

Needless to say, Eckhart's science and that of Aristotle is not the postmodern science of today. For that we turn to some thinkers who bring today's science alive for us in a spiritual context, especially the Jesuit priest and scientist, the mystic and poet, Teilhard de Chardin. Thomas Berry, a priest of the Passionist Order, was an admirer of Teilhard and for years was president of the Teilhard Society of New York. Together with his disciple cosmologist Brian Swimme, Berry studied the new cosmology and produced the book *The Universe Story*. Among Berry's other important books are *Dream of the Earth* and *The Great Work*. Swimme's most recent work is *Journey of the Universe*, which is a book and a one-hour film summarizing today's creation story via science.

I also want to mention the fine studies of the universe written by the husband-wife team of Joel Primack, an astrophysicist, and Nancy Abrams: *The View from the Center of the Universe* and *The New Universe and the Human Future: How a Shared Cosmology Could Launch a Global Society*. The latter book in particular addresses the moral issues and values that the new cosmology raises concerning the survival of our species. All these thinkers are gifting us with summary teachings — about the universe, about our future as a species, about our home, our Earth home and our cosmic home. I have no doubt whatsoever that Aquinas and Eckhart, both passionate searchers, would be salivating profusely to learn what today's science is teaching us of the universe. Their thinking was very much aligned with cosmology, microcosm/macrocosm, as above, so below. They could not conceive of humanity apart from our cosmic home.

[
"Seize God in all things, for God is in all things."
]

Once again, I turn to Rabbi Heschel to set the stage for the sacred stories of today's universe. Scientists rarely dare to allow feeling to color their facts, so we need a mystic like Heschel to put things in proper perspective:

> To a mind unwarped by intellectual habit, unbiased by what it already knows; to unmitigated innate surprise, there are no axioms, no dogmas; there is only wonder, the realization that the world is too incredible, too meaningful for us. The existence of the world is the most unlikely, the most unbelievable fact. Even our ability for surprise is beyond expectation. In our unmitigated wonder, we are like spirits who have never been conscious of outside reality, and to whom the knowledge of the existence of the universe has been brought for the first time. Who could believe it? Who could conceive it? We must learn to overcome the slick certainty and learn to understand that the existence of the universe is contrary to all reasonable expectations.

Teilhard de Chardin

Teilhard de Chardin (1881–1955) was a lover of creation his whole life. A scientist, poet, mystic, and Jesuit priest — who was banished to China by his order — Teilhard devoted his life to bringing religion and science, spirit and matter, together. He published many scientific and theological articles, but the Vatican forebade the publication of most of his books in his lifetime. He wrote in a letter to a friend about how his spiritual work drew him daily away from his paleontology digs: "A degree more of contact with the Center of things is more important than any progress in the knowledge of past Geology." Why was he called to explore the "Center of things"? Marxist philosopher Roger Garaudy, in a talk in London on Teilhard and Marxism, explained it this way:

> Ever since the first great scientific discoveries of the Renaissance man might well feel himself lost in the immensity of the universe, might well experience a fatal vertigo. The traditional outlook of the Middle Ages had accustomed man to living in a closed world. And now this universe is *deprived of its center* by astronomy, exploding the limits of Ptolemy's crystal spheres, which had thus far enclosed man and the earth in a reassuring chrysalis. Man and his planet are now no more than an infinitesimal and derisory point in the limitless infinity of the galaxies.
>
> This universe is *deprived of its center* by biology, which replaces the Bible stories of a mere six thousand years of dialogue between man and his God, by the savage epic of life in which the two million years of human history and prehistory are no more than a brief episode in the full undoing of life on our planet and the genesis of our minute planet in the cosmos.
>
> This universe is *deprived of its center* by psychology itself, since Freud has given us an image of man in which all sorts of fibers, drawn from the remote everywhere, compose our soul out of their monstrous nodes, ever ready to escape our control and become loosened.
>
> How can a man break away from the anguish of being thus thrown, like a wisp of straw, into this maelstrom of worlds, into an absurd universe, devoid of meaning, in which he is nothing?

Modern humanity has been gripped in fear and anxiety ever since we lost our center due to science's advances. Teilhard recovers this lost center. For him, the "Center of things" is Christ. The Christ of the Cosmos. The Cosmic Christ is Wisdom, who, in the words of the Book of Wisdom, "holds everything together on earth and in heaven." Wisdom was celebrated at the birth of Christianity within the cosmic hymns found in the earliest writings by St. Paul. "He is the invisible God's image, firstborn of all creation, because within him everything was created....In Christ were created all things in heaven and on earth: everything visible and invisible....

Before anything was created, Christ existed, and Christ holds all things in unity" (Colossians 1:15–17). Biblical scholar Bruce Chilton comments: "In Colossians, Christ is the center of the cosmos — natural, social, and supernatural — that created the world and makes the world new each day.... The range of Paul's thinking was literally cosmic, and metacosmic."

Paul speaks of the Cosmic Christ in his letter to the Ephesians as well. "God has made known to us in all wisdom and insight the mystery of the divine will, according to the divine purpose which God set forth in Christ as a plan for the fullness of time, to unite all things in Christ, things in heaven and things on earth" (Ephesians 1:9–10).

What has happened to this sense of cosmology and Christ? Lutheran theologian Joseph Sittler has said that the raging cosmic fire that characterized Christianity's origins has been reduced by modern religion to a mere "flickering flame" in the individual soul. Soul and cosmos are no longer married. Psyche and universe have ruptured. And humanity is confused, lost, and depressed.

The Cosmic Christ restores this lost unity, this vastness of our souls and all their relationships. Says Teilhard, "I can no longer see anything nor any longer breathe, outside that *milieu* in which all is made one." The oneness he breathes is a oneness of panentheism, which he expresses in the following prayer: "All of us inescapably, exist in you, the universal *milieu* in which and through which all things live and have their being." Panentheism sees God in all things and all things in God. God is a "milieu."

Eckhart, too, is bullish on panentheism. It is the way he saw the world and God's relationship to it. He writes: "God created all things in such a way that they are not outside himself, as ignorant people falsely imagine. Everything that God creates or does he does or creates in himself, sees or knows in himself, loves in himself." Thus it is that "all creatures flow outward, and nonetheless remain within" God. He draws an analogy with our own creativity: "When the Father begot all creatures, he begat me also, and I flowed out with all creatures and yet remained in the Father. In the same way the words that I am now speaking first spring up in me, then secondly I reflect on the idea, and thirdly I express it and you all receive it; yet it really remains in me. In the same way, I have remained in the Father." What is creative (and created) flows out but remains within.

Panentheism is a mystical way of seeing God and the world; in it dualisms are ended, and yet the transcendence or further surprises of Divinity are not squelched, as can happen in a pantheistic view. Pantheism is the idea that God is all things, as opposed to panentheism, which says God is in all things and all things are in God. Eckhart, like Teilhard, invokes Acts 17:28: "In him we live, move, and have our being." Eckhart sees God as "round-about us completely enveloping us," much like a fish in water and water in the fish. In this view of Divinity, inside and outside are done away with. Eckhart says this many times and in many ways: "God is in all things. The more he is in things, the more he is outside of things; the more he is within, all the more he is without." Also, "God is the ground and encirclement of all creatures." And, "God is in all creatures, in so far as they have being, and yet He is above them." And, "God is everywhere and equally present at all times.... No creature can fully embrace Him or mirror God's goodness in itself." We can know God through creatures, for "a person who knew nothing except creatures would never have to attend to any sermons, for every creature is full of God and is a book [about God]." This sounds very much like indigenous wisdom, which we will explore in chapter eleven.

The goodness of creatures reveals the goodness of God, which comes to us through them. Eckhart writes, "All goodness flows forth from the superfluity of God's goodness. But God's will has savor for me only in that unity wherein the repose of God's goodness is in all creatures." All goodness flows from Divinity, since "God alone is the sole fount and vein of all goodness." When Eckhart asks, "What is good?" he answers, "That is good which shares itself. We call one a good person who shares himself or herself and is helpful.... God shares the Godself most of all."

The Cosmic Christ

Teilhard talks about the Cosmic Christ as the "center of things" who is present "even in the heart of the tiniest atom" as well as encompassing the vast universe. The Cosmic Christ glows in the microcosm and the macrocosm of the universe. It names the glory, *doxa*, or radiance of the universe. It is like the Shekinah of the Jewish tradition, which was mentioned in chapter one.

Shekinah depicts the *presence* of God and the *presence* of Divine glory, localizing it and making it real. Thus the Cosmic Christ.

Far from resisting evolution as some kind of antireligious plot, Teilhard talks about the thrill evolution gives him, and he says the "new mysticism" appears to him to be a "communion with evolution." Speaking autobiographically, he writes of "that magic word 'evolution' which haunted my thoughts like a tune:...like a summons to be answered." It became his calling, his vocation, to spread the word about evolution and its deeper, spiritual meaning. The Cosmic Christ is historical. It evolves and has evolved, as does history and all beings in history.

In Teilhard's mind, a theology of the Cosmic Christ moves us beyond the centuries of debates about the human side versus the divine side of Christ to a third reality — but he complained that he found it difficult to find theologians or laypeople who wanted to discuss the Cosmic Christ. Teilhard died in 1955. Today is a different day, however, and I for one find a great deal of interest in the Cosmic Christ, especially with the dissemination of the new cosmic creation story.

Methodist liberation theologian Joerg Rieger wrote a book on the history of Christology from Paul to the present, which he concluded with a chapter on the Cosmic Christ called "Christology in a Postcolonial Empire." In it, he writes about the current historical moment: "At the end of the twentieth century and at the beginning of the twenty-first, the horizons of Christology have been broadened once again by the notion of the cosmic Christ." Rieger applies the Cosmic Christ archetype to political consciousness today insofar as it offers an alternative to imperial consciousness. He observes that "the image of the cosmic Christ might resist postmodern and postcolonial forms of empire where it directs attention to precisely those elements of the cosmos that are most overlooked and that suffer most under the pressures and exploitation of empire. If the cosmic Christ relates for instance to the environment under attack and to people who are forced to labor under inhuman conditions, Christology begins to break out of the status quo."

Teilhard believes that the West offers a "personalistic" nature to the universe; he calls this "the great western Discovery." He senses that this perspective married to today's evolutionary understanding of the universe allows us to visualize a "new dimension" of God: "the God of a moving and growing World — the true Spirit of Matter." Creativity and love lie at the core of the universe. He confesses that "the essence of my 'gospel' can be summarized by these simple words: not only 'God is love,' as Saint John used to say, but 'the World is love' and it is only fulfilled and takes on meaning to the extent that we submit to God and rejoin him (through and in the shape of all efforts and all vents) through love. Love is the superior, stable, and definitive form of all energy." Love lies at the core of the heart of the Cosmic Christ.

Teilhard attributes much of humanity's brilliance to a "cosmic sense" that flows from wonder as we confront the universe (as Heschel says). Psyche and cosmos come together. Teilhard writes: "I give the name of cosmic sense to the more or less confused affinity that binds us psychologically to the All which envelops us.... The cosmic sense must have been born as soon as humanity found itself facing the frost, the sea and the stars. And since then we find evidence of it in all our experience of the great and unbounded: in art, in poetry, and in religion."

Meister Eckhart was also thoroughly grounded in a theology of the Cosmic Christ, where "Christ is all and in all," as he cites St. Paul as saying. Indeed, he developed the Cosmic Christ theology more fully than any writer I know before or since. Eckhart draws heavily from the powerful Cosmic Christ passage of John 1: "In the beginning was the Word and the Word was with God and the Word was God." This text also echoes teachings of Wisdom, who was with God at the creation of the world and sought to set up its tent among us — and it also hints at the presence of Shekinah, as it talks about the "glory" of the children of God. Also, that the Word is the "light in all things." Eckhart teaches that "all creatures are words of God," and "the purpose of a word is to reveal." All creatures are revelatory like Christ. The word that God speaks is continuous — it is still going on, as all creation is — and it is both "spoken and unspoken," since no creature truly speaks for God and yet every creature "may indeed echo God." Eckhart writes, "All creatures want to express God in all their works; let them all speak, coming as close as they can, they still cannot speak him. Whether they want to or not, whether it is pleasing or painful to them, they all want to speak God and he still remains unspoken." This is the Christ at work in all creatures

— sometimes the Word gets spoken and sometimes it remains silent and hidden. "All creatures are gladly doing the best they can to express God."

In a sermon based on 2 Timothy 4:2, "Preach the Word," Eckhart translates the text in this way: "Announce the word, pronounce the word, produce it, give birth to the word." And then he immediately talks about words "and all creatures" that flow out but remain within. Word and creatures are one for him. That is a Cosmic Christ theology. He invokes Psalm 62 — "God spoke one and I heard two" — and comments: "That is true. God is constantly speaking only one thing. His speaking is one thing. In this one utterance he speaks his Son and at the same time the Holy Spirit and all creatures. And yet there is only one speech in God. The prophet says, 'I heard two. That means I heard God and the creature. There where God speaks the creatures, there God is.'"

There is one word, one Cosmic Christ, and that incorporates all creatures. The implications for an eco-theology, one that defends Mother Earth and all her creatures, are immense. Within the perspective of a Cosmic Christ, this teaching tells us that all beings are sacred and all life on the planet is sacred. The obvious corollary is this: to ignore the sacredness of the forests, the rivers, the oceans, and the four-legged ones is to crucify the Christ all over again. The cross is not a private, anthropocentric event but a cosmic event, a rupture in the cosmos that in fact happens whenever injustice reigns.

Eckhart also raises the ante on the human condition, for if every being is a Cosmic Christ, surely humans are also. "People think God has only become a human being there — in his historical incarnation — but that is not so; for God is here — in this very place — just as much incarnate as in a human being long ago. And this is why he has become a human being: that he might give birth to you as his only begotten Son, and as no less." Eckhart repeats often that "God is in all things," urging us to "seize God in all things, for God is in all things."

While emphasizing the immanence of God in all things, Eckhart is clear about his panentheism, but he also avoids charges of pantheism, which would reduce God exclusively to creation. He says: "God is in the soul with his nature, his being, and his Godhead, and yet he is not the soul. The reflection of the soul is God in God, and yet the soul is what it is." God and the soul are not identical, just as God and the rest of nature are not identical. They are in a subject-subject relationship.

Thomas Berry and the Ecological Revolution

For Thomas Berry, a Cosmic Christ is necessarily a Green Christ and an Eco-Christ since "ecology is functional cosmology." Like the prophets of old, Berry warns us how dangerous we humans can be and have been to ourselves and to the rest of creation: "By bringing humans into existence the Earth has created a supreme danger to all other components of the Earth community because the human can invade the region of other species with a unique range of freedom." Humans differ from other species because the other-than-human species "discover their survival context with only limited disturbance of the larger complex of life systems. They find their niche quickly, or else they perish. A certain stability eventuates. A new equilibrium comes into being, a functioning relation of things with one another." The same is not true of humans. We, of course, are not so genetically programmed as other species; we are creative, we operate by trial and error, we are curious, we roam far and wide. Our niche "is a special form of niche." Other life forms generally survive "within a limited bioregion," but we humans "can establish our human presence almost anywhere on the planet." Our very creativity and adaptability makes us uniquely dangerous.

> *"God created all things in such a way that they are not outside the Godself, as ignorant people falsely imagine."*

Our genetic coding makes culture and with it education the primary driving force of our existence and indeed survival. But what if a culture and its education are rapacious and not respectful of other life forms? What if a culture and its educational system focus on accumulating the most goods and property and control possible and are oblivious of the sacrifice and cost of other species? What if a culture and educational system numb the human capacity for reverence and respect and awareness of the nonanthropocentric world by incessantly advertising greed and comfort as primary values? What if a culture and education teach no values of responsibility or awareness of others, including Mother Earth and her forests, waters, fishes, animals, birds, trees, soil? What if religion also succumbs to the same anthropocentric agenda and narcissistic preoccupations about the salvation of the individual and about a life after death while ignoring the cosmos and with it the Earth altogether? When religion is prophetic, it will dare to challenge culture with calls to moral conscience and action — and this includes eco-action.

Berry warns us: "In some sense the human refuses to accept any particular niche, for the basic function of a niche is to set limits to the activity of a species. In this sense the human refused to accept limits imposed from without or even from within its own being." Is capitalism in grave danger of refusing to accept limits? Is it based on a "quest for the infinite" accumulation of goods and wealth? Are misers its patron saints? If so, then Meister Eckhart's teachings about "everything we have is on loan" kicks in to awaken our consciences once again. So too does his teaching about the holiness of all things, the Cosmic Christ or the image of God in all things. So too does his teaching about how to combat the temptation to greed and avarice, namely by "letting go" or detachment. (This practice, which lies at the heart of Eckhart's practical spirituality, is the focus of chapter three.) So too does Eckhart's teaching on the interconnectivity of all beings strike at the heart of ecological wantonness, as do his teachings on justice and compassion. If "God is justice," as Eckhart says, then God is eco-justice as well.

Berry draws a powerful ethical lesson from the cosmic principle of beings finding their appropriate niche: "This law of limits is among the most basic of all cosmological, geological, or biological laws. It is particularly clear in the case of biological forms." As he notes, various spiritual traditions teach about limits, forming part of their cosmic religious teachings.

In the Hindu world this law of limits is recognized as *rita* in the cosmological order or as *dharma* in the moral order. In the Chinese world it is *tao* in an earlier phase or *li* in the later neo-Confucian period. In the Greek world it is *dike* as the order of justice or *logos* establishing the intelligible order of the universe. Yet in the modern world this sense of limits imposed by the natural functioning of the universe has to some extent been overridden, at least in a temporary manner, by industrial processes created by humans.

Curiously, Berry leaves out the biblical teaching on limits that is found in Judaism, for example, the teaching of the Sabbath — letting the Earth and the animals who work the Earth be free at least one day per week and every seventh year for a year and every jubilee year also. The prophets of Israel were fierce about respecting the soil and the land for the sake of future generations and about the return to chaos that will result if humans disobey God's rules that respect creation. According to the prophet Jeremiah, catastrophe results from human actions. "Have you not done this to yourself, by forsaking Yahweh your God?" (Jeremiah 2:17). Again, Jeremiah laments: "I looked upon the earth, and lo, chaotic waste, / and unto the heavens, and their light was gone.... / I looked, and lo, there was no human being, / and all the birds of the air had vanished. / I looked, and lo, the fertile land was wilderness, / before Yahweh, before his fierce indignation" (Jeremiah 4:23, 25–26). The incarnation of the Logos that Christians honor especially in John 1 ("In the beginning was the Logos or Word") would seem to feed Berry's ethical demand richly. Eckhart's teaching of the Cosmic Christ, of the divine Logos or Word that every creature is, would also seem to support Berry's concerns as well.

Berry targets Western culture most of all when he warns that our current path is no longer sustainable.

> Our entire industrial system can be considered as an effort to escape from the constraints of the natural world. We have created an artificial context for our existence through mechanical invention and the extravagant use of energy. In this process we have so violated the norms of limitation, so upset the chemical balance of the atmosphere, the soil, and the oceans, so exploited the Earth in our use of fossil fuels, that we are devastating the fertility of the planet and extinguishing many species of wildlife. We no longer live within the organic, ever-renewing world that is the natural context of our existence.

Berry is convinced that "reverence for the sacred dimension of the natural world" was diminished over time in the emergence of modern European consciousness. This and financial speculation fed a growing abuse of nature, leading to a "direct assault on the various life-forms of the [American] continent or to subjugation for some utilitarian purpose." Here Berry addresses from a historical perspective Eckhart's principle of "living and working without a why" and Heschel's principle of "non-expediency" from chapter one. Berry writes about the European settlement of North America:

> Land was for settlement and possession. Soil was for cultivation. Forests were for timber. Rivers were for travel, for irrigation of the fields, and for power. Animals such as the wolf, the bear, and the snake were for killing. Animals such as the beaver, the deer, the rabbit, and the passenger pigeon were for the fur or the food they could provide. Fish, so abundant throughout the streams and rivers and along the shores, were for catching. North America was indeed a luxuriant continent awaiting human exploitation under the title of "progress" or "development."

A heavy dose of Eckhart's Cosmic Christ theology, a return to the reverence due all beings, would provide real medicine to combat this idol of usurpation and utilitarianism. In this context, this and similar texts from Eckhart attain their richest and fullest meaning: "If anyone were to ask life over a thousand years, 'Why are you alive?' the only reply could be: 'I live so that I may live.' This happens because life lives from its own foundation and rises out of itself. Therefore it lives without a reason so that it lives for itself."

This is surely more than utilitarian living. I have a puppy. She loves to play. To play is to work without a why. She teaches me anew that we are to live without a why. We live in order to live. Trees and fish do the same. Only humans worship an idol of expedience, sometimes carrying it to the level of idolatry, as if usefulness were the *only* value to live for. Eckhart imagines this dialogue:

> "Why do you love God?" "I do not know...because of God."
> "Why do you love the truth?" "Because of the truth"...
> "Why do you love goodness?" "Because of goodness."
> "Why do you live?" "My word, I do not know! But I am happy to be alive."

This is what he means by "loving for the sake of loving" and "working for the sake of working." When we always work for a "why or wherefore," we are "no better than mercenaries." All of life becomes a transaction.

A Spirituality of Ecology and Cosmology

Berry expresses sadness at the demise of the beauty and diversity of the Earth now occurring at the hands of a philosophy that has empowered a corporate takeover of the planet. We can respond with Meister Eckhart's worldview that all being is holy. He insists we ought to "love all creatures equally with everything which we have received from God." If there is love among species, then there must be an equality among beings as well, for, Eckhart says, "love will never be anything else than there where equality and unity are. Between a master and a servant he has there is no peace because there is no real equality." Humans cannot survive in a master/slave relationship to the Earth and her creatures. Love and peace require a different relationship, one of respect, reverence, and gratitude. One of reciprocity.

A Cosmic Christ awareness provides such a sense of respect, reverence, and gratitude. Eckhart tells the story of being alone in a desert feeling afraid and how a live animal would be most valuable in such a situation. Why? "The life within the animal will give strength. For equality gives strength in all things." And why is this? "So noble, so full of pleasure, and so powerful is life itself." So Eckhart is not cut off from the deep relationships we experience with other beings. Quite the opposite. When it comes to being, we are equals. The gift of being is the gift of being, and for Eckhart it comes "directly" from God. The same is true of the gift of life, which is "so powerful in itself " and which gives "strength" because "equality gives strength in all things." Here we have a bona fide spirituality of ecology.

Berry makes clear that "in the realm of living beings there is an absolute interdependence. No living being nourishes itself. There exists a sequence of dissolution and renewal, a death-life sequence that has continued on Earth for some billions of years."

The fuller awareness of our history as a species that is emerging from the new cosmology teaches us many lessons. Astrophysicist Joel Primack and coauthor Nancy Abrams write in their book *The New Universe and the Human Future* that the ingredients in the universe that have contributed to our existence are vast and varied. They write, "An enormous base of material and phenomena in the universe have made and will continue to make our existence possible." The fraction of stardust associated with living things is "extremely tiny," and the fraction "associated specifically with intelligent life anywhere in the universe is vanishingly small." Though we seek to find other beings on other planets who share our intelligence, "the possibility exists that it is only our eyes that see this universe."

They are not trying to be pessimistic but realistic. Part of that realism is a deep gratitude that we are, after all is said and done, here. Thanks to the assistance of ever so many beings over the past 13.8 billion years. "Intelligence can burst out only from bits of stardust. Everything we learn about ourselves in the context of the universe as a whole reinforces a fundamental fact: that from a cosmic point of view we intelligent self-reflective beings are rare and precious beyond calculation — but we are only possible because of the composition of the rest of the universe." Is this what Eckhart means when he says "all beings love one another"? And that we are all "interdependent"?

Thomas Berry talks about our new "sacred story." It's an "epic of evolution, telling us, from empirical observation and critical analysis how the universe came to be, the sequence of its transformation down through some billions of years, how our solar system came into being, then how the Earth took shape and brought us into existence." But he insists that the emergent process "is neither random nor determined but creative." Creativity lies at the heart of our existence and that of the entire universe. His recipe for survival is this: "We will recover our sense of wonder and our sense of the sacred only if we appreciate the universe beyond ourselves as a revelatory experience of that numinous presence whence all things come into being. Indeed, the universe is the primary sacred reality. We become sacred by our participation in this more sublime dimension of the world about us."

A thoroughly secular mind-set — such as that of Richard Dawkins in his book *The Blind Watchmaker* — is a world without meaning or higher significance, governed only by change. Berry challenges that pessimistic and anthropocentric worldview. He writes: "Yet a different interpretation of the data of evolution is available. We need merely understand that the evolutionary process is neither random nor determined but creative. It follows the general pattern of all creativity." Eckhart agrees, for he too sees creativity at the heart of the universe: "All creatures have the capacity to give birth. A creature without powers of birthing would not exist." And again, "God's chief aim is giving birth." And, "The noblest work of God is giving birth...."

God takes the greatest delight in giving birth." We explore his deep sense of creativity in chapters four and eight.

In Berry's view we can see a "larger arc of development" as the universe moves from lesser to greater complexity in structure and "from lesser to greater modes of consciousness." Eckhart would agree, and he would say that the greater mode of consciousness is compassion. Berry recognizes "governing principles" of evolution in its three movements, which he names as "differentiation, inner spontaneity, and comprehensive bonding." We humans have arrived at a sort of pinnacle of this journey, for we are not unfamiliar with differentiation, inner spontaneity, or bonding.

Despite our current predicament, Thomas Berry feels a genuine sense of possibility for the human species. If we can wake up now, if we can move out of our slumber and attachment to a worldview that is both boring us and destroying the planet, there is much beauty that awaits. If we learn to appreciate and live out the fact that the "universe is composed of subjects to be communed with, not objects to be exploited," and we can move beyond our compulsion to take "use as our primary relationship with the planet," then we can be sustainable. Surely Meister Eckhart's insistence that every creature is a Word of God and a Cosmic Christ moves us from use and object relationships to deep intersubjective relationships and from exploitation to reverence. Just as Eckhart teaches that "every being is a Word of God" and every being "is gladly doing its best to speak of God," Berry says: "Every being has its own voice. Every being declares itself to the entire universe. Every being enters into communion with other beings. This capacity for relatedness, for presence to other beings, for spontaneity in action, is a capacity possessed by every mode of being throughout the entire universe."

What follows from this? "Every being has rights to be recognized and revered," Berry writes. "All rights are limited and relative.... So too with humans. We have human rights.... We have no right to disturb the basic functioning of the biosystems of the planet. We cannot own the Earth or any part of the Earth in any absolute manner."

Berry calls for us to once again get "caught up in the grandeur of existence itself and in admiration of those mysterious powers whence all this has emerged." Surely the Cosmic Christ archetype is one such way to honor the ever-present grandeur that surrounds us with glory and *doxa* on a daily basis.

This waking up and this putting into practice in all our institutions and professions and relationships is what Berry calls the "Great Work" of our time:

> The Great Work now, as we move into a new millennium, is to carry out the transition from a period of human devastation of the Earth to a period when humans would be present to the planet in a mutually beneficial manner.... The Great Work before us, the task of moving modern industrial civilization from its present devastating influence on the Earth to a more benign mode of presence is not a role that we have chosen. It is a role given to us, beyond any consultation with ourselves.

For Berry, the very purpose of the universe is nothing less than "*celebration. It is all an exuberant expression of existence itself.*" Thus Berry takes Eckhart's love of isness and adds an adjective: "exuberant existence." Life is full of exuberance. I know my puppy is. Children are. Dolphins are. Roses are. Redwoods are. Creatures of the sea and sky, soil and forests, are living their lives with exuberance and generosity, with joy and power. Our power derives, Berry says, from feeling that "we are supported by that same power that brought the Earth into being, that power that spun the galaxies into space, that tilt the sun and brought the moon into its orbit." Eckhart was sensitive to this same experience: "Life lives from its own ground and gushes forth."

To drink deeply of life, to drink deeply of existence, to taste its exuberance, to connect to the farthest stars and the brightest distant galaxies, to spend time with a simple caterpillar — in so many ways we encounter the Cosmic Christ, the radiant *doxa* or glory that permeates all existence. We have so much to gain from moving from anthropocentrism and its restrictions to the expansiveness of a Cosmic Christ awareness. An encounter with the divine presence, the radiant Shekinah in our midst. Here is Eckhart's promise: "God shines forth in all things, for all things taste divinely to one who has imbibed God, and God's image appears to him from out of all things. God flashes forth in him always, in her there is letting go and letting be, and one bears the imprint of his beloved, present God."

CHAPTER THREE

THE APOPHATIC DIVINITY

Meister Eckhart Meets
Buddhism via Thich Nhat Hanh

If we can bring into Christianity the insight of interbeing and of non-duality,
we will radically transform the way people look on the Christian tradition,
and the valuable jewels in the Christian tradition will be rediscovered.

— THICH NHAT HANH

Love God as God is — a not-God, not-mind, not-person,
not-image — even more, as he is a pure, clear One, separate from all twoness.

— MEISTER ECKHART

When we speak of awe, wonder, and the glorious radiance of the universe, when we refer to the Cosmic Christ, we are speaking of the *Cataphatic* Divinity. That is to say, the God of Light, the God of all that is beautiful, the God of creation. It is also the God of history, which wants to liberate and redeem those elements of creation and of humans that are less than true to their best selves. Eckhart, as we have seen, is a champion of the Cataphatic Divinity, as when he says simply and directly: "God is isness" and "isness is God."

Here we will explore the *Apophatic* Divinity in Eckhart's teachings, which relates to some profoundly Buddhist elements. The Apophatic Divinity is the God without light, the God of darkness, the God who cannot be named or described.

I am not the first to recognize Meister Eckhart's philosophical connections to Buddhism. In 1959, the late and great Japanese Buddhist scholar Dr. D. T. Suzuki engaged the Catholic monk Thomas Merton in a dialogue on Buddhism and Christianity. Suzuki ended it by saying to Merton: "Tom, you are a typical Western dualist. The only outside chance you have of grasping Zen is to study your one Zen thinker of the West, Meister Eckhart."

"But Eckhart was condemned by the church," responded Merton.

"Well, I can't help that, can I?" answered Suzuki.

Merton thought it over, and the next year he devoted himself to doing just two things: 1) reading Eckhart and 2) reading Zen poetry. With that work, his entire life changed and surely his theology. Merton moved from being an essentially romantic and dualistic Augustinian monk to a contemplative activist and deep ecumenist. This is clear in all his subsequent writings, such as *Confessions of a Guilty Bystander*, *Mystics and Zen Masters*, *Zen and the Birds of Appetite*, and much more. In his last book, *Asian Journal*, he wrote in the margins of his journal, "Eckhart is my lifeboat, Eckhart is my lifeboat."

Merton met and admired both Thich Nhat Hanh and the Dalai Lama, and the admiration was mutual. Thich Nhat Hanh nominated Merton for a Nobel Peace Prize, and the Dalai Lama tells us that Merton was the first Christian he had ever met, and he was impressed from then on with Christ, if not all Christians. It has been my privilege to meet both Thich Nhat Hanh and the Dalai Lama and to sit at their feet on several occasions to hear them teach and to participate in meditation practices.

Often when I read or teach Meister Eckhart, I and my students are struck by how Buddhist he sounds, and other Buddhists I've known have said the same. Where did Eckhart learn his "Buddhism"? As far as I can detect, Eckhart never met a Buddhist in his life nor did he read any Buddhist texts. Rather, I believe he found his Buddhism exclusively in his in-depth practice meditating as a Dominican and Christian. This is quite startling news — but important to come by in our times of interfaith and interspirituality. To practice Deep Ecumenism, we do not have to abandon our faith traditions as such, but we do have to *go deeply into our own practices*, into our own soul journeys. Whether we travel as a Buddhist, Christian, Hebrew, Muslim, Hindu, Goddess worshipper, or other, we come to a common "underground river," to quote Eckhart, of Divine Wisdom. The deep and truly archetypal or universal truths of Buddhism are encountered via the deep and universal archetypes of Christianity. It is a wonderful thing when world spiritualities come together in practice and in understanding. As Eckhart says: "All roads lead to God for God is on them all evenly."

Eckhart on the Apophatic Divinity

For all of Eckhart's writings on the Cataphatic Divinity — for all his love of creation and all his love of the Cosmic Christ present in every being, large and small, in the universe, and for all his teaching of the immanence of God in all things and all things in God (or panentheism) — Eckhart also speaks out plainly about the limits to our knowledge of God. He talks of the Apophatic Divinity.

Eckhart talks of that side of God that is "superessential darkness that has no name and that will never be given a name." He says God "is without name and is the denial of all names and has never been given a name." Furthermore, God is hidden. "The prophet said: 'You are truly a hidden God' (Is. 45:15) who dwells in the ground of the soul where the ground of God and the ground of the soul are one ground." Being itself aims at darkness, for "the final goal of being is the darkness or the unknowability of the hidden divinity, which is that light that shines 'but the darkness had not comprehended it' (Jn. 1:5)." Deep within the Godhead lies profound and dark mystery: "What is the final end? It is the mystery of the darkness of the eternal Godhead and it is unknown and was never known and never will be known. God dwells therein, unknown to himself, and the light of the eternal Father has forever shone in there and the darkness does not comprehend the light."

> *"No one can really say what God is...the ineffable One has no name."*

I would maintain that this apophatic God is something akin to Buddhism's nontalk about God. Some Buddhists use God language (Thich Nhat Hanh is one), but others are reluctant to engage in God talk. The latter are, I believe, emphasizing the *apophatic* dimension to Divinity. This is a necessary correction and understanding of the Divine for all, East and West, for it teaches respect. In many ways Jewish teaching does the same when it forbids writing the name "God," which is sometimes written "G-d," and limits the times the sacred name can be recited. All this is to emphasize the transcendent dimension to Divinity, that which is beyond all human understanding and human control. It also reminds us of mystery itself and how mystery is not subject to human manipulation or control. We are to face mystery, not control it or deny it. Eckhart says: "God is unfathomable and so has no name, for all the names the soul gives to God are derived from her understanding....God is beyond existence [*ueberseiend*] and incomprehensible and unrecognizable, as far as natural understanding is concerned."

This reminds us of the limits of language. Eckhart stresses how God cannot be named, for "no one can really say what God is...the ineffable One has no name." God is "the Unnameable" — God is both named and unnamed, spoken (as in creatures who are God's word) and unspoken because creatures cannot fully express God. This dimension of limiting God talk is especially important today, when humility is called for among humans and their religions. Says Eckhart:

> A master says of the first cause, that it is beyond words. The deficiency lies in language....When the soul pronounces God this utterance does not comprise the real truth about His essence: no one can truly say of God what He is. Sometimes we say one thing is like another. Now since all creatures contain next to nothing of God, they cannot say much about Him. We can recognize the skill of a painter who has made a perfect picture. And yet we cannot fully know it from that. All creatures cannot fully express God, for they are not receptive to what He really is.

Paradox often comes closest to communicating what we know — and don't know — about God. Eckhart writes, "Whatever one says that God is, he is not; he is what one does not say of him, rather than what one says he is." God is "he who is without name and is the denial of all names and who has never been given a name...a truly hidden God." Again, "God is a nothing and God is a something. What is something is also nothing." We are in the interesting camp of paradox, which is one way we invent to talk of mystery. Buddhism also resorts to paradox to express the dark ineffability of mystery.

The experience we have of the divine is often without naming. Says Eckhart: "Since God has transcendent being, therefore He transcends all knowledge.... The soul tastes God... where all naming has been set aside: there it knows God most purely, there it is fully godlike. Therefore Paul says: 'God dwells in a light which is inaccessible.' God is a pure indwelling in his own essence, where there is neither this nor that, for whatever is in God, is God." When we speak of God, "we have to stammer." Thus it is best to "maintain total silence about that which is the source of all things."

Eckhart not only endorses silence but chides those who would break that silence: "The most beautiful thing which a person can say about God consists in that person's being silent from the wisdom of an inner wealth. So be silent and do not flap your gums about God, for to the extent that you flap your gums about God, you lie and you commit sin. If you want to be without sin and perfect, then do not flap your gums about God." No one, not even Eckhart, can maintain this paradoxical prohibition, but the meaning is clear: God is not to be talked of lightly.

Eckhart on Mindful Meditation

How do we get to that silence, to that Source of all things? Eckhart calls on the story of Jacob in Genesis (28:20): "'Jacob the patriarch came to a certain place and wanted to rest in the evening, when the sun had gone down.'... He says: 'To a place'; he does not name it. The place is God. God has no name of His own, and is the place and position of all things and is the natural place of all creatures." We commune with the Godhead, which is natural for us: "The Godhead alone is the place of the soul, and is nameless.... 'Jacob rested in that place,' which is nameless. By not being named, it is named. When the soul comes to the nameless place, it takes its rest. There, where all things have been God in God, the soul rests. That place of the soul which is God is nameless. I say God is unspoken." It is in repose, at night, in silence, that God's love burns the hottest. "In a God-loving soul it is evening. There is nothing there but repose, where a person is thoroughly penetrated and made

illuminated with divine love.... The soul remains in the light of God and in
the silence of pure repose, and that is evening: then it is hottest in the divine
love." Darkness holds its special power and its special attraction. God likes
a no-place, a no-where, and the soul wants to commune with God there as
well. "As long as the soul is anywhere, it is not in the greatest of God which
is nowhere." After all, "God is nowhere.... God is not here or there, neither
in time or place." Christ, too, is to be found there in a place of nothingness.
"Where is Christ sitting? He is sitting nowhere. Whoever seeks him anywhere will not find him. His smallest part is everywhere, his highest part is
nowhere."

The journey is a journey inward, for that is where the human spirit is
most at home and so too is God. Eckhart says, "God is a being who always
lives in the innermost. Therefore the spirit is always searching within. But
the will goes outward toward what it loves."

How do we go about this journey inward to a nameless and unknown
place? Eckhart says, "The Word lies hidden in the soul, unknown and
unheard unless room is made for it in the ground of hearing, otherwise it is
not heard. All voices and sounds must cease and there must be pure stillness
within, a still silence." To meditate is to collect ourselves. "The soul must
be collected and drawn up straight and must be a spirit. There God works
and there all works are pleasing to God. No work ever pleases God unless it
is wrought there." We learn to focus, for "the more the soul is collected, the
narrower it is, and the narrower it is, the wider." Great things happen in this
place of silence, which is "the doorway of God's house.... In the silence and
peace...there God speaks in the soul and utters Himself completely in the
soul. There the Father begets His Son and has such delight in the Word and
is so fond of it, that He never ceases to utter the Word all the time, that is to
say beyond time."

The journey inward into the dark and silence is a trip into simplicity,
Eckhart says, a letting go of all things — all forms and images and memories
— into the "essential mind of God, of which the pure and naked power is
understanding, which the masters term receptive. Now mark my words! It
is only above all this that the soul grasps the pure absoluteness of free being,
which has no location, which neither receives nor gives: it is bare 'beingness'
that has been stripped of all being and all beingness. There it takes hold of

God as in the ground of His being, where He is beyond all being." One lets go of all desire, which is so "far reaching" and measureless. "All that understanding can grasp, all that desire can desire, that is not God. Where understanding and desire end, there it is dark, and there God shines." The Word of God is heard there, for "to hear this Word in the Father (where all is stillness), a person must be quite quiet and wholly free from all images and from all forms. Indeed, a person ought to be so true to God that nothing whatever can gladden or sadden him or her. She should take all things in God, just as they are there." Then God will do the work and humans need only not resist. "If only the soul would stay within, all things would be present to it." Solitude is tasted, for there the soul "must be alone as God is alone."

In an amazing passage that is so Buddhist that it brings shouts from my Buddhist students, Eckhart gives the following advice:

> How then should one love God? You should love God mindlessly, that is, so that your soul is without mind and free from all mental activities, for as long as your soul is operating like a mind, so long does it have images and representations. But as long as it has images, it has intermediaries, and as long as it has intermediaries, it has neither oneness nor simplicity. And therefore your soul should be bare of all mind and should stay there without mind. For if you love God as he is God or mind or person or picture, all that must be dropped. How then shall you love him? You should love him as he is, a not-God, not-mind, not-person, not-image — even more, as he is a pure, clear One, separate from all twoness. And we should sink eternally from something to nothing into this One. May God help us to do this. Amen.

Subtraction and Letting Go

Eckhart says, "God is not found in the soul by adding anything, but by a process of subtraction." Subtraction and letting go leads us to the Divine depths. When we can let go and "sink into God," amazing things happen between God and us. "I advise you to let your own 'being you' sink into and flow away into God's 'being God.' Then your 'you' and God's 'his' will become so completely one 'my' that you will eternally know with him his changeless existence and his nameless nothingness."

God is characterized by a "nameless nothingness." Nothingness lies at the heart of Divinity — and maybe all things. Notice we are to *sink*, not strive, not ladder-climb, not ascend by willpower and determination. We "let God," as AA members talk of it. To sink is a godly act, according to Eckhart: "God alone sinks into the essences of things." When in love, we sink into each other, we let go, we don't try overly much, we trust; we don't rule by willpower.

Eckhart goes further in naming the practically unnameable union created by letting go. "When all the images of the soul are taken away and the soul can see only the single One then the pure being of the soul finds passively resting in itself the pure, form-free being of divine unity, when the being of the soul can bear nothing else than the pure unity of God." Intuition is sometimes like this; it lends us a direct knowledge of truth or God "without image, without mediation, and without likeness." Thus Eckhart promises:

> All God wants of you is for you to let go of yourself and creatures and let God be within you. The smallest creature image that takes shape in you is as big as God. Why? It deprives you of the whole of God. As soon as this image enters you, God with all His Godhead has to exit. But when the image exits, God enters.... What harm can it do you to do God the favor of letting God be God in you? Let go of yourself for God's sake, and God will let go of Himself for your sake! When these two have exited, what is left is one and simple. In this One the Father bears His Son in the innermost source.

Eckhart explains how it is that being unable to let go restricts our experience of the Divine. "True possession of God depends on the mind, an inner mental turning and striving toward God — but not in a continuous and equal thinking of Him, for that would be impossible for nature to strive for, very difficult and not even the best thing. One should not have or be content with a God one imagines, for when the image disappears, God also disappears. Rather, one should have an essential God, who is far beyond the thought of humans and of all creatures."

For Eckhart, emptying the mind is "the most powerful prayer, one almost omnipotent to gain all things, and the noblest work of all is that which proceeds from a bare mind. The more bare it is, the more powerful, worthy, useful, praiseworthy and perfect is the prayer and the work. A bare mind can do all things. What is a bare mind? A bare mind is one which is worried by nothing and is tied to nothing which has not bound its best part to any mode, does not seek its own in anything, that is fully immersed in God's dearest will and goes out of its own." A bare mind is not busy worrying, not living in the past or the future, in regret or fear. It dwells in the now.

Furthermore, this great emptying is conducted decidedly *not* to make us bliss bunnies or capable of strange spiritual or mental feats, such as levitations, bilocation, or other oddities. No, the purpose of such deep unity is to render our work and our service more effective so that it derives from our being and not our compulsion to act. This is how Eckhart puts it: "Here God's ground is my ground and my ground is God's ground. Here I live from my own as God lives from His own.... Out of this inmost ground, all your works should be wrought without Why. I say truly, as long as you do works for the sake of heaven or God or eternal bliss from without, you are at fault. It may pass muster, but it is not the best."

In this way, Eckhart cautions against turning practice, even the practice of letting go, into an idol. "Indeed, if a person thinks she will obtain more of God by

> "*I pray God to rid me of God.*"

meditation, by devotion, by ecstasies or by special infusion of grace than by being at the fireside or in the stable — that is nothing but taking God, wrapping a cloak round His head and shoving Him under a bench. For whoever seeks God in a special way gets the way and misses God, who lies hidden in it. But whoever seeks God without any special way gets Him as He is in Himself, and that person lives with the Son, and is life itself." For Eckhart the practice of letting go itself must eventually be let go, so that it is not taken as an end in itself.

As a way to help visualize what this means, Eckhart asks us to consider a tablet you would write on: "The tablet is never so suitable for me to write on as when there is nothing on it. Similarly, if God is to write the highest on my heart, then everything called 'this and that' must be expunged from my heart, and then my heart stands in detachment.... Therefore the object of a detached heart is neither this nor that."

Such an emptied heart "desires nothing at all, nor has it anything it wants to get rid of. Therefore it is free of all prayers or its prayer consists of nothing but being uniform with God. That is all its prayer.... When the soul has got so far, it loses its name and is drawn into God, so that in itself it becomes nothing.... When the detachment reaches its climax, it becomes ignorant with knowing, loveless with loving, and dark with enlightenment. Thus we may understand the words of a master, that the poor in spirit are they who have abandoned all things to God, just as He possessed them when we did not exist. None can do this but a pure, detached heart." Eckhart applies a passage from wisdom literature to God when he says: "This is God who 'in all things I seek rest'" (Sirach 24:11). The Godself seeks rest in us, but we must offer a restful place for God to reside in.

Inner Solitude Requires Practice and Discipline

One does not have to flee the world to learn and practice an inner solitude. Eckhart says, "This cannot be learned by running away, by fleeing into the desert away from external things; a person must learn to acquire an inner solitude, wherever and with whomsoever one may be. One must learn to penetrate things and find God there, and make the divine image grow in oneself in an essential way."

The practice of solitude requires discipline, like any art form. Eckhart writes, "It is just like learning to write: truly, if a man is to acquire this art, he must apply himself and practice hard, however heavy and bitter a task it seems to him, and however impossible. If he is prepared to practice diligently and often, he will learn and master the art.... Wherever his thoughts may stray, he will do the job because he has the skill." Eventually the practice becomes a habit and is done with a certain ease. "Thus a person should be pervaded with God's presence, transformed with the form of his beloved God, and made essential by Him, so that God's presence shines for him without any effort; rather he will find emptiness in all things and be totally free of things. But first there must be thought and attentive study, just as with a pupil in any art." Indeed, "this above all is necessary: that a person should train and practice one's mind well and bring it to God, and then one will always have divinity within." Eckhart urges us to "practice diligently and often" and cautions that it "requires constant watchfulness."

Eckhart spells out the training and discipline he is speaking of:

> You should learn to be able to let go in your works. Yet it is not easy for an undisciplined person to reach a point when no busyness and no work hinders him or her — it calls for diligent application in order that God is always present to one and shines unveiled all the time and in all company. Skillful diligence is required for this, and especially in two areas. One is that a person shut oneself off well inwardly so that his or her mind is protected from images from the outside so that they remain outside and do not unfittingly walk and keep company with him. One should see that they do not find a resting-place in him or her. Secondly, one should not let oneself be caught up by one's internal imagery, whether it comes in the form of images or lofty thoughts, or outward impressions of whatever is present to one's mind lest one be distracted or dissipate oneself in their multiplicity. A person ought to train and discipline all one's powers to this task and keep one's inner self present to oneself.

Learning to let go means one is capable of dealing with light or dark, joy or sorrow, with equanimity. One can go to work with a clarity of mind and purpose. "As soon as a person has weaned himself or herself from all things and distanced himself from them, then one can faithfully perform all one's works, taking delight in them or leaving them alone without any hindrance." We are fully present whether we find ourselves at work or leisure. "A person should become a God-seeker in all things and a God-finder among all kinds of persons and in all places and all ways. In this manner one can always grow and never reach an end of growing." We need to "accept all things equally from God, not ever looking and wondering which is greater, or higher, or better. We should just follow where God points out for us, that is, what we are included to and to which we are most often directed, and where our bent is." After all, "God is in all ways, and equal in all ways, for one who can take Him equally." Furthermore, paradox reigns, for "where God shines least for us is often where God shines the most. This is why we should accept God equally in all ways and in all things."

What if you have your own special practice?

Now someone might say, "But if I do take God equally in all ways and in all things, do I not still need some special way?" Now see. In whatever way you find God most, and you are most often aware of Him, that is the way you should follow. But if another way presents itself, quite contrary to the first, and if, having abandoned the first way, you find God as much in the new way as in the one you have then that is right. But the noblest and best thing would be this, if a man were to come to such equality, with such calm and certainty that he could find God and enjoy Him in *any* way and in *all* things, without having to wait for anything or chase after anything: *that* would delight me!

Thich Nhat Hanh on the Apophatic Divinity

Anyone familiar with Buddhist practice or teaching will recognize in Eckhart's writing profound Buddhist insight. Conversely, whenever I read Thich Nhat Hanh, I almost always feel I might as well be reading Meister Eckhart. They have so much in common that it would be foolish to overplay the point, so I will offer just a few of the parallels here.

Thich Nhat Hanh is very fond of talking about God as the "Ground of all being." He attributes that phrase to twentieth-century theologian Paul Tillich, but Tillich himself got it from Meister Eckhart, who often talks about "God's ground and our ground" and so on. In addition, Hildegard of Bingen actually talks about Mary being the "ground of all being," and of course she wrote a hundred years before Eckhart and eight hundred years before Tillich. So this notion of Divinity as ground is deep in the Christian mystical tradition. One reason Thich Nhat Hanh is so partial to this phraseology is that it moves us beyond the many projections we put onto God. It moves us deeper than usual God talk.

As Thich Nhat Hanh says: "All notions applied to the phenomenal worlds…are transcended. The greatest relief we can obtain is available when we touch the ultimate, Tillich's 'ground of being.'…Life is no longer confined to time and space." Here Thich Nhat Hanh talks like Eckhart when he speaks of the "Godhead." This language opens the door, we might say, to the Apophatic Divinity, and Thich Nhat Hanh is very at home with the Apophatic Divinity. Says Thich Nhat Hanh: "God as the ground of being cannot be conceived of. Nirvana also cannot be conceived of. If we are aware when we use the word 'nirvana' or the word 'God' that we are talking about the ground of being there is no danger in using these words."

Thich Nhat Hanh is very wary of the grave *danger* of living only with names and concepts of Divinity — as was Eckhart — and he explains why clinging to notions and ideas is so debilitating: It does not take us to the depth of things and into the depths of our experiences. In fact, it keeps us away. "The ultimate dimension of reality has nothing to do with concepts," he warns us. You cannot just describe and talk about apple juice — you must drink it. "Things cannot be described by concepts and words. They can only be encountered by direct experience." It is that experiential side of life and of tasting — whether of apple juice or of God — that gets overlooked in an overly rational, left-brain experience of life. Thich Nhat Hanh invokes "negative theology" or "apophatic theology" to cure Christians of too many concepts. "'Negative theology' is an effort and practice to prevent Christians from being caught by notions and concepts that prevent them from touching the living spirit of Christianity.... We are talking about the death of every concept we may have of God in order to experience God as a living reality directly."

Meanwhile, Eckhart says: "I pray God to rid me of God." How like Thich Nhat Hanh is that!

Thich Nhat Hanh cites with approval the philosopher Ludwig Wittgenstein, who said, "Concerning that which cannot be talked about, we should not say anything." Comments Thich Nhat Hanh, "We cannot talk about it, but we can experience it.... We can experience the non-born, non-dying, non-beginning, non-ending because it is reality itself. The way to experience it is to abandon our habit of perceiving everything through concepts and representations." He discusses why Buddha was reluctant to engage in a lot of God talk. "The Buddha was not against God. He was only against notions of God that are mere mental constructions that do not correspond to reality, notions that prevent us from developing our selves and touching ultimate reality." If too much God talk (or too much talk of anything) prevents us from exploring our deepest selves and reality, then clearly we need to learn some silence. Which is exactly why Eckhart recommends the same.

Thich Nhat Hanh invokes his friend, the catholic monk Thomas Merton, who points out that leaving words behind is a sign of spiritual maturity (Teresa of Avila was very explicit about this also). Thich Nhat Hanh comments: "Simple and primitive images may have been the object of our faith in God in the beginning, but as we advance, He becomes present without any image, beyond any satisfactory mental representation. We come to a point where any notion we had can no longer represent God." He says: "We must abandon our notions of God, Buddha, nirvana, self, non-self, birth, death, being, and non-being." It is necessary to "rid ourselves of all notions of God in order for God to be there. The Holy Spirit, the energy of God in us, is the true door. We know the Holy Spirit as energy and not as notions and words." After we've explored Eckhart's sense of the Apophatic Divinity and his teaching about meditation, reading Thich Nhat Hanh evokes a sense of déjà vu.

Thich Nhat Hanh actually defines nirvana as the state of being at home in the kind of space of no-words that Eckhart speaks of when he says nirvana is "the extinction of all words, ideas, and concepts." Thich Nhat Hanh repeats the well-known story of the Zen master who said to his student, "When you meet the Buddha, kill him," and he comments: "He meant that the student should kill the Buddha-concept in order for him to experience the real Buddha directly." This echoes Eckhart's teaching "I pray God to rid me of God" and his emphasis on the path of letting go. Thich Nhat Hanh writes, "The practice of Buddhism has very much to do with the removal of notions. In Buddhist practice, we aim at liberating ourselves from notions and perceptions, even notions and perceptions about our own happiness." This echoes Eckhart's teaching about living and working "without a why." Says Thich Nhat Hanh, more important "than notions and perceptions…is our direct experience of suffering and of happiness." That means that undergoing the via positiva and the via negativa precedes language and concepts and doctrines.

Thich Nhat Hanh makes clear that "in the Buddhist tradition, religious experience is described as awakening (bodhi) or insight (prajna). It is not intellectual, not made of notions and concepts, but of the kind of understanding that brings more solidity, freedom, joy, and faith." Recall that Eckhart uses the term "breakthrough," a word he invented in the newly forming

German language of his day, to describe the experience of God (as distinct from God talk). He says: "In breakthrough I learn that God and I are one." This is a statement about our deification. About that, Thich Nhat Hanh comments: "The idea of deification, that a person is a microcosm of God, is very inspiring. It is close to the Asian tradition that states that the body of a human being is a minicosmos. God made humans so that humans can become God. A human being is a mini-God, a *micro-theos* who has been created in order to participate in the divinity of God. Deification is made not only of the spirit but of the body of a human also." And he repeats what Eckhart and Thomas Aquinas both teach when he says: "Why did God become a man? So that I might be born the same God."

Mindfulness

How do we arrive at this deep state of communion with the Apophatic Divinity? Says Thich Nhat Hanh: "Mindfulness is the key. When you become aware of something, you begin to have enlightenment. When you drink a glass of water and are aware that you are drinking a glass of water deeply with your whole being, enlightenment is there in its initial form. To be enlightened is always to be enlightened about something. I am enlightened about the fact that I am drinking a glass of water. I can obtain joy, peace, and happiness just because of that enlightenment." Mindful practices return us to our source, and we become like that source. Thich Nhat Hanh says, "The substance of a Buddha is mindfulness. Every time you practice conscious breathing, you are a living Buddha. To go back to yourself and dwell in mindfulness is the best practice in difficult moments. Mindfulness of breathing is your island, where you can be safe and happy, knowing that whatever happens, you are doing your best things. This is the way to take refuge in the Buddha, not as mere devotion but as a transformational practice."

Mindfulness is a return home. "Mindfulness is the light that shows us the way. It is the living Buddha inside of us. Mindfulness gives rise to insight, awakening, and love. We all have the seed of mindfulness within us." But we need to water that seed, to give it some attention. Just as Thich Nhat Hanh can talk about the "living Buddha inside of us," so Eckhart talks about the "Christ within us" and the "seed of God within us" and the "kingdom/queendom of God" within us. Both need attention on our part.

The fruits of mindfulness practice are real. "When you practice mindfulness," Thich Nhat Hanh says, "you enjoy within you the fruits of the practice. You are happy and peaceful, and your happiness and peace radiate around you for others to enjoy." This very much parallels Eckhart's promise that we find repose in God and God in us.

For Thich Nhat Hanh, mindfulness and focusing concentration complement each other. He says: "Concentration is the food of understanding.... Concentration also has its food, which is called mindfulness. Mindfulness is to be here now. Eating mindfully, walking mindfully, sitting mindfully, and hugging mindfully is where you develop concentration. Because you are concentrated, you are able to understand." Eckhart also teaches the importance of concentration in the following story:

> A pagan scholar was dedicated to the science of arithmetic and concentrated all his powers on it. He was sitting by the fire one day making calculations when someone came by, drew his sword, and not knowing who the scholar was, exclaimed: "Tell me this instant what your name is or I will kill you!" The scholar was so engrossed in his science that he neither saw nor heard the soldier. All he needed to do to save his life was to say: "my name is such and such," but he was too engrossed to do even that. The enemy screamed loud and fierce, but he still did not answer and his enemy cut off his head. This took place in pursuit of the truth of the natural sciences. How much more ought we to direct all our powers of concentration and letting go to that foundation where our treasure lies hidden.

Nirvana and the Godhead

When Thich Nhat Hanh talks about nirvana, I cannot help but hear Eckhart talking about the Godhead, which, he says, is as different from God as is heaven from Earth. Says Thich Nhat Hanh: "In the phenomenal world, we see that there is birth and death. There is coming and going, being and non-being. But in nirvana, which is the ground of being equivalent to God, there is no birth, no death, no coming, no going, no being, no non-being. All these concepts must be transcended." Eckhart teaches that the Godhead, from whom we all come and to whom we shall all return, is of such unity that "everything within the Godhead is unity, and we cannot speak about it. God accomplishes, but the Godhead does not do so and there is no deed within the Godhead. The Godhead never goes searching for a deed. God and the Godhead are distinguished through deeds and a lack of deeds." And when one returns to the Godhead, "no one asks me where I'm coming from or where I've been. No one has missed me." Nirvana is noumenal and beyond the phenomenal, and therefore beyond words and concepts. So too with the Godhead, which is about *mystery* (God being about history and creation), about *being* rather than doing, about silence rather than words. Both God and Godhead are ways of naming the Divine, but the Godhead language respects the unnameable silence of God.

Thich Nhat Hanh teaches that "God is neither small nor big. God has no beginning or end. God is not more or less beautiful. All the ideas we use to describe the phenomenal world cannot be applied to God." Eckhart uses identical language when he says that, strictly speaking, we cannot apply words like "good, better or best" to God because God is beyond them all.

Meister Eckhart talks about "transformed knowledge" and "unknowing knowing" and "pure ignorance" so that we are rendered "unencumbered and bare." This leads us into a "desert" of "pure nothingness" and "darkness" where we are to remain still to hear God speak. In a similar vein, Thich Nhat Hanh stresses how "the Buddhist teaching of abandoning your knowledge is very important." Why? Because knowledge can be "an obstacle" to understanding. "To know and to understand are two different things." That is why Buddhists "speak about letting go of your knowledge" and moving beyond dualisms "to transcend both notions of being and non-being." Here is where paradox is born.

The Living Buddha and the Cosmic Christ

Another area where Thich Nhat Hanh and Meister Eckhart find common ground concerns the Cosmic Christ (see chapter two). One can speak of the "historical Buddha" just as one speaks of the "historical Jesus," but it is the living Buddha or the Cosmic Christ that is present to us today. Thich Nhat Hanh talks about the "ontological Buddha, the Buddha at the center of the universe." Is this not the exact language of the Cosmic Christ, the "Christ at the center of the universe"? Here is how Thich Nhat Hanh puts it:

> Dharmakaya is the embodiment of Dharma, always shining, always enlightening trees, grass, birds, human beings, and so on, always emitting light. It is this Buddha who is preaching now and not just 2,500 years ago. Sometimes we call this Buddha Vairochana, the ontological Buddha, the Buddha at the center of the universe.... The trees, the birds, the violet bamboo, the yellow chrysanthemums are all preaching the Dharma that Shakyamuni taught 2,500 years ago. We can be in touch with him through any of these. He is a living Buddha, always available.

Yes, the light in all things. Is that not familiar to one who has learned of the Cosmic Christ? I often speak of the relationship of the Cosmic Christ to the historical Jesus as one of light wave to light particle. This is how Thich Nhat Hanh describes the relation of the historical Buddha to the Living Buddha. "Shakyamuni, the historical Buddha, is the Nirmanakay, the transformation body, a light ray sent by the sun of Dharmakaya."

Thich Nhat Hanh addresses the subject of the Eucharist within the context of Cosmic Christ theology when he writes: "Not many people want to become priests in our day, but everyone is hungry. So many people are hungry for spiritual food, there are so many hungry souls." And he speaks of Jesus's words at the Last Supper, reenacted in Catholic worship:

> "Take, my friends, this is my flesh, this is my blood" — Can there be any more drastic language in order to wake you up? What could Jesus have said that is better than that? ... This piece of bread is the body of the whole cosmos. If Christ is the body of God, which he is, then the bread he offers is also the body of the cosmos. Look deeply and you notice the sunshine in the bread, the blue sky in the bread, the cloud and the great earth in the bread. Can you tell me what is not in a piece of bread? The whole cosmos has come together in order to bring to you this piece of bread. You eat it in such a way that you come alive, truly alive."

Thich Nhat Hanh is pointing out that a Cosmic Christ understanding applies very much to our worship practices, and reverence follows when one recognizes the holiness of all bread, all that goes into bread, all being.

Thich Nhat Hanh says, "When I touch a rock, I never touch it as inanimate. The tree is spirit, mind; the rock is spirit, mind; the air, the stars, the moon, everything is consciousness. They are the object of your consciousness." To say that consciousness is everywhere is another way of saying that the Cosmic Christ and Buddha nature are everywhere and in all things. Surely, Thich Nhat Hanh insists, the Buddha nature is within us and not just outside. He says: "The Buddha is not really another person. The Buddha is within us, because the substance that makes up a Buddha is the energy of mindfulness, of understanding, and compassion.... You have the Buddha nature within you.... If Shakyamuni, the historical Buddha, has Buddhahood, you yourself have your own Buddhahood." That is why one can say: "I take refuge in the Buddha within myself.... You have the Buddha nature in you, and you take refuge in that nature within you."

Time and again Eckhart stresses the point that Christ is within us and we are all other Christs, that Jesus is not the "only" son of God but we are all sons and daughters of God, that Christ took flesh not just in the historical Jesus but in humanity as a whole. Thich Nhat Hanh makes the same point when he says: "You are invited to reflect on the word 'only.' You are also a daughter or a son of God. You are Jesus. All of us are Jesus. Every wave is born from water, every wave has water as substance. In Buddhism, and especially in the Northern school of Buddhism, every one of us has Buddha nature and every one of us is a Buddha-to-be."

Similarly, Eckhart talks about our responsibility to birth the Christ in us. "What good is it to me," Eckhart asks during a Christmas sermon, "if Mary gave birth to the son of God 1,400 years ago and I do not do the same? We are all meant to be mothers of God." Thich Nhat Hanh agrees: "We practice in such a way that Buddha is born every moment of our daily life, that Jesus Christ is born every moment of our daily life — not only on Christmas day, because every day is Christmas day, every minute is a Christmas minute. The child within us is waiting each minute for us to be born again and again." Eckhart says: "The seed of God is in us.... Now the seed of a pear tree grows into a pear tree, a hazel seed into a hazel tree, the seed of God into God." But he also insists that the seed requires a "good, wise, and industrious cultivator" to grow into God. Thich Nhat Hanh also likes to talk about our carrying seeds of goodness and seeds of destruction within us and how we have to cultivate and work at growing the former.

Thich Nhat Hanh compares Jesus's "Kingdom of God" with the Pure Land, and he says with practice you discover that the Pure Land "is in your own heart, that you do not need to go to a faraway place. You can set up your own mini-Pure Land, a Sangha of practice, right here, right now. But many people need to go away before they realize they do not have to go anywhere." This language is almost identical to Eckhart's: "God is at home; it is we who have gone out for a walk." Thich Nhat Hanh tells us, "I like the expression 'resting in God.' When you pray with all your heart the Holy Spirit is in you, and as you continue to pray, the Holy Spirit continues in you.... You are resting in God, and God will work in you. For transformation to take place, you only need to allow the Holy Spirit to stay in you. The Holy Spirit is the energy of God that shines forth and shows you the way. You can see things deeply, understand deeply, and love deeply." Meister Eckhart often talks about the "repose of God" and delivered several sermons on the topic. "All things seek repose," he declares, and to seek repose *is* to seek God.

Like Eckhart, Thich Nhat Hanh declares, "You do not have to abandon this world. You do not have to go to Heaven or wait for the future to have refuge. You can take refuge here and now. You only need to dwell deeply in the present moment." Dwelling deeply in the present moment is dwelling deeply in the Kingdom of God, which is already among us. Thich Nhat Hanh says, "The seed of mindfulness is the presence of the Buddha in us, called Buddha nature (Buddhata), the nature of enlightenment.... The Holy Spirit can be described as being always present in our hearts in the form of a seed.... The Kingdom of God is in us as a seed, a mustard seed." Indeed, "Everything and everyone is dwelling in nirvana, in the Kingdom of God." The Kingdom of God is everywhere and all the time for those who are, in Eckhart's words, awake.

In an amazing passage, Eckhart writes:

I have often said that God is creating the entire universe fully and totally in this present now. Everything God created six thousand years ago — and even previous to that — as he made the world, God creates now all at once. Now consider this: God is in everything, but God is nowhere as much as he is in the soul. There, where time never enters, where no image shines in, in the innermost and deepest aspect of the soul God creates the whole cosmos.... Everything of the past and everything of the present and everything of the future God creates in the innermost realms of the soul.

Is there any distance between Eckhart's experience and that expressed by Thich Nhat Hanh, who writes: "Touching the present moment, we realize that the present is made of the past and is creating the future. When we drink a cup of tea very deeply, we touch the whole of time. To meditate, to live a life of prayer is to live each moment of life deeply." Both speak about the depths of our soul — those "innermost realms" where no light shines in, without time or image — and how it is at that depth that all things get born and reborn.

Service and Compassion

Dwelling in the Kingdom of God that is the present moment is also paying attention to the suffering of the world. Eckhart and Thich Nhat Hanh both see compassion as being the fullest incarnation of the Christhood and the Buddhahood. Thich Nhat Hanh talks about *engaged Buddhism* and Eckhart insists that compassion is the "best" of all the names we have for God and that "compassion means justice." Eckhart says this work for justice "tickles God through and through." Thich Nhat Hanh says: A good Buddhist "helps the sick and the wounded as though he is serving a Buddha or a bodhisattva." This is Cosmic Christ theology — that all beings suffer and many innocent ones are crucified, and it is our task to relieve that suffering and cease crucifying others. The suffering ones are Christ and Buddha also. "As you do it to the least, you do it to me," spoke Jesus (Matthew 25:40).

Thich Nhat Hanh equates the Holy Spirit of the West with mindfulness and enlightenment. He writes: "For me, the Holy Spirit is mindfulness itself." Speaking of the Christian Trinity, he says: "We have the capacity to recognize the presence of the Holy Spirit whenever and wherever it manifests. It, too, is the presence of mindfulness, understanding, and love, the energy that animates and helps us recognize the living Christ." A Christian invoking the Holy Spirit "is taking refuge."

Meister Eckhart has a striking passage where he tells us that not substance but *relation* is the essence of everything that exists. "Relation accordingly is present in the essence of a thing, receives its being in the essence, but does not confer distinctions on the essence itself." How Buddhist an insight this is! For Thich Nhat Hanh, this is parallel to his teaching on "interbeing," which proposes: "Is there anything that has a separate self? No. A tree that stands in the front yard does not have a separate self." Why? Because without sunshine, soil, rain, and so on, the tree does not exist.

Ultimately, Thich Nhat Hanh tells us that for him "there is no conflict at all between the Buddha and the Christ in me. They are real brothers, they are real sisters within me.... A Christian is a continuation of Jesus Christ: He is Jesus Christ, and she is Jesus Christ. That is how I see things, this is how I see people. A Buddhist is a child of the Buddha, he is, and she is, a continuation of the Buddha. She is the Buddha, he is the Buddha." Nor does Eckhart see a conflict, since "all paths lead to God for God is on them all evenly."

Thich Nhat Hanh tells us he is "very excited" about the encounter between Buddhism and Christianity in the twenty-first century, but he also calls for a "very drastic change" to occur in the Christian tradition; namely, the recovery of the Apophatic Divinity. "If we can bring into Christianity the insight of interbeing and of non-duality, we will radically transform the way people look on the Christian tradition, and the valuable jewels in the Christian tradition will be rediscovered."

I think he is right, and this insight already exists within the Christian tradition, as is clear from studying Meister Eckhart. By rediscovering Eckhart's profound apophatic theology and his unconscious Buddhism we can unlock these "valuable jewels" and launch a true interchange of Buddhist and Christian wisdom. I am very excited about bringing Meister Eckhart and Thich Nhat Hanh together in our troubled and needy times. They have so much to teach us all. Christianity needs an Eckhartian Christ Path.

CHAPTER FOUR

THE DIVINE FEMININE

Meister Eckhart Meets Adrienne Rich

Motherhood (the powerful Goddess)

— ADRIENNE RICH

The maternity bed is in the Godhead....
God lies like a woman on a maternity bed who has given birth
in every good soul that has learned to let go and is initiated.

— MEISTER ECKHART

Women's spiritual quest takes a distinctive form
in the fiction and poetry of women writers.
It begins in an experience of nothingness.

— CAROL P. CHRIST

In her profound poetry and essays, feminist poet and author Adrienne Rich offers insights from a woman's perspective that often parallel some of Eckhart's. Rich writes about "the dream of a common language" (the title of one of her books of poetry), and I propose that in Eckhart there is, at many crucial places, a common language and a common concern with women's history and language. In this chapter I will draw on both Adrienne

Rich's poetry and her brilliant study of motherhood, which qualifies as a study of the Divine Feminine — for she says, "Motherhood means the powerful Goddess." Entitled *Of Woman Born: Motherhood as Experience and Institution*, her book is a tour de force through the history of womanly power and disempowerment. In chapter five, we will also consider Eckhart's relationship to the women's movement of his day, the Beguines.

On the Divine Feminine

The Divine Feminine is celebrated by Rich first in the cosmos itself. She writes: "Prepatriarchal religion acknowledged the female presence in every part of the cosmos. The moon is generally held to have been the first object of nature-worship, and the moon, to whose phases the menstrual cycle corresponds, is anciently associated with women." The lunar deity was "first and foremost related to the Virgin-Mother-Goddess, who is 'for-herself' [that is, virgin] and whose power radiates out from her maternal aspect to the fertilization of the whole earth, the planting and harvesting of crops, the cycle of seasons, the dialogue of humankind and nature." The female presence was "once felt to dominate the universe."

Rich cites Joseph Campbell's observation: "There can be no doubt that in the very earliest ages of human history the magical force and wonder of the female was no less a marvel than the universe itself; and this gave to woman a prodigious power, which it has been one of the chief concerns of the masculine part of the population to break, control and employ to its own ends." Female figurines were, Campbell finds, "the first objects of worship by the species *Homo sapiens*. But there is a shift in the magic ritual and imagery of *Homo sapiens* from the vagina to the phallus, and from an essentially plant-oriented to a purely animal-oriented mythology." Campbell associates our first radical amazement with our awareness of "the natural mysteries of childbirth and menstruation [which] are as directly convincing as death itself and remain to this day what they must also have been in the beginning, primary sources of a religious awe."

Rich recognizes the ocean as the work of the Goddess as well: the ocean "whose tides respond, like woman's menses, to the pull of the moon, the ocean which corresponds to the amniotic fluid in which human life begins, the oceans on whose surface vessels (personified as female) can ride but in whose depth sailors meet their death and monsters conceal themselves."

In his very important sermon on compassion, Eckhart offers images galore of the womb's amniotic fluid; in fact, the word "compassion" comes from the word for "womb" in both Hebrew and Arabic. In this sermon, which I have titled "Compassion Is an Ocean — the Mystical Side to Compassion," Eckhart says: "The highest work of God is compassion and this means that God sets the soul in the highest and purest place which it can occupy: in space, in the sea, in a fathomless ocean; and there God works compassion. Therefore the prophet says: 'Lord, have compassion on the people who are in you.'" The "being-in" phraseology is common in Eckhart and is part of panentheism — all things *in* God and God in all things. This is also part of being *in* the womb of the Great Mother, being carried by the Godhead (see also Isaiah 41 about this). Eckhart continues: "What people are in God? Saint John says: 'God is love and whoever remain in love remains in God and God in her' (1 Jn. 4:16)."

"The Great Goddess is found in all water," Rich writes, and she then cites Erich Neumann: "The sea of heaven on which sail the barks of the gods of light the circular, life-generating ocean above and below the earth. To her belong all water, streams, fountains, ponds and springs as well as the rain." Eckhart talks about God as "an underground river," and he describes the idea of "living water": "This water is grace and light and springs up in the soul and rises within and presses upward and leaps up into eternity." How fountain-like, this water, that "springs," "rises," "presses," and "leaps." Living, indeed. The Goddess returns in Eckhart's consciousness and teaching.

Rich, like Eckhart, thinks cosmically. Often the stars, the nebulae, and the universe creep into her poems, even when she is talking of sleeping. "Sleeping, turning in turn like planets / rotating in their midnight meadow: / a touch is enough to let us know / we're not alone in the universe, even in sleep." She hints at the Cosmic Christ who undergoes multiple crucifixions when she writes:

And how have I used rivers, how have I used wars
to escape writing of the worst thing of all —
not the crimes of others, not even our own death,

but the failure to want our freedom passionately enough
so that blighted elms, sick rivers, massacres would seem
mere emblems of that desecration of ourselves?

Eckhart offers an amazing marriage of psyche and cosmos, or what he calls "heart and the heavens," when he discusses how just as the heart is located in the center of the body so the heavens are also "in the middle of things." The heart, he says, "is the noblest part of the body [and] lies in the center of the body from which it bestows life on the whole body. For the spring of life arises in the heart and has an effect like heaven. Heaven... bestows on all creatures their beings and their lives....If heaven were to be still, the waters would not flow, and all creatures would have no strength.... The spring of life is placed in the heart."

The Goddess, as Rich understands her, brought together in herself the via positiva and the via negativa: "The Great Mother, the female principle was originally personified both in darkness and in light in the depths of the water and the heights of the sky." The Book of Sirach, from which Eckhart cites often, also talks of Wisdom, who "walks on the vaults of the sky and the sands of the deep." For Rich, creativity and destruction were incarnated in the Goddess: "Even death was part of a movement in time, part of the cycle leading to reincarnation and rebirth. A 'dark' or 'negative' aspect of the Great Mother was thus already present from the beginning, inseparable from her benign, life-giving aspect. And, like death, violence, bloodshed, destructive powers were always there, the potentially 'evil' half of the Mother's profile, which, once completely split off, would become separately personified as the fanged blood-goddess Kali, the killer-mother Medea."

The presence of the Divine Feminine was pretty much banished when patriarchal religion took over, as Campbell has observed. According to Adrienne Rich, "patriarchal monotheism did not simply change the sex of the divine presence; it stripped the universe of female divinity, and permitted woman to be sanctified, as if by an unholy irony, only and exclusively as mother....The command of Yahweh: 'Be fruitful and multiply,' is an entirely patriarchal one; he is not invoking the Great Mother but bidding his sons beget still more sons." Rich recognizes an intrinsic contradiction in patriarchy — the "central ambiguity at the heart of patriarchy: the idea of the sacredness of motherhood and the redemptive power of woman as means, contrasted with the degradation of women in the order created by men."

Sinking, Letting Go, and the Apophatic Silence

Eckhart talks of letting go as a sinking — "We sink eternally from letting go to letting go into the One," he writes. Rich, too, speaks often of the sinking dynamic: "I sink and float / like a warm amphibious animal / that has broken the net, has run / through fields of snow leaving no print; this water washes off the scent — / *You are clear now.*" Notice how her sinking and letting go, like Eckhart's, is a cleansing affair, but a kind of rupturing occurs, a breaking of the net. The "warm amphibious animal" conjures up our bodiliness — spirituality for Rich is *not* about climbing Jacob's ladder to a sky God. It is about trust and letting go, sinking into La Mer, the sea, the mother of us all. The Great Mother.

> *"We are all meant to be mothers of God."*

Later in this same poem, called "Origins and History of Consciousness," Rich stresses the role *trust* plays in all this sinking:

> Trusting, untrusting,
> we lowered ourselves into this let ourselves
> downward hand over hand as on a rope that quivered
> over the unsearched.... We did this. Conceived
> of each other, conceived each other in a darkness
> which I remember as drenched in light.
> I want to call this, life.

Again, the journey of love she is describing is a journey "downward," and it has everything to do with trust. Similarly, Eckhart says the reason people do "not bear fruit" is that "they have no trust in either God or themselves," and "love cannot distrust" and "no person could ever trust God too much." Trust matters, Eckhart says, for "there is no better sign of perfect love than trust. For if a person deeply and wholeheartedly loves another, that inspires trust....And so, just as God could never love a person too much, neither can a person trust God too much."

Rich invokes another common theme found in Eckhart, that of darkness and light embracing each other, the light shining in the darkness. A darkness "drenched in light" in Rich's language. And this, she hopes, is what life is.

For Rich, such as in her poem "Diving into the Wreck," to dive and descend into the waters is to go down into the dark, into mystery, to trust, to explore. Eckhart advises the same: "The ground of the soul is dark," he warns. In the innermost realms of the soul, time and images do not enter and "no image has ever shed its light." Yet Eckhart advises us to go into the dark; down into the dark. Sink there. "The more a person is sunk in the ground of true humility the more one is sunk in the ground of divine being." In Eckhart's Latin language, "humility" comes from the word for "earth," *humus*.

In another via negativa poem, Rich speaks of falling and of letting go.

We cut the wires,
find ourselves in free-fall, as if
our true home were the undimensional
solitudes, the rift
in the Great Nebula.
No one who survives to speak
new language, has avoided this:
the cutting-away of an old force that held her
rooted to an old ground
the pitch of utter loneliness
where she herself and all creation
seem equally dispersed, weightlessness, her being a cry
to which no echo comes or can ever come.

Rich's language of "cutting away" and "cutting the wires" matches exactly Eckhart's word *Abgeschiedenheit*, which comes from the word for "scissors" and which we translate as "letting go."

The cutting results in a "free-fall" that is cosmic in scope, but it goes with the territory of being a new-language bearer, which is the work of the feminist poet and the medieval mystic. There is a solitude, an "utter loneliness," in the prophetic call that both Rich and Eckhart tasted. In the same poem, Rich indicates that what we do not hear is often the scariest — "and the whole chorus throbbing at our ears / like midges, told us nothing, nothing / of origins, nothing we needed / to know, nothing that could re-member us." The search for origins, the search for Source, rarely gets talked about, rarely gets taught, whether one is speaking of one's female ancestors or of one's quest for the Divine.

In the poem "Splittings," Rich talks about integrating our suffering and our living, our pain and our power, instead of allowing them to split off: "If we could learn to learn from pain / even as it grasps us." In this way she marries the via positiva and the via negativa. In the poem, she also wants to marry action and nonaction, action and contemplation: "I refuse these givens the splitting / between love and action I am choosing not to suffer uselessly and not to use her / I choose to love this time for once / with all my intelligence." Eckhart also refuses to split action from contemplation. In one famous sermon he praises the busy Martha over the contemplative Mary because Martha is more mature, since she can do two things at once — both contemplate the guest (Jesus) and do the preparations. Mary can only do one thing: sit in contemplation. Eckhart labels her "less mature," but he proposes she will one day grow up to be able to do both things at once. And Eckhart, too, combines both the pain of life with the power; he also resists the splitting of the intellectual brain from the mystical or intuitive brain.

In her poem "Cartographies of Silence," Rich addresses one of Eckhart's favorite themes, silence:

> The technology of silence
> The rituals, etiquette
> the blurring of terms
> silence not absence
> of words or music or even
> raw sounds
> Silence can be a plan
> rigorously executed

the blueprint to a life
It is a presence
it has a history a form
Do not confuse it
with any kind of absence.

This is like Eckhart, who says, "Nothing in all creation is so like God as silence." Eckhart countenances silence as letting go of all images and forms in order to entertain the one silent Word of God. For Eckhart, this Divine silence is not an "absence" but a "plan" and even a "blueprint to a life," as Rich says. Few people have so succinctly argued for the Apophatic Divinity, who is beyond all naming and all words, like Adrienne Rich when she confesses: "It was an old theme even for me: / Language cannot do everything — / chalk it on the walls where the dead poets / lie in their mausoleums." Not even poets — whose vocation is to name things, even ineffable things — can express everything with language. We all have to entertain nonlanguage and silence and death in the presence of mystery. What are the mysteries greater than our work, our words, our thoughts, that we take with us to our graves? Are they not written in silence more than in words?

At Home in Nothingness

Rich speaks of the "void," or what Eckhart calls nothingness, in the following stanzas of a poem written to a friend born in a Calvinist tradition who died of breast cancer at an early age. "You played heroic, necessary / games with death / since in your neo-protestant tribe the void / was supposed not to exist / except as a fashionable concept / you had no traffic with." In contrast, both Rich and Eckhart are very much at home with nothingness. They are unafraid to entertain the void. This includes the pregnant nothingness of God as well as of our own souls.

In fact, feminist theologian Carol P. Christ, in her book *Diving Deep and Surfacing*, describes nothingness as a common theme and focus of women writers. In *Diving Deep*, Christ celebrates five women writers, including Adrienne Rich, who focus on the spiritual quest, and in each she finds that "an experience *of nothingness*" (italics hers) is "central." She writes:

Women's spiritual quest takes a distinctive form in the fiction and poetry of women writers. It begins in an experience *of nothingness*. Women experience emptiness in their own lives — in self-hatred, in self-negation, in being a victim; in relationships with men; and in the values that have shaped their lives. Experiencing nothingness, women reject conventional solutions and question the meaning of their lives, thus opening themselves to the revelation of deeper sources of power and value.

In this way, a passage from the via negativa to the via creativa occurs. Christ continues, "The experience of nothingness often precedes an *awakening*, similar to a conversion experience, in which the powers of being are revealed.... Through awakening to new powers, women overcome self-negation and self-hatred and refuse to be victims."

Two powerful areas of awakening for women involve valuing their experiences of the Divine in nature and the "affirmation of women's bodies" in all their diversity, an affirmation girls and women rarely feel in our largely judgmental culture. She argues that we need to "develop a new understanding of being human, in which the body is given a more equal footing with the intellect and the human connection to nature is positivity valued."

To reach this more creative place, we often must first become full with nothingness. Christ compares this experience to the mystic's dark night of the soul, and she insists that it needs to be accompanied by "the courage to see." For Christ, Rich's phrase "diving into the wreck" suggests that kind of apocalyptic purification by fire and ice, including righteous anger. In Rich's poem, Christ sees a "metaphor for an interior journey to the source of her inner powers.... She is seeking the primal source." As an example, she cites these lines by Rich, which name her destination: "the wreck and not the story of the wreck / the thing itself and not the myth." Diving down, Rich finds what she is seeking and tells us, "This is the place." Her undersea exploration, Christ says, "is a pilgrimage; the diver enters the waters of transformation and rebirth.... She has reached the sacred center." Christ credits Adrienne Rich with providing, among all the writers she studied, "the clearest vision of the path toward the integration of spiritual vision into social reality."

I recognize in these reflections by Christ much synergy with Eckhart's telling of the spiritual journey. Eckhart also frequently names the nothingness experience and its potential for new birth, and in this way he speaks deeply to women's experience. He preached to women (and to minorities and peasants) in their own language, and this was no doubt one reason why he was so appreciated by them.

For instance, Eckhart describes a dream: "A man had a dream, a daydream: it seemed to him that he was big with nothingness as a woman is with a child. In this nothingness God was born. He was the fruit of nothingness. God was born in nothingness." Here, as we saw in chapter three, Eckhart shows us that his idea of "nothingness" is not something negative but something wholly Divine-like. On many occasions he says, "God is nothing." Here, Eckhart "dives down" like Rich into the nothingness of the maternal womb and comes back to proclaim the Divine Feminine.

The Primary Role of Creativity

How do we move from an unmothered world dominated by a savage sense of fatherhood to a healthier one? Rich tells us in a poem: "*This is what I am:* watching the spider / rebuild — "patiently," they say, but I recognize in her impatience — my own — / the passion to make and make again / where such unmaking reigns / the refusal to be a victim / *we have lived with violence so long*." Creativity rises above masochism, rises beyond victimhood. Creativity is empowerment. It is when the Goddess rises from within and challenges the spirit of "unmaking" and the refusal to hold creativity up as a primary value in a culture.

The need "to make and make again" was also very dear to Eckhart. In my book *Passion for Creation*, I wrote that one can "extract an almost complete philosophy of art from Eckhart's writings," and I recognized nine major sermons built around creativity, or the via creativa. For Eckhart, creativity is ongoing, perpetual, Divine, and highly personal. In one Christmas sermon he speaks to that "eternal birth" that God "accomplishes unceasingly in eternity." But, he asks, "What does it avail me if this birth takes place unceasingly and yet does not take place within myself? It is quite fitting, however, that it should take place within me." What is this birth; who is this birth? "Not only is the Son of the heavenly Father born in this darkness, but you also are born there as a child of the same Father and none other; and he also gives that power to you." He ends the sermon with a prayer: "May the God who was reborn today as a human being help us in this birth! May he eternally help us weak human beings so that we may be born in him in a divine way."

Our rebirth is a "breakthrough," and in this breakthrough, Eckhart says, "I discover that I and God are one." We ourselves take on a Divine mode as sons and daughters of God. "It would mean little to me that the 'word was made flesh' for man, in Christ, granting that the latter is distinct from me, unless he also was made flesh in me personally, so that I too would become the Son of God."

In another sermon Eckhart mixes Divine motherhood and fatherhood when he declares: "The Father's speaking is his giving birth; the Son's listening is his being born." Creativity drives Divinity. We are the mothers of the Cosmic Christ for "we are all meant to be mothers of God," and "where the Father generates his Son in me, I am that very same Son and no one else." As he often asks: "What help is it to me that the Father gives birth to his Son unless I too give birth to him? It is for this reason that God gives birth to his Son in a perfect soul and lies in the maternity bed so that he can give birth to him again in all his works." All our works are a birthing of the Cosmic Christ. Christ is the "innermost" word of God, and "God speaks once (Jb 33). He speaks in engendering his Son, for the Son is the Word. He also speaks in creating the creatures." Creatures and the Christ, beings and the Cosmic Christ, are born as one.

For Eckhart the Holy Spirit *is* the spirit of creativity. It is like a "rapid river" with "living waters that flow." A certain "intoxication" occurs in the experience of the Spirit at work in creativity. "The Holy Spirit cannot keep from flowing into every place where he finds *space* and he flows just as extensively as the space he finds there." This is why we need to be emptied, to be naked, to let go in order that Spirit can fill us. The soul must be "brought together and solidified in the noblest power found within it if the soul is to receive the divine 'river' that fills it and causes it to rejoice" — just as the apostles were "gathered together and enclosed when they received the Holy Spirit." Thus, as with Rich, the via negativa paves the way for the via creativa, and we become "coworkers with God." When the "rapid river of the Holy Spirit" moves us, "grace is mixed up with a creature, that is, with myself."

Creativity is a requisite for us. We exist to give birth. Eckhart writes, "Human beings should be communicative and emanative with all the gifts they have received from God....If human beings have something that they do not bestow on others they are not good. People who do not bestow on others spiritual things and whatever lies in them have never been spiritual. People are not to receive and keep gifts for themselves alone, but they should share themselves and pour forth everything they possess in their bodies and souls as far as possible, and whatever others desire of them." Eckhart insists that we honor our creativity. "Whatever can be truly expressed in its proper meaning must emerge from inside a person and pass through the inner form. It cannot come from outside to inside of a person but must emerge from within." He names the power of our creativity when he says, "Words too have great power: we could work wonders with words. All words have their power from the first Word."

God is "pure generation and means the same as 'a life of all things.'... His generating is at the same time his indwelling, and his indwelling is his generating." It is the nature of God to be fruitful and creative. Eckhart speaks explicitly to the maternal side of God when he writes: "The maternity bed is in the Godhead....God lies like a woman on a maternity bed who has given birth in every good soul that has learned to let go and is initiated."

We share the same compulsion for creativity, for "the soul, too, is in no way content until the Son of God is born in her." Joy is intrinsic to the creative process. "God has all his joy in giving birth, and therefore He gives birth to His Son in us, that we may have all our joy therein, and that we may give birth to the same natural Son with Him: For God has all His joy in giving birth and therefore He gives birth to Himself in us, so that he may have all His joy in the soul and we may have all our joy in Him." Our creativity is boundless, for "the soul that has God is fruitful all the time."

We are heirs of the "fearful creative power" of God and are to bear "fruit that remains" (John 15:116). What remains? "What is inborn in me remains." The artist learns to "no longer accomplish things with grace but divinely in God. Thus the soul is in a wonderful way enchanted and loses itself." It is like the annunciation story all over again when creativity is at work. Eckhart writes, "The work that is 'with,' 'outside,' and 'above' the artist must become the work that is 'in' him, taking form within her, in order towards the end that she may produce a work of art, in accordance with the verse 'The Holy Spirit shall come upon thee' (Lk. 1:35), that is so that the "above' may become 'in.'" Yet "all things beget themselves: each begets his own nature. Why does not the apple tree's nature produce wine, and why does not the vine produce applesauce? Because that is not its nature, and so forth with all other creatures."

Indian art historian and philosopher Ananda Coomaraswamy (see chapter nine) credits Eckhart with his teaching of God as Mother because "with respect to his 'staying with creatures to keep them in being' Eckhart thinks of God as a mother (the creations both of God and man are in the nature of children begotten and conceived), and it will not be overlooked that in so far as man takes care of things that have been made and preserves them from decay, he is working temporally in the analogy of God's maternal maintenance."

Thus, if Rich is correct when she identifies motherhood and the Goddess, then Eckhart is swimming in the Goddess because for him the via creativa, the call to us all to be mothers of self, of the Cosmic Christ, and of all our many birthings, is an essential part of our spiritual journey. If "the maternity bed is in the Godhead," then clearly a return to the Godhead renders us motherly, motherly in what Rich has labeled an "unmothered world," that is, a patriarchal world.

Rich points out that ancient Goddess-worshipping societies were identified as such in part because their earliest art celebrates womanly dignity and power. These artifacts "express an attitude toward the female charged with awareness of her intrinsic importance, her depth of meaning, her existence at the very center of what is necessary and sacred.... The images of the pre-patriarchal goddess-cults did one thing; they told women that power, awesomeness, and centrality were theirs by nature, not by privilege or miracle; the female was primary."

The Goddess represented the intrinsic power and sacredness of creativity itself. She embodied transformation, and one expression of this in ancient societies was the reverence for pottery making, which, Rich writes, "was invented by women, was taboo to men, [and] was regarded as a sacred process." Rich observes: "It does not seem unlikely that the woman potter

molded, not simply vessels, but images of herself, the vessel of life, the transformer of blood into life and milk — that in so doing she was expressing,
celebrating, and giving concrete form to her experience as a creative being
possessed of indispensable power. Without her...invention and skill, the pot
or vessel — the most sacred of handmade objects — would not exist."

Eckhart, too, endorses this powerful image of creativity as a transformative container. He equates the Holy Spirit with our becoming fruitful, just
as Mary became fruitful with Jesus through the Spirit's power — and as
all of creation was begotten by the Holy Spirit. As Eckhart scholar Reiner
Schurmann puts it, for Eckhart "the reception of God...in us is a gift which
must bear fruit: detachment is completed by fertility.... One sole determination joins them [humans and God] together: that of giving birth." Rich adds
that "in primordial terms the vessel is anything but a 'passive' receptacle; it
is *transformative* — active, powerful.... The transformations necessary for
the continuation of life are thus, in terms of this early imagery, exercises
of female power." This power was "not over others, but transforming
power, was the truly significant and essen-
tial power, and this, in prepatriarchal society women knew for their own." In
biological motherhood, too, as in these
other activities, "woman was not merely a
producer and stabilizer of life: there, too,
she was a *transformer*."

> *"The soul that has God is*
> *fruitful all the time."*

Rich recognizes that coming to grips with the Great Mother, including
her powers of creativity and her powers of death and destruction, is essential
to male as well as female consciousness, particularly in today's patriarchal
culture, which peddles so many negative images of women. Creativity is key
for a new vision to occur, and men must find it within themselves. Rich says:

> I am curious and expectant about the future of the masculine conscious-
> ness. I feel in the work of the men whose poetry I read today a deep
> pessimism and fatalistic grief; and I wonder if it isn't the masculine side
> of what women have experienced, the price of masculine dominance.
> *One thing I am sure of: just as woman is becoming her own midwife, creat-*
> *ing herself anew, so man will have to learn to gestate and give birth to his*
> *own subjectivity — something he has frequently wanted woman to do for*

him. . . . Women can no longer be primarily mothers and muses for men: we have our own work cut out for us.

Who can deny that Eckhart, with his immense celebration of our divine powers of creativity, is such a man who has "learned to gestate and give birth to his own subjectivity"? He invites everyone, women and men alike, to do the same. In *Passion for Creation,* I gave titles to Eckhart's sermons that explicitly focus on the via creativa, the call to creativity and birthing. These titles encapsulate how Eckhart honors the creativity of the Divine Feminine: "How Letting Go and Letting Be Are to Bear Fruit"; "Three Births: Ours, God's, and Ourselves as God's Children"; "Our Divinity and God's Divinity: To Be God Is to Give Birth"; "We Are Children of God and Mothers of God"; "The Holy Spirit, Like a Rapid River, Divinizes Us"; "Be You Creative as God Is Creative"; and so on.

As for Eckhart in his time, Rich connects these spiritual ideas to modern politics, culture, gender, psychology, and society:

> One of the devastating effects of technological capitalism has been its numbing of the powers of the imagination — specifically, the power to envision new human and communal relationships. I am a feminist because I feel endangered, psychically and physically, by this society, and because I believe that the women's movement is saying that we've come to an edge of history when men — in so far as they are embodiments of the patriarchal idea — have become dangerous to children and other living things, themselves included; and that we can no longer afford to keep the female principle — the mother in all women and the woman in many men — straitened within the tight little postindustrial family, or within any male-induced notion of where the female principle is valid and where it is not.

Compassion Means Societal Action

Both Rich and Eckhart understand that embracing the via creativa of the Divine Feminine means transforming not only ourselves but our society. It leads to the via transformativa. For both, one of the most direct expressions of this is in how we feed, and thus care for, one another.

In her poem "Hunger," Rich declares: "The decision to feed the world

/ is the real decision. No revolution / has chosen it. For that choice requires / that women shall be free. / I choke on the taste of bread in North America / but the taste of hunger in North America / is poisoning me." Eckhart also addresses hunger in stark terms in his commentary on the "Our Father" prayer. Commenting on the phrase "Give us this day our daily bread," he writes:

> Bread is given to us so that not only we might eat but that we recognize others in need, lest anyone say "*my* bread" is given to me instead of understanding that it is *ours*, given to me, to others through me and to me through others. For not only bread but all things which are necessary for sustaining this present life are given to us with others and because of others and given to others in us. Whoever does not give to another what belongs to the other, such a one does not eat his own bread but eats the bread of another along with his own. Thus when we justly eat the bread we have received, we certainly eat our bread; but when we eat evilly and with sin the bread we have received, then we are not eating our own bread but the bread of another. For everything which we have unjustly is not really ours.

Rich speaks to compassion and its active dimensions when she writes:

> But gentleness is active
> gentleness swabs the crusted stump
> invents more merciful instruments
> to touch the wound beyond the wound
> does not faint with disgust
> will not be driven off
> keeps bearing witness calmly
> against the predator, the parasite.

She speaks again to active compassion when she declares: "My heart is moved by all I cannot save: / so much has been destroyed / I have to cast my lot with those / who age after age, perversely, with no extraordinary power, reconstitute the world."

Eckhart sought to do the same by reaching out to women, the Beguines, but he also preached to the peasants about their "nobility" and "aristocracy," a lesson the aristocrats did not want the poor to hear. As we will explore in the next chapter, Eckhart paid a concrete price for supporting the poor and the women of his day.

From the Divine Feminine to Feminism

Adrienne Rich does not define modern feminism in strictly political or cultural terms. For her, feminism amounts to a radical defense and embrace of the Divine Feminine, one that would change not just society but our definitions of ourselves. For Rich, as for Eckhart, the spiritual, the personal, and the political are inextricably linked.

In an essay on Rich's vision of feminism, Erica Jong defines feminism this way: "By the *feminine* I mean the nurturing qualities in all people — whatever their sex." Rich believes that a root goal of the feminist movement should be to restore the feminine to its rightful place in society and consciousness. Truly liberating women, she writes, "means to change thinking itself: to reintegrate what has been named the unconscious, the subjective, the emotional with the structural, the rational, the intellectual...*creating a new kind of human being.*" Elsewhere, she reiterates that feminism is both societal and highly personal: Feminism "exists in many stages of development throughout the world at the most local, pragmatic levels, as a network of formal and informal communications, as a growing body of analysis and theory, and as *a profound moral, psychic, and philosophic revaluation of what it means to be 'human.'*"

Erica Jong sees Adrienne Rich's feminism as "a natural extension of her poetry because, for her, feminism *means* empathy. And empathy is the essential tool of the poet. It is akin to the quality Keats called 'negative capability' — that unique gift for projecting oneself into other states of consciousness. If Rich sees the role of the poet and the role of the revolutionary as totally compatible, it is because she understands that the most profound revolutions will come from the development of our capacity for empathy." On this, despite a distance of centuries, Rich and Eckhart certainly agree: the goal of the redefinition of the human is all about nurturing empathy and compassion.

For Rich, this compassion is born in the moral imagination of both women and men. In an essay entitled "The Anti-feminist Woman," she summed this up: "I believe that feminism must imply an imaginative identification with all women (and with the ghostly woman in all men) and that the feminist must, because she can, extend this act of the imagination as far as possible." Of this passage, Jong comments:

> The phrase "the ghostly woman in all men" is crucial. Rich is alarmed not only by the outward signs of discrimination against women in our patriarchal culture, but also by the way this culture suppresses the nurturant qualities in men, in children, and in societal institutions.... Her feminism is far more radical and far-reaching than equal-pay-for-equal-work or the establishment of fifty-fifty marriages. It envisions a world in which empathy, mothering, a "concern for the quality of life," "a connection with the natural and the extrasensory order" will not be relegated to women (who then have no power to implement these concerns on a practical level), but will be encouraged in the society at large. She is not talking only about discrimination against women, but about discrimination against the *feminine*.

Rich does not exclude men from her vision of feminism, but neither is she in denial about patriarchal dominance. Jong continues, "No 'man-hater,' the poet nevertheless refuses to blind herself to the reality of the conflict between women and men in sexist society which is sterile, 'autistic' with no reverence for life — for the female principle." Or, as Rich puts it: "The irreducible, incomplete connections / between the dead and the living / or between man and woman in this / savagely fathered and unmothered world."

Rich is explicit about the role men might play in such a revolution of creativity and compassion. "As long as women and women only are the nurturers of children, our sons will grow up looking only to women for compassion, resenting strength in women as 'control,' clinging to women when we try to move into a new mode of relationship. As long as society itself is patriarchal — which means antimaternal — there can never be enough mothering for sons who have to grow up under the rule of the Fathers, in a public 'male' world separate from the private 'female' world of their affections."

She asks the question: "What do we want for our sons?" And she answers it thus: "To discover new ways of being men even as we are discovering new ways of being women...a manhood in which they would not perceive women as the sole source of nourishment and solace. These fathers barely exist as yet." It will take men of courage to let go of the patriarchal worldview and join the spiritual battle for a maternal, that is, a compassionate, future.

Rich admires courage — including courage in men — and I think she would respect the courage Eckhart exhibited by standing up to patriarchal powers of capitalism and of church on behalf of Beguines and women and the peasants of Germany. She writes:

> If I could have one wish for my own sons, it is that they should have the courage of women. I mean by this something very concrete and precise: the courage I have seen in women who, in their private and public lives, both in the interior world of their dreaming, thinking, and caring, and the outer world of patriarchy, are taking greater and greater risks, both psychic and physical, in the evolution of a new vision. Sometimes this involves tiny acts of immense courage; sometimes public acts which can cost a woman her job or her life; often it involves moments, or long periods, of thinking the unthinkable, being labeled or feeling, crazy; always a loss of traditional securities....I would like my sons not to shrink from this kind of pain, not to settle for the old male defenses including that of a fatalistic self-hatred. And I would wish them to do this not for me, or for other women, but for themselves, and for the sake of life on the planet Earth.

This courage of creativity is the courage of the prophet. Eckhart demonstrated it, and Rich's call to creativity and compassion parallels profoundly Eckhart's call, as does Eckhart's frequent invoking of *wisdom*, which in fact he calls a "maternal name." Rich and Eckhart are sister and brother in so many respects. Together, they help to usher in a return of the Divine Feminine.

CHAPTER FIVE

LIBERATED AND LIBERATING SISTERS

Meister Eckhart Meets Dorothee Soelle,
the Beguines Mechtild of Magdeburg and Marguerite Porete,
and Julian of Norwich

Eckhart raised a bold objection that reflects the spirit
and discussion of the blossoming movement of women.

— DOROTHEE SOELLE

The day of my spiritual awakening was the day I saw and knew I saw
all things in God and God in all things.

— MECHTILD OF MAGDEBURG

God feels great delight to be our Father and God
feels great delight to be our Mother.

— JULIAN OF NORWICH

In his life, Meister Eckhart did not just incorporate the Divine Feminine in some speculative or safe manner. He actually engaged with the women's movement of his day, the Beguines, a movement very much under suspicion by the powers that be, inquisitors and popes included. He practiced what he preached. Dorothee Soelle is a fine guide to tell us this story.

Dorothee Soelle (1929–2003) was a poet, a mother, an activist in peace and ecological movements, a substantive feminist theologian, and a liberation theologian. A citizen of Germany, she taught theology for twelve years at Union Theological Seminary in New York City and was author of many books, including *To Work and to Love: A Theology of Creation*, *Theology for Skeptics*, *Suffering*, *Revolutionary Patience*, and *The Silent Cry: Mysticism and Resistance*. Especially in *The Silent Cry*, Soelle addresses the relationship of Meister Eckhart to the Beguines, a mystical tradition that resisted social injustice, and she invokes Eckhart as a supreme example of a spiritual warrior, a mystic-prophet, and a contemplative activist. Soelle also taught courses on Eckhart at Union Theological Seminary, so it can be said that she and Eckhart have already met at a profound level. What I offer in this chapter, then, is an opportunity for the reader to be a fly on the wall as Eckhart and Soelle interact still one more time. It is a conversation very much worth participating in.

Soelle on the Prophetic Dimensions of Mysticism

Soelle grew up in Germany under the Nazi regime, and she became acutely sensitive to hypocritical religion and religion that lacks courage and a prophetic voice. I think this is one reason she was so committed to hunting for the deeper meaning of religion, which she found both in the quest for social, gender, and eco-justice and in the mystical tradition that inspired many activists. In her writing, she does not hesitate to criticize the churches for having "buried the revolution" that Christ announced, and she calls on Christians to wake up and rise up. She tells us, "To feed the hungry means to do away with militarism. To bless the children means to leave the trees standing for them." For her, the Christian tradition has effectively lost its healthy mysticism, resulting in a distorted version of who Jesus is and what he taught. She writes: "The goal of the Christian religion is not the idolizing of Christ, not christolatry, but that we all 'are in Christ,' as the mystical expression goes, that we have a part in the life of Christ." There is a difference between esteeming Christ and following him. She opts for the latter.

Soelle criticizes patriarchal religion for being antimystical and supportive of the status quo: "Martin Buber said that 'success is not a name of God.' It could not be said more mystically nor more helplessly. The nothing that wants to become everything and needs us cannot be named in the categories of power. (That is why the 'omnipotent' God is a male, helpless, and antimystical metaphor that is void of any responsibility.) To let go of the ego means, among other things, to step away from the coercion to succeed. It means to 'go where you are nothing' [St. John of the Cross]."

Soelle praises Eckhart for his teachings about the nothingness of the Apophatic Divinity and about Jesus's beatitudes, which resist avarice or what Buddhists call "craving." She writes: "Meister Eckhart names the three conditions of 'inward poverty': to desire nothing, to know nothing, and to have nothing. All three forms for mystical poverty are focused on the nothing whose concrete form and most important metaphor is, in Christian mysticism, construed as becoming naked. This nothing is what can neither bind nor rule over me." For Soelle, Eckhart's sense of being must remake our consciousness. Advanced capitalism cultivates our compulsion to "have"; it reduces us to our desires. But to Soelle's great approval, Eckhart resists that.

Soelle elaborates on how mysticism challenges patriarchal hierarchies. Mysticism "comes closest to overcoming the hierarchical masculine concepts of God." Her definition of mysticism is this: "The mystical certainty that nothing can separate us from the love of God grows when we ourselves become one with love by placing ourselves, freely and without guarantee of success, on the side of love." And again, "the language of religion, by which I do not mean the stolen language in which a male God ordains and imperial power radiates forth, is the language of mysticism: I am completely and utterly in God, I cannot fall out of God, I am imperishable. 'Who shall separate us from the love of God?' we can then ask with Paul the mystic: 'neither death nor life, height nor depth, neither present nor future' (Romans 8:35 and 38)." Soelle recognizes that mysticism offers a revolutionary about-face in the language of transcendence, and it is a feminist consciousness: "In feminist theology therefore, the issue is not about exchanging pronouns but another way of thinking of transcendence. Transcendence is no longer to be understood as being independent of everything and ruling over everything else, but rather as being bound up in the web of life.... That means that we move from God-above-us to God-within-us and overcome false transcendence hierarchically conceived."

Soelle says her goal is "democratizing mysticism," and I am very much of the same ilk. From the start of my teaching over forty-three years ago,

I have said that "all of us are mystics," and I have been trying to lay out what that means and how we develop our mysticism and how we recognize it when we undergo it. Like Soelle, I seek to foster a mysticism that grows into resistance or prophetic action; time and again, I invoke a favorite phrase from American philosopher William Hocking, "The prophet is the mystic in action." Both Soelle and I have found a brother in Meister Eckhart, a true spiritual warrior-prophet and mystic, whom Soelle calls "drunk with God."

One of Soelle's favorite phrases from Eckhart is his call to act "without a why and wherefore" (*sunder warumbe*). This is an invitation, she suggests, to "a completely free choice, without duty, threat, or promise, without desires or fears that might be attached to one or the other option of the choice." A decision "to open oneself, to remove the corset, or unbuckle the armor." A movement from unfreedom to authentic freedom. Soelle, like Rich, decries how language fails us. She asks, "Why is our language so helpless? Why can we not share in communicating what we need the most?" And she answers: "I have learned much about this matter from Meister Eckhart. His concept *sunder warumbe* is for me an indispensable expression of mystical existence; it also introduces a different existential quality into the understanding of language." Eckhart writes at length about this, of which this is only a small part:

> You should perform all your deeds without whys and wherefores. I say
> in truth, as long as you perform your deeds for the sake of the king-
> dom of heaven or God or your eternal salvation, in other words for an
> external reason, things are not truly well with you.... The person who
> seeks for God without a way will find Him, as He is, in Himself; and
> such a son lives with the Son and He is life itself.... Life is lived for its
> own sake and emanates from its own sources; hence it is lived entirely
> without whys or wherefores, because it lives for itself.

As we have seen, Eckhart means this attitude to combat expediency, utilitarianism, and what he calls "the merchant spirit." For Soelle, this is all-encompassing: "It is the absence of all purpose, all calculation, every quid pro quo, every tit for tat, all domination that makes life itself its servant.... I say this with a view to the goal-centered rationality that pervades our highly technologized world. Such a rationality prohibits any form of existence for which there is no purpose: we eat certain foods in order to lose weight, we take dance lessons in order to keep fit, and we pray in order to facilitate specific wish fulfillment by God." Furthermore, "the *sunder warumbe* lies at the root of all mystical love of God."

Soelle recognizes that Eckhart is shaking up language with this saying. Language does not exist only "to appropriate something." Language is not meant merely to be a "means to win the world for myself." Rather, it ought to (at least sometimes) "celebrate joy and lament pain. It would not aim at something that I can conquer but instead aim to gather me in the now." Mysticism's contribution to language is that it "is oriented towards pure praise." Praise "always has the character of the *sunder warumbe*." It is an end in itself (such as Heschel's understanding of praise in chapter one). In praising, our craving and our notions of ego and competition are thrown out the window.

This is how God loves — without a why or wherefore — teaches Meister Eckhart. "God, too, loves us without a why or wherefore....But love has no why, no reason. If I had a friend and loved him because good things and everything I desire might happen to me, then I would love, not my friend, but myself. I should love my friend for his own goodness and his own virtue and for the sake of all that he is in himself." Soelle sees that the "original act of creation" is of this kind. It derives from love and life, not from purposefulness.

Like Rich, Soelle criticizes the language of domination. She asks: "A language free of purpose and control — is there such a thing at all?" Yet mysticism offers a way out. "All mysticism is part of the endeavor to escape from this fate of language that serves the exercise of power, control, and possession." Instead of a relationship with a God of "obedience," which gets so much press among fundamentalist preachers, mysticism offers a relationship of union. Soelle cites John's gospel: "That they may all be one; even as thou, Father, art in me, and I in thee,...that they may be one even as we are one, I in them and thou in me, that they may become perfectly one, so that the world may believe that thou has sent me" (John 17:21–22). Here, says Soelle, "all dualistic discourse of lord and servant, speaking and listening, and free and slave is left behind." In its place is a language that is "nonimperialistic and anarchistic (as the repeated use of 'in' and 'one' indicates)." Speaking and thinking this way entails political ramifications, for "this basic quandary of language of domination versus language of oneness is precisely what mystics suffered from. They kept silent and hid themselves for fear of exclusion and persecution." Eckhart, of course, did *not* keep silent or hide himself — quite the opposite. He preached in the vernacular to peasants and to women, such as the Beguines, about their royal personhood. As we will see, he shared solidarity with the poor.

Soelle also draws a parallel between the teachings of Eckhart and Thich Nhat Hanh. She cites Thich Nhat Hanh on the subject of washing the dishes: "There are two ways to wash dishes: the first is to wash dishes in order to have clean dishes; the second is to wash dishes in order to wash dishes." She comments: "What the *sunder warumbe* is in the language of Meister Eckhart is made clear here by means of a simple, everyday process." The issue is about being present; about being in the now; about not being someplace else; about not living by means only. As Soelle puts it, "The mystical relationship to time is fundamental not only for the I that is becoming attentive, but also the purposes and goals that orient our activities." This has much to teach activists who can, if too focused on purpose and results, be carried away and burn out. As Thich Nhat Hanh says, "When you are being carried off by your sorrow, your fear, or your anger, you cannot really be present to the people and things you love." Attention matters. Mindfulness matters. In themselves. So say Thich Nhat Hanh, Meister Eckhart, and Dorothee Soelle.

Soelle is very excited by Eckhart's sermon on Martha and Mary, which totally turns upside down the traditional interpretation, repeated ever since St. Augustine, that the story illustrates the superiority of the contemplative life over an active life. In the Gospel story, Jesus visits the home of Martha and Mary, and Mary sits at Jesus's feet to listen to him while Martha is busy preparing the meal. Traditionally, as Soelle puts it, "Martha is seen to be useful but somewhat limited, while her sister is seen as spiritual, refined, and more saintly.... In the course of Western intellectual history, this relationship gets passed on, according to the patriarchal gender roles, as work of the head and manual labor." But Eckhart "raised a bold objection that reflects the spirit and discussion of the blossoming movement of women." In his sermon, Eckhart proposes that Martha is actually the more "mature" of the two sisters because she can do two things at once. She can both listen and get her work done; that is, be both mystic and activist, contemplative and productive. Someday, Eckhart says, Mary will become as mature as Martha. Soelle concludes:

> This reversal is not only about rehabilitating Martha and active behavior but also about abolishing the division of human beings into makers and dreamers, activists and introverts, and the differentiation between the productivity of action and the receptivity of piety....Eckhart does away with the false superordination as well as the compulsive choice between two forms of life, the spiritual and the worldly. In this perspective of mysticism, this hierarchy is untenable. Real contemplation gives rise to just actions; theory and praxis are in an indissoluble connection. Even if one were in a state of rapture like Paul it would be better still to prepare a pot of soup for a needy neighbor!

Soelle recognizes the immediate application of Eckhart's teaching about Martha and Mary to the women's groups and especially the Beguine movement of his day. It is also an application of his Dominican spiritual heritage. The motto for the Dominicans was to "share the fruits of your contemplation" by being among the people instead of being warehoused securely in a monastery away from the cities and universities and turbulence of the world.

The Beguine Sisterhood

In Meister Eckhart's day and land, numerous women were stepping beyond male-dominated theology to express their own spiritual experience. Dominicans had included women from the very beginning of their existence, and Eckhart had plenty of interaction with Dominican women. But he also interacted with a relatively new form of female community, the Beguines, who did not take the formal vows of cloistered women, such as Dominican women did at that time. The Beguines lived in community and were essentially from the lower classes. They worked, in particular, with the poor and the young and the sick, and they often associated with the new mendicant orders, the Dominicans or the Franciscans. There is no question, as we will see, that the exchange between Eckhart and the Beguines was mutual and mutually beneficial. Eckhart on numerous occasions pictures God as feminine, beginning with his frequent use of the term "Godhead," which is a feminine word in the two languages he knew, Latin and German (*Deitas* and *Gottheit,* respectively). "God," on the other hand, is masculine in both Latin and German (*Deus* and *Gott*).

The Beguines were a woman's movement of the Middle Ages. Women who were not nuns cloistered in a convent and were not married gathered in community. It was a third lifestyle — similar to but long before the "third order sisters" who live in community and do service in the Catholic Church today. In Eckhart's day, women had what amounted to two options: they could live the cloistered life of a nun or get married. Beguines represented a "third way." Further, becoming a nun required a dowry, but this was not required to join the Beguines, so the latter were generally from the lower classes.

Often Dominican and Franciscan friars were spiritual directors to the Beguines, and in this capacity Eckhart had many interactions with them. Very often their modest-sized community houses were deliberately located near Dominican or Franciscan churches and convents. As Soelle puts it, "Coming into being at the end of the twelfth century and flourishing for nearly two centuries, the Beguine movement is one of the rarest examples of a mystically inspired new form of life created by women for women [that] distanced itself deliberately from the church's hierarchy." The movement was strong in Holland, the Rhineland, France, and Switzerland, and it numbered close to one million women, or 3 to 4 percent of the female population. "In an ocean of patriarchal, hierarchically directed injustice," Soelle says, "the Beguines created an island of freedom for women. The evolution that occurred there was spiritual. It refused to bow down to the world's secularity in relation to sexuality and property, as well as creating a new way of life that also found new forms of expressing the inner life in language and ritual." There was also a group of men called "Beghards," but their numbers and influence were far less than were those of the Beguines.

The Beguines lived in small communities, usually numbering three to twelve sisters, and they often were somewhat educated and sought out as teachers. They were committed to studying the scriptures in the vernacular, and they "preached and taught, they gave counsel and pastoral care to other women." They were a "community of learning." They often earned their living by manual labor, such as baking bread, brewing beer, making candles, spinning, weaving, and sewing. They cared for the sick and dying and buried the dead. They were also seen as a threat to many men in privileged places. Soelle writes, "Governed by no ordering rule, poor, persecuted and free: that is how one may describe these communities in which many of the great women mystics, such as Mechtild von Magdeburg, Marie d'Oignies, Hadewijch of Brabant, lived and found homes." They had what Soelle calls "a certain anarchist tendency, sometimes described among scholars as feminine, to regard institutional structures as secondary and for having little enthusiasm for handling the organizational formalities of a group."

Eckhart interacted with them and they with him — in fact, a number of his German sermons that we possess today are believed to have been memorized and written down by the Beguines. Surely their presence in his life — along with those cloistered Dominican nuns Eckhart met regularly as a provincial preacher — influenced his growing awareness of the feminine side of God.

Mechtild of Magdeburg

To illustrate this connection, let's briefly consider two Beguines who share much "common language" with Meister Eckhart. The first is Mechtild of Magdeburg (1210–c. 1280), who wrote in a journal she kept her whole life, which she called *The Flowing Light of the Godhead*. Soelle hails her work as "a language of daring passion that has left behind the terms of time and space, reason and purpose, power and impotence. It is a language of first-order amazement, a mystical praise of creation and of the bridegroom-creator who 'no longer wanted to be in himself.'"

Mechtild recognizes God as Mother, writing: "God is not only fatherly. God is also mother who lifts her loved child from the ground to her knee. The Trinity is like a mother's cloak wherein the child finds a home and lays its head on the maternal breast." Echoing the watery feminine imagery used by Adrienne Rich, Mechtild says: "The rippling tide of love flows secretly out from God into the soul and draws it mightily back to its Source." Also: "The true blessing of God flows from the heavenly flood out of the spring of the flowing Trinity." Celebrating our creativity and cocreative vocation with the Creator, she says: "I once heard the Spirit speak to the Creator, saying: 'We will no longer be unfruitful! We will have a creative kingdom.' And then I hear Jesus speak to the Creator, saying: 'My nature too must bear fruit. Together we shall work wonders so let us fashion human beings after the pattern of myself.'"

Mechtild underscores the union of God and human: "The soul becomes a god with God. Then what God wills the soul wills. Otherwise, God and soul would not be united in so beautiful a union." When one is "awakened by the light of true love, . . . she sees clearly and recognizes for the first time How God is all in all." The union of God and the soul is such that God "pours out the divine nature completely into it" and this renders the soul "speechless."

Mechtild offers this poem of the spiritual life with special emphasis on the via negativa:

Love the nothing,
flee the self.
Stand alone.
Seek help from no one.
Let your being be quiet,
Be free from the bondage of all things.
Free those who are bound,
Give exhortation to the free.
Care for the sick
but dwell alone.
When you drink the waters of sorrow
you shall kindle the fire of love
with the match of perseverance —
this is the way
to dwell in the desert.

Mechtild has tasted the dark night of the soul: "There comes a time when both body and soul enter into such a vast darkness that one loses light and consciousness and knows nothing more of God's intimacy. At such a time, when the light in the lantern burns out, the beauty of the lantern can no longer be seen. With longing and distress we are reminded of our nothingness."

Two hundred years before John of the Cross, she teaches, "Do you wish to have love? If you wish to have love, then you must leave love."

Like Rich and Eckhart, Mechtild talks of the soul's journey as a *sinking*. The soul, "on fire with its long love, overpowered by the embrace of the Holy Trinity, begins to sink and to cool — as the sun from its highest zenith sinks down into the night, thus also, do we sink, soul and body."

Like Wisdom in the scriptures, Mechtild's God is a playful God. "God takes the soul to a secret place, for God alone will play with it in a game of which the body knows nothing. God says: 'I am your playmate! Your childhood was a companion of my Holy Spirit.... Sing for joy and laugh for I the Creator am truly subject to all creatures.'" Again, "Woman, you ought to dance merrily, dance like my elected one! Dance like the noblest, loveliest, richest Queen!"

Mechtild knew panentheism, for she writes of the exquisite union between God and us: "I who am Divine am truly in you.... I am in you and you are in Me, we could not be any closer. We two are fused into one." Also: "The day of my spiritual awakening was the day I saw and knew I saw all things in God and God in all things." Her via positiva is creation based (and therefore wisdom based), as when she says: "How does God come to us? Like dew on the flowers, like the song of the birds! Yes, God gives himself with all creatures wholly to me." Mechtild asks: "What is the human soul?" And she replies: "The soul is a god with God. This is why God says to the soul: 'I am the God of all gods; but you are the goddess of all creatures.'" Her Christ is a Cosmic Christ. "God says: 'Now is the time to tell you where I am and where I will be. I am myself, in all places, in all things as I ever have been without beginning.'"

About compassion, Mechtild writes: "Who is the Holy Spirit? The Holy Spirit is a compassionate outpouring of the Creator and the Son. This is why when we on earth pour out compassion and mercy from the depths of our hearts and give to the poor and dedicate our bodies to the service of the broken, to that very extent do we resemble the Holy Spirit." She says we are like God "in so far as we love compassion and practice it steadfastly." Mechtild also links justice and compassion, and she practiced both — as did Meister Eckhart, the Jewish biblical tradition of the prophets, and so many of her Beguine sisters.

Anyone familiar with the four paths of Creation Spirituality will find them amply treated in Mechtild. A great common language ensues between Mechtild and Eckhart. Did they influence one another? It is hard to think otherwise. There seems to be a mutual give-and-take. At the least, there was "something in the air" that both drank from deeply.

Marguerite Porete

Marguerite Porete was a Beguine from northern France who composed a text that was read among Beguines for centuries. For hundreds of years, the text's authorship was unknown; some considered it possibly the work of the Flemish mystic Jan van Ruysbroeck. But recent scholarship has established that it was authored by Porete, who was condemned by the Inquisition and burned at the stake in Paris in 1310. The book is called *Mirror of the simple, annihilated souls and for those that tarry solely in desiring and demanding love.* It was too much for the Inquisition and its twenty-one male theologians to take. Probably written before 1300, it was banned by the Bishop of Cambray between 1296 and 1306 and publicly burned at Valenciennes in the presence of Porete. Soelle writes, "Nonetheless, the work found extraordinarily rapid dissemination. Like no other early mystic text in the vernacular, in subsequent years it made a triumphal march through Europe's order and Beguine houses, and it appeared in four languages, including Latin."

During the Inquisition, when the chief inquisitor demanded that Porete swear oaths required for her examination and provide information about her teachings, Porete refused. She was imprisoned in Paris for eighteen months but refused to recant. Soelle thinks that very likely politics played a role in her condemnation and subsequent burning at the stake, since it just so happened that the acting inquisitor was also the king's personal confessor. The king of France needed favors from Rome, and sacrificing a Beguine who did not have the protection of marriage or a religious order might well have won him favor with orthodox hounds in Rome.

It is said that on the way to the stake to be burned, Porete held her head high, refusing any assistance. Soelle comments: "The depth of her resistance, apparent in her refusal to testify under oath, her silence before her accusers, and her desire for nothing on the way to the stake, grows from the conviction of being at one with the *ravissant loinpres* (the ravishing far-near one)."

Porete's treatise is not without self-aware political consciousness and consequences. In her book she distinguishes between what she calls "The Great Holy Church," which is the Church of the Spirit, and "the Little Holy Church," which she calls the "empirical and scholastic church whose uncomprehending queries are more often placed on the lips of reason than are made to testify to love or the soul." The former church preaches Love; the latter church preaches rules and law and order.

Soelle and other historians recognize a direct link between Porete and Eckhart's later teachings. Soelle writes: "This freedom from every form of religious utilitarianism relates Marguerite perhaps most deeply to Meister Eckhart. He arrived in Paris one year after her death and became involved as a result of his pastoral commission with the Beguines. He took up many of Marguerite's basic ideas and gave them theological expression in a less offensive manner." For instance, Porete spoke of the Apophatic Divinity, as did Eckhart, and letting go of all will and all knowledge are phrases used by both Porete and Eckhart.

Another medieval scholar, Maria Lichtmann, has studied Marguerite's story and her relationship to Eckhart in an essay entitled "Marguerite Porete and Meister Eckhart." She comments, "It is a source of wonder that despite her condemnation and branding as a heretic, despite her having been shut out of the academic world by her gender, and despite her inability to garner sufficient ecclesiastical support for protection, Marguerite's work became known to Eckhart." Porete's book was purposefully marginal because it was written in

[

"Compassion is where peace and justice kiss."

]

the vernacular by a laywoman, a Beguine. Lichtmann says, "Addressed to a female audience and with a feminine divine, Dame Amour, at its center, Marguerite's mysticism is overtly female, entailing a set of values at odds with patriarchal norms." By describing the Little Church as "ruled by reason rather than love," Porete took on the institutional church and paid the ultimate price. "As woman, as Beguine, and as mystic, Marguerite transgressed all the appropriate boundaries. Yet, it is not unimaginable that

Eckhart overcame ecclesiastical diversions of gender and rank to recognize in Marguerite a spirit kindred to his own in audacity of expression, and more importantly in authenticity of experience."

Eckhart lived in Paris from 1311 to 1312, and he actually shared a Dominican convent with William Humbert of Paris, the inquisitor who sentenced Marguerite to death. There is speculation that Eckhart may have seen copies of her treatise that were confiscated during the Inquisition process.

As Lichtmann points out, Marguerite's book is "both Dionysian and Beguine, therefore both apophatic and cataphatic." And also, "at the heart of her apparently negative theology is the supreme value of Love as the affirmative revelation of the feminine divine." All this is also true of Eckhart, who frequently focuses on the love and compassion of God. As we saw in chapter four, compassion is very much a name of the Divine Feminine. Lichtmann sees Marguerite's teaching constituting "a profound meditation on God as feminine Amour and feminine Bonte (Goodness) which tends by the nature of love to give itself and to expand all its bounty, overflowing all boundaries."

God for Porete is an "unmanifest nothingness" reachable by "knowing nothing," "willing nothing," and having no space for God. These words are found in Eckhart's celebrated sermon on the Sermon on the Mount. Lichtmann says that Marguerite's "pervasive concept of nothingness, *le nient,* is a metaphor of the primal maternal ground of being and seedbed of all possibilities." Yet Marguerite complains, "So few folk are disposed to receive such a seed." This language also echoes Eckhart's well-developed via creativa and his celebration of the birth of the Son in the soul. Porete also affirms a body/soul integration, and this upset the Inquisition (though it was integral to both Eckhart's and Aquinas's philosophical worldview). As the mirror that is the human soul becomes empty, Lichtmann believes, "it more perfectly reflects the boundlessness of God's *Bonte*" and becomes "symbolic of the honesty and depth of the true self before, in, and becoming God." The soul becomes free of projections and free of projects, and also free of lots of religious exercises, such as fasting, prayer, masses, sermons, and intermediaries in general. Says Porete: "Those have a good and profitable time who no longer seek God only in temples or monasteries but in all places, through being in union with the divine will."

Porete writes that the soul sinks or falls as it lets go — falling "from love into nothingness, and without such nothingness she cannot be All. The fall is so deep, she is so rightly fallen, that the soul cannot fill herself from such an abyss." In the following stage the soul "no longer sees herself or God, but rather God sees God in her so that she sees that none is but God." For "there is nothing except God." Here the soul returns to her origins and "is in the stage of the prior being, and so has left three and has made of two One."

This language is strikingly like Eckhart's. Lichtmann comments that, in both Marguerite and Eckhart, "the paradigmatic relation to God is no relation but a return to the self-sufficient Source or ground of Being, what Eckhart calls the Godhead and Marguerite calls Nothingness." Of course, Eckhart calls God "nothingness" at times as well. Eckhart talks about surrendering a place for God so that God becomes the place, and Marguerite says that the soul "has no place, nor does she take into account anything that may happen to her." Lichtmann also points out that the phrase "living without a why," which figures prominently in Eckhart, occurs in Marguerite.

The parallels are so many, we have to ask if Marguerite influenced Eckhart directly. Lichtmann wisely puts the answer this way: "It is just as astonishing that Eckhart read this condemned mystic's work and appropriated it, as it is to suppose that he did not actually read it but arrived at its message through the commonality of their mystical destinies. By whatever mode of communication, Eckhart could not help but recognize in Marguerite one who knew the *wuset Gotheit* as well as the birth of Love in the soul."

But Eckhart did more than recognize a kindred spirit. From what we can discern, there is little doubt that Eckhart, arriving on the Paris scene one year after Marguerite's burning at the stake, and living in the Dominican convent along with her inquisitor, quite consciously took up the banner of the fallen warrior, Marguerite Porete. He did not hide or denounce her spirituality, but he made it his own, adapting it slightly to his own language, and he carried on the battle — a battle aimed at the excessive "rationalism" of the academic establishment and the corruption and distance of the ecclesial establishment (then as now in cahoots with the political establishment). It is interesting that Eckhart "lasted" only one year on this, his third, sojourn in Paris. One wonders, why did he leave so abruptly? Perhaps he was quite sickened by the story of the treatment of Porete and resolved to join his future with that of the Beguines henceforth. Perhaps he became a persona non grata among the academicians and their allies, the inquisitors, in early-fourteenth-century Paris. Eckhart never returned to formal academia. He shook the dust from his sandals. Afterward, he allied with the Beguines, even though Pope John XXII condemned them on seventeen different occasions. Eventually, Pope John XXII also condemned Eckhart.

Eckhart never diluted his teaching and preaching about the "aristocracy" and "nobility" of the ordinary person. If anything, it gained steam as his career advanced. His political consciousness was surely challenged and strengthened by his encounter with the work and witness of Marguerite Porete. He learned from his fallen sister, and ultimately, near the end of his life, he too was subjected to similar suspicion and charges of heresy. But Eckhart, with a Dominican Order to back him, was not put to the stake. In addition, while being interrogated in the dungeons of Avignon, where the pope was ensconced, Eckhart signed a document saying, in effect, "If I have spoken wrongly, I repent."

It is a remarkable story, the story of Marguerite Porete and her influence on Meister Eckhart. It underscores the deep and reciprocal influence he had with the Beguine movement and they with him.

Love and Compassion First

What stands out theologically in Porete is her insistence on putting Love first — ahead of rationality, ahead of legalistic games of canon law, and ahead of pastoral theology reduced to canon law and male-dominated ecclesiastical bureaucracy that claims to operate in God's name. In fact, this is a very prominent theme in other women writers of the Middle Ages, including but not limited to her sister Beguine Mechtild of Magdeburg, Hildegard of Bingen, and Julian of Norwich. Putting Love first is a not-so-subtle way of replacing the concept of "original sin" with "original blessing" (or "original wisdom," which was Hildegard's term). Hildegard writes about our origins this way:

> I heard a voice speaking to me: "The young woman whom you see is Love. It was love which was the source of this creation in the beginning when God said: 'Let it be!' And it was. As though in the blinking of an eye, the whole creation was formed through love.... The whole of

creation calls this maiden 'Lady.' For it was from her that all of creation proceeded, since Love was the first. She made everything.... Love was in eternity and brought forth, in the beginning of all holiness, all creatures without any admixture of evil. Adam and Eve, as well were produced by love from the pure nature of the Earth."

Mechtild writes: "You speak to me of my beginnings? I will tell you. I was created in love. For that reason nothing can express my beauty nor liberate my nobleness except love alone." Julian writes: "I saw that God never *began* to love us.... We have *always* been in God's foreknowledge, known and loved from without beginning.... We are kept as luminous and noble as when we were created."

Eckhart carried the banner of Marguerite Porete but with a difference. The Dominicans often argued with the Franciscans about whether knowledge or love comes first; the Dominicans insisted that you can't love what you do not know. In his writing, Eckhart himself wrestled with this debate, but he eventually abandoned that battle and came up with his own fresh, and today very relevant, solution: for Eckhart, God is neither love nor knowledge so much as *compassion*. "I say that beyond these two, beyond knowledge and love, there is compassion. In the highest and purest acts that God works, God works compassion."

This compassion equates not with mercy — but with justice. Eckhart draws heavily from the feminist tradition that puts compassion ("empathy") out front, and he also links to the Jewish tradition of compassion and justice. "Compassion means justice" he states. Compassion requires warrior energy, he says. He cites on several occasions Psalm 85:10, "Compassion is where peace and justice kiss." Compassion is very much a maternal value, as Adrienne Rich has pointed out. But it also carries a masculine and warrior energy when it extends to actions, and especially when equated with justice. For all these writers, there is a healthy yin/yang energy to the experience and practice of compassion.

Julian of Norwich

Eckhart's influence on Julian of Norwich was immense. Julian (1340–c. 1416) lived in Norwich, England, as a hermitess. She was walled up in a room adjacent to the public church, but she had access to a window along a busy trail that led from the riverfront to the city. Through this, she would counsel people of many classes who came to visit her. She composed a short and an extended version of her *Book of Showings*, which offer profound observations on the soul's journey with God. We know that Eckhart's works were smuggled into Norwich, which was a hotbed of mysticism in Julian's day, even after Eckhart's condemnation by the pope in 1329.

Julian is deeply original, but she is also in touch with Eckhart's teachings, and she adapts or expands on them. For example, where Eckhart says, "Isness is God," Julian says, "The goodness that everything possesses is God." She expresses a deep and well-developed theology of the Motherhood of God: "Just as God is truly our Father, so also is God truly our Mother." In fact, "God is the true Father and Mother of Nature," and "God feels great delight to be our Father and God feels great delight to be our Mother." She links wisdom and God as Mother when she says: "The deep wisdom of the Trinity is our Mother. In her we are all enclosed." And God speaks to her: "This I am — the wisdom of the Motherhood," and "a mother's service is nearest, readiest and surest." Furthermore, "Jesus is our true Mother in whom we are endlessly carried and out of whom we will never come." Again, "Jesus is our Mother, brother and Liberator."

Julian also links compassion to the Divine Feminine: "Compassion is a kind and gentle property that belongs to the Motherhood in tender love.... Compassion protects, increases our sensitivity, gives life and heals." Compassion is about action. "The ground of compassion is love and the working of compassion keeps us in love... nor does the working of compassion cease." Finally, she begins and ends with love, for "God wants to be thought of as our lover."

Eckhart and the Divine Feminine

In the past two chapters, we have considered some of Meister Eckhart's substantive contributions to an understanding of the Divine Feminine, as well as his on-the-ground alliance with women struggling for their own language and to balance the feminine and masculine in religion and in social institutions. His teachings about creativity and compassion, the via positiva and Cataphatic Divinity, and the via negativa and Apophatic Divinity honor the

Divine Feminine. His imaging of the spiritual journey as a "sinking" and "letting go," rather than as a climb up a vertical ladder, honors the Earth, the lower chakras, and the dark goddess. He emphasizes the role motherhood plays in all of our journeying and even in our imitating Mary by birthing and mothering God and the Cosmic Christ. All this speaks to the return of the Divine Feminine. His sharing solidarity with the controversial Beguine movement of his day also tells a story in itself about his commitment to the values and actions of women liberating themselves. Obviously, he learned from them at the same time that he was teaching them. In short, Eckhart was in his day, as he is in ours, an ally for women awakening to their own wisdom and God-given potential. And he extends an invitation to men and male-dominated institutions to develop a healthy gender balance with self and structures.

It seems appropriate to end these two chapters on Eckhart's relationship to the Divine Feminine and to women's wisdom with a powerful and nonsentimental poem from Adrienne Rich on the meaning of compassion. She writes:

> We are a small and lonely human race
> Showing no sign of mastering solitude
> Out on this stony planet that we farm.
> The most that we can do for one another
> Is let our blunders and our blind mischances
> Argue a certain brusque abrupt compassion.
>
> We might as well be truthful. I should say
> They're luckiest who know they're not unique;
> But only art or common interchange
> Can teach that kindest truth. And even art
> Can only hint at what disturbed a Melville
> Or calmed a Mahler's frenzy; you and I
> Still look from separate windows every morning
> Upon the same white daylight in the square.

This poem evokes the profound relationship between the via negativa (including our solitude and our mistakes) with art, the via creativa, and compassion. What is compassion? Knowing we are not unique, that we are in this together, our joy and suffering shared. Yet we seem destined for separateness, staring out of our separate windows every morning on squareness and light, not on the rounded and curved and dark experiences that in fact bring us together, not on the third chakra, which takes us out of our heads and into the dark of our guts where we feel the kick of injustice and where we wail the pain of grief, the place where compassion is born. When all is said and done, compassion marks the best in us, the "most that we can do for one another" on this planetary voyage through cosmic time and space, while we till by sweat of our brow this "stony planet."

CHAPTER SIX

THE HISTORICAL JESUS

Meister Eckhart Meets Marcus Borg, Bruce Chilton, and John Dominic Crossan

The parables [of Jesus] do not invoke external authority....
Rather, their authority rests...in their ability
to involve and affect the imagination.

— MARCUS BORG

Eckhart writes sermons the way the Gospel writers wrote the Gospels —
filled with stories and images that get people to see.

— DR. HELEN KENICK MAINELLI

The Kingdom was based on a community's acceptance of the poor,
the hungry, the bereaved, and the shunned.

— BRUCE CHILTON

For over 250 years, biblical scholarship has been searching to determine, as precisely as possible, who Jesus the man really was. Scholars have tried to re-create what his times were like and to distinguish which of Jesus's words and stories as recorded in the Gospels and letters that constitute the New Testament are reliably his and not words put into his mouth by enthusiastic followers decades after he died. In our time, through the use of more and more sophisticated language studies, archaeological findings, and discoveries of ancient texts, and with the collation and comparison of texts and much more, that scholarly journey has reached a certain culmination and blessed our generation with the most accurate answers to these questions yet. We owe a debt of gratitude for all the hard work that has gone into unveiling the historical Jesus.

For this book, the question arises: Did Eckhart relate to the accurate historical Jesus as well as to the Cosmic Christ? Did Eckhart preach what, and as, the historical Jesus taught? To address that question, we will consider some of the findings of three very respected scholars of the historical Jesus: Protestant theologian Marcus Borg, Anglican theologian Bruce Chilton, and Roman Catholic theologian John Dominic Crossan.

We do not want to limit ourselves just to the findings of the historical Jesus, however. The community that followed Jesus is also of significance — one might say they represent the Cosmic Christ at work, since much wisdom was passed on by persons excited and alive because of their encounter with the Jesus story and Jesus's teaching. So we will also be asking: How does Eckhart speak in the name of the Cosmic Christ as well as the historical Jesus?

Strategies of the Historical Jesus

Several striking findings have emerged from the hard work of the historical Jesus scholars (and from the many others on whose shoulders they stand). One is the realization that only about 15 percent of the words attributed to Jesus in the Gospels are truly his. Nevertheless, those words tell us a lot about the person Jesus was and the teachings, values, and messages he meant to convey. The Gospels are an extremely rich web telling the story of Jesus's public life as an adult as well as the teachings he shared with his followers — including those who turned their back on him. The writings link and weave his original teachings and his commentary on the Jewish stories and instructions from the Hebrew Bible. Of course, as a Jew in first-century Palestine, Jesus taught in a profoundly challenging milieu, a mix of ancient Jewish teachings and practices with the struggle to survive under the military occupation of the very efficient — and very severe — Roman Empire.

At an early age, Jesus himself learned, up close and personally, the hard lesson of the need to dance, weave, and bob to avoid the empire's cruel presence. His mentor, John the Baptist, with whom Jesus spent his adolescence coming of age and who inducted him into manhood and spiritual maturity, suffered a dramatic end to his life. After years of teaching and baptizing at the River Jordan and in the desert, John the Baptist was imprisoned and had his head cut off and served on a platter for the entertainment of the political bosses of his land, who were beholden to the empire. This surely made a lasting impression on Jesus, confirming the seriousness of his vocation. It also spurred his own imagination — not only to think outside the box of ordinary political and societal norms but to find methodologies for carrying on that teaching that would confront the power structure not directly but indirectly

[*"Jesus is wisdom itself."*]

With that in mind, he eventually developed three methods for his teachings: 1) parables or stories with open-ended lessons that each person could take to heart and come to conclusions about; 2) aphorisms, sharp-tongued sayings that catch both mind and imagination; and 3) table gatherings, meals where people of different classes, professions, and experiences could gather in long sessions of discussion, debate, and down-to-earth sharing that might at times result in changes of heart and consciousness as well as group action. As John Dominic Crossan puts it, open and free association at a shared table with tax collectors, sinners, and unmarried women (denounced as "whores") "clashes fundamentally with honor and shame, those basic values of ancient Mediterranean culture and society." Jesus, who chose this as a model of the "Kingdom of God," was considered to have no honor, to have no shame. But this reflected his sense of "reciprocal justice — a world in which there would never again be any boots on any necks."

These were Jesus's strategies. In his lifetime, they proved to be sometimes more and sometimes less successful. Yet afterward, they were often obscured as other cultural and political forces, as well as ideologies and historical events, shaped or distorted Jesus's memory over the centuries and millennia following his death.

Eckhart on the Historical Jesus

Eckhart often makes the distinction between the Cosmic Christ, or the risen Christ or post-resurrection Christ, and Jesus himself. For example, in his celebrated sermon based on Jesus's Sermon on the Mount, "Blessed are the poor in spirit, for theirs is the kingdom of heaven" (Matthew 5:3), Eckhart begins by making a distinction for his listeners: "Now there exist two kinds of poverty: an *external* poverty, which is good and is praiseworthy in a person willing to take it upon himself or herself through the love of our Lord Jesus Christ, because *he was himself poor on earth*. Of this poverty I do not want to speak any further. For there is still another kind of poverty, an *inner* poverty, by which our Lord's word is to be understood when he says: 'Blessed are the poor in spirit.'" Thus Eckhart reminds us, Jesus "was himself poor on earth," but earthly poverty is not the topic of this particular sermon. Instead, the lessons he offers concern the Christ born in us or desiring to be born in us here and now.

Eckhart has a powerful treatise on compassion, which is a commentary on Luke 6:36–42, "Be you compassionate as your Father in heaven is compassionate." In it, Eckhart talks about how, while Christ eternally had all things in his nature and was thus

> rich in all things — he in no way had a way of suffering nor a back which could be beaten. In this sense there is another legitimate explanation for what Paul is saying in 2 Corinthians 8: "for our sake he was made poor." For he did not have to beg for anything lacking to him, unless it be for the back which could receive blows. For the Psalms say, "sinners hammer on my back." Thus in all these ways he showed compassion. And Luke says: "Go and do likewise." And this is what he teaches and taught, after he manifested it in deed....He gives us an example or model of this compassion.

Thus, Eckhart expressed an awareness of the difference between Christ as Logos and Word of God — the Cosmic Christ we considered in chapter two — and the historical person, who lived a life in poverty and vulnerability (with a back that could be beaten) that modeled his teaching. On numerous occasions in his sermons Eckhart makes that distinction. No doubt he would welcome contemporary scholarship that clarifies the person and times and teachings of Jesus, but he would not jettison either the Cosmic Christ dimension to the lessons or the events of Jesus's life and those teachings added by his followers after his life ended. In other words, Eckhart would be very much at home with my teaching that the Christ path flies on two wings — that of the historical Jesus *and* that of the Cosmic Christ. We do Jesus's memory and our own faith life a grave disservice if we pay attention exclusively to only one or the other.

Jesus and Eckhart: Methods of Instruction

Other important lessons we have learned from today's scholars about the historical Jesus concern his method of teaching, which was provocative and participatory. As Marcus Borg puts it, "The parables of Jesus are invitational, using the form of a story.... No great storyteller tells a great story only once." These were "oral stories" repeated on various occasions, never in exactly the same way. Jesus was a "creative story teller" who invites the listener into the story in an implicit way. Borg says, "The appeal is not to the will — not 'Do this' — but rather, 'Consider seeing it this way.' As invitational forms of speech, the parables do not invoke external authority.... Rather, their authority rests...in their ability to involve and affect the imagination." His stories invite one to "see in a radically new way," Borg explains. "The appeal is to the imagination, to that place within us in which reside our images of reality and our images of life itself; the invitation is to a different way of seeing, to different images for shaping our understanding of life." Jesus himself said when asked that he talked in parables so that people who have eyes and do not see would see.

Eckhart used this approach to teaching as well. When my book of Eckhart sermons, *Passion for Creation*, first appeared, biblical scholar Helen Kenik Mainelli commented: "Eckhart writes sermons the way the Gospel writers wrote the Gospels. Filled with stories and images that get people to see." She was so right. Reading Eckhart is a lot like reading the Gospels — things happen in the process of hearing his words or his images around Jesus's words — which is pretty close to what happened when people heard Jesus speak as well.

Borg and other scholars agree that Jesus was a "teacher of wisdom."

Eckhart says the same thing. Eckhart begins his sermon on "Blessed are the poor of spirit" by saying: "Blessedness opened its mouth of wisdom and spoke...and this wisdom has declared that the poor are blessed." Notice that Eckhart calls Jesus "Blessedness" who speaks with a "mouth of wisdom." He also calls Jesus wisdom incarnate: "this wisdom has declared." He elaborates: "Everything that was ever born must remain silent when the wisdom of the Father speaks; for all the wisdom of the angels and of all creatures is sheer nothingness before the groundless wisdom of God." Here he is connecting Jesus as wisdom to the message of wisdom and to the eternal wisdom that is the Cosmic Christ or the "wisdom of the Father." He has it all. In another sermon he talks about Jesus as "wisdom itself" who reveals himself "within the soul with the immeasurable wisdom that is himself — the same wisdom with which the Father in his totally paternal ruling power himself as well as the Word, which is also wisdom itself, and all the Word contains, since God is one." We are capable of being with that very wisdom in our souls provided we have first emptied ourselves. On numerous other occasions, Eckhart refers to Jesus as wisdom and as a teacher of wisdom. It is all there.

Bruce Chilton comments on Jesus's parabolic messaging: "Jesus was known as a master of the genre of parable in its full extent, from simple adage to complicated — sometimes, as we shall see, even surreal — narrative." Examples include the stories about the divided house and the thief. "Part of the force of the comparison lies in its surprising sympathy — with the thief, rather than with the householder. Jesus compares himself to a skillful burglar and Satan to a man so wealthy he deserves the theft that is coming his way." The motif of a festal banquet is "central within Jesus' parables and sayings....Parables are not just lively stories taken from nature; the point can often turn on what is striking, peculiar, or unpredictable." Consider the parables of growth: the hidden treasure in the field; the pearl. Says Chilton: "Like the prophets, Jesus taught his hearers how to see the Kingdom as well as how to act on the basis of what they saw. Vision — the capacity to perceive God actively at work — is the prophetic foundation of calling people to work with God."

Eckhart's teachings, like Jesus's, were very parabolic. They are not so much left-brained arguments or rational in their methodology as inviting the imagination and encouraging participation. One has to participate in a sermon by Eckhart, not just think about it. You have to let go of too much thinking and swim with the images, which often tumble one into another. You have to go along for the ride, and in the end, you often ask yourself: "What has he said? What does it mean? How does it apply to me and my life and my experience?" Such a response to Eckhart's teachings parallels profoundly the method of Jesus's parables and his aphorisms. They are heart teachings before they are head teachings. They force us to bring the heart to the table. They put our right brains to work and the left brain follows.

Eckhart, like Jesus, puts intuition first. One cannot approach his teachings with the left brain alone. This is one reason why a sad number of historians and fact hunters so often mistranslate Eckhart and actually kill his soul and his message. Needless to say, this happened to Jesus's writings as well, which have been regularly mishandled over the centuries to serve the agendas of empires and bureaucracies alike. One who is out of touch with the mystic inside ought not to be translating the mystics or telling us about them. Mystics don't deny facts, but facts are a very limited dimension to our mystical lives. As Mary Oliver put it, "I want to live beyond the weight of facts."

Jesus and Eckhart as Prophets

Furthermore, both Jesus and Eckhart, in choosing to speak and teach in imaginative form, are following the ways of the prophets. The prophets speak to the moral imagination of the people to wake them up, and how can this be accomplished except with more imagination? Walter Brueggemann, a very respected scholar of the Hebrew prophets, says as much even in the title of his book *The Prophetic Imagination*. He writes: "Every totalitarian regime is frightened of the artist. It is the vocation of the prophet to keep alive the ministry of imagination, to keep on conjuring and proposing alternative futures to the single one the king wants to urge as the only thinkable one." The via creativa of the prophets, Jesus included, actually brings more awe and wonder into people's lives. "Jesus of Nazareth is the fulfillment and quintessence of the prophetic tradition. He brought to public expression the newness given by God. The response to his work and person is amazement.... That amazement gave energy, the only kind of energy which gives newness." In other words, creativity wakes people up and energy flows from that. It happened with Jesus's teachings in parables, aphorisms, and meals and by example. And it happened with Eckhart in his imaginative preaching and image making and eliciting and also in his work, listening to and standing with women and peasants in their struggles.

There never was a prophet who was not an artist. Gandhi and Martin Luther King Jr. were artists not only in the moving speeches they gave but in the actions they organized — gathering thousands of people to march to the sea or to boycott buses, to sit at segregated lunch tables and to march to Selma, to fill the jails. These were acts of prophetic imagination. They were acts of social art. Rabbi Heschel recognizes how revelation always goes beyond literalness, and he warns that "literalmindedness [is] the surest way of misunderstanding revelation." Of words about God, Heschel says, "when taken literally, they either turn flat, narrow and shallow or become ventriloquous myths." What is the proper language for revelation, according to Heschel? "In order to understand them we must part with preconceived meanings, cliches are of no avail. They are not portraits but *clues* serving us as guides, suggesting a line of thinking." Jesus and Eckhart both offer clues, suggestions, guides, and images that provoke, encouraging us to explore and awaken. In no way are they dealing in clichés.

There never was a prophet who did not speak from the imagination of the people to the imagination of the people. Isaiah and Jeremiah, Hosea and Amos, are among the greatest poets of Western culture. They operate from a deep place of creativity, imagination, and resourcefulness. That is one argument why the via creativa is so central to a prophetic spiritual journey, which undermines a status-quo consciousness — one that supports empires without questioning them, downplays the value of creativity, and often drives creativity out of education altogether. Our imaginations ask untidy questions, and prophets appeal to the disenfranchised, to anger, to potential "chaos," to the not-yet, to nothingness, rather than to rules of law and order. When Jesus says the Sabbath is for people and not people for the Sabbath, he utters just such a dangerous and potentially chaotic rule breaking — one that he also played out. He walked his talk by healing on the Sabbath, and this caused all kinds of stir.

What was the goal of Jesus's aphorisms and parables? Borg says it is "to subvert conventional ways of seeing and living, and to invite his hearers to an alternative way of life. As a teacher of wisdom, Jesus was not primarily a teacher of information (what to believe) or morals (how to behave), but a teacher of a way or path of transformation." A way out of conventional wisdom to an alternative wisdom. Eckhart is that kind of teacher as well. Information and dogma is not his preoccupation — nor even morals — but a way or path to transformation.

Jesus, Zechariah, and Eckhart on Moneylenders

In one very consequential instance, Jesus put into practice a teaching of the prophet Zechariah, "You shall not make my temple a den of thieves." In a blunt and public action, Jesus overturned the tables of the sellers in the Temple. According to Chilton, he had "a rioting mob" of two hundred people assisting him, and it was "Jesus' last public action." This event as much as any other got him killed by the high priest and the officials representing the Roman Empire, both of whom were freaked out by the brazenness of the attack and its chaotic implications for law and order. Chilton says, "This act is the key to why Jesus was crucified by the Romans, who had put their prestige behind the status quo in the Temple."

Without doubt, the action itself was a parable intended to become its own story. Who would not have been talking about this wild event in the heart of the city, in the Temple corridors, at the time of pilgrimage and passover? Jesus was not oblivious about how to make headlines. Jesus proved himself to be "a threat to Judean control — priestly, Pharisaic, and aristocratic." He paid a severe price for his teaching. And notice: We are talking about it still, two thousand years after the event.

Eckhart was also talking about it fourteen hundred years after the event. In a powerful sermon, for which he too would pay a severe price, he applied the driving of moneylenders from the Temple to what was then going on economically and politically in his own city of Cologne. At that time, Cologne was a major center for trade and goods passing down the Rhine to southern Europe and to eastern Europe. Furthermore, Cologne's very fancy late Gothic cathedral, which still exists, was then halfway built. Yet Eckhart challenged its deeper meaning from the very pulpit of that impressive edifice. For his sermon, he chose the Gospel of Jesus driving moneylenders from the Temple (Matthew 21:12) to make the point that the only temple that counts is the temple in the human soul. "This temple, which God wishes to rule over powerfully according to his own will, is the soul of a person. God has formed and created this soul very like himself, for we read that our Lord said: 'Let us make human beings in our own image' (Gn. 1:26). And this is what he did."

In the sermon, Eckhart pronounces that no creature and no object humans build is "so like to himself or resembles him as much as does the soul of a human being." He goes on to excoriate "who the merchants were then and still are today — those who were buying and selling then, and are still doing so, the ones our Lord whipped and drove out of the temple." Eckhart criticizes the "merchant mentality," and he applies his criticism to religious practices, "fasts, vigils, prayers and similar good deeds of all kinds" — if "people do these things so that our Lord may give them something," they are merely merchants. For "truth doesn't long for any kind of commercial deal. God does not seek his own interest." If we could empty our souls, they would "gleam so beautifully and shine so purely and clearly over and through everything created by God that no one could match its splendor except the uncreated God. And in all truth no one really resembles this temple except the uncreated God alone."

Eckhart may admire Cologne's new cathedral, but he is much more impressed with just one person emptying and filling the grace of her soul. In this sermon, clearly, he is displaying the *prophetic* side of his message, thus imitating Jesus. And, like Jesus, he stepped on powerful toes — can you imagine how unimpressed the bankers and bishops and erectors of the cathedral must have been by this sermon, by Eckhart's unsubtle rejection of their magnificent project in favor of the beauty of just one single ordinary person? Prophets pay a price for such rants, and Eckhart paid a severe price. He was put on trial by the powers that be in Cologne (a trial that he actually won) and later in the pope's palace in Avignon (a trial that he lost). Like Jesus, Eckhart displaced "conventional wisdom" with a different wisdom, a conventional kingdom — the Roman Empire of Jesus's day and the mercantile powers in Cologne — with an alternative kingdom.

Kingdom of God

Scholars agree that Jesus's teaching of an alternative kingdom lay at the heart of his message. Bruce Chilton reminds us: "In all Jesus' teaching no single concept is more important, more central, or more resonant than the Kingdom of God. The Kingdom of God also figures as a vital concept within the Scriptures of Israel." The focus is on God as the king of the universe (that is, the Cosmic Creator!), Chilton says, and "the promise of God's Kingdom is that people will finally come to realize divine justice and peace in all that they do, putting into action with one another the righteousness they see in God. The Kingdom is a matter of both perceiving God's will and doing God's will — on earth as it is in heaven." This means God removes all "human greed and tyranny, and replaces them with a common passion for divine justice." Chilton reminds us that in teaching the kingdom's arrival, Jesus is drawing from the Psalms and wisdom literature as much as from the prophets, for Jesus connected to Israel's wisdom tradition.

Biblical scholar Burton Mack reminds us that the issue of *basileia* (which we translate as "kingdom") was a hot one in Jesus's day. "*Basileia* is what kings and rulers had; sovereignty, majesty, dominion, power, domain. How to guarantee the just and beneficent exercise of power was a very big question through this period." John Dominic Crossan tells us that what are at sake are "power and rule, a process much more than a place, a way of life much more than a location on earth. The basic question is this: How does human power exercise its rule and how, in contrast, does divine power exercise its rule? The kingdom of God is people under divine rule,...what the world would be if God were directly and immediately in charge."

In this way, the new kingdom is about justice and compassion, and by practicing compassion, people realize the kingdom in the midst of community. Chilton says, "The Kingdom was based on a community's acceptance of the poor, the hungry, the bereaved, and the shunned." When Jesus says, "The Kingdom of God is in your midst" (Luke 17:21), the word for "your" is plural! It refers to a community and not to just a single person.

In Jesus's time, the dominant social vision was centered in holiness, which was understood as purity and following religious tenets. But Jesus held an "alternative social vision," writes Marcus Borg, "centered in compassion...."

For Jesus, compassion was more than a quality of God and an individual virtue: it was a social paradigm, the core value for life in community. To put it boldly: Compassion for Jesus was political.... He called for 'a politics of compassion.'" Jesus promised "Your kingdom will come" (Matthew 6:10) and taught us how to aid its arrival. Crossan warns that "the open commensuality and radical egalitarianism of Jesus' Kingdom of God are more terrifying than anything we have ever imagined, and even if we can never accept it, we should not explain it away as something else." He believes it sprang from an "ancient and universal peasant dream of a just and equal world."

As we have seen, compassion is also at the forefront of Eckhart's understanding of the spiritual way, and in good biblical fashion he marries justice and compassion. He says that the prayer "thy kingdom come" means that we are "bidding this very earth to become a heaven" where "goodness returns and then there will be altogether no difference between heaven and earth." He recognizes that justice is the pathway to this kingdom. He says: "The person who understands what I say about justice understands everything I have to say."

Jesus's practice very much included women and especially Mary Magdalene. But as Chilton points out, quite early in the development of the Christian church there was "a gradual conformity to the culture," particularly regarding women. For example, Luke leaves Mary Magdalene, her anointing Jesus prior to his death and her risen Christ experience, out of his Gospel. "Male dominance is everywhere in Luke's gospel," as Chilton points out. And yet, Jesus adapted the scriptures on a number of occasions, and even "manipulated and paraphrased" them "to explain his experience of God, and how God was active in what he said and did."

Early in Luke's gospel, in the synagogue of Nazareth, Jesus claims that he is indeed part of the prophetic lineage. In Chilton's translation (derived from the Old Syria Gospels, which come closest to Jesus's indigenous Aramaic), Jesus says: "The Spirit of the Lord is upon you, on account of which he has anointed you to message triumph to the poor; and he has delegated me to proclaim to the captives release, and to the blind sight — and I will free the broken with release — and to proclaim the acceptable year of the Lord." This announcement in his hometown did not go over well. The elders and others chased him out of town. These events aroused fear in his hometown and in his family; it shed bad light on them. He left the area — to everyone's relief.

Borg points out that Jesus's "subversive wisdom" challenged the "conventional wisdom" of his time and culture, and it was in direct opposition to the "encultured consciousness — that is consciousness shaped and structured by culture or tradition." Jesus "directly attacked the central values of his social world's conventional wisdom: family, wealth, honor, purity, and religiosity. All were sanctified by tradition and their importance was part of the taken-for-granted world." Jesus reverses conventional wisdom — the smug self-assurance that considers itself beyond debate or dispute. Is it any surprise that Jesus was not popular? He upset not just the powers that be but the assumed hierarchy of values across society, including those concerning family, wealth, honor, purity, and religiosity.

The Cross as Letting Go

It is clear that "letting go" and "letting be" lie at the heart of Eckhart's spiritual practice. These are my translations of the words *Abgeschiedenheit* and *Gelassenheit*, which Eckhart often uses. While some translate these words as "detachment," I feel "detachment" carries too much baggage, including hints of willpower, that are not otherwise found in Eckhart's worldview.

It is also clear, as Eckhart tells us time and again, that he derives his teaching from Jesus, both his teaching to "take up your cross and follow me" and his crucifixion. Eckhart says, "Whatever a person willingly gives up for love, he or she shall receive in nobler fashion; as Christ says: 'He who leaves anything for my sake will receive again a hundredfold' (Matt. 19:29)." The via negativa is a real part of life and of our spiritual journey. "Our whole being depends on nothing but a becoming nothing....He who would receive all things must abandon all things."

Chilton writes: "Jesus committed himself to this principle of self-annihilation as a life-long process of renewal. Jesus taught: Whoever loses one's life will save it (Mk 8.35). The world's mystical traditions center on the abandonment of the self, a dark night of the soul prior to union with God. Often that loss is a discrete event, punctuating one's life and signaling the first steps along a mystic's path....He turned it into a persistent principle.

Again and again he embraced this shattering of self." Eckhart warns that "if you want the kernel, you must break the shell," and the rich word he coined, "breakthrough" *(Durchbruch)*, embodies this sense of being broken as well.

Chilton develops the meaning of the cross since for Jesus "suffering was not to be avoided, but embraced as a prophetic sign that God's Kingdom was making its way into a world that resisted transformation. 'For whoever wishes to save one's own life, will ruin it, but whoever will ruin one's life for me and the message will save it. For what's the profit for a person to gain the whole world and to forfeit one's life?' (Mk 8.35ff, etc)." Prophets suffer! The crucifixion event "symbolized the potential of suffering to serve as the gateway to vision." Jesus asked people to let go of wealth and family (Mark 10:13–31), to ruin their lives if necessary for the message of the all-consuming kingdom. Chilton says, "Jesus framed his teaching to make hardship the gateway to vision."

Borg shares a similar vision, and in doing so sounds strikingly like Eckhart: "Death as an image of the path of transformation points to dying to the world of conventional wisdom as the center of one's security and identity and dying to the self as the center of one's concern.... Death [is] the ultimate letting go, and thus the opposite of the grasping that marks the life of conventional wisdom." In this way "the path of death is also, for Jesus, the path to new life. It results in rebirth, a resurrection to a life centered in God."

Sons and Daughters of God

There is no doubt that at the heart of Eckhart's teaching is the good news that we are indeed sons and daughters of God, who in turn birth "other Christs." This teaching has often been lost in fundamentalist Christianity, where all is to be sacrificed to the worship of Jesus as the "only son of God." But this is not the biblical teaching, as Bruce Chilton emphasizes when he comments on the transfiguration experience, wherein Jesus and his disciples heard the phrase "This is my Son, the beloved, in whom I take pleasure: hear him" (Matthew 17:5). The same message occurred at Jesus's baptism. Chilton cautions: "As in the earlier case with John, the voice that came after the luminous cloud in the Transfiguration did not speak in the exclusive language of the later doctrine of the Trinity, which made Jesus into the only (and only possible)

'Son of God.' Rather, the point was that the same Spirit that had animated Moses and Elijah was present in Jesus, and that he could pass on that Spirit to his followers, each of whom would also become a 'Son.'" Chilton recognizes the entire Gospel of Mark as "a program to train its hearers and readers for the moment of baptism, when they, too, will experience the Spirit within them and call upon God as their *Abba*, their father and true source" — that is, to see themselves as God's son or daughter.

Chilton elaborates on the term "son of God": "Contrary to a popular fallacy, the language of divine sonship is by no means a Christian invention. The term 'son' is used frequently in the Old Testament for the special relationship between God and others," including angels (Genesis 6:2), all of Israel (Hosea 11:1), and the Davidic king (Psalm 2:7). What is being signified is that such people "are indeed 'the beloved,' as Jesus became as a result of his vision." Jesus's designation as the son of God means, Chilton says, "he is of the spiritual lineage of Israel's seers, the visionaries who meditated on the chariot and were blessed with the Spirit which pours out from the Throne of the heavenly Father." When the early church took on the Roman Empire, one of the issues was that the emperor claimed to be "God's son," and Christians found this blasphemous and "silly." In that context, a certain politicization of Jesus's lineage took hold, exalting him as God's son over against the emperor.

That Eckhart puts our being "sons and daughters of God" at the center of his teaching is not without precedence. He found it in the Gospels and epistles, as in John 3:1: "Think of the love that the Father has lavished on us, by letting us be called God's children; and that is what we are." Yet this teaching has rarely been emphasized and developed as richly as Eckhart treated it.

Sacred Meals

More and more in his work, Jesus developed a practice quite unique to him "of festive celebration." He developed this "practice of holy feasts into an art form," reports Chilton. "Meals rather than manual work progressively became the focus of Jesus' journeys." Jesus was signaling in this practice the coming of the kingdom indicated by the prophet Zechariah. Jesus said: "Many shall come from east and west and recline in feasting with Abraham, Isaac, and Jacob in the Kingdom of God" (Matthew 8:11; Luke 13:29). He offended many of his contemporaries in Judaism by insisting that feasting, rather than fasting, was to be the rule of the Kingdom of God (Matthew 9:14–17 and so on). He was announcing the new prophetic era of rejoicing that Zechariah predicted (8:19). Borg adds: "Banquet imagery is central to the gospels. It is tempting to generalize and to suggest that Jesus saw life as a banquet from which many exclude themselves because of perceptions and preoccupations flowing out of their embeddedness in the world of conventional wisdom."

Crossan recognizes a deep alternative politics to Jesus's feasts: "The rules of tabling and eating [are] miniature models for the rules of association and socialization. It means table fellowship as a map of economic discrimination, social hierarchy and political differentiation" are all cut through by Jesus's practices. The practice therefore tells something about the arrival of the kingdom, for it tells a story about negating "the necessity of any hierarchy among" peoples. The emphasis by Jesus on "open commensality" in the ritual meal following Jesus's death and departure has since, however, according to Crossan, been "ruined" because "hierarchy and authority have been reintroduced into the meal."

> "The person who understands what I say about justice understands everything I have to say."

Chilton believes that in his sacred meals Jesus was launching a protest against temple worship as well as the origins of the Eucharistic liturgy. "Jesus crafted his holy feasts into the prototype of what is now called Eucharist, Mass, or Holy Communion. This new meaning made his meals into the primary technique of his mystical practice, but they were also deeply divisive." They alienated the Sanhedrin, who were the guardians of the temple and its practices. The idea of sharing a meal was a sign of the kingdom and a kind of practice in solidarity and community. "These meals were Jesus' last, desperate gesture to insist that his own meals were better sacrifices than what was offered in Caiaphas' corrupt Temple.... When Israelites shared wine and bread in celebration of their own purity and the presence of the Kingdom, God delighted in that more than in the blood and flesh on the altar in the Temple."

Saying "this is my body" over the bread and "this is my blood" over the cup brought up deep lessons from his lineage. Chilton says, "The radical meaning of his words was that wine and bread replaced sacrifice in the Temple, and that was a direct challenge to established ritual practice in Israel.... Jesus proclaimed wine as his blood of sacrifice and bread his flesh of sacrifice.... When Jesus had made his meals into an altar that rivaled the Temple's, many disciples deserted him (Jn 6:60–71)" — not just Judas but many others as well.

Most of Eckhart's sermons were preached in the context of a Eucharistic worship. Eckhart addresses the Eucharistic meal when he says: "Surely we have been invited to the greatest feast ever, where the king of heaven puts on a feast for his son's wedding (Matthew 22:1–14)." The son, says Eckhart, is all of us in touch with our divine sonship and daughtership, and the host of the banquet is "the ineffable One, [who] has no name...the person who is God." God is also the food eaten, for "in the Last Supper God gives himself with all he is as food for his dear friends." Eckhart also sees liturgy in the context of the coming of the kingdom. "Exactly there we too will find our happiness, there where his happiness lies, and whence he receives his being, in that same ground, there all his friends shall find their happiness and draw it from there. That is the 'table in God's kingdom.' That we may come to this table, may God help us."

Eckhart on the Royalty of Every Person

Eckhart writes a treatise on a topic dear to him, which he also preached about: how everyone is an aristocrat or royal person. He begins with a passage from Luke (19:12): "A man of royal birth went to a distant country to be appointed king, and afterward he returned." Says Eckhart: "Our Lord teaches us in these words how royal people have been created in their nature, how divine is the state to which they can rise through grace, and, in addition, how people are to reach that point. In addition, a large part of the Holy Scripture touches upon these words. He says that the person who is hidden within us is the inner person. Scripture calls this person a new person, a heavenly person, a young person, a friend and a royal person." This inner person is also "the soil in which God has sown his likeness and image and in which he sows the good seed, the roots of all wisdom, all skills, all virtues, all goodness — the seed of the divine nature (2 Peter 1:4). The seed of the divine nature is God's Son, the Word of God (Luke 8:11)." Thus Eckhart is talking about the son and daughter of God that we all are.

This inner person is also the creative person, the birther, the mother in us all, "the good tree of which our Lord says that it always bears good fruit and never evil fruit." Adrienne Rich points out that the tree and sacred groves were originally a symbol for the Goddess and the Great Mother in all her bounty of fruits. Only later did patriarchy appropriate it as a phallic symbol.

Our godliness is part of our inner person. We all have it, Eckhart says: "Christ's whole nobility belongs equally to us all and is equally near to us." But it takes some effort to bring it to fruition. "The seed of God is in us. If the seed had a good, wise, and industrious cultivator, it would thrive all the more and grow up to God whose seed it is, and the fruit would be equal to the nature of God. Now the seed of a pear tree grows into a pear tree, a hazel seed into a hazel tree, the seed of God into God (cf. John 3:9)." This divine seed in us may be "crowded, hidden away, and never cultivated," but it will "still never be obliterated. It glows and shines, gives off light, burns, and is unceasingly inclined toward God." It is our destiny to "take on the Son and become the Son and remain within the bosom and heart of the Father." But we have work to do, emptying, to come to that place of "no intermediaries" between us and God.

With nobility comes responsibility. In the Jewish tradition the royal household is responsible above all for justice — justice with the Earth and justice among the people. Preaching about our nobility is not just to enhance one's dignity and esteem but also to get justice rolling. In this treatise, Eckhart invokes Hosea on several occasions, such as Hosea 5:1: "Listen to this, priests attend, House of Israel, listen, royal household you who are responsible for justice." The prophet's job is to "remind the king" of the law of justice. No wonder Eckhart calls Jesus "the great Reminder." Eckhart reveals a personal awareness of the prophetic struggle when he observes:

"When people grow and become rooted in love and in God, they are ready to take upon themselves every attack, temptation, vexation, and painful suffering willingly and gladly, eagerly and joyfully." And he warns, "people should not be sorry because people are angry with them; they should rather be sorry if they merited the anger."

Eckhart concludes his teaching about our royal personhood by invoking the prophet Ezekiel, who talks about a "large eagle" — in Eckhart's German language, "eagle" (*Adler*) and "noble" (*Edler*) are nearly identical words, so he is clearly playing with language here. "What our Lord calls a royal person is named by the prophet a large eagle. Who then is more royal than one who was born, on the one hand, from the highest and best that a creature possesses and, on the other hand, from the most intimate depths of the divine nature and its wilderness? Through the prophet Hosea our Lord says: 'I am going to lure her and lead her out into the wilderness and speak to her heart' (Hosea 2:16)."

Who can deny that this sermon is one of spiritual democracy? One of the Kingdom of God, of the radical availability of our divinity? One that parallels the message of the historical Jesus while incorporating in rich detail the presence of the Cosmic Christ within us and yearning to be born within us?

Eckhart and the Historical Jesus

We find, then, in exploring today's biblical scholarship about the historical Jesus that Eckhart is surprisingly on target in many areas. First, he is at home with the distinction between the historical Jesus and the Logos or Cosmic Christ, which he develops in great depth. Second, in his preaching and teaching, he employs methods that very much mirror those of Jesus and certainly of the Gospel writers, one that is creative to the core and that appeals to the imagination and participation of his listeners. Third, he is very much cognizant of the understanding of Jesus as a teacher of wisdom as well as Jesus as incarnate wisdom.

Fourth, Eckhart is aware of the prophetic lineage of Jesus, and he challenges himself and his hearers to be prophetic as well. Fifth, he is at home with a path of feasting (via positiva) that includes a path of deep letting go and carrying one's cross (via negativa). Sixth, Eckhart recognizes Jesus as son of God *and* all of us as sons and daughters of God, and even as other Marys or birthers of sons and daughters of God, as birthers of the Cosmic Christ. Seventh, our divine sonship, like Jesus's, is centered on the practice of compassion and justice in order to bring about the Kingdom of God on earth. Eighth, he sees the Eucharistic worship as a sign of the kingdom. And last, he too angered the powers that be, the guardians of the religious and cultural status quo, the conventional wisdom, by his work and solidarity and message sharing with the women's movement and with the peasants. He dared to criticize the "merchants in the temple" of the newly constructed Cologne Cathedral with a wisdom that was subversive and nonconventional in every sense of the term.

Given this track record of Eckhart's biblical scholarship and intuitive grasp of the Gospel message from Jesus, one can imagine how excited he would be to talk with today's scholars about the historical Jesus. I believe the learning would be mutual.

CHAPTER SEVEN

DEPTH PSYCHOLOGY

Meister Eckhart Meets Carl Jung

Only in Meister Eckhart did I feel the breath of life.

— CARL JUNG

*The art of letting things happen, action through non-action,
letting go of oneself, as taught by Meister Eckhart,
became for me the key opening the door to the way.*

— CARL JUNG

*God, who is without a name — He has no name — is ineffable,
and the soul in its ground is also ineffable, as He is ineffable.*

— MEISTER ECKHART

Psychology offers much healing and insight to individuals and to human circles striving to be healed and liberated or to bring healing and liberation to others. Since its proper study is human beings, their feelings and their experiences, inner and outer, psychology is sure to overlap with the terrain that the great mystics travel. As Carl Jung put it, speaking of his own calling, "The main interest of my work is not concerned with the treatment of neuroses but rather with the approach to the numinous. But the fact is that the approach to the numinous is the real therapy and inasmuch as you attain the numinous experience you are released from the curse of pathology."

Put this way, it's evident why the great mystics cross paths with deep psychologists. Both journey to find truth in the depths of selfhood and community; they delve into the "inner person," rather than remaining on the surface with the "outer person" (to use Eckhart's and St. Paul's language). In this chapter I wish to offer some suggestive links between Meister Eckhart and Carl Jung. In the next chapter, I will connect Eckhart to the "humanistic school" of psychology through Otto Rank, who influenced many noteworthy and meaningful psychological thinkers of that lineage.

Eckhart brings much to the table of psychological insight — as Jung explicitly acknowledges. Jung invokes Eckhart often throughout his work. As one Jungian scholar put it, "Jung was no casual reader of Eckhart. One has the impression that he almost uncannily perceived in Eckhart's corpus expressions of the deep psyche." Jung speaks to the common depth that all humans share and that psychology seeks to explore: "Man is no longer a distinct individual, but his mind widens out and merges into the mind of mankind — not the conscious mind but the unconscious mind of mankind where we are all the same." Jung's understanding of the collective unconscious was, of course, his effort to name that deep place in all of us that taps into the deep place in others from which so much common experience is shared and named. But he emphasizes in this passage how what we share most deeply is in the *un*conscious mind, not the conscious mind. Who will lead us down there? Who will help us navigate a journey downward, into the dark, into the shadows, into the more-than-rational and more-than-verbal spaces and places? Who is courageous enough to make that journey and artful enough, upon return, to attempt to name it? Meister Eckhart is such a person.

The Darkness of the Soul

Eckhart knows that there is a depth to us all that is unnameable. As we saw in chapter three, he insists on the "unknowability" and fundamental "unnameability" and "ineffability" of the Godhead. But he also teaches that the human soul is, like God, unknowable, unnameable, and ineffable, and he repeats the point on numerous occasions. Obviously, it is important to him, and it is important to him that his audience grasp this basic point. He says: "God, who is without a name — He has no name — is ineffable, and the soul in its ground is also ineffable, as He is ineffable." It is not just in her ground, however, that the soul is unknowable but also at her fullest level of being. "The soul is so noble at her highest and purest that the masters cannot find any name for her.... The soul is made in God's image in her highest part." And again: "The soul, too, has no name. Just as no one can find a true name for God, so no one can find the soul's true name, although mighty tomes have been written about this. But the soul is given a name as regards its activity." He repeats this point as well, that we know about the soul from its work, from its activities. "The soul contains many powers which work in great secrecy." We need to explore those powers and secret activities. Psychology helps do that.

If alive today, Eckhart would have respected the efforts of Carl Jung and other depth psychologists to explore the hidden, dark, mysterious, and important depths of the human psyche. He would have eagerly sat at their feet to learn. Why am I so certain? First,

> *"Nothing is so near to me as God. God is nearer to me than myself....God is within, but we are outside. God is at home in us, but we are abroad."*

because Eckhart made that journey himself and came back to tell us about it, to visualize and describe it. But second, because Eckhart welcomed anyone to the table who could assist in healing our ignorance and denial, who could shine light in the darkness without denying the darkness in which we all dwell. Says Eckhart: "The ground of the soul is dark." This did not deter him from his journey any more than a counselor or psychologist today is deterred from that journey of exploration. In fact, it enticed Eckhart as it also allured Jung, who had to deal with the darkness in his own psyche time and time again. Most prominently, at the onslaught of middle age, Jung experienced a severe depression, if not a psychic break, that lasted for three long years.

Eckhart, like any depth psychologist, learned to be at home in the dark and to seek out the mysterious but vital truths lurking there and that without exploration leave us subject to their whims and control. Can one explore the Godhead and not the soul? Can one explore the soul and not the Godhead? Eckhart thought not: "The Godhead alone is the place of the soul, and is nameless." It is not an easy task to explore the nameless, but neither is it thankless. It is essential, though it presents the psychologist with the same problems of description as the mystic. At one point Jung compares the conscious to nature and the unconscious to grace. Eckhart, on the other hand, declares that all of nature is grace. Jung fished in the unconscious and drew forth images and language from its watery depths that Eckhart would have understood.

Most of all, Eckhart understood and welcomed the urge to explore the human mind and its many layers of consciousness. It is natural to want to know what is going on most deeply, most "innermost," in our psyches. Eckhart writes, "God is a being who always lives in the innermost. Therefore the spirit is always searching within. But the will goes outward toward what it loves."

Looking within, Eckhart talks about discovering a region, an intersection between the Divine and the human, that though nameless and formless still has a particular quality: "There is something in the soul in which God is bare and the masters say this is nameless, and has no name of its own. It exists, and yet it has no being of its own, for it is neither this nor that, neither here nor there."

Jung's term *synchronicity* was one way he tried to name this place.

Synchronicity

Jung's understanding of synchronicity sheds light on Eckhart's frequent references to the need to go deeper than time and space, to enter into a place where time and space do not reign. Such is the Kingdom of God. Eckhart writes: "Nothing so much hinders the soul's understanding of God as time and space. God is neither this nor that in the way of the manifold things of earth, for God is one."

Jung defines synchronicity as a "coincidence in time of two or more unrelated events which have the same or a similar meaning." The key word here is *meaning*, according to Jungian Steven Herrmann. Meaning and synchronicity intermesh. One might say that synchronicity names the central mystery of the "collective unconscious" and its enduring psychological "archetypes" that Jung explored: synchronicity is the unseen process by which humans share, through time and across cultures, common meaningful understandings about life, the universe, and the Divine.

For Jung synchronicity carries us beyond Newtonian laws of cause and effect; Jung sometimes defined it as "acausal relationship." He came to it by noting the correlation between movements of events within dreams and ancient scriptures. But its immediate insight came from discussions with physicists Niels Bohr and Wolfgang Pauli and Albert Einstein. From them he took the notion of the atom as the basic unit of the physical world and compared it to the psyche as the basic unit of the human being. Jung felt that "if great sums of energy could be released by breaking the elemental unit of the atom, equivalent sums of energy might be brought forth if the depths of the psyche could be opened in a comparable way." Noncausal but meaningful relationship is key to synchronicity.

Synchronicity also explains events that go beyond the normal or accepted nature of the psyche. Jung writes:

> The psychoid archetype, that is, its irrepresentational and unconscious essence, is not just a postulate only, but possesses qualities of a parapsychological nature which I have grouped together under the term "synchronicity." I use this term to indicate the fact that in cases of telepathy, precognition, and similar inexplicable phenomena, one can very frequently observe an archetypal situation....And since the parapsychological phenomena associated with the unconscious psyche show a peculiar tendency to relativise the categories of time and space, the collective unconscious must have a spaceless and timeless quality. Consequently, there is some probability that an archetypal situation will be accompanied by synchronistic phenomena, as in the case of death, in whose vicinity such phenomena are relatively frequent.

We see, then, that both Jung and Eckhart are busy exploring synchronicity, which takes one not only deeper than everyday time and space but also deeper than the ego itself. It takes one to a nonplace, to a space where ego no longer rules, to a place of deep mutuality where "your joy is my joy and your pain is my pain," to quote poet Bill Everson (who drank deeply from Jung's teachings, and who we will visit in chapter eleven).

With the term "synchronicity," Jung helps us name the nameless place Eckhart found, but rather remarkably, Eckhart also helps us understand the unseen process synchronicity represents. In one particular sermon, Eckhart — finally! — offers us a working definition of the soul, one he has struggled mightily to come up with. Our Divine soul may be dark, unseen and ineffable, but we can recognize it at work. He writes: "Whatever God does, the first outburst is always compassion, and I do not mean that he forgives a person his sins or that a person takes compassion on another.... The highest work of God is compassion and this means that God sets the soul in the highest and purest place which it can occupy: in space, in the sea, in a fathomless ocean; and there God works compassion. Therefore the prophet says: 'Lord, have compassion on the people who are in you.'" In other words, in some fashion, we are *in* God, and such a being-in is a land of compassion, of togetherness, of love, of nondualism, of nonpity, of union. Eckhart continues: "A master who has spoken the best about the soul says that all human science can never fathom what the soul is in its ground. To know what the soul is, one needs supernatural knowledge. We do not know about what the powers of the soul do when they go out to do their work; we know a little about this, but not very much." Of course, Jung would say that the soul creates archetypes and dreams and much more, and that these are sources of the soul's energy and work. But still, Eckhart is saying, such knowledge, while helpful, is limited. He concludes: "What the soul is in its ground, no one knows. What one can know about it must be supernatural, it must be from grace. The soul is where God works compassion."

This is stunning information from Eckhart. The unknowability, the namelessness, and the deep, dark mystery of the soul occurs because the soul is not a noun. It is a where; a place; a space where God works compassion and where the love of God is active. This sounds very Buddhist in its seeming abandonment of the soul as a thing, eternal or not. It also parallels the concept of synchronicity as a process, a how; it's the Divine, supernatural grace that provides the unconscious with its gifts of collective understanding. It names the radical level of *interdependence* that is the basis of all compassion and indeed of our whole existence. It is from this land of interdependence that Jung's collective archetypes emerge as well.

Eckhart is further implying that until we become a conduit for the Divine compassion, we do not yet have soul. Soul is something we birth, and we birth it in proportion to our developing love and compassion.

The Relativity of the God-Concept in Meister Eckhart

Jung was by no means unread in Meister Eckhart. Quite the opposite. Jung calls Eckhart the "greatest thinker" of the medieval era, and he invokes him at least thirty-eight times in his writings. In his autobiography — after relaying the sorry story of his father's hyperrational theism (and by implication that of nine other relatives who were also ministers in the Swiss Reformed Church) and Jung's own lack of any spiritual breakthrough at the time of his first communion, and after lamenting the "absence of God" especially from church and describing himself as having no relationship to God whatsoever — Jung tells us that "only in Meister Eckhart did I feel the breath of life."

Jung devotes a chapter to Eckhart entitled "The Relativity of the God-Concept in Meister Eckhart" in his volume *Psychological Types*. In it, he lucidly defines the chapter title: "The 'relativity of God,' as I understand it, denotes a point of view that does not conceive of God as 'absolute,' i.e., wholly 'cut off' from man and existing outside and beyond all human conditions, but as in a certain sense dependent on him; it also implies a reciprocal and essential relation between man and God, whereby man can be understood as a function of God, and God as a psychological function of man." The presence of God in the unconscious is an "overpowering impetus to action" that "transcends conscious understanding" and has its source "in an accumulation of energy in the unconscious." Jung continues, "From the beginning of time [God] has been the collective expression of the most overwhelmingly powerful influences exerted on the conscious mind by unconscious concentrations of libido." This brings things about that "could never be done by conscious effort." One senses why Jung calls the unconscious a place of grace and not just nature.

What Jung names with his phrase the "relativity of God" (he also talks about "the relativity of the symbol") is clearly a nontheistic deity. This is not a God who is cold, distant, and separate from creation and humans; it is not a Newtonian God who operates a mechanical universe like an engineer. Instead, Jung is celebrating an immanent God, a panentheistic deity. And of course, as we saw in chapter two, Eckhart's God is a panentheistic God. As a reminder, here is another quote by Eckhart on his sense of the presence of God: "I am as certain as I am of my own life that nothing is so 'near' to me as God. God is nearer to me than myself. My being depends on the fact that God is 'near' to me and present for me!...God is near to us, but we are very far from him. God is within, but we are outside. God is at home in us, but we are abroad." Eckhart is naming the experience of the mystics.

When Jung visited Taos, New Mexico, and Kenya, Africa, at the age of fifty he returned home to say: "Today we are obliged to view the miraculous in a somewhat different light." Elsewhere, Jung comments: "I believe that, after thousands of millions of years, someone had to realize that this wonderful world of mountains and oceans, suns and moons, galaxies and nebulae, plants and animals, *exists*." Jung goes on to share what he calls his "confession of faith":

> From a low hill in the Athi plains of East Africa I once watched the vast herds of wild animals grazing in soundless stillness, as they had done from time immemorial, touched only by the breath of a primeval world. I felt then as if I were the first man, the first creature, to know that all this *is*. The entire world round me was still in its primeval state; it did not know that it *was*. And then, in that one moment in which I came to know, the world sprang into being; without that moment it would never have been.

It is clear that Jung underwent a profound spiritual conversion amid the native peoples of America and Africa in these journeys. Is this not Eckhart's teaching on how "isness is God" and the impact of encountering the Cataphatic Divinity, and the via positiva? Does this not answer Jung's complaint that "nothing is holy any longer."

In his essay on Eckhart, Jung calls Eckhart "the great relativist" for honoring how "life itself flows from springs both clear and muddy. Hence all excessive 'purity' lacks vitality....Every renewal of life needs the muddy as well as the clear." As evidence of this, Jung cites this statement by Eckhart:

God is willing to bear the brunt of sins and often winks at them, mostly sending them to those whom he has destined for great things. Behold! Who was dearer and nearer to our Lord than the apostles? Not one of them but fell into mortal sin; all were mortal sinners. In the Old Testament and in the New he has shown this to be true of those who afterwards were far the dearest to him; and still today one seldom finds that people come to great things without they first go somewhat astray.

One can only imagine how refreshing Eckhart's nonmoralizing was to a son (and grandson) of a Swiss preacher whose moralisms constituted the bulk of the Christian ideology of his youth. What freedom and sense of grace Eckhart must have brought to Jung's soul! And with it Jung felt a permission to pursue a parallel path of psychological and spiritual explorations outside the confines of institutional religion. Jung offers many citations from Eckhart to support this. In one passage, Eckhart writes: "Christ says, 'The kingdom of heaven is like a treasure hid in a field.' This field is the soul, wherein lies hidden the treasure of the divine kingdom. In the soul, therefore, are God and all creatures blessed." Jung comments: "This interpretation agrees with our psychological argument: the soul is a personification of the unconscious, where lies the treasure, the libido which is immersed in introversion and allegorized as God's kingdom. This amounts to a permanent union with God, a living in his kingdom."

In Jung's work, the "libido" refers to life force — a life force that is a "hidden treasure," one hidden in the "field" that is the "soul." How to awaken that life force? The key is found in Eckhart's awareness of the presence of God *within,* thus the "relativity" of God. Previously the libido was "invested in objects, and this made the world seem all-powerful. God was then 'outside,' but now works from within, as the hidden treasure conceived as God's kingdom." Instead, God is now the "power working within the soul and perceived by it." And Jung enthusiastically adds, "Eckhart even calls the soul the image *of God.*" Why is this such news to Jung? Obviously, his exposure to Christianity before Eckhart was shallow and mystic-less, indeed. God was something exclusively "outside." Jung speaks of "life at its most intense," and the experience of such a God results in what Eckhart calls a "blissful" state. This Jung defines as "a state of intense vitality." Jung says this blissful state is "strongly reminiscent of that of the child on the one hand,

and of the primitive on the other, who is likewise highly influenced by the unconscious. We can safely state that the restoration of the earlier paradisal state is the cause of this blissfulness." Citing Eckhart's play on words, *Gott ist selig in der Seele* ("God is blissful in the soul"), Jung asks, "Whence comes this 'blissful' feeling, this ecstasy of love?" Jung also recognizes "the ecstasy of a non-temporal state in which present, past, and future are one...a state of feeling" — clearly Eckhart not only goes to that place of bliss and ecstasy but invites others as well to enter the "kingdom," which is an experience of the eternal now in which "everything of the past and everything of the future" is present in the soul now. Much of the healing that Eckhart accomplished for Jung is his invitation to put aside a God of theism (a God outside) and to enter into the God of panentheism (us in God and God in us). This theology of panentheism was utterly lacking in the Christianity Jung inherited from his father.

Jung, Eckhart, and the Via Creativa

Eckhart also challenges the patriarchal God of Jung's Calvinist ancestors when he insists on the birthing or maternal dimension to our God experience. As Jung says, creativity comes "from the land of the mothers" — and Eckhart knew this and emphasized it. Jung is moved deeply by the via creativa, which Eckhart identifies with the role of God and the soul operating together. The dynamic Divine relationship Eckhart describes inside the individual soul is directly analogous to how Jung envisions the archetypal dynamics of the unconscious. "The determining force (God) operating from these depths [of the unconscious] is reflected by the soul, that is, it creates symbols and images, and is itself only an image. By means of these images the soul conveys the forces of the unconscious to consciousness; it is both receiver and transmitter, an organ for perceiving unconscious contents. What it perceives are symbols. But symbols are shaped energies." Jung is excited that for Eckhart "the happy state is a *creative* state," and he cites the following "noble words" by Eckhart:

> If anyone should ask me, Wherefore do we pray, wherefore do we feast, wherefore do we do all manner of good works, wherefore are we baptized, wherefore did God become man, I would answer, So that

> God may be born in the soul and the soul again in God. Therefore
> were the Holy Scriptures written. Therefore did God create the whole
> world, that God might be born in the soul and the soul again in God.

Jung comments: "Here Eckhart states bluntly that God is dependent on the
soul, and at the same time, that the soul is the birthplace of God." He says
that the symbol of God's birth used by Eckhart is "equivalent to a renewal of
life." Jung rightly recognizes that for Eckhart "God's birth [is] a continual
process."

Both Jung and Eckhart honor image making and creativity. Therapist
Dr. John Conger, who wrote about Jung, says that "images are to the psyche
what energy is to the body; they form a functional identity." Eckhart is not
at all parsimonious about images but brings them forth often in torrents of
creativity. Indeed, in one sermon he describes the Holy Spirit, the spirit of
creativity, as a "rapid river" rushing into and through our souls, and I suspect he is speaking of his own experiences of creativity. Eckhart says:

> Saint John says that from all of those who have a faith enlivened by
> divine love and who prove it by their good works "living waters will
> flow" (cf. Jn. 7:38). In this way, he wishes to point to the Holy Spirit.
> The prophet...calls the Holy Spirit an "intoxication" because of its
> quick emanation, for the Spirit flows just as completely into the soul as
> the soul empties itself in humility and expands itself to receive him. I am
> certain of this: God would...completely fill the soul with this "river."

Eckhart reminds us that the Holy Spirit is a "gift" and he tells this story:
"We read about a woman who received a gift from Christ. The first gift
which God gives is the Holy Spirit; in that gift, God gives all of his gifts:
That is 'the living water, whomever I give this to will never thirst again.'
This water is grace and light and springs up in the soul and rises within and
presses upward and leaps up, into eternity."

Jung asks: "How does one come to terms in practice with the unconscious?" He answers his question through the method he devised called
"active imagination." He writes: "But the supreme meaning is the path, the
way and the bridge to what is to come. This is the God yet to come. It is
not the coming of God himself but his image which appears in the supreme
meaning. God is an image, and those who worship him must worship in the

images of the supreme meaning." Thus both Eckhart and Jung agree on the redemptive and healing powers of the via creativa, what Jung calls "the land of the mothers" or "that sea of creativity which mythology as humanity's first psychology knows as the great Goddess or Mother," who is mother of all. Both Jung and Eckhart trust the imagination and the Holy Spirit to impregnate it. Both recognize that a great emptying (the via negativa and even nothingness) makes way for a great birthing (the via creativa).

However, according to Eckhart, before this great birth, the via creativa is preceded by the via negativa (as we saw in chapter three). This part of the journey is not a blissful one, though what follows with the birth is a blessing. Says Eckhart, "With the birth you discover all blessing."

This relationship is embodied in Eckhart's distinction between God and Godhead, of the Cataphatic Divinity who is the God of Light and the Apophatic Divinity, or the unknowable, unnameable Godhead. Jung finds this to be an important distinction. He writes: "God is a function of the soul, just as the soul is a function of Godhead. Godhead is obviously all-pervading creative power or, in psychological terms, self-generating creative instinct, that neither knows nor possesses itself, comparable to Schopenhauer's universal Will." The soul along with every creature "declares" God. In Eckhart's dynamic of God and Godhead, "God disappears as an object" and becomes "a subject which is no longer distinguishable from the ego. In other words the ego, as a late product of differentiation is reunited with the dynamic All-oneness (the participation mystique of primitives). This is the immersion in the 'flood and source.'" In other words, when God is no longer "out there," God "disappears" as an object and we become "co-creators" (Eckhart) with God.

> "Isness is God."

Jung on the Shadow

One of Jung's most enduring and important concepts is "the shadow," or what his longtime associate, Marie-Louise von Franz, called "the dark, unlived, and repressed side of the ego complex." However, Jung sweepingly says, "The shadow is simply the whole unconscious."

The concept of the shadow presents a paradox. If the unconscious represents what we aren't conscious of knowing, or what we actively keep ourselves from knowing, then how can we ever become self-aware of what it contains? Jung says by letting go, by letting be and letting happen without judgment. In fact, Jung gives complete credit to Meister Eckhart for teaching him this practice when he says: "The art of letting things happen, action through non-action, letting go of oneself, as taught by Meister Eckhart, became for me the key opening the door to the way. We must be able to let things happen in the psyche. For us this actually is an art of which few people know anything. Consciousness is forever interfering."

Just as Jung challenges us by drawing attention to our personal and collective shadows, Eckhart challenges us with his similar concept of nothingness, but first, let's look at the shadow — how the idea arose and what it meant for Jung. According to therapist Dr. John Conger, in his rich book *Jung & Reich: The Body as Shadow*, Jung's father taught him only about the Cataphatic Divinity. Jung's father believed that "Christ is all good and Christians are expected to see no value in 'sin.'" But very early it dawned on Jung that the darkness of life must be given its due; otherwise it will assert itself in powerful and negative ways. Jung was always grateful to his mother, who, when he was a child, suggested that he read Goethe's *Faust*, which became, Conger writes, a "guiding myth for his life, a story that did full justice to the integration of the dark side." Without the awareness that everything under the sun also casts a shadow, we reduce three-dimensional reality to a mere two dimensions. The shadow, as Conger points out, stands for not just "what we dare not see but our potentiality, what we are becoming." As Jung put it, "that future personality which we are to be in a year's time is already here, only it is still in the shadow." If, in one sense, we are always in the process of birthing ourselves, then that future self is already partially present, unseen, in our unconscious shadow. Says Dr. Conger: "Psychology teaches us to enter more easily into the shadows so that we can cooperate with nature and ourselves." According to Jung, the unconscious is a much larger "sea" than our consciousness; it contains "a wealth beyond our fathoming," an "endless and self-replenishing abundance of living creatures."

How do we access it? "The only way to get at them in practice," Conger writes, "is to try to attain a conscious attitude which allows the unconscious to cooperate instead of being driven into opposition."

In other words, we have to let go, and this is a good thing. The shadow, observes Conger, "holds the essence of what it is to be alive....It gives us weight and credibility, grounds us in space and time." This is the dialectical power of the shadow, and of Eckhart's conception of God and the Godhead: while there is an interior realm beyond time and space, we still very much live in an embodied world. Our bodies live in a specific time and place. Therefore, both Eckhart and Jung urge us to live dialectically, in both worlds concurrently; indeed, one might say that the more time one wants to dwell beyond time and space, the more one should be grounded in time and space. The shadow helps us to ground ourselves, to remain close to "earth." This is how Eckhart understands the word "humility." It is our capacity to stay grounded. It is not about putting oneself down or allowing one to be put down by others (Eckhart says: "Despise being despised") — but about remaining connected to Earth, which exists in time.

Conger elaborates on the nature of the shadow. He says it is

imagined, unseen, primitive, archaic, instinctual, primordial, unpredictable, confused, rebellious, unstructured, unaccepted, unrelated, uncivilized, unstable, unavailable, mad, the left hand, the antithetic mask, the Dionysian, the underside of things, the Chthonic side, the background, the peripheral, the perverse, the yearned for, that which holds back and stands back, that which is glimpsed at out of the corner of the eye, that which looks bad, is magical, denied, unusual, mercurial, elusive, deadly, underground, the roots of the tree.

One can feel here a link with one of Eckhart's favorite terms, which he used over and over: God as the *ground* of being, the search for the *ground* of the soul, and the coming together of "God's ground and my ground" to make one "ground." Once again we see that Eckhart is in no way afraid of the dark (for the underside and the roots of the tree are in the dark); in fact, he seeks it out and urges us to do the same.

Jung warned that most people try to live "without a shadow," and civilization often encourages that, as if we are only what we care to know or believe about ourselves. But this is the path of denial, and it presents great danger — especially if the society as a whole wants to see itself entirely in the light. When we deny a quality in ourselves, we typically project it onto others, who become our scapegoats as they play our shadow for us.

Says Jung: "Modern man must rediscover a deeper source of his own spiritual life. To do this he is obliged to struggle with evil, to confront his shadow, to integrate the devil. There is no other choice." The shadow comes to us, observes Conger, "in the area of our greatest blindness and area of inferior development where we are least able to defend ourselves." Yet this very darkness, Jung says, is what provides "the door into the unconscious and the gateway of dreams....A man who is possessed by his shadow is always standing in his own light and falling into his own traps." When we repress or deny the shadow, it responds, Conger says, "explosively and catastrophically," and we want to rid ourselves of it. Instead, the shadow can be an ally, maybe even "our best teacher, reflecting back to us our blind side." It is the opponent "who sharpens our skill."

Jung believes that Hitler personified the German shadow in the 1930s. He wrote, "In Hitler every German should have seen his own shadow, his own worst danger." That they did not allowed the tragedy of World War II and the Holocaust. Few of us, Jung believes, even today, are open enough to entertain the shadow. Instead we settle for lives of conformity and living out the so-called values of mass culture and living them out uncritically. We are set up for the dangers of denial.

Eckhart on Divine Nothingness

Meister Eckhart is constantly asking people to enter or face the shadow, and he does so with surprising language and paradox. He says "God is not good" because God cannot be better or best. He says: "I pray God to rid me of God." And of course (as we saw in chapter three), he talks at length about the Apophatic Divinity, the dark Godhead that cannot be named. One might say, the Divinity that dwells in the shadow.

Another way he urges us to face the shadow is in his frequent discussions of nothingness. "Our whole being depends on nothing but a becoming-Nothing," he says. He urges us to pay attention to our weak side. "It is very silly for a person who fasts a lot, prays and performs great works and spends time in solitude, if he does not mend his ways, and is impatient and angry. One should find out one's greatest weakness, and devote all one's energy to overcoming that." But God is also nothing. "God is nothing. It is not, however, as if he were without being. He is rather neither this thing, nor that thing that we might express. He is a being above all being. He is a beingless being." God is a no-thing, a nonobject.

Commenting on Paul's conversion experience when he fell off his horse and was blinded (Acts 9:8), Eckhart says, when Paul rose from the ground, he "saw nothing, and this nothingness was God. Indeed, he saw God and that is what he calls a nothingness....I cannot see what is One. He saw nothing, that is to say, God. God is nothingness, and yet God is something." Notice how Eckhart presents this Divine nothingness as an *experience*, a conversion experience, one of the most influential experiences in human history — because without Paul's awakening, Christ's message would very likely have not extended very far into the empire of the day. The kind of nothingness Eckhart is inviting us into is an experiential nothingness. "All creatures are a mere nothing," he says. By that he means that we did not create our own being. That was done for us. We come into being on the work of others. Only God is independent Being. Eckhart also calls God a "nameless nothingness."

He also sees the human intellect as pure potentiality, thus it is "nothing." It takes us beyond what is. Creativity is truly about something new, birthing something that hitherto has been a nonbeing. Just as a mirror has to be emptied, or rendered blank, so that it can accomplish its task of reflecting an accurate image, so our minds must also revert at times to nothingness and emptiness to be with reality as it is. To be with God, nothing to nothing. To be in the presence of sacred nothingness.

Is Eckhart's invitation into nothingness comparable to Jung's invitation into the shadow? I suspect they share a lot in common around this important experiential reality. By calling God a "nameless nothingness," Eckhart is extending permission to all humans to face their own nothingness and anything else the shadow may carry with it. All darkness, all regrets, all pain, all mistakes, all projections. Or as Conger put it, all that is "imagined, unseen... underground, the roots of the tree."

Eckhart is challenging us to integrate nothingness, to entertain it and spend time with it and not run from it — whether it be our personal nothingness or the nothingness of our work, our death, our limits; the nothingness of our country or of our species. These are meditations worth practicing, especially today when so much Something, so much Self-Righteousness and Surety, so many Idols, so many Consumer Goods, flood us, seeking our attention and our false worship.

I suspect that the experience of nothingness for Eckhart was deeply felt his entire life. As a Dominican, he knew intimately the story of his brother Thomas Aquinas, who died just two years before Eckhart entered the order as a young man. Aquinas was a genius by anyone's reckoning. He was an intellectual freak, a giant among men, and a prodigious scholar and writer who died at only forty-nine years of age. But the final year of his life, he went mute. He told associates that he had a mystical experience that taught him that "all he had written was straw." What an immense letting go resulted from that experience! Surely this story — that the greatest theologian in all of Christianity put down his pen, saying that all it produced was "straw" — could not help but influence Eckhart's awareness of the nothingness of all things. A nothingness, however, that was also balanced with the godliness of all things, the light in all things, the Cosmic Christ in all things. Eckhart danced the dialectical dance 'tween light and dark, via positiva and via negativa, cataphatic and apophatic. Nothingness was not the last word. But one returns to it often because there one gets grounded and emptied and faces an authentic truth and gets readied for the return of Spirit, which "makes all things new." Even nothingness. Eckhart was fond of citing John's Gospel, "the light shines in the darkness and the darkness grasps it not."

The Kabbalah, a medieval Jewish mystical work, also talks of the soul and its experience of nothing (or *ayin* in Hebrew). In it, we learn how important stillness and solitude can be in order to get to know the soul: "Your deep soul hides itself from consciousness. So you need to increase aloneness, elevation of thinking, penetration of thought, liberation of mind — until finally your soul reveals itself to you, spangling a few sparkles of her lights." For this tradition, as for Eckhart, the soul is unknowable. As the Kabbalah states, "No one knows anything at all about the human soul; she stands in the status of nothingness, as it is written: 'The superiority of the human over the beast is ayin.'" There is a certain "glory" in being in touch with one's nothingness. "By means of this soul, the human being ascends higher than all other creatures and attains the glory of Ayin." Ayin, or nothingness, and wisdom travel together. "God generates all of existence. The beginning of existence is the secret concealed point, primordial wisdom, the secret conceptual point. That which abides in thought yet cannot be grasped is called wisdom: Hokhmah...Hakkehmah. Since you can never grasp it, hakkeh, 'wait,' for mah, 'what' will come and what will be." Nothingness takes us to a place of equality and equanimity — just as Eckhart teaches. "Wait... for What." That seems like a practical way of being in silence, with nothing, without projections, without a why or wherefore, just being with being. Wisdom as waiting for nothing, waiting for whatever....

The Kabbalah continues: "If you think of yourself as something, then God cannot clothe himself in you, for God is infinite. No vessel can contain God, unless you think of yourself as Ayin." For this, a great emptying is required, a real letting go. "This is the sublime, primordial wisdom emerging out of Ayin. Think of yourself as Ayin and forget yourself totally. Then you can transcend time, rising to the world of thought, where all is equal: life and death, ocean and dry land." Was Eckhart familiar with the Kabbalah? If not directly, certainly he came to similar teachings about Ayin, or nothingness.

Recently I saw a picture taken from outer space, just at the edge of our solar system. Earth was in the picture only as a dot in the distance. Is Earth only a dot? Is it even less than that, if seen from the fuller view of all the galaxies with which we share this universe? In a way, yes. We are a receding dot and little more. But from another perspective, no. We are water; we are oceans with amazing fishes and whales and porpoises. We are mountains and polar bears, elephants and redwood trees; we are puppies and kittens and roses and lilies; we are forests and rocks; we are humans with our music and poetry and films and rituals and costumes and religions and scholarship and comedy. We are amazing. We are something. But we are also very close to nothing. That is part of the vision of Eckhart and his invitation to visit nothingness and talk about it. It is integral to everything we are — and, in his view, to everything God is also.

If the Earth is just a dot, what about the ego? The self? How ephemeral, how impermanent, how tiny is that in the scope of all things? Yet, we humans are, as Aquinas put it, *capax universi*, capable of the universe and the Cosmic Christ archetype that Eckhart invokes so often. Jung lamented how the rupture between psyche and cosmos occurred during the modern era: "The development of Western philosophy during the last two centuries has succeeded in isolating the mind in its own sphere and in severing it from its primal oneness with the universe." We are both/and; we are nothing and something; we are tiny and dependent beyond belief, but we are also Cosmic Christs in touch with the macrocosm of the universe. That is Eckhart's view, one seemingly confirmed by today's scientific findings on the vastness and the continuously self-generating, evolutionary nature of our 13.8-billion-year-old universe.

To name nothingness and urge us to journey into it — as both Eckhart and Jung do — names something physical as well. It is another way of talking about our lower chakras, those that take us down into Mother Earth or, as we saw earlier, into authentic humility (*humus*). It is about returning to our first chakra, which connects us to Earth and the cosmos and all beings that vibrate; to our sexuality in the second chakra; and to our outrage and power for centering ourselves as found in the third chakra. This is important. One reason our culture, including media and education, is incapable of teaching us about shadow and nothingness is that the left brain cannot under-

> *"Just as no one can find a true name for God, so none can find the soul's true name, although mighty tomes have been written about this."*

stand it. The left brain entertains things and words but not emptiness and space and nothing. Also, in the dark we are more one; there is less differentiation and less individuality; we are closer to the Godhead, where all is one, than to God, where differentiation of creation takes place. Here is how Jung puts it: "The deeper 'layers' of the psyche lose their individual uniqueness as they retreat farther and farther into darkness. 'Lower down,' that is to say as they approach the autonomous functional systems, they become increasingly collective until they are universalized and extinguished in the body's materiality, i.e., in chemical substances....Hence 'at bottom' the psyche is simply 'world.'" Eckhart also talks about the "world" being the "soul."

Conger concludes his study on Jung with the following wisdom: "Man's liberation is not divorced from the heart of darkness within and around him.... There is no nirvana in undeveloped nature, and we need the dialogue with the shadow at our core to individuate.... If we release the devil to a secondary level, there can be no profound ongoing struggle in our psyche, no alchemy in which we are tried and tested at our core in the fires of hell.... Nevertheless, the question of whether darkness follows us into our deepest center of being is not easily resolved in favor of Jung." We do need, Conger feels, the presence of the "God of light" that comes with the good news of Christ. The via negativa calls for a via positiva.

Is there any shadow without light? Is a shadow not 100 percent dependent on the light, on the sun even? And is a shadow not one-dimensional (lacking two, much less three, dimensions), even though it may, as Conger proposes, lay the groundwork for our three-dimensional existence? There lies something beyond shadow, and that surely is our powers of creativity, of birthing new light, into the world.

Return to the Mother Goddess

In a passage strikingly like Eckhart's sermon, quoted above, about the sea and compassion, in which he defines the soul as the place "where God works compassion," Jung writes:

> The meeting with oneself is, at first, the meeting with one's own shadow. The shadow is a tight passage, a narrow door, whose painful construction no one is spared who goes down to the deep well. But one must learn to know oneself in order to know who one is. For what comes after the door is, surprisingly enough, a boundless expanse full of unprecedented uncertainty, with apparently no inside and no outside, no above and no below, no here and no there, no mine and no thine, no good and no bad. It is the world of water, where all life floats in suspension; where the realm of the sympathetic system, the soul of everything living, begins; where I am indivisibly this and that; where I experience the other in myself and the other-than-myself experiences me.

Like Eckhart, Jung comes to the realization that compassion is the culmination — even of the way of the shadow, the way of soul growth in the via negativa. In invoking the "world of water," Jung, like Eckhart, is invoking the Great Mother.

Indeed, Jung is explicit that our return to nothingness is a return to the Mother Goddess. As Jungian scholar John Dourley puts it, "Much of his [Jung's] psychology is devoted to the description of the base dynamic of individuation as repeated immersion in her restorative nothingness and the prelude to a life of enhanced compassionate activity in the world she also authors. This is the numinous maternal in the most extended sense." Life is renewed through reconnecting with "the Great Mother as the creative nothing from which all consciousness is born." Thus Eckhart's frequent invitation to honor nothingness and not flee from it is still another invitation to return to the Divine Feminine — and out of this return there will be born a new Christ in each of us, just as his dream foretold. Dourley recognizes that "Eckhart identifies with the mother, herself formless, from whom all form and the drive to form derive. A moment of dissolution in the nothing frees Eckhart from the compulsion of form, of mind, and their projection of form on matter or others. It is at the heart of his doctrine of resignation or letting be. His dissolution in the mother is the height of the numinosity of the night."

The Collective Unconscious and Interfaith, Interspirituality

Jung recognizes in Eckhart a deep ecumenical mind — one that links to prehistory as well as to the wisdom of the East. We saw an application of this ecumenical consciousness when we discussed Thich Nhat Hanh in chapter three, and we will see it anew in chapters nine, ten, and eleven. Jung even says that Eckhart's finding of universal truths "proves" the reality of archetypes and a collective unconscious. "The numerous analogies with Eastern ideas are immediately apparent, and they have been elaborated by writers more qualified than myself. In the absence of direct transmission this parallelism proves that Eckhart was thinking from the depths of the collective psyche which is common to East and West. This universal foundation, for which no common historical background can be made answerable, underlies the primitive mentality with its energic conception of God." Jung says that Eckhart embodies a "return to primeval nature and mystic regression to the psychic conditions of prehistory," which is common to all religions "in which the impelling *dynamis* has not yet petrified into an abstract idea but is still a living experience." In the process "the original state of identity with God is re-established and a new potential is produced." By reconnecting the individual to God, it "creates the world anew."

When Jung analyzes the pathologies of Western civilization and calls for an "approach to the numinous" as the appropriate method for our deep healing, one can see why Eckhart offers him (and us) so much juice for starting anew. Speaking of organized religion, Jung decries how "the bridge from dogma to the inner experience of the individual has broken down." Of course, Eckhart's entire effort could be seen as healing that broken bridge and trying to restart Christianity as something experiential. He represents and articulates the mystical experience par excellence. Jung cautions that Christianity is threatened with "complete oblivion" because "it is of the highest importance that the education and 'enlightened' public should know religious truth as a thing living in the human soul and not as an abstruse and unreasonable relic of the past." Surely Eckhart has set his sights as preacher and teacher on rekindling what is "living in the human soul." And Eckhart speaks to Jung's great concern, which Jung describes as follows:

> Too few people have experienced the divine image as the innermost possession of their own souls. Christ only meets them from without, never from within the soul....So long as religion is only faith and outward form, and the religious function is not experienced in our own souls, nothing of any importance has happened. It has yet to be understood that the mysterium magnum is not only an actuality but is first and foremost rooted in the human psyche. The man who does not know this from his own experience may be a most learned theologian, but he has no idea of religion and still less of education.

To which Eckhart responds: Amen.

CHAPTER EIGHT

PSYCHOTHERAPY AND THE "UNIO MYSTICA"

Meister Eckhart Meets Otto Rank

Human nature is at bottom irrational....
The epitome of the irrational [is] the marvel of creation itself.

— OTTO RANK

If anyone were to ask life over a thousand years, "Why are you alive?"
the only reply could be: "I live so that I may live." This happens because
life lives from its own foundation and rises out of itself.
Therefore it lives without a reason so that it lives for itself.

— MEISTER ECKHART

The individual is not just striving for survival
but is reaching for some kind of "beyond."

— OTTO RANK

I n addition to Carl Jung as a primary representative of depth psychology interacting with Meister Eckhart, I also wish to consider Otto Rank. Unfortunately, Rank is only today finally receiving some credit for his important influence on the entire "humanistic school" of psychology, which includes notables such as Abraham Maslow, Rollo May, and Carl Rogers.

I discovered Rank, who died young in 1939, when (Pulitzer Prize–winning author Ernest Becker, who wrote *Denial of Death*, said that Rank's *Art and Artist* was the most important book he had read in his entire life.) Since then, I have studied Rank and taught courses on him for over thirty years, and I have been moved time and time again by his depth, his insight, his humanity, and his courage — in short, by his spirituality.

Rank's work carries with it a deep social consciousness. In his last and brave book, *Beyond Psychology*, published posthumously, he begins with a chapter "Psychology and Social Change," which includes observations on the accomplishments of Karl Marx. In the chapter "Feminine Psychology and Masculine Ideology," he offers a deep analysis of women's psychology, demonstrating a feminist awareness way back in 1939.

In *Psychology and the Soul*, published in 1930, Rank declares himself thus: "I believe that we have entered a new phase of spiritual development, one that affects both physics and psychology." How telling that Rank, in proposing that our "spiritual development" is the next evolutionary step for our species, sees spirituality as providing the larger context for physics and psychology, which will each be changed by it — and not the other way around. There is no reductionism of spirituality; we are not bowing at the feet of the god of psychology. Spiritual development is key.

Freud, who was Rank's mentor, ridiculed mysticism, but Rank respected mysticism and included it in any view of a whole and healed personality. Now let us consider several areas in which Rank emerges as a bona fide mystic in Meister Eckhart's tradition.

Honoring the Irrational

Rank respects both the limits of language and the apophatic tradition. In fact, he praises religion because "it admits *the Unknown*, indeed recognizes it as the chief factor instead of pretending an omniscience that we do not possess." Of course, Rank is talking about a religion that is in touch with the apophatic, not one that has all the answers in its dogmatic certitude.

In attempting to name the mystical, Rank often employs the term "irrational." By this, he means much more than merely "illogical" or "nonsensical," or the opposite of the rational. Rank is standing up to and calling our attention to the *excessive rationality* of the modern era and its science of mechanism and reductionism, of Freud, of Newtonian causality — indeed, of patriarchy itself.

An analogy would be between the rational left-brain intellect and the irrational right-brain intuitions and emotions, or between thoughts and sensations, reason and instinct. What would Rank categorize as irrational? How about the following: dreams, music, dance, art, ritual, sex, love-making, babies, laughter, play, massage, drumming, singing, the smell of newly cut grass, the tastes of spicy foods, silence, grief, color, creativity, peace, clowning, nature, wilderness, prayer, fear, animals, angels or spirits, children, beauty, paradox, myth, stories, games, campfires, chant, darkness, tenderness, forgiveness, meditation, God, birds, trees, plants, flowers, and food. And, Rank adds, "legitimate foolishness," the folly that accompanies wisdom. Holy folly.

What would life be without these? Where would we derive our reasons for living, our zest for carrying on? The irrational includes the "dynamic forces governing life and human behavior." In our culture, these forces are often still stigmatized as "irrational."

By this definition, animals are irrational and the winds and the sea and the stars and the planets and the rocks. Yet they all speak to us. And they often speak of the Unknown and the mystery behind all things. All kinds of beings — beings that an anthropocentric civilization *chooses* to ignore — live their wonderful lives with little or no rationality. Furthermore, humans, too, live our lives far more irrationally than modern science and modern education would have us believe. Rank believes that values count — but values are not born of rationality. Nothing deep is, in Rank's view. Like Einstein, Rank believes values are born of the "irrational," or of feeling and intuition.

What is at the heart of the irrational? Rank declares that "the epitome of the irrational is the marvel of creation itself." Here, Rank, in his own poetic way, names the unnameable, for he points to *where* we will find experience that is worthy of being named "spiritual." It is in nature.

Wonder is irrational, not rational. This Jewish spiritual consciousness is echoed in Rabbi Heschel (see chapter one), who speaks of "radical amazement" and reminds us that "awe is the beginning of wisdom." The rational gives us knowledge, but wonder gives us wisdom. Rank sought wisdom; he had seen enough of knowledge (and the rationalizations of body counts and "bottom lines"). Whole civilizations, such as the Roman Empire, have fallen because they chased after the rational at the expense of the irrational, Rank argued. These were societies that pursued a patriarchal agenda (for the rational is part of the masculine) at the expense of the matriarchal (for intuitions and feelings are part of the feminine, of the "more than rational").

For Rank, ideology represents the shadow side to irrationality; a wolf in sheep's clothing, ideology cloaks itself in the scientific, the objective, and the rational. But scratch the surface, and you find that what often drives ideology is unconscious fear, dread, guilt, and the compulsion to control. This demonstrates the power of the irrational: repress it, forget it, deny it, and it will come up in other forms to bite us.

"Vital human values" — ethics itself — derive from the irrational, from our experience of what matters, of what is truly vast and vulnerable and worthy of our attention and protection. In other words, what is truly *marvelous*. The irrational is that which "does not fit into our scheme of things" — it takes us beyond our personal, private, tribal, anthropocentric agendas into a vaster world, a cosmic place.

Rank observes that life would not be life without the irrational. "Rationalistic psychology was only an outgrowth of the mentality of our age which is, or rather, was up to recently, so highly rationalized that the irrational had only the neurotic form of expression." Repress the healthy irrational and neurosis will sting you — and sting all of culture. What is the cure to excessive rationality? "To attempt to cure this result of rationalism by more rationality is just as contradictory as a war to end wars, or an effort to strengthen a weakening democracy by more democracy."

The cure is to step out of excessive rationality and make room for the power of life itself. Rank says, "The only remedy is an acceptance of the fundamental irrationality of the human being and life in general, an acceptance which means not merely a recognition or even admittance of our basic 'primitivity,' in the sophisticated vein of our typical intellects, but a real allowance of its dynamic functioning in human behavior, which would not be lifelike without it." What is lifelike *is* irrational, and we ought to be paying attention to this first and foremost. This may mean getting off our intellectual high horses. When Eckhart says that "God is life," and we are to live life "in order to live," he is also championing putting the irrational first.

Rank doesn't propose that the irrational replace the rational, but they need to be balanced. "When such a constructive and dynamic expression of the irrational together with the rational life is not permitted, it breaks through in violent distortions which manifest themselves individually as neurosis and culturally as various forms of revolutionary movements which succeed *because* they are irrational and not in spite of it." Notice that Rank does not abandon the rational — he describes the rational in a "constructive and dynamic" relationship with the irrational. Without this, without an appreciation of the irrational, our lives and our culture run into peril. Neurosis arises, as does revolutionary ideology, which take us over even as they undermine us — *anything to bring alive the irrational*. Rank believes that Karl Marx succeeded because he offered *hope* to the poor. Hope is irrational. It keeps people in dire straits alive.

We need, says Rank, a whole new civilization — one that includes the irrational — because "human nature is at bottom irrational." While Eckhart speaks of finding the *ground* of our souls, Rank says the truth is at the "bottom" of our beings. Because society is rational (or pretends to be), we suffer from its "rational ideology," which is in fact born of an "inhibited negation of life." Instead, why not a community celebration of life? This celebration of life, this optimism, begins with awe and wonder, with marveling at creation itself.

Rank is a creation-centered mystic of the highest order. The via positiva — a rediscovery of the awe and wonder, the delight and joy, of existence itself — is the basic cure for self and society's tiredness and pessimism. A new falling in love with life is the medicine prescribed by Rank and other creation-centered mystics. Consider, for example, Thomas Aquinas: "Joy is the human's noblest act" and "God is supremely joyful and therefore supremely conscious."

The Beyond

Rank says: "The individual is not just striving for survival but is reaching for some kind of 'beyond.'" Beyond is something we reach for that is not here yet. One might say it is "eschatological," or in the future. It is what beckons us, reaches out to us. The word "beyond" implies *being yonder*, being at a frontier, at an edge, and then stretching or growing into it. Eckhart says: "God is delighted to watch our souls enlarge." By enlarging, our souls cross a "beyond"; we travel a distance, go over a horizon, start an adventure. We go "beyond" ourselves when there is something great to strive for, something great to welcome us in or welcome us home. It can be a homecoming, a return to our origins. The archetype of the "kingdom of God" that was so dear to both Jesus and Eckhart is an invitation to make the beyond present. To make the not-yet happen now.

In *Art and Artist* Rank insists that the passion of the ancients for developing our *relationships* to the macrocosm, so fully experienced by way of ritual, can be our passion today. Humanity's will, its power to choose to create, is called forth by struggle and survival issues. Our species, which is so deeply troubled by its own mortality, seeks still to reach "for some kind of beyond." It is, in Rank's view, that very reaching that characterizes us as a species. Call it a desire for immortality, or perhaps a wish to overcome the fear of death. In our children, our monuments, our creativity, our art, this drives us, or beckons us, to reach some kind of beyond. We cannot escape it.

Rank speaks of the need to move *beyond psychology*. How is this done? "Man is born beyond the psychological era only through vital experience of his own — in religious terms, through revelation, conversions, or rebirth." This sounds strikingly like Eckhart's effort to return religion to experience, the experience of the revelations of God in nature and in breakthroughs. Vital experiences take us beyond, wake us up, feed us with revelation and rebirth. Vital experiences include the experiences of ecstasy and union, joy and beauty, that no one can take from us. They are, as Dr. Elisabeth Kübler-Ross famously reported, those moments people remember on their death beds when they die peacefully. They are grace. Grace breaks through. These are mystical moments. Mysticism is our breakthrough experiences of union, of ecstasy, sometimes hot or orange ecstasies, and sometimes cool or green/blue ecstasies. They are what nourish the soul, for soul is, says Rank, our "power of rebirth." They make us young again, new again. Eckhart says the first gift of the Spirit is *newness*.

Rank believes that we "negotiate with the problem of the Beyond" in at least two deep instances: art and love. Our experiences of union overcome separateness. As Jungian scholar Robert Kramer puts it, "in the jointly created — and endlessly re-created — 'moment' of empathy between artist and enjoyer, lover and beloved, I and Thou, client and therapist, separateness is dissolved only to be rediscovered, enriched, and renewed by the dissolution of the individual into the void. 'Love abolishes egoism,' said Rank, 'it merges the self in the other only to find it again enriched in one's own ego.'" Beauty does this to us, and the experience of truth and art do the same. These "beyond experiences" dissolve our individuality, not just into "the void," Ranks says, but into "a greater whole."

Unio Mystica: Love and Cosmos

What is this "greater whole"? Rank described this mystical experience in 1924 in *The Trauma of Birth*, and the book got him expelled from Freud's circle. Rank says the mystic "cries out in beloved ecstasy: 'The I and the You have ceased to exist between us, I am not I, You are not You, also You are not I; I am at the same time I and You, You are at the same time You and I.'"

Rank saw separation from the cosmos as the greatest issue besetting our species. This cosmic separation is temporarily healed by our experiences of mystical union, the return to an original identity of union with the cosmic process that "has to be surrendered and continuously re-established in the course of self-development." When we surrender ourselves in art or in love, we undergo a "potential restoration of a union with the Cosmos, which once existed and was then lost. The individual psychological root of this sense of unity I discovered (at the time of writing *The Trauma of Birth*, 1924) in the prenatal condition which the individual in his yearning for immortality strives to restore. Already, in that earliest stage of individualization, the child is not only factually one with the mother but beyond that, one with the world, with a Cosmos floating in mystic vapors in which present, past, and future are dissolved." This passage echoes Eckhart when he talks about our pre-origins in the Godhead, where the unity is so great that no one will have missed us when we return.

Rank believed that premodern and ancient peoples saw physics (that is, nature, or the macrocosm) and psychology (human nature, or the microcosm) as one. All of life was a celebration of this union of psyche and cosmos. For Rank, people still seek "an identity with the cosmic process," and rediscovering cosmology provides the surest healing for our deepest woes, which stem from our separation from the cosmos. Ranks calls this the *unio mystica* (the mystical union) or "being one with the All" and "in tune with" the cosmos. The earliest humans knew all this intimately. "This identification is the echo of an original identity, not merely of child and mother, but of everything living — witness the reverence of the primitive for animals. In man, identification aims at re-establishing a *lost identity with the cosmic process*, which has to be surrendered and continuously re-established in the course of self-development." Rank instructs us to look to indigenous peoples — in this instance, to the wisdom they derive from animals and the "reverence" they hold for animals. But there is also the issue of a cosmic awareness (as discussed in chapter two). Says Rank: "Psychology is searching for a substitute for the cosmic unity which the man of Antiquity enjoyed in life and expressed in his religion, but which modern man has lost — a loss which accounts for the development of the neurotic type." Much of the neurosis of our time, Rank feels, is due to the loss of our connection to the cosmos. We will explore more of indigenous wisdom and awareness in chapter eleven.

For Rank, the world "bears the mark of infinity." Rank's world is not a rational world that humans make but the *whole world* that constitutes the very meaning of the Greek word *cosmos*. French philosopher Gaston Bachelard, in his moving book *The Poetics of Space*, describes what living in a cosmos is like and in his way expands on Rank's insight. The soul experiences *immensity* and *grandeur in the context of the cosmos*. We are at home with solitude, for great things well up in the soul because of solitude. "Immensity is within ourselves. It is attached to a sort of expansion of being that life curbs and caution arrests, but which starts up again when we are alone.... We are elsewhere; we are dreaming in a world that is immense." Our soul is a *vast* place full of hidden grandeur. In our experiences of unity or grace, "we discover that immensity in the intimate domain is intensity, an intensity of being, the intensity of a being evolving in a vast perspective of intimate immensity." Intensity, immensity, intimacy — in the human, they all occur at once. There follows a new level of self-appreciation and gratitude for being here. "Slowly, immensity becomes a primal value, a primal, intimate value. When the dreamer really experiences the word *immense*, he sees himself liberated from his cares and thoughts, even from his dreams. He is no longer shut up in his weight, the prisoner of his own being."

According to Eckhart, the feeling of ecstasy results in a taste of profound *voluptuousness*. Eckhart says, "God is voluptuous and delicious." Liberation and healing follow. I believe Rank saw all this. This is why, as does Eckhart, Rank champions so fiercely the reunion of microcosm and macrocosm.

The Now

For Rank, as for Eckhart, the experience of union with the cosmos includes the suspension of time — "present, past and future are dissolved." Rank says, "In the psychic realm, the only reality is the *Now*, the same Now that physicists find so incomprehensible, useless, and even unthinkable." Rank criticizes Freud for dwelling in the past, for "in so doing, he neglects the truly psychic element — the present, active self, and its corresponding Now." For Rank the creative process, the choice to give birth that is the basis of all ethics, happens *only in the now*. Creativity is not of the past; therefore our healing will come not from knowledge of the past but from current choices made in the present moment.

Rank practiced what he preached (or did he preach what he practiced?) when he applied his philosophy to his "dynamic therapy." This therapy shifted focus "from the past to the *present*, in which *all* emotional experience takes place." In the healing paradigm Rank created, the "eternal now" is reenacted. This emphasis on the now dictates a trust of what is really going on. This sounds very Zen-like. Meister Eckhart talks similarly when he says that God is creating everything of the past and everything of the present and everything of the future in the depths of your soul now. Eckhart adds: "God is in this power as in the eternal now. Were the spirit at every moment united with God in this power, people could never grow old.... There everything is present and new, everything which is there. And there you have in a present vision everything which ever happened or ever will happen.... Everything is present and in this ever-present vision I possess everything."

Another creation mystic, the historical Jesus, also speaks of the importance of the now when he says: "The kingdom and queendom of God *is* among you." It is from these experiences of the eternal now that our memories are stamped forever with what we truly cherish. Therefore it is from these glimpses of a restoration of a primal unity (Eckhart talks about our return to our "unborn self") that our truest values emerge. Without honoring these now experiences, we do not have values in common. We have no shared ethic.

Letting Go

Eckhart says, "We sink eternally from letting go to letting go into the One." Similarly, Rank talks about the constant separations that life asks of us:

> I have learned that the capacity to separate is one of life's major functions. Life in itself is a mere succession of separations, beginning with birth, going on through several weaning periods and the development of the individual personality, and finally culminating in death — which represents the final separation. At birth, the individual experiences the first shock of separation, which throughout his life he strives to overcome. In the process of adaptation, man persistently separates from his old self, or at least from those segments of his old self that are now outlived. Like a child who has outgrown a toy, he discards the old parts of himself of which he has no further use.

If we fail to learn to let go, the result is neurosis. The neurotic, Rank says, "is unable to accomplish this normal detachment process. He cannot live through and emancipate himself from the various fundamental separation stages in life. Owing to fear or guilt generated in the assertion of his own autonomy, he is unable to free himself, and instead remains suspended upon some primitive level of his evolution. He stays fixated, so to speak, upon a particular worn-out part of his past that he cannot sever himself, and his whole present behavior is directed and symbolized in terms of this *unaccomplished* separation." Thus the neurotic never tastes the now. He is too busy living in the wounds, imagined or real, of the past, and he is bracing himself for an imagined angst-ridden future. In either case his imagination is eating him alive. Rank attributes all neurosis to the "artiste manqué," our failed creativity and the misuse of our imagination. *The neurotic is not just the artiste manqué; he is also the mystique manqué.* That is, he is frustrated and unfulfilled in his most important effort, union with the Divine. Rank is not only a mystic himself — he calls us all to the *unio mystica* and to the "marvel of creation," to the irrational and the beyond, to the now and to deep and constant letting go. To fail to respond is to invite loss of soul.

Mysticism is our "yes" to life. Rank proposes that neurosis is by definition a refusal to say yes; thus it is a refusal to be a mystic. He writes, *"All neurotic reactions can be thus reduced to one Big No that men hurl at life."*

Creativity

Rank's entire psychology might be called an exegesis of our existence as "images of God the Creator."

This is how he distinguishes himself from other psychologists in his circle: "Neither Freud, nor Jung, nor Adler sufficiently considers the creative part of our personality: that which is *purely individual*, not biological, racial, or social. This I consider the most important part not only for understanding personality but also for therapy and for the individual's adaptation." Rank applied this sense of a creative work of art, living and alive, to his practice as a therapist. He says, "I don't explain my psychology to the patient but let him develop himself, express himself. . . . My aim is to enable the individual first to find himself and then to develop himself. . . . I think the neurotic type is a *failure of a creative type*." The proof of good results is also creativity. "If the therapist achieves a real therapeutic result, the patient will not only be able to adjust himself but sometimes he *adjusts the circumstance to himself* — which means creation. . . . His chief job is to create himself and then to go on and create externally."

Indeed, he attributes most neurosis to an internal *artiste manqué*. We misuse our creative imaginations or use them to beat ourselves up, instead of probing what Eckhart would call our divine nature, the image of God in us. Rank includes therapy itself in this concept of life's artistry. Each encounter with a client is itself a work of art; a patient-client relationship ought to be not "father knows best" but mutual, creative interaction. This methodology became very useful and prevalent when it was adapted by such persons as Rollo May, Abraham Maslow, and Carl Rogers.

Rank puts the via creativa to work. In doing so, I believe, he subtly raises the question about how all of our work ought in some way to be creative if it is to be human and satisfying. But creative toward healing — not just toward enhancing the ego. This hints at how we can redefine work, which was an issue that Eckhart was keen on. Eckhart says: "United with God and embraced by God, grace escapes the soul so that it now no longer accomplishes things with grace but divinely in God. Thus the soul is in a wonderful way enchanted and loses itself...[and] draws all its being from nowhere else but from and in the heart of God."

Honoring the Child

In a lecture at the University of Minnesota in 1938, a year before he died, Rank repeated his call for a feminine psychology and a children's psychology. "We do not possess a real psychology of the *woman* nor do we understand the *child* psychologically." What we have in psychology, he said, "is in essence *man*-made: that is to say, man has projected his own psychology into the woman and into the child." In this, Rank was ahead of his time. He pointed to what we might call adultism — the projection of adult attitudes into children. The implications for society's education are immense.

Rank suggests that adults ought to learn from the children (Jesus offered the same subversive advice). The child is more mystical, more at home with the irrational. "The child lives mentally and emotionally on an entirely different plane: his world is not a world of logic, causality, and rationalism. It is a world of magic, a world in which imagination and creative will reign — internal forces that cannot be explained in terms of scientific psychology." To honor the child's wisdom is to recover a respect for nature itself. "The child lives in a world of magic, where no logical or rational — that is, man-made — laws govern, but where the irrationality of nature herself, of which the

> "The soul now no longer accomplishes things with grace but divinely in God.
> In a wonderful way the soul is enchanted and loses itself [and] draws all its being from nowhere else but from and in the heart of God."

woman is still so much a part, predominates." Instead of projection of adult ideologies into children, Rank proposes a radical alternative: the way of love. This love isn't sentimental or anthropocentric but compassionate. We cannot remove a child's fear or insecurity, but we can "alleviate [them] by love, *a love that connects the tragically separated individual again with cosmic life*" (italics his). Of course, for this to happen, adults must themselves possess a relationship to the cosmos.

Rank continues: "Instead of psychologizing the child, we should respect his irrational nature and learn from him to accept it humbly in ourselves as well. We are not in the least more secure than he is, we are not less irrational at bottom. All we do is pretend to be; that's our tragedy, our false heroism."

How much room is there in education today for the "irrational," for art, music, theater, dance?

The Interference of the Prophet

Rabbi Heschel teaches that the first work of the prophet is to *interfere*. Rank did that, as did Eckhart. Rank combined his mysticism with his prophecy in the very title of his last work, *Beyond Psychology*. Rank proposed to take us beyond his own profession as it was then conceived and, by going beyond psychology, to interfere with what was accepted and transcend it.

As noted above, Rank names many areas and ways in which we must move "beyond." We must move not only "beyond psychology" but beyond rationality, patriarchy, and masculine ideology. In fact, he called Freud's psychology man's "last attempt to control nature, this time his own."

Rank calls us beyond anthropocentrism with his love of cosmos and his "reverence" for animals, and he calls us beyond the *hubris* of the modern era, or the arrogance toward indigenous peoples. He calls us beyond the superficial "art mania" of modern culture, beyond boredom, beyond adultism. Rank signed his own letters as "Huck," as in Huck Finn, whose childhood he believed was worth remembering. Rank calls us beyond neurosis and beyond the artiste manque.

Prophets, when they interfere, often pay a price, socially, culturally, politically, and personally. We saw this with Meister Eckhart, and Rank paid for his commitment to a bigger view of the world and of the psyche. When

Rank went "beyond Freud" — a term he used himself — beyond his mentor, friend, and father-figure, he was rejected by Freud and his followers. These included his wife, who divorced him and stayed in the Freudian camp. He was vilified by his former Freudian brothers, who told his publisher, Knopf, that if they published more of his books, they would not get any more of Freud's. His name was practically erased from the psychoanalytic history. He found it very hard to find work. As with many prophets, Rank was not honored in his own village. Indeed, he was vilified. But he did not respond in kind.

Rank was not a practicing Jew, but he was always faithful to the heart of Jewish spirituality. That is, in my opinion, the marriage of mysticism (our yes to life in spite of all its obstacles) and prophecy (our interference, or our no to injustice and falsity). The two impulses blend beautifully in Rank's work. Consider, for example, how he insists that the fear of death prevents us from living fully. Or when he names the neurotic impulse as using our creativity falsely, when we employ it to escape life and even to beat ourselves up with self-accusation. Rank dares to challenge the artist to live an artful life and even to renounce "objets d'art" to accomplish this. Rank concludes, along with Eckhart and biblical teaching, that we are all made in the image and likeness of the creator. We are all cocreators and must get on with our task.

Social workers in America, people who work daily with the poor and neglected of society, responded warmly and deeply to Rank's message. The Schools of Social Work in Philadelphia and in New York welcomed him to their cause. He married the personal and the social, as any sacred activist must, and as Meister Eckhart did.

Rank recognizes how he broke with Freud:

In *The Trauma of Birth* (1924), extending Freudian determinism from object to subject — from patient to therapist, psychoanalytically speaking — I jolted Freud's "physical" standpoint by analyzing the *relationship* [italics in original] between research subject and observer in the analytic situation itself. This relativistic orientation led in my more recent publications to a relativity-based psychology in which there is no longer a fixed position for the observer — that is, consciousness — but only the moment-to-moment dynamic relation of the twosome.

Rank extends this Einsteinian perspective to the very definition of psychology, which appears on the final page of *Psychology and the Soul*: "Psychology has less to do with facts than does physics.... [Psychology] is a science of relationships — a way of observing relationship and relativities." Rank proposes that we can't isolate the individual, who can yield certain "scientific results," but that *all living psychology is relationship psychology.* This applies whether the relationship is between two persons or between multiple persons in larger family or social groups. Thus, Rank names the very essence of a feminist philosophy and applies it to his profession: everything exists in *relationship*. Rank credits Einstein for this perspective: "I consider psychology to be a *science of relations* and interrelations, or a science of relativity. There is nothing fixed in the field of psychology, everything changes, it is constantly moving.... *There are no facts*. The facts are interpretations." Eckhart agrees, as when he says, "Relation is present in the essence of a thing."

Rank's daring act was to apply critical judgment and prophetic interference *to his own profession and his own livelihood*. Many are the intellectuals who critique every system but their own, every structure but the one that is feeding them. Rank dared to critique his very "family," just as Eckhart criticized his fellow preachers and churchgoers. In the process, Rank paid the price of a prophet, but without succumbing to regret or guilt.

Rank and the Four Paths of Creation Spirituality

Rank offers some refreshing and challenging insights about the four paths of Creation Spirituality: the via positiva, via negativa, via creativa, and via transformativa. Rank was clearly at home along the via positiva and his call to "marvel at creation itself." But we shouldn't underestimate the effort this takes in the midst of culture's many betrayals. In fact, in Rank's view, the "new hero" will be one committed to the via positiva: "The new hero, still unknown, is the one who can live and love in spite of our *mal du siècle*."

Rank speaks to the via negativa when he trusts the one suffering (the client in therapy) to undergo his or her pain and to be with it. He also countenances, as we have seen, the principle of continuous separation or letting go. He insists that difference need not be negatively conceived. The via negativa is, among other things, about accepting difference. The neurotic refuses to let go: "he is unable to accept this — *his difference* — positively. He is compelled by a deep-rooted self-denial to interpret his difference negatively, as inferiority." It is only by letting go of this self-denial that we move on. Consider Eckhart: "God is the denial of denial." The via negativa for Rank includes letting go of denial and self-hatred and fear of being different.

After the filling of the via positiva and the emptying of the via negativa, the via creativa leads to what Rank would call "rebirth" and what Eckhart would call "breakthrough." We connect to our primal will, which is our capacity for creativity. "The individual is both creator and creature," declares Rank, but for the neurotic, "the creative expression of will is a negative one, resting on the denial of the creator role." It is for this reason that he feels so much of neurosis is an issue of the *artiste manqué*. If we don't create, we are in trouble. Eckhart echoes this when he promises that in the birth "you will discover all blessing," but "neglect the birth and you neglect all blessing." This rebirth, in which the individual realizes he or she is "both creator and creature," is also Eckhart's rebirth when he says we become "mothers of God."

For Rank creativity is a choice, as all morality is. We face life and death every day and we are free to choose either on a daily basis. Rank cites Deuteronomy 30:19: "I put before you life and death — choose life," and then adds himself: "Do not be reluctant to give birth." Creativity became the linchpin to Rank's therapeutic method. It offered the patient "a much more *active* role than being merely an object upon whom the therapist operates, like a surgeon. Thus, my concept allows for operation of the patient's own will as the most constructive force in the therapeutic process." By "will," Rank means the choice to give birth. Rank first noted "the absence of a creative driving force in Freudian theory" in his 1905 book *The Artist*:

> I meant by artist the creative personality, and using Freud's psychology and terminology I tried to explain this creative type — but I found it was impossible without going beyond Freud. The chief difference already showing in my book was that, in contrast to Freud, I emphasized not the biological and external factors, but this *inner* self of the individual, something in the individual that is creative, that is impelling, that is not taken in from without but grows somehow within.

Compare this to Eckhart: "Whatever can be truly expressed in its proper meaning must emerge from inside a person and pass through the inner form. I cannot come from outside to inside of a person but must emerge from within."

Rank practices the via transformativa when his work interferes with sadness and degradation, with abuse and soul loss, through what he calls "empathy" and "identification" in the therapeutic process. He writes, "Correct understanding is one of empathy based on identification, whereas intellectual understanding is again projection to a certain degree, a *compelling of the other* to our own thought, our own interpretation." Surely empathy and identification are forms of compassion. Rank practiced this and spoke of it: "Love abolishes egoism, it merges the self in the other to find it again enriched in one's own ego." All psychologists — and indeed all workers — felt the original call to this noble vocation of compassion. The trick is to get it back. While Freud used the term *analysis,* which he derived from the language of chemistry, because he cared "more about research than helping," Rank preferred the term *psychotherapy.* He even called himself "a philosopher of helping," since *therapy* derives its meaning from "serving, care and healing." Rank felt that in Freud's more rigid scientific biological determinism, choice is often as lacking as creativity. According to Rankian scholars James Lieberman and Robert Kramer, Rank sought out "an inner principle, the individual's *own self-creative power....* We are no longer living on a purely biological principle. We are living on a moral principle." They define Rank's naming of our psychological rebirth as our "evolution from creature to creator."

Rank, like Eckhart, wants people to live life fully, which means creatively and compassionately. Lieberman and Kramer summarize Rank's work by saying that, for Rank, "the post-Freudian challenge is creating a person — life as an individual art work. By engaging the will, overcoming anxiety and guilt, one puts the loan of life to good use. The neurotic, a failed artist in Rank's view, tries by inhibiting life to deny death, which is repayment of the loan."

Eckhart also talks about life and all its accoutrements as being given to us "on loan." In this and all the other ways that the preceding two chapters have explored, in Meister Eckhart's teaching and that of Jung and Rank and the field of depth psychology and psychotherapy, we find how Eckhart's preaching about the "ground" of human existence remains very much in tune with, and even still challenging to, psychology in our time. Eckhart brings mystical and prophetic theology together with an in-depth psychology, rendering him a mystic-warrior for our time.

CHAPTER NINE

WISDOM OF HINDUISM

Meister Eckhart Meets Ananda Coomaraswamy and Father Bede Griffiths

Eckhart's Sermons *might well be termed an Upanisad of Europe....*
Eckhart presents an astonishingly close parallel to Indian modes of thought;
some whole passages and many single sentences read like
a direct translation from Sanskrit.

— ANANDA COOMARASWAMY

In Hinduism everything turns to experience.
It is the aim of the Upanishads to awaken this experience,
and it is the aim of every devout Hindu to have this experience of God.

— FATHER BEDE GRIFFITHS

The divine nature is repose....
Nothing resembles God in all creation so much as repose.

— MEISTER ECKHART

Meister Eckhart's work has deep resonances with the Hindu tradition. Since it is unlikely that Eckhart read any sacred Hindu texts, this resonance seems to demonstrate, as Jung believes, Eckhart's deep connection to the archetypal mystical experiences that define Eastern spirituality. It's also true that part of this interplay can be explained by the Celtic presence among the Middle Age Rhineland mystical movement. In my recent study on Hildegard of Bingen, who was raised in a Celtic monastery on the Rhine River, I note that it is generally believed that the Celts came from India, and many themes common to Celtic spirituality — including a cosmic awareness and an emphasis on the Divine Feminine and on "birthing" — are common to both traditions. Whatever the reasons for this deep resonance, it behooves us to explore it more deeply. The likenesses between Eckhart and Hinduism can assist us in understanding Eckhart's language and concepts and also help us, in this time of a global and interspiritual practice, to marry more consciously the wisdom of East and West.

Coomaraswamy on Eckhart

Ananda Coomaraswamy, a Hindu, first introduced me to Meister Eckhart when, in 1976, I read his classic book *The Transformation of Nature in Art*. That book, published in 1934, dedicates a chapter to Meister Eckhart and his view of art, which I found deeply striking. I had recently published an article, and yet here were quotes by Eckhart that matched entire sentences I had written. This experience of convergence spurred me to explore Eckhart further, as it surely must have done with Eastern spiritual leaders and thinkers. It is telling that Indian thinkers were taking Eckhart seriously before very many Westerners did. Remember that it was Japanese Buddhist philosopher D. T. Suzuki who, in 1959, first introduced Eckhart to the Catholic monk Thomas Merton (see chapter three).

Ananda K. Coomaraswamy (1877–1947) was born in Sri Lanka of an English mother and Sri Lankan father. When his father died, he was sent to England, where he studied geology, botany, and languages. When he refused to join the military to serve in World War I because the English still occupied India, he was "exiled" to the United States. There he served as curator of Indian art at the Boston Museum of Fine Arts for many years. Coomaraswamy has been described as a "unique fusion of art historian, philosopher, orientalist, linguist, and expositor" whose knowledge of Asian art was "unexcelled" and whose monographs on art "revolutionized entire fields of art." He knew thirty-six languages and was convinced that primitive, medieval European, Indian, and classical experiences of truth and art "were only slightly different dialects in a common universal language."

In the chapter on Meister Eckhart in *The Transformation of Nature in Art*, Coomaraswamy writes: "There was a time when Europe and Asia could and did actually understand each other very well. Asia has remained herself; but subsequent to the extroversion of the European consciousness and its preoccupation with surfaces, it has become more and more difficult for European minds to think in terms of unity, and therefore more difficult to understand the Asiatic point of view." So keenly does Coomaraswamy see the similarities between Eckhart and Indian thought (which applies to Thomas Aquinas as well) that he says: "Eckhart presents an astonishingly close parallel to Indian modes of thought; some whole passages and many single sentences read like a direct translation from Sanskrit." As I've said, Eckhart did not directly read Hinduism's rich scriptures, nor does Coomaraswamy think he did. He adds: "It is not of course suggested that any Indian elements whatever are actually present in Eckhart's writing, though there are some Oriental factors in the European tradition, derived from neo-Platonic and Arabic sources. But what is proved by the analogies is not the influence of one system of thought upon another, but the coherence of the metaphysical tradition in the world and at all times." Of course, this is exactly what Jung proposed, that there are universal archetypes held in common.

[*"Nothing resembles God in all creatures so much as repose."*]

Coomaraswamy found a deep understanding of art in medieval thinkers. Even if they rarely wrote about art directly, he says, "there is nevertheless a far-reaching theory of art to be found in their writings." Among these, no one was more universal, more profound, or more distinguished by vigorous clarity than Meister Eckhart. Offering Eckhart the highest praise, Coomaraswamy says that "Eckhart's *Sermons* might well be termed an Upanisad of Europe." Another writer has said that the Rhine should be considered the "Ganges of the West." Coomaraswamy recognizes in Eckhart a trait common to all true artists: "What is remarkable in him is...a great energy or will that allows him to resume and concentrate in one consistent demonstration the spiritual being of Europe at its highest tension. Toward his theme he is utterly devout, and his trained mental powers are the author of his style, but otherwise, in his own words spoken with reference to the painter of portraits, 'it is not himself that it reveals to us'; 'What I give out is in me…as the gift of God.'"

Coomaraswamy feels that Buddhists and Hindus can understand Eckhart more readily than can Protestants or Western philosophers. "The real analogy between Eckhart's modes of thought and those which have long been current in India should make it easy for the Vedantist or Mahayana Buddhist to understand him, which would require a much greater effort on the part of a Protestant Christian or modern philosopher." This is because modern Western consciousness has left behind the sense of the whole, the mystical experience, and intuition.

Among modern Western thinkers, Coomaraswamy says, "Eckhart's nearest and natural descendant is Blake; for example, Jesus and his Disciples were all Artists; Praise is the Practice of Art; Israel delivered from Egypt is Art delivered from Nature and Imitation; The Eternal Book of Man is the Imagination; the gods of Greece and Egypt were Mathematical Diagrams; Eternity is in love with the production of time; Man has no Body distinct from his Soul; If the doors of perception were cleansed, all things would appear to man as they are, infinite; in Eternity All is Vision."

Coomaraswamy recognizes that Eckhart considers our lives to be works of art, and Eckhart uses aesthetic ideas and terms to convey theology and the Divine. This is also true among indigenous peoples, who very often have no word for "art" but only for "beauty." Here, Coomaraswamy pulls relevant quotes from Eckhart:

> Eckhart's whole conception of human life in operation and attainment is aesthetic: it runs through all his thought that man is an artist in the analog of the "exalted workman," and his idea of "sovran good" and "immutable delight" is that of a perfected art. Art is religion, religion art, not related, but the same. No one can study theology without perceiving this; for example, the Trinity is an "arrangement" of God, "articulate speech," "determined by formal notions," "symmetry with supreme lucidity." Eckhart is writing, not a treatise on the arts as such,

though he is evidently quite familiar with them, but sermons on the art of knowing God. Ignorance is "lack of knowledge...brutish."

In a remarkable passage that in many ways echoes Eckhart's own style of rushing images and running thoughts that are ecstatic in their connections, Coomaraswamy ends his substantive essay with the following summation that draws from over fourteen of Eckhart's sermons. One gets a taste of Coomaraswamy's enthusiasm for Eckhart, the Upanishadic writer of the West, as he recounts this litany of Eckhart's descriptions of the aesthetic experience and creativity, which include

> recollection, contemplation, illumination (*avabhasa*), the culminating point of vision, rapture, rest. In so far as it is accessible to man as a rumor or foretaste, passing like a flash of lightning, it is the vision of the world-picture as God sees it loving all creatures alike, not as of use, but as the image of himself in himself, each in its divine nature and in unity, as a conscious eye situated in a mirror, might see all things in all their dimensions apart from time and space as the single object of its vision, not turning from one thing to another but seeing without light in a timeless image-bearing light, where "over all sensible things hangs the motionless haze of unity." That is a seeing of things in their perfection, ever verdant, unaged and unaging: "To have all that has being and lustily to be desired and brings delight; to have it all at once and whole in the undivided soul and that in God, revealed in its perfection, in its flower, where it first burgeons forth in the ground of its existence... that is happiness," "a peculiar wonder," "neither in intellect nor will,... as happiness and not as intellection," not dialectically but as if one had the knowledge and the power to gather up all time in one eternal now, as God enjoys himself.

Father Bede Griffiths on Deep Ecumenism

Father Bede Griffiths (1906–1993) is an especially reliable bridge builder between Hinduism and Christian mysticism because, though educated at Oxford and later in the Benedictine monastic tradition, he lived in India for over fifty years and drank deeply from the wisdom of that place. He brought both left brain and right brain to his explorations of Hinduism and his own

Christian spiritual roots, such as in his books *The Marriage of East and West*, *Return to the Center*, *Christ in India*, *The Golden String*, *River of Compassion*, and *The Cosmic Revelation*. He also had a deep knowledge of the Cosmic Christ tradition of the West and of Creation Spirituality. Thanks to Father Bede, we do not have to start from scratch or reinvent the wheel, for he already illuminates Eckhart's relationship to the wisdom of Hinduism.

To begin, Bede opts for interspirituality as an experience in "sharing one another's riches" — but he warns that this sharing must take place primarily at the level of *experience*. Indeed, we must share what lies "in the cave of our hearts" for "if one starts with doctrines the arguments are endless.... But when one comes to the level of interior experience that is where the meeting takes place.... It is in this cave of the heart that the meeting has to take place. That is the challenge." After all, he points out, this is where Hinduism begins. "In Hinduism everything turns to experience. It is the aim of the Upanishads to awaken this experience, and it is the aim of every devout Hindu to have this experience of God." Bede emphasizes that, while we are looking for like-nesses between Eckhart's Christian mysticism and Hinduism, each has its own "uniqueness." But Father Bede is convinced that "they are complementary" and that they need "to meet and to share."

To put experience first, Bede emphasizes that we must let go of some concepts and names, some dogma and doctrines. Early Christianity couched itself in highly sophisticated Greek wording, which still dominates Christian dogma — such categories as "person" and "nature," for example, which "translate the mystery of Christ into rational terms." Rather, Bede says, "if we would know the mystery, we must share in the experience of Jesus. We must know ourselves as sons of God, eternally coming forth from the Father as words of God expressing his mind. We have to know ourselves as God, God by participation in the divinity of Christ, as we participate in his humanity." Can we not hear Eckhart's language and imagery at work in this?

Bede observes:

> Each religion has its own particular insight and its own particular limitations. We have to learn to detect the insight and to recognize the limitations. The limitations come from time and place and circumstance, from economic, social and political conditions; the insight comes from the eternal Wisdom reflected in them. The eternal Truth has to be

expressed in the forms of space and time, under social and historical conditions, yet these very forms will always tend to betray it.

As an example, Father Bede compares the Law of Moses and St. Paul's attitude toward the law. The law was indeed "a divine revelation" uniting the people "with the eternal Ground of being. But the historical conditions, social and political and religious, of Israel were continually changing, like those of every other people." He draws a parallel with the church today. While Jesus intended the church as "the nucleus of a people, leading them into all truth," yet "in the course of time this Church inevitably developed according to the historical conditions in which it was placed. It left its Jewish matrix and grew up in the Graeco-Roman world, developing its theology through contact with Greek philosophy, its organization according to the patterns of the Roman Empire, and its ritual accord to the customs of the time." But over time it "lost its capacity for creative growth. This is the challenge to the Church today. The structure of doctrine and ritual and organization which it has inherited are no longer adequate to express the divine Mystery."

Bede challenges Christianity to get over much of its Hellenistic and Roman accretions, so that it can become less exclusively Western and more universal. He also critiques the sociological forms that the institutional church has taken on through history:

> The fact that Rome became the center of Christendom is an accident of history and the Bishop of Rome only acquired his present position after many centuries.... There is no reason to believe that the present structure of the papacy is permanent, or that the Church may not acquire a new structure in the context of future history. In the same way, episcopacy as a system of government was only gradually established and there is no reason to hold that the present structure...should always remain. All church structures are subject to the law of historical growth.

Bede urges a demythologizing and a remythologizing. "We have to go beyond all these historical structures and recover the original Myth of Christianity, the living truth which was revealed in the New Testament. But this cannot be done by the Western mind alone." Thus, the deep importance of interfaith sharing. "We have to open ourselves to the revelation of the divine mystery, which took place in Asia, in Hinduism and Buddhism, in

Taoism, Confucianism and Shintoism," as well as among indigenous peoples everywhere.

Bede also challenges the East to undergo its demythologizing as well:

It would seem that Hinduism, like every other religion, will have to undergo a process of "demythologization." All that is fanciful and no longer meaningful will have to be removed and the ancient symbols interpreted in the light of modern man's experience of the world. But this cannot be the work of "reason," of learning and scholarship; it has to grow out of a mystical experience, in which the primordial meaning of the ancient symbols is recovered and their relevance to the world today is discerned. It is this process... which each religion has to undergo.

Bede warns that "it is not sufficient to return to the Bible to discover the original source of Christianity. The biblical revelation has to be seen in the context of history as a stage in the manifestation of the Word of God, of the eternal Wisdom, which has been present to the world from the beginning. This same process of critical evaluation needs to take place in each religion. No religion can now remain in isolation. The revelation of the Vedas, of the Buddhist Sutras and of the Koran have to be evaluated in the light of the biblical revelation and of one another." While each needs to be respected as unique, nevertheless each is also limited by historical conditions. The "essential Truth," which is ultimately One, needs to be discovered. "But this essential Truth cannot be put into words. It is not to be discovered by any process of dialectic. It is known in the silence, in the stillness of all the faculties, in the depth of the soul, beyond word and thought." It will come in different languages and expressions. "In Hindu terms it is the knowledge of the self, the divine Saccidananda. In Buddhist terms it is in the experience of Nirvana. In Muslim terms it is *fana* and *baqa* — the passing away and the life in God. For the Jews it is the knowledge of Yahweh, for a Christian it is the knowledge of 'the love of Christ which surpasses knowledge.'"

Brahman and the Apophatic Divinity

While recommending that different religions meet in the cave of our hearts, Father Bede also talks about "the 'house of the womb,' the source of life, or the *mulasthanam*, the inner sanctuary which is always dark. The meaning of this is that God, the ultimate mystery, dwells in the darkness, beyond the light of this world. In the little temple in our ashram we follow the same pattern: the inner sanctuary is always kept in darkness with only an oil lamp burning before the tabernacle." When I hear about caves and houses of the womb, I think of sweat lodges. There I have often found a shared ultimate truth and shared presence of the Holy.

To talk about "the house of the womb" is to invoke a sense of the Apophatic Deity and an association with Mother Earth. Thus, early in one's encounter with Hinduism, the apophatic side of God asserts itself. Just as one cannot understand Eckhart without acknowledging the dark and unknown side of God, so too with Hinduism — where Brahmin is the term one uses for the Godhead, which is, in fact, without a name. Bede says, "It is a mystery which cannot be named.... Brahman cannot properly be named. It is without name or form." Bede elaborates: "There is nothing higher than this, than if one says, 'not this, not this.' This is negative theology. We cannot name Brahman. It is 'not this, not this.' Whatever word we use, whatever image, whatever concept, we have always to go beyond.... One cannot stop with any name of God.... We are all seeking that inexpressible mystery beyond, and that is Brahman, which is *neti, neti*, 'not this, not this.'" For readers of this book, the similarity of this description with Eckhart hardly needs pointing out.

Bede recognizes in Brahman the mysterious Godhead that Eckhart talks about along with the nothingness he offers as a name for God. Father Bede writes, "The Father is *nirguna* Brahman, the naked Godhead, the abyss of Being, the divine darkness, without form and void, the silence where no word is spoken, where no thought comes, the absolute nothingness from which everything comes, the non-being from which all being comes, the One without a second, which is utterly empty yet immeasurably full, wayless and fathomless, beyond the reach of thought. He cannot be named, cannot be expressed, cannot be conceived." Bede explains that "the absolute plenitude of Being [is] so far beyond thought that it appears to us as a darkness, a void, an abyss of nothingness." Eckhart's words exactly. This is Eckhart's "unmanifest" Divinity.

Bede states that "the essential truth of Hinduism is the doctrine of the

Brahman. The Brahman is the Mystery of Being, the ultimate Truth, the one Reality. Yet it also can only be described by negatives.... It is unseen, unrelated, inconceivable, uninferable, unimaginable, indescribable." Yet it can be experienced "in the depth of the soul as the very ground of its being. It is the Atman, the Self, the real being of man as of the universe. 'I am Brahman,' 'Thou are that,' 'All this [world] is Brahman.' These are the *mahavakyas*, the 'great sayings,' of the Upanishads, in which the Mystery of being is revealed."

How similar these great sayings are to Meister Eckhart — who says we too learn, in the experience of "breakthrough," that "God and I are one," that "every creature is a word of God and a book about God," that "God's ground and my ground are one ground," and that the Godhead "has no name and will never be given a name."

The Sacred Cosmos and the Cosmic Christ

In the West, science searches for the substance of reality. Bede says, "We reduce everything to atoms, then we come to electrons and protons — we are always trying to find what is behind it all. What is it all woven in? At last one comes to something which cannot be named, cannot be seen — the hidden mystery. That is Brahman, on which everything is woven. The world of the gods, the world of the sky and of the earth are all woven on Brahman. He is the One pervading all." For this reason there exists a "sacramentality" to the entire universe. "The whole creation is pervaded by God.... The Hebrew begins always with the transcendence of God.... For the Hindu it is the exact opposite. God is immanent, immanent in every created thing — in the earth, in the water, in the fire, in the air, in the plants, in the animals, in people."

One can recognize here a Cosmic Christ theology, what Eckhart calls the Logos, or Word of God, operating in all beings. In answering the question "Where is God?" Bede says, "all the Hindus pointed to their breasts: 'God is in the heart.' God is immanent. Present within creation and within the human. The Upanishads say: 'To that God who is in the plants, to the God who is in the trees, to the God who is in the earth, to that God who is in everything, adoration to Him, adoration to Him.'" Father Bede agrees with Eckhart that this is panentheism: God in all things and all things in God. He says, "God's manifestation in the world of creation...can be called panentheism. God is in everything.... First of all God is in the whole creation by His power, because He sustains everything by His power...Shakti, the 'Power of God.'...He is in everything by His Presence. God is present in everything."

Thus, in the Upanishads, Bede finds not only the unnameable Apophatic Divinity but the many-named Cataphatic Divinity. Brahman, Bede says, "is the source of all creation, of all the diversities of nature. It pervades all things 'from Brahman (the creator) to a blade of grass.' The whole world, the earth, the water, the air, the sun, the moon, the stars, the gods (the cosmic powers) and their creator, are all 'woven' on this Brahman. He is the 'honey,' the subtle essence of everything. In a sense he is every thing. 'All this (world) is Brahman.' And yet he is nothing: he is 'not this, not this' (*neti, neti*). There is nothing higher than if one says, 'he is not this.'" It is interesting that Eckhart also talks about the "honey-sweetness of things" revealing the Divinity.

Bede writes about the rich tradition in Hinduism of Purusha, "the cosmic man, of whom it is said 'one fourth of him is here on earth, three quarters are above in heaven.'" Bede compares him to the "Son of Man" tradition of Israel, as well as to an "archetypal man" or "Universal Man." Says Bede: "This is one of the most profound symbols of the ancient world. It is based on the recognition that man embraces both heaven and earth. Though his body occupies only a little space on a small planet, his mind encompasses the universe." We need to return to this vision, "that the universe is a unity and man is a mirror of the universe." Thus, we are a microcosm of the macrocosm. "Purusha is the cosmic person, who contains the whole creation in himself and also transcends it. He is the spiritual principle, which unites body and soul, matter and conscious intelligence in the unity of a transcendent consciousness." The basic structure of the universe is mirrored in him. Is this not Paul calling Christ "the pattern that connects everything in heaven and everything on earth"? Is this not the Cosmic Christ who is so fundamental to Eckhart's teaching?

Father Bede recognizes a likeness between the image of the Dancing Shiva in Hinduism and that of the resurrected (and Cosmic) Christ in Christianity:

Shiva Nataraja, the Dancing Shiva...is one of the great figures of Indian mythology. He is represented with four arms dancing in a circle of fire, dancing at the heart of creation. It is a cosmic dance: it represents the power which permeates the whole universe. The idea is that God is dancing in the heart of creation and in every human heart. We must find the Lord who is dancing in our hearts; then we will see the Lord dancing in all of Shiva....The whole figure (Shiva) can be seen as a beautiful symbol of the Risen Christ. Christ is at the heart of the universe. St. Paul says, 'In and through and for Him all things consist. All things hold together in Him.' He sustains the whole universe. This holding of the universe is a kind of dance, the dance of the universe, and He is dancing in every human heart.

So both macrocosm (the whole universe) and microcosm (the human heart) are part of the dance of the Cosmic and risen Christ; the human heart expands to include the whole cosmos and the cosmos becomes personalized and joyful within the human heart. Outside becomes inside, inside becomes outside. Surely, Eckhart would be happy to join such a dance.

In my opinion, one of the most beautiful passages in Hinduism speaks to the experience of the Cosmic Man. The Upanishads say: "In the center of the castle of Brahman, our own body, there is a small shrine in the form of a lotus-flower, and within can be found a small space. We should find who dwells there, and we should want to know him. The little space within the heart is as great as this vast universe. The heavens and the earth are there, and the sun, and the moon, and the stars; fire and lightning and winds are there; and all that now is and all that is not: for the whole universe is in him and he dwells within our heart." Eckhart says something similar when he talks about the human soul as a "city" and a little stone that contains the whole universe. Also Julian of Norwich describes how God showed her "a little thing round as a ball about the size of a hazelnut" and she was told: "It is everything that is created," and "everything has being because of God's love."

Journeying into Darkness, the Via Negativa

In his book *The Marriage of East and West*, Father Bede cites what he calls "the heart of the teaching of the Upanishads." Bede says, "The wise man,

who by means of meditation on the self, recognizes the Ancient who is difficult to be seen, who has entered into the dark, who is seated in the cave, who
dwells in the abyss, as God, he indeed leaves both joy and sorrow behind."
Of this passage, Bede comments:

> This is the death we have to undergo, to go beyond the rational under-
> standing, beyond the imagination and the senses, into the primeval dark-
> ness, where God, the divine mystery itself, is hidden. It is a return to the
> womb,...to the original darkness from which we came. But now that
> darkness is filled with light, it is revealed as God. The senses, the imagi-
> nation and reason by itself cannot pierce through that darkness, but when
> we die to ourselves, to the limitation of our mind which casts its shadow
> on the light, then the darkness is revealed as light, the soul discovers itself
> in the radiance of a pure intuition; it attains to self knowledge.

How like Meister Eckhart this sounds. Eckhart says the darkness is overcome by the light, and he reminds us often of Jesus's teaching that we take up
our cross to follow him — and this following, Eckhart insists, is not that of a
falcon following a woman carrying tripe home from the butcher shop. It means
something deeper, something more generous, more deliberate, more chosen.

To fully enter into the sacred dance of the universe one undergoes a kind
of death; the via negativa is part of the deeper journey. In the Hindu tradition
there exists a sacrifice by fire, and in Christianity baptism itself is a kind of
sacrifice. Bede writes:

> If you want to reach your true Self, if you want to find God, you have
> to die. In the Christian tradition baptism is death. To be baptized is to
> participate in the death of Christ. The ego has to undergo this death....
> He has eventually to return and be reconciled with his past, with the
> tradition of his family and people. One enters a fire. The fire sacrifice
> signifies the offering of everything in the Cosmic fire, the fire of life.
> Every created thing has to be sacrificed, that is, offered to God, if it is
> to become a source of blessings.

The Kingdom of God

In chapter six, we discussed how the theme of the "Kingdom of God" was
central to both Jesus's and Eckhart's preaching and teaching. Father Bede

concurs, but he asks, "What is this kingdom of God?" Bede suggests that Hinduism and other religions teach it as well: "Let us say that it means the divine life among men. This is the essential message of all religion. The infinite, transcendent, holy Mystery, which is what is signified by 'God' or 'Heaven,' is present in the world, has its kingdom, its reign, its indwelling among men. Is not this the message of all scriptures? 'This Brahman, this Self, smaller than the small, greater than the great, is hidden in the heart of every creature' (Svetasvatara Upanishad, III.20)."

Father Bede insists that we do not have the language for such a mystery; the language must come from our meditation and heart. "These are only words which point to the Truth. We cannot properly say what 'God' is, what is this Brahman, what is this Truth, this noble Wisdom, what is the kingdom of heaven. We have to meditate on these words in the heart, until the Truth shines out and enlightens us, until we experience the presence of God, the kingdom of heaven, within."

What we do know, however, is that the Kingdom of God is not the same as the institution of the church. He says, "All external religion, with its rites and dogmas and organization exists for no other reason but to lead men to the knowledge — which is also the experience — of this inner mystery. The Church exists for the sake of the kingdom of God. This kingdom is universal, it is the presence of God among men. It has existed from the beginning, in all times and in all places. Every religion bears witness to it." Furthermore, the essence of the revelation is that "the mystery of being reveals itself as a mystery of love." The church "has no other purpose than to communicate this love, to create a community of love, to unite all men in the eternal Ground of being, which is present in the heart of every man." It is by this criterion that the church is to be judged. When its institutions obstruct this message, Bede says, "it has ceased to fulfill the purpose for which it was instituted." Simply, "it has continually to renew itself" and "find new ways of expressing its doctrines to make it meaningful, new forms of ritual which will embody the inner experience of the Spirit." This reality presses itself upon all religions in our day. "Every religion today is in the process of renewal. It has to discover again its original message, to define it in the light of the present day, to manifest its power to transform men's lives."

The Role of Intuition

Father Bede learned from living in India for over half a century that one of the biggest lessons the West has to absorb from the East is to get over its idolatry of rationalism and to give proper due to our powers of intuition. Jung made a similar point, as did Albert Einstein when he talked about resisting the "god of the intellect" in favor of "intuition and feeling." The intellect gives us methods, Einstein said, but not values. Bede also connects intuition to a feminine awareness he learned in India but felt was lacking in the West. He writes: "The Western world — and with it the rest of the world which has succumbed to its influence — has to rediscover the power of the feminine, intuitive mind, which has largely shaped the cultures of Asia and Africa and of tribal people everywhere. This is a problem not only of the world as a whole, but also of religion." He felt "all the Christian churches, Eastern and Western, have to let go of their 'dominantly masculine character' in order to recover their balance and evolve an authentic form of religion."

How does Bede understand intuition and our way to recovering it? He says: "Intuition is a knowledge which derives not from observation and experiment or from concepts and reason but from the mind's reflection on itself." It is the mind's "power of self-reflection" that makes it so unique. "The human mind is so structured that it is always present to itself.... I know not only what I know, but also myself as knowing." The self-awareness that accompanies our actions "is not conscious in the ordinary sense. It is often referred to as 'unconscious.'" While giving Jung credit for the concept of "the knowledge of the unconscious underlying all conscious knowledge," Bede finds this still "an unsatisfactory term." He is more at home with the term "subliminal," meaning "beneath the threshold (*limen*) of consciousness." "Intuition belongs not to the sunlit surface of the mind, but to the night and the darkness, to the moonlit world of dreams and images, before they emerge into rational consciousness."

In trying to understand intuition more fully, Bede invokes the medieval language of "active intellect" and "passive intellect." The former provides rational concepts and scientific theories, and the latter "receives the impressions of the experience of the body, the senses, the feelings, the imagination.

This is the source of intuition." It allows us to go "beneath the surface of [our] mind and explore its depths." This, Bede grants, is what psychoanalysis attempts to do in the West, but he laments that Western psychology "rarely goes beyond the level of the dream consciousness and that of repressed emotions, whereas in the East, in Hindu and Buddhist and Taoist yoga, *they have penetrated to the depths of the psyche and discovered its original ground."* He feels this is an important lesson that the East has to teach the West — discovering the original ground of the psyche.

Did Eckhart undertake such explorations? Is that why he and Buddhism, Hinduism, and Taoism find so much common insight? It would seem so, for Bede continues: "Intuition, then, is the knowledge of the passive intellect, the self-awareness, which accompanies all action and all conscious, deliberate reflection. It is passive: it comes from the world around me, from the sensation of my body, from my feelings and spontaneous reactions. That is why intuition cannot be produced. It has to be allowed to happen. But that is just what the rational mind cannot endure. It wants to control everything. It is not prepared to be silent, to be still, to allow things to happen."

> *"All creatures are words of God...they all want to speak God and God still remains unspoken."*

Here, of course, we come to Eckhart's teaching of letting go, letting be, and letting happen, which was precisely the teaching that gave Jung the "key" to the unconscious. Bede instructs us to tame that "activity of the mind which is grasping, achieving, dominating," in favor of an activity that is "receptive, attentive, open to others. This is what we have to learn."

Bede recognizes two aspects of the mind: "the intuitive which grasps the whole but does not distinguish the parts, and the rational which distinguishes the parts but cannot grasp the whole. Both these powers are necessary for the functioning of the human mind." He celebrates how ancient languages such as Sanskrit in the Vedas (as well as Aramaic, Jesus's language) "contain a multiplicity of meanings." He says, "The imagination, which is the faculty of primitive thought, expresses itself in symbols (literally, from the Greek, that which is 'thrown together'), which reflect this multiplicity of meanings in a single word. In other words, primitive thought is intuitive; it grasps the whole in all its parts." We need both the rational and the intuitive, for "intuition without reason is blind; it is deep and comprehensive but confused and obscure. Reason without intuition is empty and sterile; it constructs logical systems which have no basis in reality." Father Bede takes delight in the fact that "in the Vedas there is a marvelous meeting of the intuitive and the rational mind."

Repose

Bede invokes the Tao Te Ching: "'Attain to the utmost emptiness, hold firm the basis of Quietude. To return to the root is repose.' These are the principles which underlie the wisdom of the East, which the West has to discover…to find its balance."

Eckhart preached an entire sermon on "repose" that begins with his citing three times from the Book of Sirach (Sirach 24:11, 12, 15), which he calls "the book of wisdom." He says to consider these words "as if the eternal wisdom were conducting a dialogue with the soul." Eternal wisdom speaks first: "I have sought repose in all things." Then the soul responds: "He who created me has rested in my tent." Next the eternal wisdom says: "My repose is in the holy city."

Eckhart goes on to explain how the "divine nature is repose," the "origin of all creatures" is repose, and God "seeks his own repose" in all creatures. Indeed, "nothing resembles God in all creatures so much as repose." Eckhart pretty much eschews many religious practices, such as "vigils, fasting, prayer, and all forms of mortification," which God does not "heed or need." What God needs, Eckhart says, "is nothing more than for us to offer him a quiet heart. Then he accomplishes in the soul such secret and divine deeds that no creature can serve them or even add to them." Knowledge can take God "into the soul and leads the soul to God. But it cannot bring the soul into God." What then does? "After knowledge has conducted the soul to God, the highest power comes forward — this is love — and penetrates God and leads the soul with knowledge and with all its other powers into God, and is united with God." The soul then becomes "submerged in God and baptized into the divine nature. It receives there a divine life and takes on the divine order so that it is ordered according to God." Furthermore, all creatures have been allotted this taste of the divine repose. Repose is the goal of the Creator; of the Holy Trinity; of the soul; and of all creatures who seek it in "all their natural efforts and motions."

Bede teaches that Brahman, or the Mystery of Being, is known

> not by intellect, or by reason, or by learning; it is known in pure consciousness (*cit*), a pure intuition in which the knower, the thing known, and the act of knowing are one. There is here no duality, all differences have been transcended, there is only that one "without a second." And this is an experience of infinite bliss (*ananda*). All desires are here fulfilled, the soul has entered into its rest, it attains to peace — *shanti* — the peace that passes understanding. This is the supreme goal, the ultimate state, which the Bhagavad-Gita calls "the Nirvana of Brahman."

It would seem that Eckhart has experienced this Hindu teaching, and that by heeding and following Eckhart, we would find the balance that Father Bede instructs us all to recover.

The Living Word

Eckhart often talks about the "living word of God." He speaks of how "God is a Word but an unexpressed Word," how "God is a Word which speaks itself," how "God is spoken and unspoken," how "the Father speaks the Son from his entire power and he speaks him in all things," how "all creatures are words of God," and how "all creatures want to express God in all their works; let them all speak, coming as close as they can, they still cannot speak him. Whether they want to or not, whether it is pleasing or painful to them, they all want to speak God and he still remains unspoken." All this emphasis on the Creator as word would not be lost on the Hindu tradition.

Bede tells us that the word "Brahman" derives from the root *brh*, "which means to swell or to grow. This seems to have signified originally the rising of the word from the depths of the unconscious, the growth into consciousness." Sri Aurobindo describes it as the "voice of the rhythm which has created the world." This is not unlike Genesis 1, which says, "God said, 'Let there be light,' and there was light," and it echoes John 1: "In the beginning was the Word." Says Bede: "Brahman is the mysterious power in nature which comes into consciousness in the word." The Upanishads say: "In the beginning this was Brahman, one only."

A word is creative, language is creative, born of the unconscious. Indeed, all creative expression — whether poetry or dance, music or drama, film or painting — are also the Divine Word at work in the world, the uprising of the unconscious, the mark of the artist within our deep-down selves. Eckhart saw this. The Upanishads celebrate it as well. Coomaraswamy helps explain the relationship between the via negativa, the letting go, and the via creativa, giving birth, for Eckhart: "The arising of the image is not by an act of will whether human or divine, but of attention (*dharana*) *when the will is at rest....* The aesthetic process is threefold, the arising of the idea in germ, its taking shape before the mind's eye, and outward expression in work." Rest is required; as we have seen, "repose" is key to Eckhart's naming of the journey. Creativity is not so much a willful gesture as a surrender to what is deep within us, a sinking, a resting. From this rest, God is born.

This is part of what Otto Rank means when he calls us to pay more attention to the child, and why the child has so much to teach the adult. The child honors intuition. Reason follows rather than dominates. Scholar Norman O. Brown defines the artist as one who can recover childhood at will. The artist draws from the inner child, the intuitive self, and brings it to the table to be pondered and to render delight. Poetry, Bede asserts, preceded prose in human evolution. He writes, "All the evidence of history shows it. The further we go back in time the more we come not on prose but on poetry. The literature of India begins with the hymns of the Rig Veda, that of Greece with the poems of Homer. The Bible itself is as much poetry as prose, and its earliest strata are all poetic. The reasons for this are obvious. Poetry is the expression of the whole man. It expresses not merely his mind but his sensations, his feelings, his 'heart's affections.'" But modern consciousness has "broken" the link between mind and heart, intellect and sense, thought and feeling. The rational human has cut the connection where humans have so long dwelled, Bede says, "in the world of the imagination, that is the world of integral wholeness." Such a world was a world of myth. We need to return to those deep places where the world speaks through us once again. I think Eckhart helps take us there — by his language and images as well as his message.

Work and the Word of God

Then again, as Eckhart says, our lives themselves are also art; our actions
are also poetry. They too emerge from the deep unconscious informed as
it is by our passion for values. Thus the world of our work is holy ground.
Father Bede describes three ways of yoga, the way of action (*karma*), the
way of devotion (*bhakti*), and the way of knowledge (*jnana*). He comments:
"For most people the way to self-discovery, to union with God, is by action.
This was the great discovery of the Bhagavad-Gita. At first it was thought
that the way to union with God, the path of salvation, was to be found in the
practice of asceticism, in silence and solitude, in prolonged meditation. But
the Bhagavad-Gita declared that the householder doing the ordinary duties
of his life could attain salvation no less than the ascetic in the forest. Man
could be saved by work."

This was Eckhart's way also. After all, he was a very busy man. He was
an administrator, a counselor or spiritual director, and a manager of people
and properties, in addition to being a very public preacher and teacher and
always a studious researcher. He also took on the great powers of his day,
financial, political, and of course ecclesiastical. He understood the path of
action. He preached about the holiness of work, as in his startling sermon on
Martha and Mary (see chapter five), in which he praised Martha, who could
both listen to Jesus and do her work at the same time, over Mary, who is the
epitome of devout, pure contemplation.

In that sermon, Eckhart instructs people to learn to be "among things
and not in things,...among cares but not within cares." Martha's strength
was that she "possessed a mature, well-established virtue and an undisturbed
disposition that was unhindered by all things." Indeed, "Martha was so real
that her works did not hinder her." Work can be just as sacred as a retreat
in the desert because work "carries us just as close as possible to the highest
thing, except for the vision of God in his pure nature." Work and Word so
marry that our work is accomplished "divinely in God." We take our love of
God to our work. "Who 'honors' God? He or she who intends to honor God
in everything he or she does." Being a Dominican, Eckhart was committed
to this action-contemplation dialectic that in the thirteenth century deliberately confronted the monastic tradition that honored contemplation alone.

Eckhart was committed to preaching to people busy in the world of action, including Beguines and other laypeople.

Bede makes the same distinction as Eckhart regarding the correct way to walk the path of action: that it "be done with detachment. It is work which is done with attachment, that is, with selfish motives that binds the soul. We must not seek the 'fruit' of work. We have to make the offering of the work to God, then it is not we who act but God who acts in us." This, Bede tells us, is Hindu teaching. It also reflects Eckhart's insistence on our "working without a why or wherefore." What Eckhart teaches as letting go and letting be, Bede calls "detachment"; it also resonates with Bede's teaching of karma as sacred work. Eckhart's teaching that we become "co-workers with God," with the "rushing waters of the Holy Spirit" working through us, is also resonant with this Hindu teaching and practice. When pursued in this way, our works then derive, Eckhart says, "from the heart of God" and become "enchanting" work.

Coomaraswamy also talks about Eckhart's understanding of work and compares it to the teaching of the Upanishads:

> God "must do, willy-nilly," according to his nature, without a why. In man this becomes what has been called the gratuitousness of art: "man ought not to work for any why, not for God nor for his glory nor for anything at all that is outside him, but only for that which is his being, his very life within him" (cf. Brhadaranyaka Upanisad, IV, 5, 6); "have no ulterior purpose in thy work," "work as though no one existed, no one lived, no one had ever come upon the earth"; "all happiness to those who have listened to this sermon. Had there been no one here I must have preached it to the poor-box." "I should do my works in such a way that they entered not into my will....I should do them simply as the will of God," "Above all lay no claim to anything. Let go thyself, and let God act for thee."

Coomaraswamy offers an important warning about Eckhart's phrase "work for work's sake." In doing so he makes the connection between Eckhart and the Bhagavad Gita:

> "Working for work's sake" sounds to modern ears like art for art's sake. But "art" and "his ideal" have not here their modern sentimental

connotations, they represent nothing but the artist's understanding of his theme, the work to be done; working for "the real intention of the work's first cause" is not working for the sake of the workmanship, as the modern doctrine implies; "working for work's sake" means in freedom, without ulterior motive, easily.

Thus we see the deep links between Eckhart and the wisdom of ancient Hinduism, which were easily recognized by those, like Ananda Coomaraswamy and Father Bede Griffiths, who actually lived, loved, and studied those traditions. In Coomaraswamy's striking language, we can see Eckhart's "astonishingly close parallel to Indian modes of thought," in which "whole passages and many single sentences read like a direct translation from Sanskrit." In fact, these analogous conceptions — which allow Eastern thinkers to understand Eckhart readily while Western, modern Christians have some catching up to do — is precisely why one writes a book like this: to invite Eckhart to assist us in finding our mystical brains once again.

CHAPTER TEN

ECKHART AS SUFI

Meister Eckhart Meets Rumi, Hafiz, Ibn El-Arabi, and Avicenna

Ah, one spark flew
and burned the house of my heart.

— RUMI

In the spark of the soul there is hidden something like the original outbreak of all
goodness, something like a brilliant light which incessantly gleams, and something like
a burning fire which burns incessantly. This fire is nothing other than the Holy Spirit.

— MEISTER ECKHART

Love is the creed I hold: Wherever turn
His camels, Love is still my creed and faith.

— IBN EL-ARABI

I have made the journey into Nothing.
I have become that flame that needs
No fuel.

— HAFIZ

When *Passion for Creation*, my book of sermons by Meister Eckhart, appeared in 1980, the very first response I received was not from a Christian theologian or preacher but from a Sufi. His correspondence was long, and it surprised me, pleasantly so. At that time, like most in our culture, I was less aware of Sufism. Today, the West is much more familiar with it, thanks to the dissemination of Rumi's stunning poetry, to Hafiz's amazing work, and to the Dances of Universal Peace inspired by Samuel L. Lewis, which has moved (literally and spiritually) so many people around the world.

Here is the portion of Eckhart's sermon that so moved the Sufi. Eckhart says:

> Love is nothing other than God. God loves himself and his nature, his being, and his divinity. In the same love, however, in which God loves himself, he also loves all creatures, not as creatures but he loves the creatures as God. In the same love in which God loves himself, he loves all things. Now I shall say something I have never said before. God enjoys himself. In the same enjoyment in which God enjoys himself, he enjoys all creatures. With the same enjoyment with which God enjoys himself, he enjoys all creatures, not as creatures, but he enjoys the creatures as God. In the same enjoyment in which God enjoys himself, he enjoys all things.

This brief passage, out of a book of 580 pages, so inspired this Sufi that he immediately sat down, composed a ten-page "Sufi exegesis" working from his tradition, mailed it to me, and in his accompanying letter declared, "Eckhart is a Sufi."

What Is a Sufi?

What is a Sufi? Who are the Sufis? Sufis represent the mystical tradition of Islam, and for centuries they have practiced their faith, sometimes amid considerable opposition. As mystics, they seek to *taste* God and not just pronounce about God or think about God. Sufis want to do the deep *inner* work of the soul and not settle for the outer trappings of religion. They do not want to jettison religion so much as to explore the deeper and multiple meanings of doctrine and dogma, rites and rituals, life, death, and resurrection.

Idries Shah (1924–1996) was an eminent historian of Sufism, a Grand Sheikh of the Sufis, and eldest son of the Nawab of Sardana, near Delhi in India. In his book *The Sufis*, he asks: "Exactly how old is the word 'Sufism'?

There were Sufis at all times and in all countries, says the tradition. Sufis existed as such and under this name before Islam." Sufis themselves call it "a science, an art, a knowledge, a Way, a tribe — but they do not call it Sufism." Shah likes the term "the Path of the Sufi." In addition, "the Sufi is known as the Seeker, the Drunken man, the enlightened one, the good, the Friend, the Near One, the dervish, a *Fakir* (humble, poor in spirit), or *Kalandar*, knower (gnostic), wise, lover, esoterist." The Sufi tradition is not monastic — it does not propose leaving the world or taking vows of celibacy. Sufis like to consider themselves "a leaven (Sufism is yeast) within all human society." Sufism is "an adventure in living, a necessary adventure," according to the tradition.

Rumi (1207–1273) died when Eckhart was thirteen years old, and Rumi's spiritual genius, as expressed in his prodigious output of poetry, is without parallel. Thanks to people like Coleman Barks, Robert Bly, Andrew Harvey, and others, he has become the best-known Sufi in our time. Rumi offers this simple poem about Sufihood.

> Destroy your house, and with the treasure hidden in it
> You will be able to build thousands of houses.
> The treasure lies under it; there is no help for it;
> Hesitate not to pull it down; do not tarry!

In these four lines, Rumi distills the central imperative of Sufism, using language that echoes that of many thinkers in this book. The message to seek and find a treasure is also Jesus's message (and Eckhart's); for them, it is seeking the Kingdom of God. Yet the treasure is hidden below, under our house. It takes work to uncover, and it is in the ground. This recalls Eckhart's "ground," Mother Earth, the lower chakras, Jung's unconscious, and even Rank's "beyond." To "destroy" and "pull down" our house is the via negativa, the letting go and the rupture that lead to Eckhart's "breakthrough," to the via creativa and via transformativa. Eckhart says: "If you want the kernel, you must break the shell," and the kernel is the realization that "God and I are one." Is this not a treasure that could build "thousands," and infinite thousands, of houses?

What is this "house" that needs to be torn down? Idries Shah describes

Rumi's "house" this way: "Within mankind is a 'treasure,' and this can be found only by looking for it. The treasure is, as it were, inside a house (fixed thinking-patterns) which has to be broken down before it can be found.... Man sees only pieces of things because his mind is fixed in a pattern designed to see things piecemeal." It is our "fixed thinking-patterns" that need to be let go of, our idols, our frozen mind-sets, which include seeing the world only through anthropocentric, not cosmic, glasses. This sounds very close to Father Bede Griffiths's teaching as well.

The Sufi way puts experience first. Says Rumi: "He who tastes not, knows not." Wisdom comes from tasting, even from "sucking," as the Kabbalah speaks about it. As this book shows, direct experience of God is key to any religious or spiritual awakening. This was certainly Eckhart's consistent purpose — to wake people up to their capacity for the Divine, to the inner reality of their being a "son of God, a daughter of God." This direct experience is distinct from knowledge alone. Historically, Sufism has struggled with those theologians, scholars, and academics who live more in their left brains than their right brains, for whom "tasting" is less important than conceptualizing. Ghazali (1058–1111) lived in Central Asia and wrote a book called *Destruction of the Philosophers* in which he took on the powerful scholastics (also called "schoolmen") of his day. Ghazali says: "Apart from incapacity itself, other shortcomings prevent the reaching of inner truth. One such is knowledge acquired by external means." Knowledge is not wisdom; and knowledge by external means does not lead to the hidden treasure, the meaning of life.

The long, ongoing struggle between the Sufi (or Love) dimension of Islam and the scholastic theologians sheds light, I think, on the tensions in medieval Europe between the Franciscans (who opt for love first) and Dominicans (who argue that knowledge comes first, since you can only love what you know). This battle waged in Eckhart's time and in his consciousness. He brought the topic up often and sided with his Dominican lineage, prizing knowledge. However, in a sermon that I believe was delivered very near the end of his life, Eckhart comes to a surprising conclusion: He overthrows both God as love and God as knowledge in favor of... God as compassion! "I say that beyond these two, beyond knowledge and love, there is compassion. In the highest and purest acts that God works, God works compassion." As we saw in chapter five, this major and original breakthrough led Eckhart, at the end of this sermon, to put forth compassion as the very meaning of soul: "The soul is where God works compassion. Amen." He returns not to our knowledge of God but to our *practice* of God's essence, which is compassion.

Hiding the Mystical Heart: A Survival Mechanism

Throughout Islamic history, as happened to mystics in Christian history as well, Sufis were often attacked and even persecuted by religious officials and political powers and academicians who were subservient to them. Thus, the early poetic expressions of Sufism often embodied a political strategy; they were an indirect way of talking about experienced truth within a controlled society and religion dominated by conceptual thought, much as how, during the slavery days in America, Negro spirituals were often coded messages about liberation. But the poetry, full of analogy and metaphor, was also meant to thwart easy understanding, which might reduce hard-won Sufi wisdom into a few facile "truths."

Says Shah, "Writing often under threat of inquisitorial persecution, Sufis have prepared books reconciling their practices with orthodoxy and defending the use of fanciful imagery. In order to obscure the meanings of ritualistic factors, or for the necessary purpose of appearing mere compilers of Sufi compendiums, they have handed down manuscripts for which the Sufi essence is to be distilled only by those who have the necessary equipment." Robert Graves makes a similar point: "The poets were the chief disseminators of Sufi thought, earned the same reverence as did the *ollamhs*, or master poets, of early medieval Ireland, and used a similar secret language of metaphorical reference and verbal cipher.... This language was a protection both against the vulgarizing or institutionalizing of a habit of thought only proper to those that understand it, and against accusation of heresy or civil disobedience." Graves describes how Ibn El-Arabi was once called before an Islamic inquisition at Aleppo. Graves says that, in his defense, El-Arabi "pleaded that his poems were metaphorical, the basic message being God's perfection of man through divine love." This is the same message as is found in the Bible's "Song of Songs."

Indeed, we can see the same techniques in Eckhart's work — his playful-
ness with language, his humor, his oft-repeated phrase "Now pay attention,"
his paradoxical statements, his surprising and even shocking sayings ("I pray
God to rid me of God"). These were often spontaneous but they were also
a way to put inquisitor types off his trail, and they worked for a number of
decades during his preaching vocation. (I also followed a parallel strategy
when I named my early books after dreams and nursery rhymes. It gave me
breathing room from inquisitor types who tend to be quite underdeveloped
in areas of humor and childlikeness.) Eventually, of course, the dominant
powers caught up with Eckhart and sponsored two trials against him late in
his life. Thus, as we can see, diverting inquisitorial attacks through poetic
metaphor is another strategy he shares with Sufis.

Sufis like to say: "This is not a religion; it *is* religion," or "Sufism is
the essence of all religions," which provides "a belief in an inner teaching
beyond formalized religion." In other words, Sufism puts spirituality first
— getting to the heart of the matter, the lived experience of the Divine.
Eckhart does the same; he tried to get deeper than the "formalized" version
of Christianity. Sufism explicitly practices what I call Deep Ecumenism, honoring the essence of religious teaching and the lived experience of Divinity,
found in all religious traditions.

Idries Shah points out that Ibn El-Arabi (1164–1240), called "the greatest Master" or Sheikh, "confused the scholars" because he practiced Islam as
a "conformist in religion while remaining an esotericist in inner life." This
is not unlike the case with Father Bede Griffiths, who remained a Christian
Benedictine monk while seriously critiquing the institutional church, or
Eckhart, who stayed true to his Dominican vocation to the end. Shah says
that Ibn El-Arabi, "like all Sufis,... claimed that there was a coherent, continuous and perfectly acceptable progression between formal religion of
any kind and the inner understanding of that religion, leading to a personal
enlightenment. This doctrine, naturally, could not be accepted by theologians, whose importance depended upon more or less static facts, historical
material and the use of reasoning powers."

Not too much changed between El-Arabi's day and Eckhart's, nor in
my opinion has much changed between Eckhart's day and ours. Still today
we have academicians ignoring and mistranslating and belittling the mystics.

The same was true in Jesus's day. As we saw in chapter six, Jesus also developed art forms, stories, parables, and aphorisms to confound the legalistic and pharisaical minds of his day.

Robert Graves remarks that love and ecstasy are central to Sufi teaching, but that "whereas Christian mystics regard ecstasy as a union with God, and therefore the height of religious attainment, Sufis admit its value only if the devotee can afterward return to the world and live in a manner consonant with his experience." Regarding this distinction, Meister Eckhart is perhaps one exception who proves the point (along with other Christians as well, including those committed to liberation theology, like Dorothy Day and many others). As we have seen, Eckhart teaches the same Sufi ideal about merging action and contemplation. To some degree, the Sufi teaching may have been integrated into the Dominican ideal that Eckhart lived and espoused, that of "sharing the fruits of one's contemplation." St. Dominic, after all, was a Spaniard and very much exposed to both the scholastic dimension to Islam and Sufi devotional practice. This may have expressed itself in the story of his having invented the rosary and in the Dominican devotion to Mary and the Divine Feminine.

St. Francis and the Sufis

Idries Shah makes a very convincing argument that Sufism deeply influenced St. Francis and the Franciscans. Among Shah's proofs: Francis spoke Provençal, which was the language used by the troubadours, who were descendants of Saracenic musicians and poets (a pre-Islamic nomadic people). On a number of occasions when Francis was a child, Francis's businessman father traveled to Provençal areas and sometimes took Francis with him. Francis's own poetry, Shah writes, "so strongly resembles in places that of the love poet Rumi that one is tempted to look for any report which might connect Francis with the Sufi order of the Whirling Dervishes. Such a story exists in Franciscan lore — that Francis was walking through Tuscany with Brother Masseo one day and came to a fork in the road not knowing which way to go. Francisco commanded Brother Masseo to 'turn round and round as children do, until I tell you to stop.' After much twirling and dizziness the brother was told to stop and was aiming toward Siena. 'Then to Siena we must go,' said Francis."

Several times Francis tried to travel to Muslim areas, first to Syria, where the Whirling Dervish movement was very strong. But he only got partway, ran out of money, and had to return to Italy. Then, heading for Morocco, he traveled through the kingdom of Aragon in Spain, which at that time was "very much penetrated with Sufi ideas and schools." But Francis got ill and never arrived in Morocco. Then he set out for the Crusades, where the siege of Damietta was taking place. Francis went to see the sultan Mali el-Kamil, who was encamped across the Nile; he had a very favorable visit with the sultan, who invited him to return. What was going on with these efforts by Francis? Says Shah: They were "a troubadour looking for his roots" in the heart of Sufi activity. Francis did not convert any Muslims, but he did try to convince the Christians not to attack the enemy. Later, the Crusaders were repelled from the walls of Damietta amid great losses.

Francis's "Song of the Sun" was composed after this journey. It proved to be the first poem in vernacular Italian, and Shaw compares it to Rumi's many poems dedicated to the Sun. Shah also compares Francis's order to a "dervish organization." The "remembering" practices in both; the dress of the order with its hooded cloak and wide sleeves are those "of the dervishes of Morocco and Spain." Francis's refusal to become a priest, thus teaching and preaching as a layperson, was Sufi-like. It was a democratic impulse. Furthermore, Shah says, "like the Sufis and unlike the ordinary Christians, his followers were not to think first of their own salvation. This principle is stressed again and again among the Sufis, who consider regard for personal salvation to be an expression of vanity." Francis would begin his preaching almost always with a salutation that he said God revealed to him: "The peace of God be with you!" This is, Shah points out, "of course, an Arab salutation." Nevertheless, Shah laments that the Franciscan order (like the Dominicans) did eventually take on the role of inquisitors — not exactly a feather in the cap or consistent with their claim to be imitating St. Francis, who was gentle even with wounded wolves.

Shah makes the point that there is archaeological evidence of a Sufi initiatory society among the Celts of Ireland as early as the ninth century. If that is the case, it too might shed light on the Rhineland mystic movement, which included Hildegard of Bingen, Albert the Great, Thomas Aquinas, Mechtild of Magdeburg, and Meister Eckhart. The source for this movement may have been from Celtic origins along the Rhine. Sufi history is diverse. "They have been hailed as saints, executed and persecuted as heretics. They teach that there is only one underlying truth within everything that is called religion." This Deep Ecumenism, or "interspirituality" in today's parlance, made it easier for others to embrace Sufi ideas. Ibn El-Arabi composed the following altogether ecumenical poem:

> My heart is capable of every form:
> A cloister for the monk, a fane for idols,
> A pasture for gazelles, the votary's Ka'ba [temple],
> The tables of the Torah, the Quran.
> Love is the creed I hold: wherever turn
> His camels, Love is still my creed and faith.

Rumi's path

Rumi traveled with Ibn El-Arabi, who was a mentor to him, and he also gives us a deeply ecumenical teaching when he sings:

> Cross and Christians, end to end, I examined. He was not on the Cross. I went to the Hindu temple, to the ancient pagoda. In neither was there any sign. To the heights of Herat I went, and Kandahar. I looked. He was not on height or lowland. Resolutely, I went to the top of the Mountain of Kaf. There only was the place of the 'Anqa bird. I went to the Kaaba. He was not there. I asked of his state from Ibn Sina: he was beyond the limits of the philosopher Avicenna.... I looked into my own heart. In that his place I saw him. He was in no other place.

Rumi takes on academicians when he writes:

> You claim skill in every art
> and knowledge of every science,
> Yet you cannot even hear
> what your own heart is telling you.

Until you can hear that simple voice
How can you be a keeper of secrets?
How can you be a traveler on this path?

Shah surprises us when he tells us that for Rumi "poetry was only a second-ary product," since "what he had to communicate was beyond poetry." Rumi also brought forth music and dance, as well as poetry, in the dervish gatherings. "Harmonious development, through the medium of harmony, might be a description of what Rumi was practicing," Shah says. This is the via creativa.

Yet Rumi is very clear: the greatest love is not poetry; it is silence. Silence, the via negativa, is always present. Indeed, silence is very often the crescendo of true creativity. We say, one gets "moved to silence." Awe shuts us up as it opens up the heart. Divine ecstasy cannot be expressed. Thus Eckhart says: "Nothing in all creation is so like God as silence."

And Rumi:

Secretly we spoke,
that wise one and me.
I said, *Tell me the secrets of the world.*
He said, *Sh...Let silence*
Tell you the secrets of the world.

Hafiz (1320–1389), another Sufi poet, also chimes in about the value of silence.

Noise is a cruel ruler
who is always imposing Curfews,
While stillness and quiet
Break open the vintage bottles,
Awake the real band.

And here is Hafiz again:

When the words stop
And you can endure the silence

that reveals your heart's pain
Of emptiness
Or that great wrenching-sweet longing,
That is the time to try and listen
to what the Beloved's eyes
most want to say.

Rumi speaks often of the power of silence to take us to what we are look-ing for. In one poem he says:

We search for him here and there
while looking right at Him.
Sitting at His side we ask,
"O Beloved, where is the Beloved?"

Enough with such questions! —
Let silence take you to the core of life.

All your talk is worthless
When compared to one whisper
of the Beloved.

The last stanza would seem to describe what happened to St. Thomas Aquinas when he underwent the mystical experience that drove him to silence. As I described in chapter seven, after this experience, Aquinas declared, "all I have written is straw," and said and wrote nothing over the last year of his life. For Aquinas, "one whisper" changed everything.

Avicenna and Eckhart's "Spark of the Soul"

In his sermons, Eckhart often refers to the teachings of Persian-born Muslim philosopher Avicenna (980–1037). With Walshe's help, I count at least eleven references. Eckhart calls him a "master" on numerous occasions, and sometimes "a very great master," and he explicitly credits Avicenna with the teaching of the "spark of the soul." This is of considerable importance because Eckhart's use of "spark of the soul" is a core teaching in his theology. He sometimes equates it with the Holy Spirit.

> There is something in the soul in which God is bare and the masters [Avicenna] say this is nameless, and has no name of its own. It is, and yet has no being of its own, for it is neither this nor that nor here nor there.... For in this the soul takes its whole life and being, and from this it sucks its life and being. This nameless thing is all in God, but the soul is outside here, and therefore the soul is accordingly always within God, unless it takes this nameless thing outward or extinguishes it within itself.

Eckhart also credits Avicenna with naming the "two faces of the soul." He says the "masters" — by which he means Avicenna — say the soul has two faces: her upper face "gazes at God all the time," and the lower face looks down somewhat and guides the senses. The upper face is "the apex of the soul, is in eternity and has nothing to do with time: it knows nothing of time or of the body." From the spark or apex or "peace of the soul there flow forth two powers," Eckhart says. "The one is will, the other intellect, and her powers' perfection lies in the highest power, which is the intellect." The soul does not seek God but the Godhead; it "seeks to have God there where God has no name: it wants a nobler, better thing than God who has a name.... It wants him as the marrow from which goodness comes, it wants Him as the kernel from which goodness flows, it wants Him as a root, as a vein whence goodness springs: only there is He the Father." Eckhart calls the spark of the soul at times the "Holy Spirit" and at times an "uncreated something." We all have it.

Idries Shah quotes a twentieth-century Muslim sheik in northern India who, in his instructions to a young seeker, speaks about the link between us and God in language that is very similar to Eckhart's. This provides important information regarding Eckhart's use of the phrase "spark of the soul":

> What we have to do is detach from both intellect and emotions.... We do not regard intellect as sufficient. Intellect, for us, is a complex of more or less compatible attitudes which you have been trained to regard as one single thing. According to Sufi thinking, there is a level below this which is a single, small, but vital one. It is the true intellect. This true

intellect is the organ of comprehension, existing in every human being. From time to time in ordinary human life it breaks through, producing strange phenomena which cannot be accounted for by the usual methods. Sometimes these are called occult phenomena, sometimes they are thought to be a transcending of the time or space relationship. This is the element in the human being which is responsible for his evolution to a higher form.

Notice the phrases "breaks through," "transcending...time or space," "the true intellect." Is synchronicity also being spoken of here? These all echo Eckhart's understanding, as does the sheik's following comment: "You cannot just believe such a reality exists," you can't take it on trust, or "you could very well lose it. No, you have to experience it. This means, of course, that you have to feel it in a way which you feel nothing else." The sheik also says, "You have chosen one single method of approaching truth. This is not enough. We use many different methods, and we recognize that there is a truth which is perceived by an inner organ." Eckhart says the same: "God has not bound man's salvation to any special way. Whatever has one way does not have another, but God has endowed all good ways with effectiveness and denied them to no other good way. For one good does not conflict with another good." And again: "God is in all modes, and equal in all ways, for him who can take Him equally."

The "spark of the soul" for Eckhart is the manger, the "maternity bed" where God is born. It is an "uncreated something" that links what is created in us to what is uncreated, what links God the Creator to the Godhead, which is deeper and more hidden and darker than all of creation. Therefore it links being and doing, nonaction and action. The spark of the soul is where the "now" of time encounters the "eternal now" of eternity. Eckhart says: "People know in the now of time. The now of time is the least thing there is. But take away the now of time, and you are everywhere and you have the whole of time." This is how the angels perceive; they "perceive in a light that is beyond time and is eternal. They therefore perceive in the eternal now." In another place Eckhart says that "spirit is the highest part of the soul, where it dwells in community and close companionship with the angels in angelic nature. Angelic nature is not in contact with time, nor is the spirit which is the man in the soul; it is free from time." The seventh chakra is about community, including our relationship to light beings or angels.

The spark of the soul is that which connects with the "living water" and therefore with the Holy Spirit. It is where spirit (human) meets Spirit (God). The spark seeks the Godhead itself. Eckhart says: "In every way the spark in the soul is borne up in the light and in the Holy Spirit and carried right up into the primal source, and it becomes so fully one with God, and seeks the One so fully, that it is more truly one with God than the food is with my body — indeed far more, insofar as it is far more pure and noble." Eckhart says the spark of the soul encounters God as "bare" and "naked." In the spark of the soul there is "hidden something like the original outbreak of all goodness, something like a brilliant light which incessantly gleams, and something like a burning fire which burns incessantly. This fire is nothing other than the Holy Spirit." It is the "simple power that recognizes God":

> This spark...wants nothing but God naked, just as He is....This light is not content with the simple changeless divine being which neither gives nor takes: rather it seeks to know where this being comes from, it wants to get into its simple ground, into the silent desert into which no distinction ever appeared, of Father, Son or Holy Spirit. In the inmost part, where no one is at home, there is where that light finds satisfaction, and there it is more one than it is in itself: for this ground is a still stillness, with no motion in itself, and by this immobility all things are in motion, and all those receive life that live of themselves, being endowed with reason.

Eckhart scholar Reiner Schurmann correctly teaches that the "spark of the soul" is in a human faculty and is not the faculty itself. Intuition fits that criterion. It is in the intellect or spirit but is not the intellect or spirit as such. Eckhart calls it a "something": "There is something in the soul which is only God and the masters say it is nameless, having no proper name of its own. It is and has no existence of its own since it is neither this nor that, neither here nor there. For it is what it is in another and that in this." It overlaps with God's Spirit. "Herein the soul takes its whole life and being and from this source it dares its life and being, for this is totally in God." It is the place of the image of God in us, as Schurmann attests: "In this spark, as the higher part of the spirit is located the image of God that the mind is." It is "something like a spark of divine nature, a divine light, a ray, an imprinted picture of the divine nature." Schurmann calls this "an interior knowledge by intuition."

> *"God enjoys the Godself. In the same enjoyment in which God enjoys himself, God enjoys all creatures."*

The spark is in the ground of the soul where God is "with all his divinity." And it is, Eckhart says, "so closely related to God that it is a unique indivisible unity, and bears within itself the images of all creatures, image without image, and image above image." When the spark is allowed to flourish, we become young again. Eckhart says, "God is in this power as in the eternal now. Were the spirit at every moment united with God in this power people could never grow old.... There everything is present and new...and in this ever-present vision I possess everything." One wonders if Eckhart is not talking about our powers of imagination, our powers of creativity and intuition.

The Spark of the Soul in Medieval Jewish Mysticism

The expression "spark of the soul" used by Eckhart and found in Avicenna is familiar to the medieval Jewish tradition as well. It's found throughout Sufi mystical poetry, and it's found in the Kabbalah and the Zohar, the mystical books of Judaism that were circulating in Germany in Eckhart's day. The word *zohar* actually means "radiance, splendor, brilliance" and designates "the hidden power of emanation," according to Jewish mystical scholar Daniel Matt. This sounds very much like the *doxa*, or glory and radiance, associated with images of the Cosmic Christ (see chapter two). Matt says, "The spark of emanation flashes again and Keter, the aura, transmits the impulse to Hokhmah, the point of Wisdom."

Thus, the sparks touch and even ignite Wisdom herself. Wisdom accompanies creation, and so the sparks play a role in the unfolding of creation itself — might we even call them the "original fireball"? Sparks play a role in the creation of all things, including the elements of the universe — fire, air, water, and earth, "from which evolved the states of mineral, vegetable, animal, and human," Matt writes. Thus the sparks precede the cosmic forces and feed them. When things came into being as mineral, vegetable, animal or human, "some of the sparks remained hidden within the varieties of existence." The Zohar, referred to as a "mystical novel of the Torah," interprets the creation story by the Elohim author of Genesis: "In the Beginning" meant that "a blinding spark flashed within the Concealed of the Concealed / from the mystery of the Infinite." Yes, we are to touch the "mystery of the Infinite" and spread the sparks, for nature is busy spreading them from north to east to west to south, in the heavens and on the earth.

> Sparks burst into flashes, up high and down below
> then quieted down and rose up high, beyond, beyond....
>
> The spark expanded, whirling round and round.
> Sparks burst into flash and rose high above.
> The heavens blazed with all their powers;
> everything flashed and sparkled as one.

Furthermore, it is our responsibility to bring heaven and Earth, cosmos and psyche, together, teaches the Zohar, in order to "raise those sparks hidden throughout the world, elevating them to holiness by the power of your soul." Our minds and creativity are to unveil the hidden sparks of the world, for they lie hidden everywhere. They are in our hearts, for "love and sparks from the flame of your heart will escort you." They are present in all things as "sparks of holiness" that "intermingle with everything in the world, even inanimate objects." They come to us in all manner of our activities, even "by eating, you bring forth sparks that cleave to your soul.... When you eat and drink, you experience enjoyment and pleasure from the food and drink. Arouse yourself every moment to ask in wonder, 'What is this enjoyment and pleasure? What is it that I am tasting?' Answer yourself, 'This is nothing but the holy sparks from the sublime, holy worlds that are within the food and drink.'"

The Kabbalah tells us that "there is no greater path than" to bring sparks alive in life, to educe the spark that lies within. Ordinary things become extraordinary. The profane becomes sacred. The Kabbalah states: "When you desire to eat or drink, or to fulfill other worldly desires, and you focus your awareness on the love of God, then you elevate that physical desire to spiritual desire. Thereby you draw out the holy spark that dwells within. You bring forth holy sparks from the natural world. There is no path greater than this. For wherever you go and whatever you do — even mundane activities — you serve God."

This is also what Eckhart teaches: those who experience the divine are always in the right place and at the right time.

Hafiz on the Divine Feminine

Sufism employs many images of the Divine Feminine. Idries Shah explains that a "new realization of love, maternity, art, color, verve" strongly marked the "ideas and activities" of the Sufis in twelfth-century Spain. This same feminine impetus was found in the Gothic architectural revolution and the cathedral movement in twelfth-century Europe. Consider this poem from Hafiz:

> The sun's eyes are painting fields again.
> Its lashes with expert strokes
> Are sweeping across the land.
>
> A great palette of light has embraced
> This earth....
>
> What excitement will renew your body
> When we all begin to see
> That His heart resides in
> Everything?
>
> God has a root in each act and creature
> That He draws His mysterious
> Divine life from.
>
> His eyes are painting fields again.
> The Beloved with His own hands is tending,

Raising like a precious child,
Himself in
You.

Hafiz touches on so many themes dear to Eckhart: the Cosmic Christ,
present in all things; the maternity of God; and the invitation to birth the
Cosmic Christ within. The emphasis on a fecund Earth ready to give birth
implies the Divine Mother and the sacred powers of creativity. These are all
elements found in abundance in Eckhart (see chapter four especially).

However, the Sufi tradition is also very much at home with the experience of nothingness. As described by Eckhart, it is an experience of fullness,
not negation. Hafiz says:

I have made the journey into Nothing.
I have lit that lamp that
Needs no oil.
I have cried great streams
Of emerald crystals
On my scarred knees, begging love-making

To never again let me hear from
Any world

The sound of my own name,
Even from the voice of divine thought

Or see that pen you gave me, God,
In the sun's or sky's skillful hand
Writing
Anything other than the word —
One.

I have made the journey into Nothing.
I have become that flame that needs
No fuel.

Beloved,
Now what need is there to ever
Call for Hafiz?

For if you did,
I would just step out
of *You.*

The Path of Service

The Sufi path is not just about seeking mystical experiences, however rapturous they are. It is about service. It is about returning to help with a sense of compassion and justice. This applies to all beings. "All creatures are God's children, and those dearest to God are the ones who treat His children kindly." Kindness to animals, respect for all of God's creation, are enjoined. If an animal is to be killed, it must be done swiftly and in a merciful manner. Tyranny and oppression of any of God's creatures, including by a ruler or government, are very strictly prohibited and constitute very grave sins. Generosity and hospitality are thus highly valued qualities among Muslims in every part of the world. "To be a dervish (Sufi) is to serve and to help others, not just to sit and pray. To be a real dervish is to lift up those who have fallen, to wipe the tears of the suffering, to caress the friendless and the orphaned." Mohammed was told about a man who spent all his time in the mosque praying. He asked, "Then who feeds him?" "His brother," was the reply. "Then his brother is better than he," he said. People are to rejoice at one another's good fortune and share in one another's grief. "A man does not believe until he loves for his brother what he loves for himself." Belief takes one into one's heart to a place where compassion is felt deeply. Here, too, we see Eckhart in agreement with Sufi teachings.

Muslim author Ibrahim Abdul-Matin, who was a policy adviser on long-term sustainability issues for New York mayor Michael Bloomberg, recently published a book on Islam's attitude toward environmental issues called *Green Deen: What Islam Teaches about Protecting the Planet*. In it, Abdul-Matin offers six principles of Islam that bear on environmental sustainability: understanding the oneness of God and His creation (*tawhid*); seeing signs

(*ayat*) of God everywhere; being a steward (*khalifah*) of the Earth; honoring
the trust (*amana*) we have with God to be protectors of the planet; moving
toward justice (*adl*); and living in balance with nature (*mizan*). His book
treats each of these elements as part of an "environmental ethos of Islam."

Abdul-Matin begins with a teaching of a "basic tenet of Islam" that he
learned on camping trips with his father: that "the Earth is a mosque, and
everything in it is sacred." The term *ayat*, or "sign," means a sign of the
presence of the Creator. An *ayat* can refer to any of the verses of the Qur'an
"or the same word can mean the signs around us — the mountains, the trees,
the seas. These signs are evidence of God." This sounds to me like Eckhart's
teaching that "every creature is a word of God and a book about God." Says
Abdul-Matin: "We can fine-tune our attention to see every aspect of creation as being a divine message.... We are immersed in the amazement of
the sign Allah has spread out before us. These experiences can lead us into a
state of awe. Our awe is our sense that we are part of the amazing beauty of
those signs." Awe, amazement, reverence, gratitude — these are the starting
points for Abdul-Matin's spiritual journey, just as they are for Eckhart, and
for Rabbi Heschel, as we saw in chapter one.

Ultimately, it is not for me to say that Eckhart is a Sufi. But a Sufi has
already made that claim, opening my eyes to the connections that I have
presented in this chapter. Let us close with Rumi's song about the "spark in
the soul":

Ah, one spark flew
and burned the house of my heart.
Smoke filled the sky.
The flames grew fierce in the wind.

The fire of the heart is not easily lit.
So don't cry out: "O Lord, rescue me
from the burning flames!
Spare me from the army of thoughts
that is marching through my mind!"

O Heart of Pure Consciousness,
You are the ruler of all hearts.
After countless ages
you brought my soul
all it ever wished for.

CHAPTER ELEVEN

INDIGENOUS WISDOM AND SHAMANISM

Meister Eckhart Meets Eddie Kneebone,
Black Elk, and Bill Everson

*The round form of the drum represents the whole universe and its steady,
strong beat is the pulse, the heart, throbbing at the center of the universe.
It is as the voice of Wakan-Tanka, and this sound stirs us and helps us
to understand the mystery and power of all things.*

— BLACK ELK

*The aspect of being at one with the universe...is included in our lives. It is a part of us.
...For me, Creation Spirituality...is like the Dreamtime in the way that it brings
the entire cosmos into our lives, making it a part of us, and us a part of it.*

— EDDIE KNEEBONE

*God loves all creatures equally and fills them with his being. And we should lovingly
meet all creatures in the same way. We find this attitude among the pagans,
people who came to this sense of love-filled equanimity.*

— MEISTER ECKHART

The shamanistic tradition has always been about fostering, or restoring, our intimate connection with the cosmos and all the life within it. It teaches reverence for and identification with animals and creation. Shamanism is found almost universally among ancient and indigenous peoples, and evidence of it ranges from the Arctic to the southern tip of South America, from East to West and points in between. Shamanism speaks deeply to our ancient memory of how, in ages past, humans and animals "shared the same language" — meaning we humans were closer to our animal roots and more alert sensually to the mysteries of nature, be they the rock world, the plant world, the winged world, or the world of the four-legged ones. We were keen observers and translators, one might say, of the signals of other creatures. For our ancestors, this was surely a survival mechanism, but it was also a spiritual reality.

You can sense this in the presence of the figures of Lascaux Cave, which are some forty thousand years old. Or in the ancient Aboriginal paintings in the Australian desert. These are clearly sacred places. The paintings are not just memories of animals; they are not "art for art's sake." They are art for Spirit's sake. This was art as action, bringing Spirit present and alive into the tribe. Much of the art no doubt was employed in shamanic rituals and rites of passage. It was, and should be, taken seriously. The late Catholic monk Thomas Merton tells us that "no art form" stirred or moved him "more deeply" than Paleolithic cave paintings. Why is that?

> The cave painters were concerned not with composition, not with "beauty," but with the peculiar immediacy of the most direct vision. The bison they paint is not a mere representation of an animal, it is a sign, a *gestalt*, a presence of the unique and peculiar life force incarnated in this animal — in terms of Bantu philosophy, its *muntu*. This is anything but an "abstract essence." It is dynamic power, vitality, the self-realization of life in act, something that flashes out in a split second, it seems, yet is not accessible to mere reflection, still less to analysis. Cave art is a sign of pure seeing, nothing else.

Reading Eckhart can also take one into places of "pure seeing, nothing else." It can prove to be a quasi-shamanistic experience. Eckhart himself frequently invites us to bring our "naked self" to the "naked Godhead." Merton's language helps us to grasp the meaning of these deep experiences, which I have also had while praying with indigenous peoples. Whether in sweat lodges or during sundances or powwow dances or with the sacred pipe, whether with eagle whistles or hawk feathers or Lakota singing and drums, with rattles or heated rocks — there is a peculiar life force that is called forth. This is ancient prayer. It is shamanistic prayer, and its appeal is as old as our souls — for all our ancestors, for thousands of years, prayed such prayers. One shamanistic scholar believes the roots of shamanism date back fifty to seventy thousand years!

Thomas Berry believed that the shamanistic spirit is returning in our time, and it is a sign of hope, a reality that may prove key to our survival as a species. He writes:

> In moments of confusion such as the present, we are not left simply to our own rational contrivances. We are supported by the ultimate powers of the universe as they make themselves present to us through the spontaneities within our own beings. We need only become sensitized to these spontaneities, not with a naive simplicity, but with critical appreciation. This intimacy with our genetic endowment, and through this endowment with the larger cosmic process, is not primarily the role of the philosopher, priest, prophet or professor. It is the role of the shamanic personality, a type that is emerging once again in our society.

Meister Eckhart as Shaman

In many ways, Meister Eckhart reveals himself to be a "shamanic personality." For one thing, Eckhart's use of language, his rhythms and repetitions, display the musical qualities of a preacher or poet. It takes sensitive English translations of his original German to bring this out, such as the following passage: "God dwells in the innermost dimension of the soul and in the highest aspect of the soul. And when I say 'innermost,' I mean the highest. When I say 'the highest,' I mean the innermost region of the soul. The innermost and the highest realms of the soul — these two are one." A student of mine commented that this passage "sounded like a black preacher, the beats and the repetitions." It is useful in this regard to read Eckhart out loud — after all, his sermons were delivered that way. One finds this shamanic beat in contemporary rap as well. Eckhart's language is that of the "poet-shaman," such as Walt Whitman and Emily Dickinson, according to Whitman scholar Steven Herrmann.

Robinson Jeffers was a California poet steeped in a shamanistic soul akin to the land and rock and sea where he lived and where he wrote and built his "Tower." Of the antiquity of poetry and its shamanistic musculature, he says, "Poetry is more primitive than prose. It existed before prose and will exist afterward; it is not domesticated; it is wilder and more natural....It belongs outdoors, it has tides as nature has....The brain can make prose; the whole man, brain and nerves, muscles and entrails, organs of sense and germination, makes poetry and responds to poetry." One feels the truth of this on reading and praying Meister Eckhart. Something primitive lurks there, something chthonic, from the deep and ancient past. It is more than prose that the rational mind proposes. The "whole person" — all the chakras — are affected both in the making and in the responding. Often the experience is closer to shamanic chanting than theological rhetoric, and it has an effect on the whole body.

Eckhart's theology of the Word of God is clearly rich in shamanistic philosophy. The teaching that "every creature is a word of God" and "every creature is doing its best gladly to speak God" is pure Earth-based, shamanistic theology. When he says, "God is in all things," and in "the innermost and highest aspect of the soul God creates the entire cosmos" — this is shamanistic philosophy and cosmology. Eckhart's explicit commitment to panentheism, the presence of the Divine in all things and all things in the Divine, is also shamanistic. His premodern appreciation for the necessary marriage of psyche and cosmos reflects a shamanistic relationship to the world.

For instance, consider this beautiful passage by Lakota elder Black Elk: "We should understand that all things are the works of the Great Spirit. We should know that He is within all things: the trees, the grasses, the rivers, the mountains, and all the four-legged animals, and the winged peoples; and even more important, we should understand that He is also above all these things and peoples. When we do understand all this deeply in our hearts then we will fear, and love, and know the Great Spirit, and then we will be and act and live as He intends."

Defining Shamanism

What is a shaman, and what is shamanism? Scholar Mircea Eliade, in his classic work *Shamanism: Archaic Techniques of Ecstasy*, says that shamans are persons who stand out in their respective societies by virtue of characteristics that in the societies of modern Europe, represent the signs of a vocation or at least of a religious crisis. They are separated from the rest of the community by the intensity of their own religious experience. In other words, it would be more correct to class shamanism among the mysticisms than with what is commonly called a religion.... Shamanism always remains an ecstatic technique at the disposal of a particular elite and represents, as it were, the mysticism of the particular religion.... This small mystical elite not only directs the community's religious life but, as it were, guards its "soul." The shaman is the great specialist in the human soul; he alone "sees" it, for he knows its "form" and its destiny.

Eliade considered the ecstatic experience to be a "primary phenomenon" that is "fundamental in the human condition, and hence known to the whole of archaic humanity; what changed and was modified with the different forms of culture and religion was the interpretation and evaluation of the ecstatic experience." Often it was experiences of solitude that fed the shamanistic breakthrough. Eliade found "examples of genuine mystical experiences of shamans, taking the form of 'spiritual' ascents and prepared by methods of meditation comparable to those of the great mystics of East and West." His definition of shamanism is tied up with ecstatic experiences: "The shaman, and he alone, is the great master of ecstasy. A first definition of the complex phenomenon, and perhaps the least hazardous, will be: shamanism = technique of ecstasy." The primary work of the shaman is healing, and he or she is often accompanied by helping spirits. The shaman is often adept at "mastery over fire, magical flight, etc. The shaman specializes in a trance during which his soul is believed to leave his body and ascend to the sky or descend to the underworld." The shaman often undergoes an intense "spiritual crisis that is not lacking in tragic greatness and in beauty." This deep religious experience often creates a new life (and new vocation) that separates him or her from others in the tribe. An experience of an "inner light" also plays a part, as is well documented in Eskimo shamanism.

The shaman not only heals the community but also defends it. The shaman plays the role of a spiritual warrior. Eliade says, "The shamans have played an essential role in the defense of the psychic integrity of the community. They are preeminently the antidemonic champions; they combat not only demons and disease, but also the black magicians.... The military elements that are of great importance in certain types of Asian shamanism... are accounted for by the requirements of war against the demons, the true enemies of humanity. Shamanism defends life, health, fertility, the world of light against death, diseases, sterility, disaster, and the world of 'darkness.'" Ultimately, "what is fundamental and universal is the shaman's struggle against what we could call 'the powers of evil.'"

Aboriginal Dreamtime and Meister Eckhart

Eddie Kneebone (1947–2005) was an Australian Aboriginal and activist whom I hired to teach with myself and my faculty when we led a weeklong workshop in Australia in 1990. When I cited Eckhart's saying that "God is creating the entire universe, fully and totally, in this present now," Eddie responded: "This is the Dreamtime, *now*." Eckhart says we are to live "in the eternal now," and that, too, is Dreamtime teaching. In fact, Eddie told me, there is no word for "time" in the Aboriginal languages. We are already living in the Dreamtime. This seems very close also to Jesus's teaching that the "kingdom/queendom of God *is* among you." Not will be or has been but *already is*. Eddie Kneebone observes that what Dreamtime gives people is a powerful identity, a sense of their importance and a belief that they are valuable for what they are. A sense of already having arrived, a sense of being there.

Eddie Kneebone once sat down for an interview on Aboriginal cosmology that was published in a book called *Creation Spirituality and the Dreamtime*, which was based on our summer institute. Here are some points he emphasized. "Aboriginal spirituality is the belief that all objects are living and share the same soul or spirit that Aboriginals share. Therefore all Aboriginals have a kinship with the environment. The soul or spirit is common — only the shape is different, but no less important." Thus "everything is equal and shares the same soul or spirit from the Dreamtime."

This sounds a lot like Eckhart's teaching about the "equality of being." Eckhart says:

> God poured his being in equal measure to all creatures, to each as much as it can receive. This is a good lesson for us that we should love

all creatures equally with everything which we have received from God....God loves all creatures equally and fills them with his being. And we should lovingly meet all creatures in the same way. We find this attitude among the pagans, people who came to this sense of love-filled equanimity through the knowing faculties given them by their basic human nature. It is a pagan teacher who tells us that a human being is an animal which is naturally gentle.

It is interesting that Eckhart credits "pagan teachers" with reminding us of the equality of being; it's possible he has in mind shamans. Eckhart applies Jesus's teaching in John's Gospel (13:34) — "I give you a new commandment: love one another, just as I have loved you" — to all of creation. He reminds us that "Christ himself said to his disciples: 'Go forth, and preach the gospel to all creatures.'" For Eckhart, this means love applies to all of creation equally. He writes: "A flea, to the extent that it is in God, is nobler than the highest angel is himself. Now in God all things are equal and are God himself....The highest angel, the mind, and the gnat have an equal mode in God." We saw earlier how Eckhart reminds us that "equality gives strength in all things," and that this is why a child or even a dog can be so satisfying a companion when life presents us with stress or terror.

Eddie Kneebone criticizes church buildings when they are presented as the only place to worship God; this is like Eckhart (chapter six) critiquing Cologne's cathedral in favor of the cathedral of every human soul. Says Eddie: "I have found peace of heart — but not in a building. I was told to 'Go to church, that is where you will find God, inside the church.' I have also realized that man created the buildings that he calls churches, God created the world. If I look for God, then it will be in the environment that he built."

Developing the richness of the meaning of "Dreamtime," Eddie elaborates:

> The aspect of being at one with the universe — not just the little piece of land that we stand on, not simply the environment around us, or the country that we live in — but the universe. It is included in our lives. It is a part of us. During the daytime we can look outside and we see trees, birds, rivers, the wind in the clouds and the sunshine. This is the environment that is revealed during the daylight hours, that we take for granted.

Yes, this is the Cataphatic Divinity that comes out during the day, and Eddie's description echoes Eckhart's teaching of the Cosmic Christ.

Eddie goes on:

> But at night the other half of our environment is revealed — the universe. Every clear night we can look up and see millions of stars. That is also a part of our lives. It is an important part of our lives that we forget about and don't include in our way of thinking. In Aboriginal spirituality, however, it certainly was included. We look up and see the stars shining above and we say: 'They are the bright suns and around them there are planets — possibly with people that we will never see.' The Aboriginals looked up at night and they didn't see the stars — they never saw stars. They only saw the campfires of their ancestors on their journey. The bright stars were the ancestors who were not long gone; the dimmer stars were the ancestors further on the journey. They imagined that the ancestors sitting around their campfires were looking back and seeing the campfires of the living, physical Aboriginals at their own campsites. The Aboriginal looked up and really believed that their eyes could meet. So for me, Creation Spirituality as Matthew Fox talks about it, is like the Dreamtime in the way that it brings the entire cosmos into our lives, making it a part of us, and us, a part of it.

No doubt the cosmic spirituality of Aboriginal Australians derives directly from their experience of the land — Australia's forbidding desert. Veronica Brady, a Catholic sister and professor of English at the University of Western Australia, writes: "If mysticism is found in all cultures, it ought to belong very specially in Australia, for this is a land which compels silence, and the mystic (*mustes*) is one who is sworn to silence, drawn to a mystery which is essentially unspeakable, at least in words." In the desert, she maintains, we acknowledge the limits of our own power and reason and learn "to bow down in awe, drawn by the 'mysterium tremendum et fascinans,' the sacred as that which is both terrifying and supremely fascinating. Here we understand the sheer audacity of existence, the wonder that life should exist at all where we in our arrogance find it so difficult to exist." Yet for the Aboriginals "the desert is fertile and life-giving because they can read its signs."

Eckhart, too, recognizes the mysticism of the desert. He said: "In the desert God and creature are one. There is no room for two in the desert." Eckhart also taught about letting go and silence, about the emptying and the subtraction that enlarges the soul. Aboriginal writer Patrick White says that in the Australian landscape the "state of silence, simplicity and humility...is the only proper state for the artist as for the human being." Further, Veronica Brady says we need to restore this Aboriginal (or shamanic) sense of connection and respect for the desert in order to move beyond the Western compulsion to exploit the land. Instead, Australia's desert is "a place of the encounter with the living God who figures in the Exodus story as the desert God. In this story the desert becomes rather the place of the Covenant, where the mutual bonding of God and his people is sealed."

Bill Everson on Shamans

To speak of shamanism and the wisdom of indigenous peoples is not to suggest that we return to or try to re-create a lost or romantic past. Rather, these can be guides to how we, as everyday people today, can encounter the Divine in our everyday lives.

Poet Bill Everson (1912–1994) was a Dominican, like Eckhart, for sixteen years and also an influential poet and literary critic. Everson was deeply appreciative of Eckhart; he studied the archetype of the shaman in considerable depth; and he expressed the power of a spirit-filled nature in moving fashion. For instance, Everson writes: "The ordinary man sees God in Nature or he sees Him not at all. By extension, the God-thirsting man sees Him everywhere, for Nature is omnipresent....Emerson said that nature is the language of God. It is fittingly spoken, for 'in the beginning was the Word.' And in that beginning is its end. The Word, then, is all." Everson continues:

> Nature itself holds the clue to the divine. In its myriad forms, the great plenitude of being is poured out, streaming from the womb of potentiality, exploding into act. A kind of meta-physical combustion seems smoldering in the fabric of things, a surge of incipient energy, breaking out of the bounds of its nuclear forms, and disappearing into the beyond. It is this transformation the poet celebrates.

Everson considers the shaman's journey to be essentially a descent. The shaman operates in the "underbelly," and "the totem of the shaman is usually some sort of diving bird, or a burrowing or hibernating animal, symbolizing the going down into the unconscious, where the tribe is troubled." Everson feels that the poet and the shaman share a similar journey, for "the shaman and the poet both trace this link down to atavistic forces, the deeps of instinctual response, in an effort to resist an excessive cerebral consciousness." They share a common beat or rhythm — "the basic mode is rhythmic. The drum and the rattle constitute the shaman's essential implementation, undercutting the horizontal plane, the entry into the visionary netherworld."

An American poet who preceded Everson, Walt Whitman, sings of "dancing yet through the streets" while "beating the serpent skin drum." One commentator suggests that "the drum beat works for him as a transporter to the Divine...because he is a poet-shaman," indeed "the greatest poet-shaman who ever lived." Rhythm and beat involve body and animal instinct, and shamanism includes both. This same body awareness is celebrated in Eckhart's message ("the soul loves the body") and the rhythm and beat of his words.

Also, the poet and the shaman (and the prophet), says Everson, share the "primacy of the Word. In the focus of all charismatic acts it is the utterance, the voice, that holds the clue to the inflection of creative release." One might say they are all engaged with the fifth chakra.

As for poets who engage the shamanistic today, Everson says: "The whole function of the poet as shaman is to maintain the aesthetic, not in the Modernist view, the hypothesized aesthetic object, but to maintain relevance to the archetypal world, the transcendental world, which is non-political, and sacral....It is in the secular context that the aesthetic dimension becomes the link to the transcendental."

Eckhart fulfills Everson's poet-shaman criteria. He descends, as in his talk of the "dark God," the "darkness" of the depths of the soul, and God as "ground" and "hidden." He descends to an inward region — the intellect "searches inwards," he insists, always inwards, and we are to travel there, to the "innermost part of the soul" and find God, who "creates the entire cosmos there" and is the "ground of being." Eckhart is shamanistic in his respect for rocks — "the existence of a stone reveals God." Eckhart, as we have seen, practices as well as preaches the primacy of the Word. He says: "In the first outpouring, when the truth pours out and springs forth, in the gate of the house of God, the soul should stand and should express and bring forth the Word. Everything that is in the soul should speak and praise." He sees every creature as uttering — or trying to utter — the Divine Word. After all, "God is a Word but an unexpressed Word." God is spoken and unspoken, known and unknown, expressed and unexpressed. "All creatures are words of God. My mouth expresses and reveals God but the existence of a stone does the same and people often recognize more from actions than from words.... All creatures may echo God in all their activities. It is, of course, just a small bit which they can reveal."

Jesus as Shaman

If Eckhart was shamanic, then was Jesus also, in some respects, a shaman? New Testament scholar Bruce Chilton believes he was: "Jesus clearly exercises shamanic powers in the gospels — when he stills the storm, appears to his disciples walking on water, and joins Moses and Elijah in the glory that surrounds God's chariot-throne, for example." Among the "highest prophetic attainments of the Hebrew shamans," according to Chilton, are "Elijah, Elisha, the Galilean mystics who joined the heavenly ascent of Enoch, and Jesus himself.... The shamanic prophets not only have visions; they themselves became visions for their disciples." Then, of course, at the very beginning of Mark's Gospel (1:12–13), Jesus's vision quest is described: following his baptism, Jesus is driven out into the desert for forty days to pray and wrestle with angels and Satan and the wild beasts. Might we say his was a shamanic vision quest?

Bill Everson believes that "Christ was perhaps the greatest of all shamans.... Forty days in the desert, the carrying of the cross as a Sun Dance." Everson cites Jesus's relationship to the "animal powers" and the very notion of incarnation, spirit becoming flesh. Consider the *descent* that Paul names in Philippians, to abandon the sky and God of the sky to join the Earth community — Christ was the "wounded buck." The shaman also traditionally holds a wound, as of course the Cosmic Christ does, the deep wounds of the crucified Christ. According to Everson, Jesus remained close to the Earth his whole life long — "He never identified with patriarchy. He kept the persona of a workman, or a craftsman. This is a very humbling thing." Everson draws a comparison between the sundance pole and the cross of Jesus; in the sundance, the participants are attached to a pole by cords in their chest, and they rip away from the pole at a high point in their prayer. The consequent pain and blood are a sacrificial offering for the community.

Jungian writer Steven Herrmann cites how Jung talks of "climbing the tree" as a "very ancient shamanistic motif. The shaman, in ecstasy, climbs the magical tree in order to reach the upper world where he will find his true self....To the eye of the psychologist, the shamanistic and alchemical symbols are a projected representation of the process of individuation." Jesus "climbed the tree" of the cross, but before that he also climbed the hill where the Transfiguration took place, and he taught his Beatitudes on a hill as well. Both the sundancer and Jesus are, in Everson's words, playing out the "archetype of the suffering redeemer."

Jesus addressed the "primordial wound" of the human species — not necessarily "original sin," since that was a latecomer in Christian theology, which appeared with Augustine in the fourth century. Instead, to use Otto Rank's term, it was the "original wound," which was that of separation. The first Lakota sundancer, a man named Kablaya (according to Black Elk), is said to have declared: "I shall offer up my body and soul that my people may live." Everson names the "basic psychological function of the shaman" as trance. Leading people to a state of trance, such as using silence as a trance-like technique, a method Everson employed in poetry readings, is a kind of poetic shamanism.

Herrmann comments on Eckhart's movement or *descent* leading us into the Godhead.

> The connection between Christ and the shaman is important for us to meditate upon. What comes to mind here are Eckhart's writings on the Godhead. For Eckhart, the descent into the Godhead is suggestive of a movement back, to that pantheistic level where the shaman reigns; where the Animal Powers and the instinctive forces are submerged; in that part of the psyche that is only psyche-like — the psychoid unconscious Jung spoke of. One gets the impression that Eckhart was talking in his sermons about a descent to atavistic forces of the collective

unconscious....There is a definite sense of Nature, the earth, the ground and soil of the Godhead. It seems that this movement is itself the movement that the shaman makes, away from the traditional image of God to the unformed Godhead.

Everson agrees with Herrmann that the shaman operates at the psychoid level and that it is the shaman's "familiarity with the spirits" that is the source of his power. Jung also described the shaman as a "conjurer of spirits." Says Everson: "For both shaman and poet, this calling depends upon his relation to his pain, and if he should become cured, that is, rendered insensible to his obsession, his shamanizing will cease."

Ruth-Inge Heinze, in her book *Shamans of the 20th Century*, provides other criteria for a shaman that further confirm Eckhart's shamanistic approach. According to Heinze, a shaman "can access alternative states of consciousness at will," that is, trance. The poet does this, and Eckhart does this clearly in his sermons. A second criterion is that they "fulfill needs in their community which otherwise are not met." Eckhart also did this — and does it to this day, inviting us all into the realm of our mysticism. And third, shamans "are in fact, the mediators between the sacred and the profane." As we have seen, Eckhart often tried to bridge that separation, and with just the purpose that Mircea Eliade describes: the shaman, through his or her efforts, "abolishes the present human condition and, for the time being, recovers the situation as it was at the beginning. Friendship with animals, knowledge of their language, transformation into an animal, are so many signs that the shaman has re-established the 'paradisal' situation lost at the dawn of time."

Eckhart underscores this journey when he says, "Just as every created thing follows and pursues its end, so likewise it follows its beginning." Eckhart is very much at home speaking of the "unborn self" and of our origins in the Godhead, which is thoroughly grounded in Earth imagery. Further, he describes extremely shamanlike spiritual journeying: "When I was still in the core, the soil, the stream, and the source of the Godhead, no one asked me where I wanted to go or what I was doing. There was no one there who might have put such a question to me. But when I flowed out from there, all creatures called out: 'God!' I was asked, 'Brother Eckhart, when did you go out of the house?' For I had been inside. In this way all creatures speak about 'God.'"

Finally, in chapter ten, we discussed Eckhart's "spark of the soul" in relation to Sufi mysticism. But is it also an indicator of shamanism? Is it, as one indigenous shaman described, the same as the shamanic "mind on fire"? The shaman said: "Every real shaman has to feel an illumination in his body, in the inside of his head or in his brain, something that gleams like fire, that gives him the power to see with closed eyes into the darkness, into the hidden things or into the future, or into the secrets of another man. I felt that I was in possession of this marvelous ability." Herrmann speaks of the "lightning symbolism" common to much of shamanism — and Eckhart, too, invokes lightning as a symbol of the breakthrough. Eckhart tells us that in our souls there is "hidden something like the original outbreak of all goodness, something like a brilliant light which incessantly gleams, and something like a burning fire which burns incessantly. This fire is nothing other than the Holy Spirit."

Black Elk

Black Elk (1862–1950) was a famous shaman and medicine man of the Lakota nation. He first had visions at the age of four, and at the age of nine, following a serious illness, he was granted powerful visions on a South Dakota mountaintop that he knew would help heal his people. Afterward, Black Elk underwent a deep experience of mission or vocation; in particular, he helped revive the sundance ceremony among the Lakota and respect for the sacred pipe. And he strove to revive the spirit of his oppressed people. His call, he felt, was "to bring to life the flowering tree of his people," but it "haunted Black Elk all his life and caused him much suffering." He deeply lamented the "broken hoop" of his nation, even as he traveled abroad to learn more about white ways and history while operating with Buffalo Bill's Wild West Show in Italy, France, and England.

Black Elk was born when his people still had the freedom of the plains and hunted bison, and he fought against the white soldiers at Little Bighorn and at Wounded Knee. He was a cousin to the famous chief and holy man Crazy Horse, and he knew Sitting Bull, Red Cloud, and American Horse. Near the end of his life, his mentor Elk Head gave Black Elk permission to share stories of their ceremonies because, according to Joseph Epes Brown,

Black Elk felt the "people will live for as long as the rites are known and the pipe is used. But as soon as the sacred pipe is forgotten, the people will be without a center and they will perish." Black Elk spoke no English, but with his son translating, he described his life to writer John G. Neihardt, who published these interviews in the classic 1932 book *Black Elk Speaks*. Years later, Black Elk also described sacred Lakota ceremonies to Joseph Epes Brown, who published these descriptions in the 1953 book *The Sacred Pipe*.

Much of Black Elk's and Eckhart's teachings resonate with each other. One of the more striking ways is in their celebration of the circle as a symbol of spiritual connection. Black Elk talks often about the "sacred hoop," which is the universe, but which is also found everywhere in nature as well as in the human community itself. He says: "I saw that the sacred hoop of my people was one of many hoops that made one circle.... But anywhere is the center of the world." He teaches: "There can be no power in a square. You have noticed that everything an Indian does is in a circle, and that is because the Power of the World always works in circles, and everything tries to be round.... The sky is round, and I have heard that the earth is round like a ball, and so are all the stars. The wind, in its greatest power, whirls. Birds make their nests in circles, for theirs is the same religion as ours. The sun comes forth and goes down again in a circle. The moon does the same and both are round. Even the seasons form a great circle."

Meanwhile, Eckhart says that "being is a circle for God," and he calls the soul a "circle of the world," and he calls on humans to be a "circle...filled with the spirit of the Lord." He says, "Heaven runs constantly in a circle; therefore it has to be round so that it can run more swiftly in a circle. For it bestows on all creatures their being and their lives." He connects psyche and cosmos, heart and the heavens, when he says: "Where should we begin? With the heart.... Begin with the heart, which is the noblest part of the body. It lies in the center of the body from which point it bestows life on the whole body. For the spring of life arises in the heart and has an effect like heaven." The heart matches the heavens insofar as the heart "is active constantly in a circular manner.... The spring of life is placed in the heart." Eckhart's advice to "begin with the heart" is echoed in the teaching of Black Elk, who says for peace to occur, "understanding must be of the heart and not of the head alone. [I wish] to help in bringing peace upon the earth, not only among men, but within men and between the whole of creation."

Black Elk links cosmic awareness with inner peace, which is the beginning of communal peace:

> The first peace, which is the most important, is that which comes within the souls of men when they realize their relationship, their oneness, with the universe and all its Powers, and when they realize that at the center of the universe dwells *Wakan-Tanka*, and that this center is really everywhere, it is within each of us. This is the real peace, and the others are but reflections of this. The second peace is that which is made between two individuals, and the third is that which is made between two nations. But above all you should understand that there can never be peace between nations until there is first known that true peace which, as I have often said, is within the souls of men.

Eckhart also talks of the peace or "repose" that was the "Creator's aim when he created all creatures." Repose is the "divine nature," and God seeks to draw all creatures "back again to their origins, which is repose." Thus God seeks "his own repose in them."

In Lakota ceremonies, and in the ceremonies of other Native American nations, the sacred pipe represents a marriage of heaven and Earth, sky and ground, cosmos and psyche. Smoking it is a sacred act of universal connection. Black Elk explains: "The whole universe was placed in the pipe." The tobacco represents the plant world and Mother Earth, the bowl is made of the clay of the Earth, and the smoke rises to the heavens. The keeper of the pipe prays: "O *Wakan-Tanka*, behold the pipe! The smoke from this herb will cover everything upon the earth, and will reach even to the heavens.... You have taught us that the round bowl of the pipe is the very center of the universe and the heart of man!... There is a place in this pipe for You, and for all Your sacred things and peoples! All together as one we send our voice to *Wakan-Tanka*." God and all creation come together in the pipe.

In the ancient days of nomadic living, the keeper of the fire was a very important person, as he was assigned to keep the fire going by carrying the fire in a log as the tribe moved. Here, too, the sacred pipe also carries a profound statement about the fire of the human heart, or what Eckhart calls the "spark of the soul" or "the Holy Spirit" that burns in the depths of all souls.

Black Elk says the pipe's stem symbolizes the walking of one's spirit path: "Running through the stem of the pipe there is a little hole leading straight to the center and heart of the pipe; let your minds be as straight as this Way." Is this like Jesus telling about entering the "narrow gate" to the Kingdom of God?

Almost certainly, the Lakota sundance is that narrow gate.

Experiencing the Sundance Firsthand

It has been my privilege over the years to pray and undergo sacred ceremonies with Native American peoples, most often with the Lakota. Buck Ghosthorse, a profound spiritual leader among the Lakota people, had dreams for years instructing him to work with white people, and one day he and his wife showed up at my Institute of Culture and Creation Spirituality at Holy Names College, asking to teach with us. They stayed for three rich years, holding sweat lodges on campus regularly for our students, staff, and faculty as well as teaching classes on the Red Way. Then they moved on to Goldendale, Washington, where they had a flourishing spiritual community and conducted sweats and sundances regularly. Before he left Oakland, Buck gifted me with a great gift: the sacred pipe with which he had prayed for twenty-five years.

During the time I was silenced by the Vatican, my first act was to go to his place in the mountains near Seattle to undergo a vision quest. It was a powerful and memorable experience, which I wrote about in some detail, with Buck's permission, in my autobiography. I have also been blessed to attend sundances on several occasions, and on the most recent occasion, I even joined in the dance. Buck has since passed on, but his community thrives thanks to his two sons and his wife and extended family, who carry on the sundances and ceremonies.

The sundance came about, according to Black Elk, from Kablaya, the young man with the vision for this dance, who explained to the elders: "Long ago *Wakan-Tanka* told us how to pray with the sacred pipe, but we have now become lax in our prayers, and our people are losing their strength. But I have just been shown, in a vision, a new way of prayer; in this manner *Wakan-Tanka* has sent aid to us."

At the modern sundance where I was invited to join the dancer, wearing a long, pink skirt and blowing an eagle whistle, I had a striking experience in which my Christian roots and my native roots (everyone imbibes Native American spirits on the land that they have long inhabited) came crashing together. In some sense, it's this same experience I'm trying to evoke in this book: the convergence of complementary spiritual paths in a single lived experience.

The sundance is conducted in a circle, in the center of which stands the tree, represented by a pole, which Kablaya spoke of this way: "One of the standing people has been chosen to be at our center; he is the *wagachun* (the rustling tree, or cottonwood); he will be our center and also the people, for the tree represented the way of the people. Does it not stretch from the earth here to heaven there?"

For me, the sundance pole, which for the Lakota represents the axis mundi, the tree at the center of the world, was clearly also a cross, for it was a sacred center of sacrifice "that the people may live." That is how Black Elk put it when he wrote of the "brave dancer" who dares to offer him- or herself "as a sacrifice" and who prays, "O *Wakan-Tanka*, be merciful to me. I do this that my people may live."

As we danced around the tree, singing and praying, chanting and being supported by those in the circle surrounding the sundancers, surrendering to the moment, the sun glowed very white, and it stood above the sacred tree. Black Elk says about the sun: "As you know, the moon comes and goes, but *anpetu fi*, the sun, lives on forever; it is the source of light and because of this it is like *Wakan-Tanka*." As we danced, I saw this great marriage, for the brightly lit white sun was a *host*, what Catholics call the "blessed sacrament," which is the sacred host of the Eucharist, the cosmic bread of the Cosmic Christ. They came together in this Native American ritual for me in an unforgettable way, the pole of the native sacrifice and the cross of Jesus's sacrifice and the host of Jesus's last supper, round and white like the sun, the food of the universe.

Part of the power of a sundance is the singing and drumming circle surrounding the dancers. This creates the first-chakra connection to the Earth by way of beat and invokes the ancient shamanistic practice of chanting and dancing. Black Elk says that the drum is "especially sacred and important to us. It is because the round form of the drum represents the whole universe and its steady, strong beat is the pulse, the heart, throbbing at the center of the universe. It is as the voice of *Wakan-Tanka*, and this sound stirs us and helps us to understand the mystery and power of all things."

Before and after this sacred rite at the sundance, I participated in sweats along with other sundancers. In one of them, my spiritual director of fourteen years, my dog Tristan, who had died three years previously, appeared to me. In the second, my father, who had been deceased for ten years, appeared to me amid the hot and fiery stones that form the center point, one might say the altar, of the sweat lodge. Black Elk teaches this about the sweat lodge: "The fire which is used to heat the rocks represents the great power of *Wakan-Tanka* which gives life to all things; it is as a ray from the sun, for the sun is also *Wakan-Tanka* in a certain aspect.... The round fireplace at the center of the sweat lodge is the center of the universe, in which dwells *Wakan-Tanka*, with His power which is the fire." Psyche and cosmos come together in such a ritual, as indeed they need to in all rituals worthy of the name. Black Elk shares the following prayer, which is said in a sweat lodge: "O *Wakan-Tanka*, this is Your eternal fire that has been given to us on this great island! It is Your will that we build this place in a sacred manner. The eternal fire always burns; through it we shall live again by being made pure, and by coming closer to Your powers."

Here, again, we have a symbol of the shamanic "mind on fire," which sounds very much like Eckhart's talk of the light within that "burns incessantly." Whether, or in what way, the sundancer experiences a spirit journey — or experiences Eckhart's "breakthrough" by encountering the "spark of the soul" — upon leaving a sweat lodge one feels refreshed in the deepest of ways; one feels one has tasted wisdom. Black Elk puts it this way: "The most sacred rite has now been finished, and those who have participated are as men born again, and have done much good not only for themselves, but for the whole nation.... We, too, leave behind in the *Inipi* lodge all that is impure, that we may live as the Great Spirit wishes, and that we may know something of that real world of the Spirit, which is behind this one."

The aim, then, is to be born again by the meeting of cosmos and psyche in the individual. This is what the sacred rites among the Lakota people, the sweat lodge and the sundance and the drum, *all* invoke. There lies their healing power, and there lies their power to expand the soul, to move beyond the quotidian burdens of everyday life — what Eckhart calls "time and space" — that most interfere with Spirit. We might even reach what Black Elk calls "that real world of the Spirit, which is behind this one."

Shamanism is not dead. It is returning. Many are feeling the call, the vocation, in our times. It undergoes new life through the wisdom of indigenous peoples from Australia to North America and beyond, from Eddie Kneebone to Black Elk, from Bill Everson to Thomas Berry. With its depth and its descent into the deep, it holds the energy to arm us with a warrior-hood that addresses the issues that threaten the sustainability of our species and the very planet. It calls us to resacralize our existence on the Earth. As an archetype, it represents what Jungian teacher Steven Herrmann calls "one of the first symbols of the Self," an ancient symbol of wholeness. As Joan Halifax puts it, "At that moment when the shaman song emerges, when the sacred breath rises up from the depths of the heart, the center is found, and the source of all that is divine has been tapped."

There is little doubt that Meister Eckhart assists us in finding our center and tapping into the divine and in exploring the Self and, therefore, in singing our shamanic song anew.

CHAPTER TWELVE

WARRIORS FOR ECOLOGICAL AND ECONOMIC JUSTICE

Meister Eckhart Meets Dorothy Stang, Karl Marx, David Korten, Serge Latouche, Anita Roddick, and Howard Thurman

*The person who understands what I say about justice
and the just person understands everything I have to say.*

— MEISTER ECKHART

*The old economy of greed and domination is dying. A new economy of life
and partnership is struggling to be born. The outcome is ours to choose.*

— DAVID KORTEN

*Why not improve life for the world's poorest first?
Is it so impossible to move business from private greed to public good?*

— ANITA RODDICK

*Christianity as it was born in the mind of this Jewish teacher and thinker
[Jesus] appears as a technique of survival for the oppressed.*

— HOWARD THURMAN

When Eckhart declares that justice is at the heart of his spirituality, he means it. Why else would he say, "The person who understands what I say about justice and the just person understands everything I have to say"?

After all, he, like Jesus and the Buddha, calls us to compassion, and then he declares: "compassion is the same as justice." Studying Eckhart's spirituality — as we have done so far through the varied lenses of other thinkers and spiritual traditions — does not suffice. Eckhart did not pursue spirituality in an armchair. He did not speak from a safe and comfortable position of tenure in an academic ivory tower. In fact, as we have seen, he abandoned academia in Paris to work among the people in Germany and elsewhere.

Eckhart engaged the world of his time and sought to translate his spiritual experience of compassion into action. Like his master, Jesus, he was, one might say today, a "sacred activist," or a mystic-prophet, or a mystic-warrior. He urges us to be the same. The stakes today are high and involve the very survival of our planet as we know it, as well as the survival of our species, and Meister Eckhart's words speak loudly to principal issues of our time. If all Jesus or Eckhart had sought to teach was finding "personal peace," would Jesus have been crucified or Eckhart hounded by the Inquisition and condemned? Of course not. They were, in fact, disturbing *the peace* — in Jesus's case the pseudo-peace of an empire that oppressed others, and in Eckhart's case the pseudo-peace of an ecclesial, patriarchal powerhouse that was dangerously closed in on itself.

We face similar choices today. We live in a time when the Earth and her ecosystems are being destroyed in the name of multinational imperialism. We are gripped by an anthropocentric narcissism, a species closed in on itself. A recent political cartoon captured this succinctly. It showed the earth blowing up with a heading: "We found 715 other planets and only lost one." At the bottom, a further comment reads, "except you can't get there from here." This is the reality in which we find ourselves today.

Our era is not a time for business as usual, for politics or economics as usual, for religion as usual. Modern-day prophets are calling us to "wake up" and face today's evils. In this and the next chapter, I will present a range of activists, thinkers, warriors, and prophets who speak to the principal, and often interrelated, issues of ecological, economic, and educational justice. In this chapter, we will hear, in particular, from Dorothy Stang on ecological justice and from the diverse thinkers Karl Marx, David Korten, Serge Latouche, Anita Roddick, and Howard Thurman on the related strands of economic and social justice. Along with Adrienne Rich, Dorothee Soelle, and the other female mystics we discussed in chapters four and five — which lay out a framework for Eckhart's approach to gender justice — all these people show us how heeding Meister Eckhart could transform our world, here and now.

Eckhart's Call to Compassion and Justice

We have seen how important compassion is to Meister Eckhart's spirituality. In addition to the sermons we have considered, he devotes a long and substantive Latin treatise to an exegesis of Jesus's words (Luke 6:36): "Be you compassionate as your Creator in heaven is compassionate." He recognizes compassion as being the presence of God in us, for "compassion divinely adorns the soul, clothing it in the robe which is proper to God." He cites St. Gregory, who says, "It is proper to God to be compassionate."

Meister Eckhart writes extensively and profoundly about justice and compassion, and he defines compassion as "justice" on a number of occasions. For him, "compassion means justice." Elsewhere he writes, "What is compassion is also justice," and Jesus is the "Son of Justice" and "unbegotten justice itself," for God is "*Justissumus,*" the Most Just One. There is a kind of continuous, ongoing process of justice. "The just man is always in process of being born from justice itself." It is never completed. Eckhart likes to cite Psalm 85:10: "Justice and peace have kissed" — that is his definition of compassion. Compassion is the "robe of Divinity" we are all called to wear because we are all called to our divinity. Eckhart also often cites a passage from John's epistle (1 John 4:16, 17): "Anyone who lives in love lives in God, and God lives in him.... Even in this world we have become as he is."

In this respect he is simply echoing the deep teaching of the prophets of the Jewish tradition. Eckhart writes, "We read in Proverbs 21 that those who follow compassion find life and justice and glory. Life pertains...to oneself; justice pertains...to the neighbor; and glory pertains...to God." Justice heals, and a healing life, he says, is a "living life," for Isaiah (58) says: "Your healing will spring up speedily and justice will go before your face and the glory of the Lord will surround you." As applied to one's neighbor, "compassion is just to the extent that it gives each one what is his." Eckhart cites

St. Isidore of Seville (c. 560–636), who wrote: "It is a great crime to give the wages of the poor to the rich and from the livelihood of the poor to increase the luxuriates of the powerful taking water for the needy earth and pouring it into the rivers." Eckhart cites Ecclesiasticus: "Having compassion toward your own soul, you are pleasing to God." He responds: "How then can anyone be compassionate toward me or toward you who is not compassionate toward himself? [Jesus] want us to be compassionate even to our own body and soul."

Since compassion incorporates justice, it also requires both left- and right-brain thinking. Justice requires judgment as well as intuition. Eckhart says: "We therefore are compassionate like the Father when we are compassionate, not from passion, not from impulse, but from deliberate choice and reasonable decision. For Psalm 84 says: 'Compassion and truth meet one another' — that is passion and reason. And again in Psalm 32: 'He loves compassion and judgment.'... The passion does not take the lead but follows, does not rule but serves." Clearly, by incorporating knowledge and intuition, Eckhart challenges us to use all our faculties in extending compassion. "We should be very much on the alert lest the force of passion dominate our actions." We must corral our emotions, not let them run free. "Those whom passion dominates are very much like horses. It is against this that it is said in Psalm 32:9: 'Don't be like the horse and mule.'"

In this treatise Eckhart several times refers to Isaiah 58, where the teachings of the "Works of Compassion" are laid out by the prophet. Isaiah complains about businesspeople who "oppress all your workmen" and "strike the poor man with your fist" but still carry on their religious fasting. "Is that the sort of fast that pleases me, a truly penitential day for men?" Certainly not. Isaiah says: "Is not this the sort of fast that pleases me — it is the Lord Yahweh who speaks — to break unjust fetters and undo the thongs of the yoke, to let the oppressed go free and break every yoke, to share your bread with the hungry, and shelter the homeless poor, to clothe the man you see to be naked and not turn away from your own kin?...If you do away with the yoke, the clenched fist, the wicked word, if you give your bread to the hungry and relief to the oppressed, your light will rise in the darkness....Yahweh will always guide you, giving you relief in desert places" (Isaiah 58:6–10). Here lie the roots of Eckhart's justice-centered passion for compassion.

Eckhart also invokes Psalm 21, which is a hymn to the royal person, and the royal person is responsible for justice (Psalm 21:3, 15, 21): "To act virtuously and with justice is more pleasing to Yahweh than sacrifice.... For the virtuous person it is a joy to execute justice, but it brings dismay to evildoers.... He who pursues virtue and compassion shall find life, justice, and honor."

Clearly, for Eckhart, compassion is based not on feeling sorry for others and not on taking pity (or mercy) on another. It involves an awareness of our shared interdependence and our obligation to assist one another. Says Eckhart: "God's peace prompts fraternal service, so that one creature sustains the other. One is enriching the other, that is why all creatures are interdependent." This echoes Thomas Merton's final teaching — delivered a few hours before he died — in a lecture entitled "Karl Marx and Monasticism," when he defined compassion as a "keen awareness of the interdependence of all living beings which are all part of one another and all involved in one another." Or as poet Angelus Silesius would put it in the seventeenth century: "There are no objects of compassion because there are no objects." This is the teaching of contemporary, postmodern science as well. All is interdependent. Thus no objects, only subjects interrelating.

Justice Transforms through Action

Eckhart preaches a sermon rich and challenging all about justice. He bases it on a line from the Book of Wisdom (5:16), "The just will live forever and their reward is with the Lord," which he exegetes this way:

> The just person is one who is conformed and transformed into justice. The just person lives in God and God in him. Thus God will be born in this just person and the just person is born into God; and therefore God will be born through every virtue of the just person and will rejoice through every virtue of the just person. And not only at every virtue will God rejoice but especially at every work of the just person however small it is. When this work is done through justice and results in justice, God will rejoice at it, indeed, God will rejoice through and through; for nothing remains in His ground which does not tickle Him through and through out of joy.

This is just the opening paragraph of the sermon! I once was giving a retreat on Eckhart in Toronto, and a priest who had been working in the slums of Toronto nonstop for nine years spoke up. He said: "I would like nothing more than to take a six-month retreat to meditate on just that one line you cited from Eckhart: 'For the just person as such to act justly is to live; indeed, justice is her life, her being alive, her being, insofar as she is just.'" Yes, when we commit to justice it very often becomes our life, our being alive, our very being. That is why people risk death for the sake of justice; one cannot be alive without it. This willingness to risk all personally for the sake of justice for others defines our social heroes: Dr. Martin Luther King Jr., Malcolm X, and others in the civil rights movement, Mahatma Gandhi, Nelson Mandela, Oscar Romero, Sister Dorothy Stang, and many others. There is something about justice that both makes God "rejoice and be tickled" and makes humans generous and brave. Justice is something worth fighting for and dying for. Justice takes us to the edge of daring and risk, and God to the edge of joy and laughter.

Eckhart stresses that when we work for justice we work "without a why" — our efforts should not be undertaken for the specific desired results alone. Our intention to see justice done is also important, as is our giving and sacrifice and our focus on community. Compassion in action is God's work, so it is deeper than any human judgment about success or failure. We work in order to work, and we do justice in order to do justice; let the chips fall where they may. Eckhart elaborates on this, saying there are dead works and there are living works, and we must go through the letting go of the via negativa before our works come to life: "For all works are surely dead if anything from the outside compels you to work.... Even if you take God as your goal, all such works which you do with this intention are dead and you will spoil good works." Rather, we are to "first make contact with this nothingness" and work out of our nothingness. "Enter into your own ground and work there and these works which you work there will all be living. And therefore the wise person says: 'The just person lives.' For because he is just, he works and his works live."

Furthermore, such works are the birthing of the Christ into the world. "The Father gives birth to his Son as the Just One and the Just One as his Son; for all virtue of the just and every work of the just which are born from the virtue of the just person are nothing other than the event of the Son being born from the Father [who] always runs and hurries in order that the Son be born in me, as the Scriptures say: 'For Zion's sake I will not hold my peace and for Jerusalem's sake I will not rest, until the just are revealed and shine forth like a flash of lightning' (Is. 62:1)." Our works come from our deepest place within — that is where the Son is born and Justice is born. "If your works are to live, then God must move you inwardly, in the innermost part of the soul, if they are really to live. There is your life and there alone you live."

The passion of these truly brilliant teachings from Meister Eckhart is evident. They deserve to be put in poetic form, as they contain the impact and force of poetry. They bore into our minds and hearts, into our consciousness, where, hopefully, they give birth to action. That is what Eckhart sought: he wanted to move people to action, and to actions that are nothing less than the son of justice being born in all of us, the Christ being born in us all, the Christ of Compassion that Isaiah was calling for. After all, Eckhart says, "God and justice are one."

Ecology: Justice toward Earth

Eckhart's sermons and teachings about justice and compassion contain a clear imperative: We are here to *do* compassion, not just meditate on it. We are meant not only to understand justice but to accomplish it. One area that confronts us today and calls for action is ecology.

In chapter two we considered the teaching of Thomas Berry, who is clearly an ecological prophet for our time. What he calls the "Great Work" is a clarion call for all of us to revise how we see the world — to see it anew, not in human terms alone, but in the context of everything the Earth offers and everything the cosmos that birthed and nurtures the Earth offers. He writes: "In relation to the earth, we have been autistic for centuries. Only now have we begun to listen with some attention and with a willingness to respond to the earth's demands that we cease our industrial assault, that we abandon our inner rage against the conditions of our earthly existence, that we renew our human participation in the grand liturgy of the universe." He says we can no longer trust our "cultural resources" but must create a new culture. "In this context a completely new type of creativity is needed. This creativity must have as its primary concern the survival of the earth in its functional integrity." This goal, be believes, can "bring the nations of the world into an international community."

One person whose life and death speaks to such a commitment to eco-justice and reinvention of culture in our time is the late Catholic sister Dorothy Stang. "Dot," as she was known, lived and worked among the peasant farmers of the Amazon trying to defend their land and the rain forest from the waste and pillage of powerful industrial forces, which were bent on seizing the land and abusing the forest. For her dedication to defending those who loved and lived on the land, she was murdered by assassins hired by powerful landowners. She died a martyr on the land she defended. As I write this book, Dot's book on Hildegard of Bingen, which was marked up by her and found at her bedside in the Amazon, sits in my office not ten feet from my computer. Hildegard taught that "the earth must not be injured, the earth must not be destroyed." Dot's book was gifted to me recently by her brother, and attached to it is blood-stained dirt from where she lay dying on her beloved earth. Dot had studied Thomas Berry and Meister Eckhart and Hildegard of Bingen in our University in Creation Spirituality a few years before she returned to Brazil and died there.

Dot knew that her life was in danger. She had become something of a leader in a very dangerous area. But she refused to leave. She said: "I don't want to flee, nor do I want to abandon the battle of these farmers who live without any protection in the forest. They have the sacrosanct right to aspire to a better life on land where they can live and work with dignity while respecting the environment." At her funeral, held in the jungle where she is now buried, one peasant said: "We are not burying you, Sister Dorothy. We are planting you." People around the world who have heard of Dot's generous witness "are keeping her memory alive by lobbying for land reform, for social justice, for simpler and fairer ways of living, for better care of our planet," says her biographer, Binka Le Breton. Dot is a model of courage and commitment to eco-justice and social justice.

Whether you call what is currently happening "climate change," "global warming," or "an extinction spasm unparalleled in the last sixty million years" — the truth is that our planet is undergoing a profound upheaval.

Why do I say this? Among other evidence, we know that the ice caps are melting at both the North and South Poles, sea levels are rising, giant storms and hurricanes are increasing, deserts are expanding, crops are failing, soil is being swept away by erosion and floods, one out of four animal species is at risk of going extinct, seventeen of the nineteen ocean fisheries are essentially fished out, bees are disappearing, and more. As I was writing this, a news story was published about how the Earth is losing 300 billion tons of ice each year. A ten-year study at Bristol University's Glaciology Centre found that two massive ice sheets in Greenland and Antarctica contain 99.5 percent of the Earth's glacier ices. The author wrote that along Antarctica's coast you can actually see "hints of grass and other plant life — green evidence that in part of the long-frozen continent the ice is thinning, and fast." Ice sheets in Antarctica have melted faster in the past twenty years than in the last ten thousand years, and "even conservative scientists say sea levels are rising 60 percent faster than what the Intergovernmental Panel on Climate Change predicted in 2007."

We are living in a cataclysmic, even apocalyptic moment, and part of the pathology of our time is that these facts are often downplayed or ignored. By this I don't mean that we should focus on only this devastating problem 24/7. A big story like this, a truly global problem, is hard to tell and hard to listen to — but that does not mean we should fail to face the truth. The truth can be difficult to conceptualize, and one could just freeze or go into a depressed state on hearing it.

Of course, corporations also resist telling this story. They encourage us to ignore it because they are invested in the way things are. To change on the level required to solve this impending global catastrophe means significant change by everyone in almost every way: personally, politically, economically, and so on. Those invested in the current system do not want to sound the alarm by telling the truth, since everything would change. Yet this entire book with its rich teachings from Meister Eckhart alerts us to our responsibility and our nobility as a species — to dwell on mysticism is to dwell on empowerment. Contrary to the myths of the dominant and illusory culture, we are all empowered to do something about the many economic and ecological injustices that are threatening our very survival.

Humans are very capable of practicing *denial* in the face of unwanted realities. Denial can get us through the day, the month, the year, or even a lifetime. Denial makes things easier; in denial we create our own world. But it is a dangerous world. Not only does it ignore what we know to be true, but this willful refusal is harmful to others, especially generations to come. It perpetuates injustice. Compassion does not happen in a state of denial. Eckhart says very bluntly: "God is the denial of denial." In other words, to live in denial is to abandon any God presence in our lives. To deny denial is to let Divinity flow again. One cannot live in denial and be in any way spiritual.

Thomas Aquinas taught that for humans to be ignorant of something we ought to know about is a "mortal" or deadly sin, the sin of chosen ignorance. That is what denial is: a refusal to face the truth, a choice to remain ignorant. The Internet and its wealth of information can work to our favor and cut through denial. On the other hand, denial can be so strong a worldview that even the Internet cannot change it, since almost by definition denial exists despite evidence to the contrary. There is less and less excuse to remain ignorant of important things.

Fortunately, when it comes to climate change, not everyone is in denial, particularly younger people. Nor are younger people running from spirituality that grounds itself in both personal and societal transformation. My recent book *Occupy Spirituality* — written with Adam Bucko, leader of the Reciprocity Foundation, which is devoted to helping young adults living on the streets of New York — published interviews with many young people around America and found that a very high percentage are eager for a spirituality that combines action and contemplation. Of course, many young people have less of an investment in politics and economics as currently practiced. As one leader of the Occupy Movement in Oakland put it, "It is time for the spiritual people to get active and the activist to get spiritual so that we can have a total revolution of the human spirit.... We need to combine this inner revolution with the outer revolution to have the total revolution of the spirit."

A 2013 bipartisan study conducted by the League of Conservation Voters found that 66 percent of young independent voters, ages eighteen to thirty-four, "accept as dogma that man and his dirty deeds are causing, and will continue to cause, climate change." Seventy-four percent of Independents and 53 percent of Republicans used the words "ignorant, out of touch, or crazy" to describe climate deniers. Only 26 percent of those polled bought into the argument that action in climate change would "kill jobs" (which is the mainstay argument of those who want to do nothing), while 65 percent felt that action on climate change would create jobs. Comments the author: "Say what you will about us millennials — we're a wilting bouquet of narcissistic, socialistic, overeducated, underemployed, tatted-up hipsters who still live at home — but, from this day forward, don't you dare say we're climate change deniers."

The truth of ecological devastation will not go away; it stares us in the face daily. How can Eckhart help? Eckhart helps in many ways. He helps by showing us ways out of denial, such as meditation and letting go and facing nothingness. He helps because he calls for the warrior-prophet in us all to stand up and be willing to "interfere" and tell the truth and to work with others creating allies. He helps because he instructs us to fall in love with Earth and life and existence and to seek a God of creation and justice, a "God of life."

Eckhart's God is a God fully present in nature and thus suffering when nature suffers. Eckhart assists us when he pushes us to be creative, to use our fertile imaginations, to reinvent things — from language to religion to education to energy to economics. Who is holding us back but ourselves? We are all born for creativity, to birth not only the Christ but the Christ who is "justice itself," the Christ of the polar bear or the rain forest or the whale or the redwoods — all threatened with extinction. The Christ being crucified all over again by an empire different from the Roman Empire of Jesus's time, but an empire nonetheless. An empire of financial speculators who appeal to greed to satisfy their own greed, an empire of consumer capitalism that takes no prisoners, that rapes Main Street, then borrows from Main Street, and then goes back to abusing Main Street again. Eckhart helps because he tells us to take seriously our experiences of beauty and awe and wonder and not to fall asleep but to wake up when beauty and health are endangered.

Overturning an Economy of Greed

I propose that the driving forces behind consumer capitalism are greed and avarice and envy. Greed or avarice is what consumer capitalism is built on, and neither is healthy for our happiness or for justice, because both easily become addictions; one never has "enough," and this automatically leaves others out of the picture. They appeal to individualism but not to the common good, not to what will work for everyone.

As consumers, we are deluged with media advertising 24/7, which relentlessly repeats the mantra to buy, buy, buy — to act on greed: "*I want more! I've got to have the latest style, the latest car, the latest refrigerator! Enough is never enough!*" That message is presented in very sophisticated ways; it looks slick and attractive and is conjured up in ads that are designed to seduce us. To live a balanced life, a spiritual life, a life of justice, we have to resist that message. We have to simplify our lives, not indulge. "The soul grows by subtraction, not by addition," teaches Eckhart. Consumer capitalism is all about addition. It is all about "more." It is outer directed, not inner directed.

If one end of the game is consumption, the other is investing — making money by gaming the capitalist system. Wall Street is the "buying" end, and it is just as much driven by greed and envy as consumption. Of course, capitalism is not in itself evil, but, like anything humans do, it has a huge shadow, and the shadow can swallow us up. Capitalism does not serve us today; we serve it, without realizing the spiritual price we are paying. Our economy has to evolve differently today if we are to survive as a species.

No religion has ever proposed that avarice is healthy. Avarice is not good for the soul, for children, for society, or for the planet. It makes madmen of adults. Avarice is the ultimate addiction. Yet we honor it! We rationalize our economic system and justify its abuses. We glorify as heroes those who can make the most money, even when those riches have been gathered at the expense of the greater good, or at the expense of our own welfare. Our only choice, even though the deck is stacked against us, seems to be to try to play the game everyone's playing and get what we can for ourselves.

This is how self-interest comes to drive our lives even when we understand that compassion is the opposite. How do we break this cycle and this trap? We have to resist. We have to scream if necessary. Were Jesus here today, I think he would be screaming!

He would also act. He would try to wake people up to how, by playing along, they are undermining their own lives. In chapter six, I told the story of Jesus driving the moneylenders from the Temple in Jerusalem. He did not do this alone. Bruce Chilton believes that Jesus organized a whole team of two hundred people to go into the Temple and turn over the tables of the moneylenders. This was a team effort, an *action*, that upended the status quo and was intended to wake the people up. Flipping tables is not going to over-turn an economy of greed, but convincing people not to play along with that economy certainly can.

Eckhart also screamed in his day; he saw a growing gap between rich and poor, and he took action. He stood up to what he called the "merchant mentality" of his day, a mentality that he felt is so damaging to the soul that it bleeds into everything else we do and value. His sermon is based on Matthew 21:12: "Jesus then went into the temple and drove out all those who were selling and buying there." In his sermon, Eckhart tells us that the "tem-ple" is "the soul of a person"; he confirms that the first economic revolution has to occur inside ourselves. "For this reason God wishes the temple to be empty so that nothing can be in it but himself alone." If our inner life is already full with buying and selling, then there is no space for God. "Now listen to me closely! I shall preach now without exception only about good people. Nevertheless, I shall at this time show who the merchants were then and still are today — those who were buying and selling then, and are still doing so, the ones our Lord whipped and drove out of the temples."

Eckhart says that the religious people who fast, hold vigils, pray, and do similar good deeds in order that God "give them something....All these people are merchants." They are "bargaining" with God. They forget that "whatever they are, they owe to God, and whatever they have they have from God and not from themselves. Therefore, God is not at all in debt to them....They achieve nothing by themselves. As Christ himself says: 'Without me you can do nothing' (Jn. 15:5)." The bottom line is that "truth does not long for any kind of commercial deal. God does not seek his own interest. In all his deeds he is unencumbered and free, and accomplishes them out of genuine love. The person united with God behaves in the same way." That is why living and loving and working without a why or wherefore are so important.

In this context, it means working without profit as the sole motive. It means contributing to the common good. God upholds the soul in its noth-ingness. "God places himself with his uncreatedness beneath the soul's nothingness and upholds the soul in his substance. The soul has dared to come to nothing, and cannot with its own power come back to itself again — so far has the soul left itself before God places himself beneath the soul." A silence takes over the soul and Jesus speaks: "What does the Lord Jesus say? He declares what he is. What then is he? He is the Father's Word." The Cosmic Christ is revealed there, in the dark, in the silence. "At another time Jesus reveals himself within the soul with the immeasurable wisdom that is himself — the same wisdom" that the Father knows. The soul then "is brought into a pure, clear light, which is God himself....For God becomes known to God in the soul. Then the soul knows itself and all things with the same wisdom."

Eckhart is talking about filling our minds and souls with real treasure. He is talking about mindfulness. Mindfulness cannot happen if we are not empty, if we are filled with projects and projections. We need time and space for emptying, for being, for living and working without a why.

I feel that the Occupy Movement has been an effort to turn things upside down and wake people up today. The younger generation is not buying into the propaganda of Wall Street and the corporate-owned media. Pancho Ramos-Stierle is a member of Occupy Oakland who has written eloquently of his generation's resistance. He has also practiced eloquently, offering non-violent resistance even when carried away by police. Ramos-Stierle writes that modern poverty "boasts two kinds of slaves: the intoxicated — the prisoner to the addiction of consumption, and those who aspire to get intoxicated — the prisoner of envy." What does the Occupy Movement mean to him? "We are the early adopters of a revolution in values, and we are the evidence that the totalitarianism of corporate capitalism, the machine that has devastated the planet and human beings — we are the demonstration that the system doesn't work and that we need a new system."

Nathan Schneider is a journalist who early on lived among the Occupy Wall Street crowd in Zuccotti Park in New York City. In a fine book commenting on the experience, he makes many points apropos to what Eckhart teaches about living lives of justice. He writes, "In the rupture of the ordinary that characterized those early days, everything felt in some sense religious, charged with a secret extremity and transcendence — secret, because the rest of the world hadn't yet become aware of what was happening down at Liberty Square. Whenever I came back to Liberty after some time away, there was a feeling of entering sacred ground." He reports on Muslim Occupiers on their knees praying in Mecca's direction five times a day; on a speech in which the message was "Occupy your heart not with fear but with love!" Schneider is not romanticizing the movement — he sees its morphing into many other directions. But he honors its dream of a better social order and its ability to seize the moral imagination of thousands — "particularly those in my young and unsettled generation, discovering better parts of themselves than they'd known before, claiming a politics more of their own making and driven by their formidable creativity." He offers the following wise observation: "Protest movements can and do change the world, though it takes time and never happens quite the way anyone expects."

Karl Marx: Socialism and Meister Eckhart

Philosopher Ernst Bloch has credited Meister Eckhart with influencing the thinking of the German philosopher Karl Marx (1818–1883). Today, of course, Marx is out of favor, particularly in the West, where capitalism for capitalism's sake dominates. But Marx's passion for economic justice was at base born of the spiritual values that lie at the heart of biblical teachings. As psychologist Otto Rank noted, Marxism appealed to the poorest of the poor because it offered hope to the disenfranchised.

Marx's socialist critique and ideas influenced labor and politics across the globe, including in the United States. However, his ideas were sometimes appropriated by others and made to serve dictatorial, totalitarian regimes, such as by Lenin, Stalin, and the Soviet empire. It's important to note that Communism as it was realized in the Soviet Union was not Marxism as Karl Marx conceived it. Instead, Marx critiqued what he saw as the inherently divisive and exploitative nature of capitalism, which led to an entrenched, self-reinforcing class structure. This was antithetical to a compassionate society, and he felt it would inevitably lead to violent conflict between rich and poor.

How did Meister Eckhart influence Marx to develop these ideas? Bloch, who was an expert on Marx, says that Eckhart's teaching did not serve "the ruling class," and "in Eckhart the heretical, antiecclesiastical lay movement of the late Middle Ages became articulate in German, which is a decisive factor in any socialist evaluation." Eckhart scholar Reiner Schurmann agrees with Bloch. Schurmann says Eckhart's theology provides a "mysticism of the left [that] would designate the appropriation by man of his authentic good when he is alienated by the dogma of an inaccessible heaven." Eckhart's teaching, like Jesus's, was about this world primarily. Eckhart warns: "If I am a rich man, that does not make me wise. But if I am transformed and conformed to the essence and nature of wisdom and become wisdom itself, then I am a wise man." Eckhart criticizes the "merchant mentality" for the consciousness it creates — an inability to receive, a reducing of things to objects for use, which creates, to use his word, "alienation." We have serious work to do, God's work, and this alienation and distraction and misplacement of consciousness seriously interferes with it. "Just as little as I can do anything without God, He cannot really accomplish anything apart from me."

Eckhart's medicine for the merchant mentality is contained in two words: *Abgeschiedenheit* (a term he created) and *Gelassenheit*. I translate these words as "letting go" and "letting be." Others sometimes translate them as "detachment," "disinterest," "solitude," or "releasement." This letting go applies to God as well — letting God be and things be in order to let experience truly happen. The merchant mentality relates to any conscious grabbing and hoarding, possessing and clinging, to any compulsive having, be it related to religion, politics, economics, or privilege.

Eckhart's preaching that "everyone is an aristocrat" elevates the poorest of the poor to their own nobility. "How nobly humans are constituted by nature," he says, "and how divine is the state to which he can come by grace." We are all born of such nobility, just as the prophet talks about the "great eagle" (the words *eagle* and *noble* are closely akin in German). "Who then is nobler than he who is born, on one hand of the highest and the best that the creature has, and on the other hand from the inmost ground of the divine nature and of His desert?" By continually defining redemption as "divinization" (as the non-Augustinian Eastern Christian tradition does), Eckhart presents the political implications of an original-blessing (as opposed to Augustine's original-sin) theology. "How should man know that he knows God, if he does not know himself? For certainly this man does not know himself or other things in the least, but God alone, when he becomes blessed and is blessed in the root and the ground of blessedness."

The political implications of this spiritual attitude are partly what inspired Marx to suggest, with socialism, that every worker is equal, and should be treated equally and receive a fair share of the wealth his or her labor creates. It was especially the radical Protestants of the sixteenth century, Hans Hutt, Sebastian Franck, and Hans Denck, who picked up on Eckhart's teaching of "every creature as a word of God" and found this teaching to strongly support the peasant movements of their day. For if every creature is a word of God, truth does not lie exclusively with the academic elites or the literate ones. Or, as Bloch was moved to say:

> One thing is certain: Eckhart's sermon does not intend to snuff man out for the sake of an Otherworld beyond him:...The revolutionary Anabaptists, those disciples of Eckhart and Tauler, showed afterwards in practice exactly how highly and how uncomfortably for every tyrant. *A subject who thought himself to be in personal union with the Lord of Lords provided, when things got serious, a very poor example indeed of serfhood.*

David Korten: A Just Economic System

Economic prophets like David Korten are also standing up, speaking out, and working hard for an alternative economics such as Eckhart calls for, one that puts justice and community before the private gain of a few. Korten is well qualified to speak on the subject of economic justice. Currently president of the People-Centered Development Forum, chair of the board of *YES!* magazine, a board member of the Business Alliance for Local Living Economies, and cochair of the New Economy Working Group, Korten taught economics at Harvard Business School as well as working abroad and learning the results of monetary practice in third-world countries up close and personal.

To overview his perspective and concerns, one might begin by meditating on the titles of some of his books. For instance: *When Corporations Rule the World*. This 2001 book explains how corporations *are* ruling the world and striving to increase their control. They tell nations what to do and not the other way around. In the United States, corporations have powerful allies throughout government, and even on the Supreme Court — whose "Citizens

United" ruling, which held that corporations are "people" under the law, allows corporations to exercise the same rights of free speech, meaning they can spend whatever they want to support politicians and to buy media time. In this way, American democracy has become a corporate oligarchy.

Or consider *The Great Turning: From Empire to Earth Community*. In this visionary work (published in 2007), Korten incorporates the information we now hold about the universe and how our Earth came into being, the new cosmology, into a love of the Earth and its ecosystems, which are so vital to both our spiritual health and our physical survival. Korten goes far beyond "economics as we know it" to place economics within a larger, more authentic context. He learns from ecologists and cosmologists and spiritual leaders like Joanna Macy and Thomas Berry, and he challenges Americans to wake up to what our empire is doing to itself and to others around the world.

Or: *Agenda for a New Economy: From Phantom Wealth to Real Wealth*. Published after the American economic collapse of 2008, it lays out both a philosophy of economics and a practical guide to a new economics, one that could work "for everyone" — not just all humans but all beings on the planet. He wrestles with the authentic theological issues of economics as well, not unlike Eckhart. He faces down the pseudo-values that empires preach in favor of authentic community values, that is, the "common good." Korten writes:

> In the Wall Street economy, money is both means and end, and the primary product is phantom wealth — money disconnected from the production or possession of anything of real value. The Main Street economy is largely engaged in creating real wealth from real resources to meet real needs. Wall Street is very good at making rich people richer, but it has no concern for the health of people, community, or nature except as sources of short-term profit.

He spells out what we have learned from the recent global financial collapse:

> Draw back the curtain, as the credit collapse has done, to reveal the inner workings of Wall Street, and it begins to look less like a legitimate business enterprise and more like a criminal syndicate running a lucrative extortion racket. The nearest equivalent in nature is a cancer that

drains the body's energy but produces nothing useful in return. You don't "fix" a cancer; you excise it and rebuild the healthy tissue. Main Street is the healthy tissue and the foundation of the New Economy.

Working with the New Economy Working Group, coordinated by the Institute for Policy Studies in Washington, DC, Korten offers some history on how we have come to where we are, financially speaking. Their report, called "How to Liberate America from Wall Street Rule," begins with a question: "How is it that our nation is awash in money, but too broke to provide jobs and services?" It continues: "The dominant story of the current political debates is the government is broke. We can't afford to pay for public services, put people to work or service the public debt, yet as a nation, we are awash in money. A defective system of money, banking, and finance just puts it in the wrong places." Instead of imagining that taxing the rich or implementing financial reforms will solve the whole issue, they call for "a deep restructuring of the institutions to which we as a society give the power to create and allocate money." The key is to "rebuild a system of community-based and accountable institutions devoted to financing productive activities that create good jobs for Americans and generate real community wealth."

The report makes clear that over the past thirty years "virtually all the benefit of U.S. economic growth has gone to the richest 1 percent of Americans." Even after the crash of 2008, "the financial assets of America's billionaires and the idle cash of the most profitable corporations are now at historic highs. Their biggest challenge is to figure out where to park all their cash." Few are committed to long-term investment that can put people to work. That is hardly on the radar for those for whom the only "value" is making more money. "The substantial majority of trades in financial markets are made by high-speed computers in securities held for fractions of a second."

After the Great Depression, financial reforms established banking and investment based on community banks, mutual savings and loans, and credit unions, which provided services for local Main Street economies. "This system which Wall Street interests dismiss as quaint and antiquated financed the U.S. victory in Word War II, the creation of a strong American middle class, an unprecedented period of economic stability and prosperity, and the

investments that made America the world's undisputed industrial and tech-
nological leader."

In the 1970s Wall Street interests pushed a deregulation agenda that led
to a transfer of financial power from Main Street to Wall Street. Instead of
investing in businesses, they created a new business model that "now specializes in charging excessive fees and usurious interest rates," provides lever-
age for speculators speculating on their own accounts, entices the unwary
into mortgages they can't afford, bundles junk mortgages and sells them as
triple A securities betting against their very clients, extracts subsidies and
bailouts from government, launders money from drug and arms traders, and
uses offshore accounts for "their profits to avoid taxes." While the middle
class melts away, "Wall Street profited at every step and declared its experiment with deregulation and tax cuts for the wealthy a great success."

Korten believes that our thirty-year "experiment with trickle-down economics that favored the interest of Wall Street speculators over the hard-
working people and business of Main Street has proved it doesn't work."
He calls for a "new economy based on a value-based pragmatism that recognizes a simple truth: If the world is to work for any of us, it must work for
all of us."

The values Korten espouses are "the health and well-being of our children, families, communities, and the natural environment." He says, "Like
a healthy ecosystem, a healthy twenty-first-century economy must have
strong local roots and maximize the beneficial capture, storage, sharing, and
use of local energy, water, and mineral resources. That is what we must seek
to achieve, community by community, all across this nation, by unleashing
the creative energies of our people." These values are very much in line with
those of Meister Eckhart, who warns that no one can love money or gold or
eat it. Gold would kill the heart, he says, if it were inserted in it.

Korten warns that we live currently in a "global suicide economy," which
is "a product of human choices motivated by a love of money. It is within our
means to make different choices motivated by a love of life."

The New Economy Working Group put forth a six-point agenda for
a new economics, which makes clear how we can move out of our current
system that benefits only a few and into a system that works for all beings
and all humans on the planet. This agenda includes breaking up megabanks

in favor of cooperative or for-profits owned by nonprofit foundations; establishing state-owned partnership banks in all states that are patterned after the Bank of North Dakota and serve to fund local farms and businesses; render the Federal Reserve more transparent; direct all new money created by the Federal Reserve to a Federal Recovery and Reconstruction Bank; and more.

Korten calls for moving from the "old economic paradigm worldview," in which "nature is a mere commodity," to the New Development Paradigm: "Earth is the sacred source of life and the natural systems on which all living beings depend are beyond price. It is our sacred responsibility to respect and care for the system in the interest of all living beings for generations to come." He believes this is a moral choice. "The old economy of greed and domination is dying. A new economy of life and partnership is struggling to be born. The outcome is ours to choose."

Korten's discussion of the sacredness of our natural systems and the Earth, and his call to choose to work to give birth to something new and sustainable and to put community ahead of individualism, certainly sounds Eckhartian to me. It embodies for our times what it would mean to drive the sellers and buyers from the temple, so that life might thrive. The call is to put the common good ahead of rugged individualism and to close the crazy gaps between the haves and have-nots. This is a moral imperative, for, as Eckhart says, we all carry "human nature equally."

Serge Latouche and the De-growth Movement

Serge Latouche is a French philosopher and economist who is one of the spokespersons of the "de-growth" movement, which is described as a political, economic, and social movement founded on principles of ecology and anticonsumerism. The movement calls for the downscaling of production and consumption whose excess lies at the root of long-term environmental perils and social inequalities. At the heart of this economic "utopia" or social imagination lies the conviction that de-growth requires not individual martyrdom or a decrease in well-being but a redefinition of well-being — one that maximizes happiness through redefining how we live and work and enjoy life. By consuming less and living a more simple lifestyle, and by working less frantically, we can devote more time to conviviality, relationships, art, music, family, culture, and community. By working less compulsively and fewer hours and consuming and wasting less, we can put more people to work and the planet itself will breathe more easily.

Latouche argues that we need to rethink from the very foundations the idea that our societies should be based on growth (including the GNP as a measure of healthy economics). A society of de-growth is not the same thing as negative growth — it is a rejection of growth and growth for growth's sake as an idol or an economic cult.

He argues that a finite planet can obviously not sustain an infinite quest for growth and that we all pay a price for a "fundamentalist belief in growth," a belief built on greed that imperils the future of humans, other beings, the planet itself, and future generations. He talks of a "serene, convivial and sustainable contraction" that will allow humans to more fully develop their contemplative as well as active souls. He calls for a "virtuous circle" of eight Rs that can bring about this quiet revolution: reevaluate, reconceptualize, restructure, redistribute, relocalize, reduce, reuse, and recycle.

Latouche asks: "Where are we going? We are heading for a crash. We are in a performance car that has no driver, no reverse and no brakes and it is going to slam into the limitations of the planet." Thanks to Rachel Carson, the Club of Rome, the Worldwatch Institute, Al Gore, and others, we are fully aware of what is at stake. But we refrain from asking deeper questions because we live in a bubble, a society "that has been swallowed up by an economy whose only goal is growth for the sake of growth." The machine in which we find ourselves "is based upon excess, and it is leading us into a blind alley," which no vague talk of "sustainable development" can paste over. The very "logic of systematic and dramatic growth (which is driven by finance capital's compulsive addiction to growth) has to be called into question, as does our way of life," even though it raises "taboo subjects." The de-growth movement is gaining steam in France, Italy, Spain, and Belgium. The goal of de-growth "is to build a society in which we can live better lives while working less and consuming less. It is an essential proposition if we are to open up a space for the inventiveness and creativity of the imagination, which has been blocked by economistic, developmentalist and progressive totalitarianism."

Latouche cites economist Kenneth Boulding as one of the "few" economists who recognized the bigger picture when, in 1966, he contrasted what he called the "cowboy economy" of the maximization of consumption and the pillaging of natural resources with a "spaceman economy," in which the Earth is like a single spaceship with limited resources. Boulding concluded that "anyone who believes that exponential growth can go on forever in a finite world is either a madman or an economist."

Latouche identifies three ingredients necessary to a consumer-driven economy: advertising, credit, and products with built-in or planned obsolescence. "Advertising makes us want what we do not have and despise what we already have. It creates and re-creates the dissatisfaction and tension of frustrated desire." A survey of CEOs of big American companies found that 90 percent of them admitted that it would be impossible to sell a new product without an advertising campaign; 85 percent stated that advertising "often" persuaded people to buy things they did not need; and 51 percent said that advertising persuaded people to buy things that they did not really want. Advertising is now the "second biggest budget in the world" — the first being weapons for war. Latouche cites American market analyst Victor Lebow, who as early as 1955 warned of the spiritual dangers of making a drug of consumerism. Said Lebow: "Our enormously productive economy demands that we make consumption our way of life, that we convert the buying and use of goods into rituals, that we seek our spiritual satisfaction, our ego satisfaction, in consumption.... We need things consumed, burned up, replaced and discarded at an ever-accelerating rate." Warns Latouche: "If growth automatically generated well-being, we would now be living in paradise. We are in fact going down the road to hell."

Latouche endorses the "slow food" movements, the "slow city" movements, and the "new commune" movements that are springing up around Europe. He sees in them a "laboratory for critical analysis" of how to put de-growth philosophy into practice.

Like David Korten, he endorses local economies and agriculture wherever possible, and he notes that small and organic farming creates many good jobs. Indeed, statistics show that in France the appearance of supermarkets did away with 17 percent of bakers in France, 84 percent of grocers, and 43 percent of hardware dealers; five sustainable jobs in local shops were lost for every one created in mass-market stores. Says Latouche, citing Ivan Illich: "The recipe lies in doing more, and doing better, with less." We can cut the depletion of natural resources by 30 percent by reducing "final" consumption by 50 percent and create an appropriate ecological footprint for our one planet and still "the improvement in our quality of life would be out of all proportion to the measures that are needed."

Latouche addresses the "massive" failures of so-called development policies in the "South," that is, the third world or developing countries. These policies have "resulted in corruption, incoherence and structural adjustment plans that have turned poverty into misery." Instead, what the South needs is "self-organized societies and vernacular economies" and de-growth can help them — but de-growth begins in the North with affluent societies ceasing to import "foodstuffs to feed our animals when famine is raging" and rain forests are burning. Colonization, development, and globalization, he feels, have interrupted the organic economies of Southern cultures. He cites a Guatemalan peasant leader who said: "Leave the poor alone and stop talking to them about development."

There are many similarities among the thoughts and proposals of David Korten, Serge Latouche, and Meister Eckhart and the constituencies they represent. An economics of compassion is not an esoteric subject. It is in the air, as our current economic systems are so failing us (meaning 98 percent of us). As Andre Gorz put it in the early 1990s: "Capitalist civilization is moving inexorably towards catastrophic collapse. There is no longer any need for a revolutionary class to overthrow capitalism; it is digging its own grave, and that of industrial civilization in general." It deserves debate in our homes and community gathering places, in the media, in academia, in legislative halls, and in political discourse.

Anita Roddick: A New Business Ethic

Another warrior in the business arena in our time was Anita Roddick (1942–2007). Anita started the "Body Shop" in a garage near Haight Street in San Francisco in the late sixties, even though she had no experience in business whatsoever. Since then, the Body Shop has grown into a major international business with over seventeen hundred stores serving 84 million customers in twenty-four languages. What made her famous, though, wasn't so much her business success as her vision and her business ethics. Anita was a visionary

— pursuing business practices based on fair trade, environmental aware-ness, animal protection, respect for human rights, and social campaigning. In addition, she founded an MBA program at the University of Bath that reflected her ethics, which included two bottom lines in addition to the usual monetary one: an environmental bottom line and a community bottom line. Anita stubbornly insisted that her business always address these questions: What are the effects of our work and employment on the environment, and what are the effects on the larger community?

To her credit, she earned great respect from many business colleagues for her emphasis on business ethics. For example, *Inc Magazine* wrote that "this woman has changed business forever." *Business Week* wrote, "Few entrepreneurs have tied their product to a social cause with better effect." *The Observer* wrote, "Most CEOs aren't fit to lick peppermint lotion off Anita's feet." And *USA Today* observed, "A Body Shop isn't just a shop. It's an arena of education."

Anita was an environmental activist and a business activist. She said that business is the most powerful force on the planet — so it needs a conscience; it needs values; it needs criticism; and it needs to work in a way that's respect-ful of all life. Anita was born in 1942 to Italian immigrants in Littlehampton, England. From her rugged upbringing, as a minority in wartime England whose mother ran a pub, Anita learned frugality, a certain toughness, and a disrespect for authority. Anita also had a nose for injustice. I once asked her where she got her energy, since I had never met anyone with so much, and she replied: "From two places. First, tomatoes. All Italians live on tomatoes. Next from my anger at injustice. I think I came out of the womb angry at injustice."

Anita raised questions for business that, particularly in the 1970s and 1980s, were rarely addressed. She asked: "Why does business have to work this way? Why not harness the market to eliminate poverty? Why not improve life for the world's poorest first? Is it so impossible to move busi-ness from private greed to public good?" She did not consider this a pipe dream; rather, it is a matter of choice, of ethics. "We have the resources. I sense that in the growing vigilante consumer movement, we have the popu-lar will and — God knows — there is plenty of inspiration in the small-scale grassroots initiatives that women have been so instrumental in establishing in the majority world."

Anita raised issues of gender equality in the workplace — as well as working for greater gender equality everywhere. On the one hand, she describes essential "masculine rights," the ones that are usually promoted, and rightly so: political and civil rights, freedom of speech, freedom of worship, freedom to own property, and so on. But, she says, "read the Universal Declaration of Human Rights and you'll find other rights which aren't referred to nearly so often. They include the right to a family, the right to rest and leisure, the right to an adequate standard of living, the right to a cultural community. These basic economic, social and cultural rights address the particular concerns of women. They are as fundamental a right as free speech." She spent a lot of time on the road visiting communities in Africa and indigenous peoples in South America. One conclusion she drew was this: "I treasure the company of women. I love their laughter. I am astounded by their ability to keep communities together around the world."

Anita dared to bring spirit talk to business while growing a very entrepreneurial corporation. "My vision, my hope, is simply this: that many business leaders will come to see a primary role of business as incubators of the human spirit, rather than factories for the production of more material goods and services." Values matter. A business that satisfies only the monetary bottom line is not adequate. Anita elaborates:

> There is more to all this than measurement and that brings us back to the word "reverence." There is a spiritual dimension to life that, for me, is the real bottom line. It underpins everything.... To me it is a very simple attitude that has nothing to do with organized religion. It means that life is sacred and awe-inspiring. In my travels around the world, I have been grounded — as millions also have — in the most fundamental of insights: that all life is an expression of a single spiritual unity. We are not, as humans, above anything, contrary to what Christianity tells us; instead we are part of everything. This interconnection has to be sacred, reverent and respectful of different ways of knowing and being.... The business of business should not just be about money, it should be about responsibility. It should be about public good, not private greed.

When I hear Anita speak, I hear the passion both of Meister Eckhart and of Jesus driving moneylenders from the Temple. Her very definition of spirituality parallels Eckhart's, which we saw in chapter one: awe at and gratitude for living. Life itself is sacred. She also clearly distinguishes between organized religion and spirituality. She talks of bringing "reverence" into our discussions of work. How like Eckhart this is when he calls for a work that brings justice and compassion in its wake. She writes about the role of conscience in our work worlds: "Leaders in world business are the first true global citizens....In terms of power and influence, you can forget the Church and forget politics, too. There is no more powerful institution in society than business. It is more important than ever before for business to assume a moral leadership in society." Business must move away from "commerce without conscience," she says. There lies the "key to the way out." She says: "My biggest fear is seeing not just the planet's business, but also the planet, being controlled by a handful of gigantic transnational corporations. You can see the beginning of this in the way that global brands are starting to raise our children. They entertain them, feed them, clothe them, medicate them, addict them and define the way in which they relate to each other.... This kind of global monoculture wreaks a soulless kind of destruction. Not just on families but on family farms." She warns that these "large faceless organizations" need careful watching and reporting about lest they accomplish evil deeds under the cover of darkness.

In her biography, *Body and Soul*, Anita talks about how she tried to live the values she preached for her company and for business in general. She says she and her husband "have no intention or desire to stack up a pile of accumulated wealth which goes on and on, *ad infinitum*, for generation after generation. We believe it would be obscene to die rich and we intend to ensure we die poor by giving away all our personal wealth, through a foundation of some kind.... The accumulation of wealth has no meaning for me; neither has the acquisition of material riches. I believe we impoverish ourselves by our tendency to undervalue all the other riches that come from our life experiences — the ones that can't be bought." Much of the Roddicks' philanthropy has been to birth social and environmental projects that are "self-financing" and sustainable. Such projects are "more significant than money."

In the end, Anita said, growth and the pursuit of profits are not inherently bad, but they become bad "when they become an end in themselves," especially when multinationals "just trade, make money and gobble up other companies." There needs to be a bottom line that is far broader than mere profit and loss.

Global companies do not have to be impersonal and blind to values. A global company that honors values, she said, is a company that is "responsible, it is multi-cultural, it has an anthropological and spiritual tone." She believed that the "mainstream" can and is "going green" and that consumers themselves must be leaders in a new and sustainable consciousness.

It is sad that Anita died so young, at age sixty-four. We miss her. Her outrage and creativity are still needed. Anita was a spiritual warrior and a giant in the world of business — fun, original, womanly, passionate, brilliant, and with a real conscience. It was a privilege to know her.

Howard Thurman: Civil Rights and Meister Eckhart

African American theologian Howard Thurman (1899–1981) was in many ways the spiritual genius behind the civil rights movement. Thurman's book *Jesus and the Disinherited* was a huge influence on Martin Luther King Jr., who took the book with him each of the thirty-nine times he went to jail.

Thurman studied Meister Eckhart as a young man from Quaker teacher Rufus Jones, and he cited Eckhart often, especially Eckhart's "spark of the soul" that lies in every person and cannot be snuffed out by hostility or fear or anger or oppression. Thurman writes, "What Eckhart calls the 'uncreated element' in [a person's] soul...was an assumed fact profoundly at work in the life and thought of the early slaves. This much was certainly clear to them — the soul of man was immortal. It could go to heaven or hell, but it could not *die*." What gives hope to the downtrodden, Thurman felt, is "the great disclosure: that there is at the heart of life a Heart," and "the most daring and revolutionary concept known to man" is that "God is not only the creative mind and spirit at the core of the universe but that He...is love." Not only is God the creator of all things, but, "more importantly, God is the Creator of life itself. Existence is the creation of God; life is the creation of God. This is of more than passing significance." In this, Thurman echoes

Eckhart's God talk, in which the "God of life" takes precedence over the God of religion. As did Eckhart, Thurman felt that Jesus's teachings have often been "betrayed" by the institutional church, which too often readily ignores those whose backs are "up against the wall."

The teachings of the historical Jesus were important within the civil rights movement. Thurman says:

> The basic fact is that Christianity as it was born in the mind of this Jewish teacher and thinker appears as a technique of survival for the oppressed.... 'In him was life, and the life was the light of men.' When this spirit appears, the oppressed gather fresh courage; for he announced the good news that fear, hypocrisy, and hatred, the three hounds of hell that track the trail of the disinherited, need have no dominion over them.

After Jesus, Thurman says, the Christian church "became, through the intervening years, a religion of the powerful and dominant, used sometimes as an instrument of oppression." But that does not reflect the mind or life of Jesus. Thurman shared with Eckhart the core belief that being a "son or daughter of God" has profound political ramifications: "The awareness of being a child of God tends to stabilize the ego and results in a new courage, fearlessness, and power. I have seen it happen again and again." Indeed, for him as for Eckhart, "the core of the analysis of Jesus is that man is a child of God, the God of life that sustains all of nature and guarantees all the intricacies of the life-process itself." And, like Eckhart, Thurman believed humanity itself needs to realize it is part of the cosmos: "The individual must have a sense of kinship to life that transcends and goes beyond the immediate kinship of family or the organized kinship that binds him ethnically or racially or nationally.... As a human being, then, he belongs to life and the whole kingdom of life."

Thurman also repeats on many occasions his stark naming of the via negativa, such as when he says that ours is a journey wherein the "human spirit [is] stripped to the literal substance of itself before God." Thurman sounds very Eckhart-like when he declares that his primary concern is to remove "the last barriers between the outer and the inner aspects of religious experience." My marrying the via positiva and via negativa (inner) with the via creativa and via transformativa (outer) is focused on the same task.

One sees in Thurman — and by extension in his student Martin Luther King Jr. — an application of Eckhart's deepest teachings, including that of the divine spark in every person, cosmic awareness, and his speaking truth to economic, political, and religious powers. It is a teaching that compassion and justice are one.

Clearly, Dorothy Stang, Karl Marx, David Korten, Serge Latouche, Anita Roddick, and Howard Thurman are warriors who challenge us to engage in social, environmental, and economic justice, which Eckhart helped lay the ground for. After all, as Eckhart said, God "*is* justice itself," and "the closer one is to justice, the closer one is to freedom."

CHAPTER THIRTEEN

WARRIORS FOR A DEEPER EDUCATION

Meister Eckhart Meets YELLAWE, Theodore Richards, M.C. Richards, and Lily Yeh

The schooling that we seek is full within.
It rises to the surface as we move....
Our planet is our school, and far beyond.

— M.C. RICHARDS

People called inner-city North Philadelphia "the badlands" because of its prevailing decrepitude, poverty, drug dealing, and violence. But this area contained invaluable hidden treasures.... It was there that I realized that art is a powerful tool for social change and that the artist can be at the center of that transformation.

— LILY YEH

Living offers the most noble kind of knowledge.

— MEISTER ECKHART

When Eckhart scholar Reiner Schurmann declares that Eckhart's work is "not a theoretical doctrine but a practical guide," he is inviting us to make it real in the world by taking it as a point of direction or a guide. I believe this is especially so when we speak of education. Our species is in a new and dangerous place. We are facing our own demise. Education is obviously a big part of the problem as well as a big part of the solution. Can Eckhart help us to transform education?

In his own day Eckhart watched the decline of education happening all around him. A century earlier, the invention of the university, a radical concept introduced from Islam, had launched an intellectual revolution, but it was losing steam. Part of the revolution had been moving the center of education from the monastic establishment in the countryside to cities, where dozens of universities sprang up in a fifty-year period. But in Eckhart's day learning was on the decline; universities were serving vested interests of the privileged more than inspiring love of learning. This is one reason Eckhart abandoned his esteemed position at the University of Paris in favor of working, learning, and teaching among the lower-class Beguines and peasants of Germany.

Eckhart exclaimed that "living offers the most noble kind of knowledge." Eckhart was, before all else, a student of life, and he urges us to be the same. "What is life? God's being is my life," he declares. All his work is a study of life and a study of God and our relation to both. Is education today a journey into life?

The Dalai Lama, among others, has proclaimed that in our day "education is in crisis the world over." I fully agree. It is only denial that refuses to look at the facts — such as that about 65 percent of black boys are not graduating from high school in the United States, that many young people are simply bored at school, and that more and more boys are getting in trouble and being diagnosed with "conditions" and "diseases" because they are not content sitting at a desk for seven hours a day. Children are alive and mystical, and our educational system ignores this almost by choice. Learning is as pleasing to the human mind as good food is to the stomach — but you would hardly know it judging from most educational experiences young people are having in school. Where has the joy of learning gone?

Humans have lots of growing up to do, lots of training to undergo, from potty training to tying one's shoes, from learning a language to standing up straight, from eating correctly to finding one's talents, reading, writing, and lots of arithmetic — and on and on. Humans need culture, we need others around us and from the past (our ancestors) whose experience can instruct us. We need guidance. We have so many choices in life, and we don't have time to try them all out by trial and error. Our lack of DNA programming means we need educating from the elders, from our parents, from culture. Meister Eckhart is such an elder. His teachings offer, I believe, what is most missing in education today.

I am speaking of a sense of awe and wonder, of gratitude and reverence (see chapter one). I am speaking of an awareness of silence and emptiness and darkness and letting go (see chapter three). I am speaking of a relationship with the universe, of bringing psyche and cosmos together again (see chapter two). Maria Montessori, an esteemed and accomplished educator early in the twentieth century, put the importance of learning cosmology this way:

> If the idea of the universe be presented to the child in the right way, it will do more for him or her than just arouse his interest, for it will create in her admiration and wonder, a feeling loftier than any interest and more satisfying.... The knowledge the child then acquires is organized and systematic; her intelligence becomes whole and complete because of the vision of the whole that has been presented to her, and his interest spreads to all, for all are linked and have their place in the universe on which his mind is centered.
>
> The stars, the earth, stones, life of all kinds form a whole in relation with each other, and so close is this relation that we cannot understand a stone without some understanding of the great sun!

I am speaking of values that matter, such as justice and compassion and certainly creativity. Pulitzer Prize–winning author Ernest Becker wrote a book on education called *Beyond Alienation: A Philosophy of Education for the Crisis of Democracy*, and in it he makes clear that the bottom line of education is values. The central issue and the historical issue is "the need for a secular moral creed." Education is and always has been about the older generation passing on values to the younger ones. How well are we doing? How can Eckhart assist us?

The Spark of the Soul

Eckhart honors intuition as the highest of all faculties. Eckhart calls it "the spark of the soul," a term we examined in chapter ten that derives both from

Sufi and from Jewish mysticism of the Middle Ages. It implies wisdom —
and is that not the direction education needs to move in? Away from knowledge factories and toward wisdom schools? Wisdom incorporates heart and
head, body and feeling, intuition and values. Einstein warns us that intellect
gives us not values but only methods. Values derive, he says, from intuition
and feeling.

It is our responsibility, as teachers and students, to bring heaven and
Earth, cosmos and psyche, together in order to, as the Jewish medieval
mystical book the Zohar puts it, "raise those sparks hidden throughout the
world, elevating them to holiness by the power of your soul." Our minds and
creativity unveil the hidden sparks of the world, for they lie hidden everywhere — in our hearts and in all things.

The Kabbalah tells us that "there is no greater path" than to bring sparks
alive in life and to educe the spark that lies within. Ordinary things become
extraordinary. The profane becomes sacred. Here lies an insight to Deep
Education: its etymological meaning is to educe, to discover inner wisdom,
to, as the Kabbalah says, "draw out the holy spark that dwells within." Is
this not Eckhart's teaching, that we are to birth the Christ in all our works?
Wouldn't it be wise to aim high and to seek to educate along a path that is
"greater" than all other paths? This is the kind of Deep Education we need.

I am convinced that what Eckhart means by the "spark of the soul"
is what we mean today by "intuition." Eckhart's term derives from the
Christian language of the *doxa*, or divine radiance (or Cosmic Christ), coming alive in all things as sparks. Eckhart develops his own version of the
"spark of the soul" concept throughout his sermons. He refers to the term
time and again, though he never fully defines it for us. In two sermons he
calls it "synderesis," which means a prelude or threshold to conscience. It
is not conscience but it is a doorway into conscience. For Thomas Aquinas,
conscience is a judgment, a decision, and synderesis is the intuition we have
that precedes our acts of conscience.

Moreover, Eckhart repeatedly relates the "spark of the soul" to the presence of angels, and according to Aquinas, angels learn only by intuition.
Therefore, to speak of angels and the sparks that accompany them is to speak
of intuition. Furthermore, Eckhart names this special place where the spark
exists as the "apex" of the intellect (or mind or human spirit); it's a special,

powerful "corner" of our consciousness. One might say it is the "sweet spot" where the human mind or spirit links up to the Divine Spirit (in the presence of angels); it also equates to the seventh chakra, which represents a kind of apex or culmination of our spiritual and physiological powers, and from which our light pours forth into the world to link up with other light beings in community making. Eckhart also refers to the spark as the "kingdom of God," meaning the place where justice and compassion flow.

Thus, for me, Eckhart's greatest contribution to education is his emphasis on intuition, which is what Einstein felt was so lacking in our culture. Returning intuition to the center of education would mean a revolution in teaching. A truly transformative event. Eckhart, by repeatedly mentioning the "spark of the soul where God is born," is telling us that we need to democratize intuition and conscience, giving them the prominence they deserve in our lives and consciousness and culture.

The great ecumenical Catholic monk Thomas Merton speaks of the spark of the soul in almost the exact language Meister Eckhart uses — one more proof of Eckhart's deep impact on Merton. In *Conjectures of a Guilty Bystander*, Merton writes:

> At the center of our being is a point of nothingness which is untouched by sin and by illusion, a point of pure truth, a point or spark which belongs entirely to God, which is never at our disposal, from which God disposes our lives, which is inaccessible to the fantasies of our own mind or the brutalities of our own will. This little point of nothingness and *of absolute poverty* is the pure glory of God in us.... It is like a pure diamond, blazing with the invisible light of heaven. It is in everybody, and if we could see it we would see these billions of points of light coming together in the face and blaze of a sun that would make all the darkness and cruelty of life vanish completely.... I have no program for this seeing. It is only given. But the gate of heaven is everywhere.

An awakened education will make room for the ancient and indigenous forms of education, which worked for tens of thousands of years. By that I mean ceremony and ritual. Ceremony and ritual are how our ancestors taught the younger generation the important stories of life, including creation stories and stories of what it meant to become an adult (rites of passage), what values mattered, and more. A rebirth of ritual and ceremony is essential for a rebirth of education in our time, for that is the bedrock of community awareness and the sharing of joy, grief, transformation, and creativity. Values are named and practiced in ceremony and ritual.

A truly Deep Education would train the intuition, the mystical brain, the place where, as Einstein teaches, values are born and conscience takes hold. Intuition is where wisdom is born, where the Divine Feminine plays and from which creativity emerges.

Few educators I know and few serving on our all-powerful and all-mighty accrediting bodies are daring to ask the real questions: What are we educating for? What values do we want to communicate? Who is profiting from education as we execute it today? Are people happy educating and being educated? Where is the joy? As the Dalai Lama observes, "Education is in crisis the world over." The forms and structures we have so mightily constructed for about 150 years in the West are not up to the task. Values and creativity are rarely addressed; instead, politicians shout for "more tests" and "more math" and "more science." Today, the Internet's potential for sharing information is obvious. But can it also impart values? More to the point, what values are important, in education and in life, that we need to pass on for the sake of our, and our planet's, survival?

Ancestral Wisdom: YELLAWE

For twenty-nine years I designed, administered, and taught an alternative educational model that focused on teaching worthy and significant values. In many respects Eckhart's teachings played a deep role in the design and implementation of this pedagogy. First, our teaching was driven by a conscious awareness that we had to step out of the given values of our society, the values of patriarchy and control and domination, and embody alternative values: those that celebrated life and creativity, joy and mutuality. We insisted on including the body in all our training, for that is where the heart is, after all. In many ways we were incorporating more of a feminist philosophy of education, as the current system is heavily patriarchal — wisdom and compassion were our goals. All this would have made Eckhart feel at home. We lived out this experiment over a twenty-nine-year period, first in Chicago and then in Oakland, California, and did so with adults in master's programs and certificate programs and finally in a doctor of ministry program. The response was profound — it changed people's lives in very deep ways.

I exited my own university, the University of Creation Spirituality, after twenty-nine years in order to translate for youth the pedagogy and philosophy that were so valuable for adults. Further, I focused on inner-city youth who were "on the edge," where up to 65 percent of youth were not graduating from high school. We held our first two-year pilot program in Oakland, California, which afterward birthed three new offshoot programs in Chicago, along with the continuing program in Oakland. We called the program Youth and Elder Learning Laboratory for Ancestral Wisdom Education, or YELLAWE. I also wrote a book describing my philosophy of education, *The A.W.E. Project: Reinvention Education, Reinventing the Human.* "Ancestral Wisdom Education" is what I believe we need — fewer knowledge factories and more wisdom schools. I believe Eckhart would agree wholeheartedly.

"Ancestral" means several things. In part it honors our ancestors, especially our premodern ones, who truly held a cosmological worldview and who put wisdom ahead of mere knowledge. "Ancestral" also honors the cosmos itself: the supernovas and galaxies and the original fireball, all of which have guided and accomplished our existence. Our lineage is literally 13.8 billion years long. As I discussed in chapter one, awe and wonder count and come first — even and especially when it comes to education. We should begin education with awe, from preschool through graduate school. What is "awesome," for example, about being a doctor, a scientist, a teacher, a priest, a painter, a dramatist, a carpenter, a mechanic? The younger generation has a right and need to hear stories of awe from their elders. Every vocation is awesome. The awe of a creation story, for example, can unite us and inspire us and challenge us to contribute to the "Great Work," as Thomas Berry calls it, the work of surviving and even thriving on this Earth with all her creatures, including us.

At the heart of our YELLAWE program is the passing on of values, and I have deliberately created a schema that is compatible with a public school context — it is deliberately not religious in language because we are employing it in the public school system, yet I do not know any religion that would not agree to the basic values named therein. I call it "the 10 Cs," and I have found that teachers do not need to climb a mountain to get students to discuss, tell stories, debate, create theater, film, paint, write poetry, and otherwise challenge themselves to understand and express these universal values. I believe the 10 Cs could reground education. I will name them here briefly:

1. *Cosmology/Ecology:* Where do we come from, and how did we get here? And where is "here"? Our universe is our home, and science has a whole new creation story to share with us today. What does it all mean? Furthermore, since "ecology is functional cosmology," what can we do about the ecological crises we all face together?

2. *Contemplation:* The need to calm the reptilian brain is universal; unless we can deal with our own action/reaction response, our tendency toward violence and aggression, we cannot be our deepest selves. Learn to be. Learn silence and "to make silence," to quote Maria Montessori. We teach some kind of tai chi or martial arts method for getting into one's body and finding silence there.

3. *Chaos and Darkness:* My experience has been that inner city youth live amid daily chaos — they have PhDs in chaos. Family structures vary and can be marked by upheaval; youth live with grandparents, aunts and uncles, friends' parents, alone, on the street, and on and on. For them to learn the new teachings of chaos theory, that there is great potential in chaos, which is a habit of nature, that birthing and creativity invariably include chaos, is a revelation for them.

4. *Creativity:* Creativity lies at the heart of our program. The entire curriculum is centered around creative expression— making a movie, painting, dancing, singing, and writing poetry — all to find the wisdom inside. As Eckhart says, "The truth comes from inside out, not from outside in." One year, a young black man who was a senior said to me: "This is the first time in four years of high school that anyone has asked me to express myself creatively."

5. *Compassion:* We all possess compassion, and it includes gender justice, eco-justice, racial justice, political and economic justice. Let us get to work.

6. *Community:* The modern era gave us a passion for the rights of the individual and that is a fine advancement in human evolution; however, we must balance individualism (which advertisers fan into a monster of ego) with community, the larger context.

7. *Critical Thinking:* Rediscovering awe as a primary value, honoring intuition and mysticism, does not mean that we abandon or belittle our analytical left brains. We must hone our critical thinking, the ability to critique, to define, and to delimit our choices and positions. An authentic education honors both right *and* left brains.

8. *Chakra and Character Development:* What is character, and how can we develop it in ourselves? Who are the people we honor for their exemplary character, and how can we who are imperfect strive to be better? With the Eastern categories of the chakras, a new language is introduced to talk about ethics and morality beyond the tired rhetoric of "do's" and "don'ts."

9. *Courage:* There is no warriorhood without courage, no character development. Whom do we admire as courageous? How do we develop courage and move beyond fear and self-doubt to become empowered?

10. *Ceremony and Celebration:* For most of human existence, we educated our young *not* in schools, at desks, or with books but in ceremonies, with drumming and dancing on the earth and under the sky. African spiritual teacher Malidoma Patrice Somé says, "There is no community without ritual." To re-create community, we must find and create common rituals that speak to the hearts, bodies, and souls today.

I am happy to report that I still encounter students from our original program five years ago who, having finished high school and gone on to other experiences of work and school, tell me their time at YELLAWE was "the high point" of their school experience. Our recent director and instructor, Rose Elizando, took the YELLAWE program to Mexico to work with educational leaders of indigenous tribal people near Oaxaca. Our current instructor in Oakland, Dr. Broderick Rodell, is using the dance and martial arts practice capoeira, from Brazil, as an emphasis on "Contemplation" as

well as music and other expressions of creativity. The 10 Cs owe much to
Meister Eckhart, who treats them all in depth, as this book shows.

Theodore Richards

A warrior in the field of education who carries on a battle in the spirit of
Meister Eckhart is Theodore Richards. Ted was at one time the director of
the YELLAWE program in Oakland, California, and he is now founder and
executive director of the Chicago Wisdom Project, operating in Chicago's
South Side. Recently he authored the book *Creatively Maladjusted: The
Wisdom Education Movement Manifesto*, which I consider to be an excellent
summary of the disease in contemporary education that also provides the
necessary medicine to render a new version of learning.

Richards takes the title from a favorite line of Dr. Martin Luther King
Jr.: "Human salvation lies in the hands of the creatively maladjusted." Ted
comments on that line: "Salvation, for Dr. King, is communal. And it is not
by conforming to society that we find salvation, but by transforming it....
For King, like any prophet, the highest calling is not conformity to society's
norms. If we are maladjusted to a corrupt system, our task is not to become
'well adjusted,' but to use our maladjustment as a creative, not a destructive,
force."

Ted says, "Our school system, like pretty much any school system, serves
the primary purpose of conformity." The best response to such enforced
conformity is creative maladjustment. Rather than trying work within or fix
a corrupt system, maladjustment is "a reasonable, moral response....Our
educational system today is as broken as Jim Crow. To succeed in such a system, one must participate in a dying culture. We put children on medication
in our schools because they don't want to sit in chairs all day and learn to take
tests — that is, because they are maladjusted."

In his analysis of education's woes, Ted wants to begin at the roots by
asking "first what is wrong with our civilization....For it is industrial capitalism spread throughout the world by colonialism and globalization, which
has defined modern education." This very methodology seems to me a new
expression of Eckhart's and Jesus's effort to drive the moneylenders from
the Temple, in this case the temple of education. Ted feels the result of our

current education system has been a "crisis of injustice" that breeds wars, violence, and suspicion; an ecological crisis that threatens the entire planet; and a crisis of meaning. "For all the wealth some of us have amassed, our lives feel empty. We feel lost and alone." We need to educate selves and others to relate in "more meaningful ways to live more profoundly, not just [to] acquire more money, which only feeds the three crises." Ted wants to dig deeper than the corporate, mechanistic, and capitalist paradigm that currently frames the discussion on education. First, we need to answer "more fundamental questions about the meaning and purpose of education." We need to address values and our wrong assumptions about how we learn. He calls for a "radical change," not "mere reform," in the way we currently educate our children.

Regarding values, Ted cites Walter Feinberg, who said that educators from Plato to Dewey all saw that "the first and most important limitation on education was the values projected and manifested in the day-to-day activities of the people in the society." Yet modern education proceeds oblivious of values as such, Ted says, "with the recent emphasis placed on empirical research." The values of American education derive, Richards feels, from the Industrial Revolution. Schools are modeled on the factory, shuffling each "student through a conveyer belt of disconnected subjects. The object was for them to get enough information to pass the test, to be a finished, marketable product." That is, to return to the factory. He draws a parallel between the factory school and the factory farm, which arose also in the late nineteenth century. In fact, Wendell Berry said, for the animals, the factory farm resembles a prison, "the aim of which is to house and feed the greatest number in the smallest space at the least expense of money, labor and attention." Today, of course, students graduate not for the factory but for the office. Those who don't graduate find jobs in neither factory nor office but instead go to prison. Incarceration is very often the result of educational failure.

Ted goes on to lay out an alternative, wisdom-based education that honors creativity and imagination, nature, the intellect, the body, the soul, and practice. He is currently working to bring inner-city children to a farm property gifted to his organization on a regular basis to till the land, learn permaculture, build structures to stay in, and do rites of passage. His work brings together body and soul, mind and heart, cosmos and psyche (he received a doctorate in cosmology from the California Institute of Integral Studies). It is very much in the tradition of Meister Eckhart.

M.C. Richards and "Nontoxic Education"

For many years, one of my colleagues at the Institute of Culture and Creation Spirituality and later at the University of Creation Spirituality was the poet, potter, painter, and philosopher M.C. Richards (1916–1999). M.C. devoted a great deal of her life to reinventing education in practice and in theory. Among her books are *Centering in Pottery, Poetry, and the Person*; *The Crossing Point*; *Toward Wholeness: Rudolf Steiner Education in America*; *The Public School and the Education of the Whole Person*; *Imagine Inventing Yellow*; and *Opening Our Moral Eye*. I will always be honored that she found in my school a companion effort. Briefly, here is her story in her own words:

> Because I was bright and had a library card when I was four and a half, the experts said I was an intellectual type and kept shoving me into programs of verbal study. (They didn't notice that I read only books with pictures in them. And later they didn't believe me when I said poets are really inarticulate.)
>
> Thank God I was a mischievous and irreverent child with a strong inner life or I might have been lost forever in a collective stereotype. I grew up thinking there were two kinds of people: bright and dumb. You could tell by their grades....It took me a lifetime to discover out of school, that human beings are unclassifiable because we are on the move, and because we live as much in an invisible, indefinable realm as we do in a visible one.

As a young woman, upon graduating from the University of California in Berkeley, M.C. landed a prestigious teaching position at the University of Chicago, but she felt stifled there. The atmosphere was defined by, she says, "duplicity, sneers, sarcasm, oneupmanship, ambition, greed, joyless intellectual gluttony, and behind-the-scenes heartbreak. Students would not allow me to spend time in class on material which did not prepare them for their comprehensive examinations. Talk about tunnel vision, ech. Nobody looked healthy or happy. It was a drag. The pay was good, the status was good, but the work and the life were juiceless and joyless."

M.C. speaks to education as it is still playing out with the following observation. "They put the student through a battery of punitive examinations, which, if he survived, made him feel superior to others. He then went into the adult world sarcastic and arrogant in turn, with his brain honed to play games to win and to escape traps and to set them for others. His character tended to be concealed and explosive. I didn't like it."

In contrast, M.C. was a serious student of Rudolf Steiner, whose philosophy of education I very much admire and consider to be quite Eckhartian, since it too brings creativity and cosmology to the fore. M.C. discussed Rudolf Steiner's educational philosophy in her book *Toward Wholeness: Rudolf Steiner Education in America*. In it, she tells us what drew her to Steiner. "I am interested in Steiner's work and the schooling that has grown out of it because of the totality of the vision — and because everything is connected with everything else. This spirit reflects the direction in which modern consciousness is evolving. The grammar of interconnections is a new discipline of our age." She observes that nature's processes are less "cause and effect" than "metamorphosis," and she applies this principle to education, where "we're connected to the past and grateful for all the earnest human effort, and we're open to the unfolding of the next form. We're not locked into anything." M.C. loves how Steiner's Waldorf education nourishes the teachers and not just the children! "Their growth is mutual." She credits Steiner's work with providing a "common archetypal ground for art, science, and religion. The whole is found in every part." Documenting and contemplating both have a role to play. She welcomes how "in its forms it provides a search for a renewal of a feeling for who we human beings really are, and for reconnection with the universe — inwardly as well as outwardly." Clearly we see here a celebration of psyche and cosmos, heart and mind, that parallels Eckhart's values as well.

M.C. soon abandoned the University of Chicago in search of a "nontoxic" educational experience, which she found in the experimental Black Mountain College in the hills of North Carolina. Among her fellow faculty members were Merce Cunningham, John Cage, and Buckminster Fuller, with whom she maintained a good relationship all her life. She loved Black Mountain for its emphasis on the centrality of art in a liberal arts education, on community, on John Dewey's principles of education, as well as on interdisciplinary learning. An informal and collaborative spirit imbued the college, though as M.C. points out, human nature often asserted itself in less benign expressions. The school existed from 1933 to 1957, when unfortunately it closed its doors, but it sowed seeds for other educational institutions. Her deepest lesson from this was that "the values and behavior of persons" are what make the difference in an institution.

Eventually, her 1964 book *Centering in Pottery, Poetry, and the Person* was such a success that she was able to pretty much surrender academia and live by conducting workshops and selling her pottery. This book has become a classic, and we were privileged one year when she was working with us in the Bay Area to host a gala event at Fort Mason in San Francisco in honor of the twenty-fifth anniversary of it. In attendance were her friends from Black Mountain, Merce Cunningham and John Cage, both of whom presented memorable offerings.

When M.C. went to college and later graduate school, majoring eventually in English and languages, she felt something was missing in her education. In studying literature, for example:

> Myths were regarded as fictions rather than as true stories of the ordeals of the human soul. We were taught to criticize but not to experience. We stood outside the words. There was silence or disdain about everything that could not be rationally validated. I have had to work hard to correct this miseducation and to learn to enter life from the inside. I know now that words are not the poetic source. The source precipitates into language; to love the language and not to experience the source, the poetry of insight, is a sort of weird "touch but don't feel anything" approach. I since have developed my ear for the objective realm of the human psyche, personal and collective, and for the truths of spirit, and can stand my ground. I have learned that poetry is a spiritual offering. It is a way of entering into one another's reality. It is a form of community. When we are children we make poems easily because we offer ourselves so readily.

One can sense in this passage a great deal of the spirit of Eckhart — how the "ordeals of the soul" matter and are not to be taken as fiction alone; how rationality can deny us access to a larger world where psyche meets cosmos, that our creativity is "a spiritual offering," how the child in us is eager to be generous.

In 1977, M.C.'s book *Centering* very much caught my eye; I read it about the time I was starting up my "post-European" model of education designed to teach spirituality. Key to my pedagogy was what I called "art as meditation," wherein we honored the via creativa and brought the heart and right brain alive through dance, painting, music, and photography as meditation. Reading her book, I felt I had discovered a sister. She confirmed my conviction that art had to be at the center of all healthy and holistic education. I published an essay on her book entitled "Art as Meditation," in which I praise her work, which integrated art and moral imagination. She showed how art cut through dualisms to create healthy dialectics as it developed, in her words, "discipline for freedom," discipline with order. She poses the question: "How does transformation come about? Not only of consciousness but of character?" And she proposes that images taken from the potter's craft, centering and the ordeal by fire, are the way. She credits Quakers with grasping "centering" as "a feeling of flowing toward a common center in their meetings for worship." What is centering? "To feel the whole in every part.... Centering has nothing to do with a center as a place. It has to do with bringing the totality of the clay into an unwobbling pivot, the equilibrium distributed throughout in an even grain."

After M.C. heard about my article, which was originally published in *Spirituality Today*, she and I started to correspond. We met and, in time, became sister and brother. M.C. taught with us when I moved the program to Holy Names College, where she also took my class on Meister Eckhart, who very much entered her consciousness. She was especially drawn to his teachings on letting go and his respect for the artist, as well as his passion for awe and for justice.

She moved to Oakland for a semester, and for several years she moved in with the Holy Names sisters on campus. To her delight (and surprise) she found she got along fine living in a convent for the very first (and last) time in her life. She enjoyed the company of these well-educated sisters, many active, a few in retirement. M.C. lived the last fifteen years of her life in Camphill Village in Pennsylvania, a village that followed the teachings of Rudolf Steiner and was dedicated to supporting residents with developmental disabilities. She first encountered such a community in 1963, and writing about it in a review of Paul Goodman's Community of Scholars for *Liberation Maga\ine*, she called it:

> The purest example I know of a "village" movement, where young adults and their teachers live together in deepest life-commitment to work, mutual service, artistic fulfillment and spiritual festival....I do not mean that the hope of the world lies in mental illness. I mean that if we teachers are serious about serving an idea of community we should realize that there may be handicaps even normal intelligent people have to overcome. Intellect itself may act as a handicap to humane endeavor. There may be a competitive and unyielding pride.

Years later, after she joined the Camphill Village community, it was my pleasure to visit her on at least two occasions. It was clear in what high esteem she was held by all who lived there and how reciprocal was their interaction and respect. We traveled to Australia along with a number of my faculty to lead a weeklong workshop; on a visit to Ulhuru, M.C. was so inspired that, at the age of seventy, she took up painting. Her three paintings of the Great Rock, the navel of the earth, were her first paintings.

M.C. shared Eckhart's respect for experience and for intuition or mysticism. In a poem, M.C. writes:

> when we are children, we experience the
> world as of the same nature as ourselves.
> for the world is to be of the same order
> as oneself means that it too is alive, thinks, feels, acts,
> laughs and cries — is all the things one is
> for out of it one has been created — what one is must be in it.
> The discovery of the world then is
> like the discovery of oneself, a delicious secret.
> It feels good. It feels important. One is not cut off.

But growing up does bring demarcation and knowledge of difference and separation, and we seek

a second coming into innocence…
a beginning of goodness
We pass through cruel ordeals on the way. Estrangement, coldness,
despair. Death.
By going through the experience faithfully, we may come through
on the other side of the crossing point,
and find that our faithfulness has born a new quality into the world.

To think of the earth's body as part of one's own will help
to renew the arts
of caring for the land and the air and water, the art
of growing and preparing food, a feeling for
the seasons and their festivals.

Surely, M.C. went "through the experience faithfully." She was a most
beloved teacher. Her classes "Clay as Meditation" and "Word, Color and
Clay" — in which students created a book from paper and painted it and
filled it with thoughts and poetry — always met with "rave" student reviews.
People's lives were changed by her teaching and her presence. She was ever
so fond of a class she taught at Camphill Village called "The Renewal of
Art through Agriculture," whose goal was "to help the students (the farmers and gardeners) lift their perceptions into the Imagination, where perceptions may be enriched by a 'spiritual feel' and reconnected to Source." M.C.
bespeaks her philosophy of education in a poem called "Opening Anthem":

The schooling that we seek is full within.
It rises to the surface as we move.
It has the face of angels, human speech.…
Our planet is our school, and far beyond:
our church, our shop and study, and our fields.
We are all learning to awake:
awake in dream, in meditation and in prayer.
Inspired awake! Inspirited awake!
We feel it thus: one mighty school, the teaching everywhere.

In our last conversation before she died she said to me that she felt that the University of Creation Spirituality was a sort of reincarnation of Black Mountain College, and she hoped it would have a more benign ending.

Lily Yeh and the Barefoot Artists

Lily Yeh is an amazing artist and community activist who cofounded the Village of Arts and Humanities in the inner city of North Philadelphia in 1986. There, amid over two hundred abandoned lots, she set up community art places where citizens would come to express themselves, often using the materials straight from the streets — broken bottles and tossed beer cans, needles and the rest — to create art and foster community and learning. One of her handpicked leaders was a drug gang leader, and with Yeh's help, he turned around his life and the lives of many others. Yeh has worked with communities in dire straits around the world, including in Rwanda, China, Ecuador, Haiti, Ghana, Kenya, Syria, and Italy. She also founded Barefoot Artist, a volunteer organization that uses the power of art to revitalize impoverished neighborhoods.

She writes: "When I see brokenness, poverty, and crime in inner cities, I also see the enormous potential and readiness for transformation and rebirth. We are creating an art form that comes from the heart and reflects the pain and sorrow of people's lives. It also expresses joy, beauty, and love." I believe Yeh is showing us the way to recover the "enormous potential and readiness for transformation" that education can be. She is not just reinventing lost neighborhoods but is shining a beacon on reinventing education. By putting the via creativa in the center, she is echoing the wisdom of Meister Eckhart to honor our "fearful creative powers" as well as that of Hildegard of Bingen, who said, "There is wisdom in all creative works." Notice: We are not reinventing schools of knowledge. What we seek is a do-over, schools of wisdom.

Robert Shetterly is a portrait painter who created an ongoing series called "Americans Who Tell the Truth." He asked to paint Lily's portrait as part of the series, and she in turn invited him to accompany her to Rwanda to a village of survivors of the horrible massacres there. Expecting a scary scene, Robert was amazed at the amount of joy and celebration that welcomed Lily back to the village. Shetterly says, "They all began running, shouting around the village, on the hard dirt between the unfinished houses that had recently been painted with murals designed by these same children under Lily's direction. Bird and beast and decorative murals transformed the depressing gray mud brick.... What had happened in this land of grotesque violence to provoke such joy?"

Shetterly answers his own question this way:

> Lily's magic. Accountable art. Healing art. No snake oil, no secret elixirs. It's an art that fans the dim embers of spirit in diminished humanity. It's one thing to decry injustice, to expose trauma, to write a report that tells a true history. It's another to witness a small Chinese-American woman with an iron will, a bag of paint brushes, profound compassion, and unshakable belief that damaged people can heal themselves with their own art, come into a terribly depressed situation and beg to fix it — begging with the irrepressible spirit of orphaned children. The children, in a sense, give re-birth to the adults, to adult hope and adult responsibility. After the art comes co-operative work, the will to heal, the will to start over.

In her book, *Awakening Creativity: Dandelion School Blossoms*, Yeh tells the story of just one of her projects — that of the Dandelion School for the children of migrant workers outside of Beijing, where she worked for five years with teachers and children with amazing results to create "a school like no other in the world," converting a school of dreary concrete that mirrored the social disregard of the children's lives. Shetterly writes, "William Sloane Coffin said, 'The highest form of spirituality is justice.' Lily's art is the pursuit of justice and it raises everyone's spirit. Her art insists on accountability — the artist to the community and then the community to itself."

In her book, Yeh shares her story and her philosophy of education. She speaks lovingly of the eighteen years she spent in the Village of Arts and Humanities in Philadelphia, where she worked with hundreds of teachers and students from the primary grades to high school creating everything from banners to murals, gardens, mosaics, dances, stories, poems, and even a fully costumed theater performance. But above all they were creating a "vital, joyful community" from a broken neighborhood. Visiting schools in Philadelphia, she often found them paved with gray cement and encircled with cyclone fences. "Entering a school there often felt like entering a place of confinement. It does not inspire learning." Her project in China was a challenge to turn a concrete jungle into an engaged community.

Lily's own story of transformation began as an art student at Taiwan University. Later, she graduated from the School of Fine Arts at the University of Pennsylvania. After some years experimenting in Western art techniques, she sensed "a strong urge to go home — not the physical home of my parents and siblings, but the spiritual home of ease and enchantment revealed to me through my study of Chinese landscape paintings." Through them she arrived at a "place of wonder and mystery,...a place potent in stillness and tranquility. The Chinese call this the 'dustless world.' Here the word 'dust' does not refer to anything physical. It points to the mental pollution of desire, longing, attachment, and greed, all emotions emanating from the ego." She traveled to Europe as well as to China in an effort "to return 'home' to that 'dustless' world." But, surprisingly, "it was in the dilapidation of North Philadelphia that I found my path of return." Notice how her journey began where Eckhart begins — with "wonder and mystery," which moves into "stillness and tranquility" and the "dustless world" of letting go of mental pollutions. Then, as she became transformed by her experience in Philadelphia, she also transformed the city. Lily writes:

> People called inner-city North Philadelphia "the badlands" because of its prevailing decrepitude, poverty, drug dealing, and violence. But this area contained invaluable hidden treasures. Numerous abandoned properties and vacant lots offered creative opportunities. The transformation of abandoned lands into art parks and gardens became the bone structure of our art project....During my sojourn there from 1986 to 2004, the Village staff, community residents, and volunteers transformed over two hundred empty lots into seventeen parks and gardens, inducing a two-acre tree farm. The Village became a national model for urban revitalization through land transformation, creation of beauty, and grassroots actions. It was there that I realized that art is a powerful tool for social change and that the artist can be at the center of that transformation.

Yeh has gone on to create and re-create similar resurrections in depressed settings around the world. Who can witness Yeh's work and not be inspired?

I find it all thoroughly grounded in her Buddhist and Taoist lineage — but also in that of Meister Eckhart, for she successfully marries the via positiva and the via creativa; the via negativa does not get her down — rather, she finds solutions in creating the via transformativa. She is an agent of transformation through a new vision of education. Shouldn't we all be doing such work?

What the programs and educators we have discussed in this chapter all have in common is a passion for justice and creativity and the necessity to underpin all education worthy of the name in values that matter. We do not teach in order to make smarter villains in the marketplace. We teach to see that justice happens. That is something Eckhart, no less than Jesus and Isaiah and the Buddha and many others, inspires and understands. Eckhart, who was living in a time of academic and religious decadence, insisted that life is the greatest teacher. "Living offers the most noble kind of knowledge. Living causes pleasure and light to be better known than everything we can attain beneath God in this life." Eckhart, like the educators mentioned in this chapter, deliberately chose to leave the comforts of academia to work with the lower classes — the Beguines and the peasants, choosing to speak to the latter in their own German dialect. M.C. Richards summarizes this teaching wonderfully when she writes:

> The fallen / The criminal / The unfaithful / The foolish / The barren / The blind, ill, demented, violent: *these* are the Christ in each of us. If we do not love them, we do not love Him. "I was a stranger," He said, "and ye knew me not." The stranger within, who is unacceptable; the unknown god. "I was the stranger, and ye knew me not." Must we not take this counsel seriously, and reach out our hand to the one whom we fear?

Many of the principles for regenerating education we have discussed in this chapter are currently being put to work at the Academy for the Love of Learning (ALL) in Santa Fe, New Mexico. ALL was started by musicians Leonard Bernstein and Aaron Stern, who is the current president specializing in transformational learning, through myriad programs and projects. The goal of ALL is "to awaken, enliven, nurture and sustain the natural love of learning in people of all ages," and their methods include the arts, contemplative traditions, transformative learning, organizational consulting, and leadership courses that emphasize "leading by being."

Though his era was characterized by pessimism, Eckhart never led from that dark place. He insisted that the via positiva and the via creativa were available to us all. What we have to do is wake up and see and find the images and wisdom we carry inside us. Such an educational philosophy of *educing* our inner wisdom to address suffering and become agents of transformation beckons us still.

CONCLUSION

Where Might Eckhart Take Us?

Eckhart is a mystic among mystics, a prophet among prophets, and a warrior among warriors. He speaks profoundly today to both heart and mind, to person and community, to Christian, Jew, Hindu, Buddhist, Muslim, Goddess worshipper, shaman, and atheist. He speaks to depth psychologists and healers of many stripes, saying a "living life is a healing life." He speaks to activists seeking justice for the environment and in economics, politics, and education. He speaks less in dogma than in images and aphorisms that entice and alert, in language meant to awaken a slumbering species. As the fifteenth-century Indian mystic Kabir puts it, "Why not wake up this morning, you have slept for millions and millions of years."

Beyond Religion

Just as Otto Rank calls us to go "beyond psychology," it is fair to say, Eckhart calls us to go "beyond religion." He calls us beyond religion as structure, dogma, institution, sectarian tribe, and ethnic identity to something more internal, more deep, more real. He speaks to the "inner person" rather than the "outer person" (a phrase he attributes to St. Paul); he focuses on the essence of religion rather than its surface layers. He calls us to spirituality, mystical experience, and prophetic action. He calls us away from external dogma so we might enter the "cave of the heart" and experience the "spark of the soul," which is an experience of the Holy Spirit. He calls for prophetic interference to help end war, tribalism, and the rapaciousness of corporate empire building. He calls for an end to using religion to legitimize the status quo. Instead, he calls us to put our sacred activism, our love energy, to work on behalf of social, economic, ecological, and gender justice. And to honor and foster the mystical dimension of religion, the experiential and intuitive dimension.

Meister Eckhart calls us to go beyond purgation, illumination, and union as the structure of our spiritual journey. Instead, he names our deepest spiritual experiences along the four paths of the via positiva, via negativa, via creativa, and via transformativa. He calls us to follow the mystics to the frontier of consciousness, to enter humanity's next evolutionary stage. He calls us to consider heart and intuition as, in Einstein's words, "a sacred gift," to which our robust rational and intellectual life is a "servant." In this way, in our religious life, we heed the warning of Father Bede Griffiths, who said that in all religious systems "the danger...is that the logical structure and rational doctrine will obscure the mystical vision, so inherent is the tendency of the rational mind to seek to dominate the truth which it should serve." Instead, Eckhart calls us to be the mystic-prophets and mystic-warriors who are needed at this critical moment in human and planetary evolution.

Are we ready to hear Eckhart's words? Are we ready to wake up to the God within and the God who protests? If so, where might Eckhart be inviting us to travel at this critical moment when so much is at stake? What waits for us beyond this present moment?

Speaking frankly, we need to accomplish a new stage in our evolutionary journey. We need to honor and balance both our mammal and compassionate brains, and our creative and analytic brains. We need to go beyond history. In many ways, Eckhart takes us *to the edge*. He encourages us to find the edge of consciousness, the edge of chaos and order, the edge where creativity happens and where evolution can take new leaps of consciousness and action. He takes us to the edge of understanding, where self-criticism and cultural criticism meet. He takes us to the edge of the four paths of joy, grief, birthing, and justice making.

This is another way of saying that Eckhart insists that we do more than rub the surface dimensions of culture and self; we must go *deeply* into them, to the edge of our understandings and experience — as in Carol Christ's phrase, "diving deep and surfacing." It is not enough to wade in, to just get our feet wet. We need to go down deep into the darkness, into the mystery, into the shadow, into the forgotten parts of ourselves as individuals and communities and as a species. Nor is it enough only to go down, whether into the earth, the collective unconscious, or our lower chakras — we must also surface. We must come back, changed and ready to make change. The days of the professional praying class — when individuals entered monasteries to explore the soul in deep contemplation within cloistered communities — are over. That is not the future.

The future requires all of us to dive deep and return, surfacing with the wisdom, the mysteries, and the truths we learned from diving. In this way, we help birth a new culture — in business and economics, in politics and religion, in art and engineering, in community and agriculture, in the media and law — one that, to use Dorothy Day's phrase, "makes it easier to be good." One that makes it easier to be sustainable and to survive as a species.

Surely there is enough folly and pain in evidence all around us to awaken our moral outrage and shout: "Enough is enough. Crazy is crazy. We cannot continue fouling and destroying our very special home, our Earth, the only nest we can survive in. Let us get on with reinventing ourselves before it is too late."

The Four Es

As I mentioned in the introduction, and as I've described throughout, Eckhart assists us in this reinvention in four particular areas — what I call the "Four Es." These are Deep Ecumenism (or interspirituality), Deep Ecology, Deep Economics, and Deep Education. They are deep because they carry with them a newer realization of the sacred. We encounter them not on the surface of things but within the depths of things. Together, they represent the evolutionary leap that we must undergo as a species.

We have encountered them all during our journey with Meister Eckhart. Let us summarize that journey here.

The First E: Deep Ecumenism (or Interspirituality)

When I first coined the term "Deep Ecumenism" twenty-five years ago in my book *The Coming of the Cosmic Christ*, my purpose was to emphasize that the wisdom of the world's spiritual traditions cannot be confined to doctrines and dogmas and institutions and religious garb. I was saying that there is a far deeper layer to religion that must bind us together. That layer is *experience* of the Divine; this is "the cave of the heart" where interspirituality lives. A cave is in the earth and underground; it represents a journey into mystery, not an in-the-light, on-the-page sort of encounter. In another book I explored eighteen myths and teachings that all religions share, and I offered another analogy for interspirituality: "one river, many wells." As Eckhart puts it, Divinity is a "great underground river that no one can dam up and no one can stop." This underground river is the shared wisdom that all religions hold in common. The way I picture it, each religion has its own well that draws from this common river, so we need to honor different wells, then journey deep into whatever well we choose till we come to the one river, the source that is beyond all names. As Nicholas of Cusa says: "Even though you are designated in terms of different religions, yet you presuppose in all this diversity *one religion which you call wisdom*."

These images and namings are efforts to describe the religious/spiritual pilgrimage we need to embark on today. In this effort, Eckhart is out in front, leading us, shouting, "Come along. It's okay. Come to the well; come down to the river, to the underground river."

The example of Eckhart's leadership is everywhere in this book. By placing Eckhart in dialogue with great thinkers and spiritual movements of the past and of today, we see how he anticipated and pollinated and helped connect our current efforts at interspirituality. In chapter one, on the very first step of our journey — the experience of awe, reverence, and gratitude — Eckhart expresses the Jewish tradition embodied by Rabbi Abraham Joshua Heschel. Eckhart links the West to the East (chapters three, nine, and ten), to the mystical teachings of Buddhism, Hinduism, and Sufism, to the experience of nothingness and the Apophatic Divinity and the "spark of the soul." Eckhart is on the same page with cosmological scientists such as Teilhard de Chardin and Thomas Berry (chapter two), as well as with depth psychologists Carl Jung and Otto Rank (chapters seven and eight). Eckhart journeys along with Adrienne Rich to honor the ancient tradition of the Goddess, the Divine Feminine (chapter four), and he reached out to embrace his female contemporaries, the Beguine sisters (chapter five). Eckhart expressed a vision commensurate with that of the historical Jesus that modern scholars Marcus Borg, Bruce Chilton, and John Dominic Crossan have since described (chapter six). Eckhart's deep, critical thinking on Christology surprises us in the number of ways his and today's scholarship are in agreement. Eckhart saw what mainstream scholarship has only recently admitted: that the Christ is all of us, that wisdom was Jesus's tradition as well as his name, that the Cosmic Christ is at the heart of authentic Christianity.

Conversely, we have also seen Eckhart claimed by and embraced by others. Hindu scholar Ananda Coomaraswamy calls Eckhart's sermons a "Western Upanishad." Father Bede Griffiths says Eckhart expresses the "cave of the heart" of Divine revelation. Muslim Sufi scholars have considered Eckhart a fellow Sufi along with people like Rumi, Hafiz, and Ibn El-Arabi. Aboriginal Australian shaman Eddie Kneebone sees in Eckhart the presence of shamanic wisdom. Howard Thurman praises his teachings, which helped name his own deep mystical intuition, and so on.

Thus, Eckhart invites us into Deep Ecumenism. He is telling us not to hold back, for "God is on all paths, and equal in all modes, for the person who can take Him equally."

The Second E: Deep Ecology

Earth survival, human sustainability on the planet, requires an Earth-based spirituality. We cannot survive as a species on the path we are on — only a worldwide commitment to values that respect Mother Earth and all her creatures can give us even an outside chance of survival beyond the twenty-first century. What Thomas Berry calls the "Great Work" and what Teilhard de Chardin calls the "mysticism of evolution" stare us all in the face. They are the universal vocation, the community calling, beckoning us all. No matter what our *particular* profession or circumstance in life — whether we are journalists or teachers, miners or farmers, business owners or preachers, parents or singles — no one can escape this vocation to save Mother Earth as we know her. Climate change affects us all. The health of the oceans, the air, and the rain forests affects us all. When pollution in Chinese cities wafts over North America, and nuclear reactor meltdowns in Japan spread poison to Russia and Europe and America, it affects us all. Drought, famine, floods, more-frequent hurricanes and tornadoes, rising sea levels, melting glaciers — these affect us all. Mother Earth is the common denominator — she is the one cauldron and vessel, the holy chalice, the holy grail, that sustains us all. Do we have the will and the moral imagination to reinvent the way we live on the Earth? To let go of our ties to fossil fuels? Do we have the imagination to move to a new level of creating sustainable energy on the planet?

Meister Eckhart assists us in Deep Ecology in several ways. First, his teachings on the Cosmic Christ and the Christ of the Earth (chapter two) state bluntly that the universe is the Christ (or, if you prefer, the Buddha Nature, the Cosmic Person, the Mother, and so on). He reminds all of us that we live in a sacred world that requires respect, reverence, and responsibility. Can we live in this way? Can we let go of wars with one another and bring that warrior energy to create a unity of purpose that transcends all nations, ethnicities, religions, economic systems, and ideologies? Eckhart, through his Cosmic Christ theology, reminds us how empires can repeat the very crucifixion of the Christ — understood today as Mother Earth and her creatures — that the Roman Empire accomplished two thousand years ago in nailing Jesus to the cross.

To live with reverence for a sacred Earth, we must overcome some of the deep hurt, the shadow attacks and wounds, that prevent our creativity from flowing. Eckhart helps us do this, too, as we saw in his encounters with Carl Jung (chapter seven) and Otto Rank (chapter eight).

Bringing the Divine Feminine back (chapters four and five) is also a big part of honoring the spirit of Mother Earth. Eckhart also leads us to honor wisdom, justice making, and creativity — in society, economics, and education — as we see in chapters twelve and thirteen. And of course, the alignment of his teachings with indigenous wisdom from around the world (such as in chapter eleven) helps us honor the feminine and the "aboriginal mother love" of planet and all creatures. This love and wisdom has been practiced for tens of thousands of years longer than any of the dominant religions in the world today.

The Third E: Deep Economics

If business reigns in our time as the "most powerful force" on the planet, as Anita Roddick maintains, then obviously economics deserves the attention of all of us. Most importantly, we must overthrow the "merchant mentality" Eckhart describes that pervades human society and whose message we absorb daily from the media, while living in an economic bubble of a very few winners and billions of losers. As Eckhart preached from the Cologne cathedral (chapter six), we must cleanse our temples of "moneylenders" who are addicted to power in favor of an economic system that works for all humans and all beings on the planet. We are fully capable of this.

We can envision and create a deeper economics that reflects justice and sustainability, such as that embodied by David Korten, Anita Roddick, and Karl Marx (chapter twelve). We must create a world that works for everyone. An economics that works for everyone. An economics that puts the poorest of the poor before the enabling of the mighty, as Jesus proposed: "Do it to the least and you do it to me.... My house is meant to be a house of prayer and you have turned it into a den of thieves" (Matthew 25:40; 21:13). We must create a world where not only does justice matter but it's the norm, where, as Eckhart says, "justice is one's being, one's being alive, one's life." As Eckhart taught: "If you are in a rapture as great as Saint Paul once experienced, and a beggar came to the door, leave your rapture and give him the soup he needs."

We can "cease the denial," as Eckhart puts it, and recognize what our current economic and political systems are doing to destroy the Earth while lying about it. We can cease the denial and see what military overkill is doing to our financial resources. An economics where justice matters means an economics that works for the Earth and all creatures — not only humans, but water and soil, forests and air, giant leviathans and birds and everything that lives. It is an economics that also works for the future and the generations to come.

This new economics begins within. It must be *deep*. It will arrive when we practice having "enough," when we put aside shallow wants. We need an economics that appeals not to greed but to need, that satisfies justice and compassion first. It will create wealth to share, supporting communities, not merely to gather and keep for ourselves, supporting only individuals. It will contribute to, not obfuscate, the soul growth of others. It will acknowledge that delight and celebration and sharing of rituals are key to the survival of human life rather than an unending barrage of "entertainment" that numbs us to reality. Deep Economics uplifts the spirit of people and celebrates gratitude and community building. Deep Economics is less about earning money than it is about fostering and preserving our lives and our common good.

The Fourth E: Deep Education

Eckhart guides us to honor values, not information. With his help, we can put behind us education for silliness, education for militarism, education for an industrial world of the nineteenth century, education for taking tests, education for boredom, education for anthropocentrism and narrowness, education for the empire. This begins by embracing wonder at our bigger selves, our biggest context, the cosmos as we are now getting to know it, a cosmos awash in creativity and expansion and silence and dark mystery. Why wouldn't education mirror the wonders and imagination of the universe itself? How else can we fit into the universe if we are not learning its wonders and its ways?

As we saw in chapter thirteen, many educators today, including Theodore Richards, M.C. Richards, and Lily Yehare, are seeking ways to bring this wisdom and wonder and creativity into the classroom. They are seeking to replace the bean-counting bureaucrats ruling over fiefdoms of knowledge, over factories of education that deaden the soul. Eckhart can be an instigator of such a revolution for he, as much as anyone, made clear by the teaching and model of his life how creative we all are and how central creativity is to our humanity. He can be a model for the type of wisdom schools that could replace the knowledge factories!

Further, Deep Education is holistic. It honors and encourages our creative right brains as well as our analytic left brains. It combines intellect with values, intuition, and feeling. A values-based and wisdom-based education is a synthesis of body and mind, of heart and head, of wonder and curiosity. As Einstein said, "There is no true science which does not emanate from the mysterious. Every thinking person must be filled with wonder and awe just by looking up at the stars."

An awakened education will make room for the ancient and indigenous forms of education, which worked for tens of thousands of years. By that I mean ceremony and ritual. Ceremony and ritual are how our ancestors taught the younger generation the important stories of life, including creation stories and stories of what it meant to become an adult (rites of passage) and more. A rebirth of ritual and ceremony is essential for a rebirth of education in our time, for that is the bedrock of community awareness and the sharing of joy, grief, transformation, and creativity.

A truly Deep Education would train the intuition, the mystical brain, the place where, as Einstein teaches, values are born and conscience takes hold. Intuition is where wisdom is born, where the Divine Feminine plays, and from where creativity emerges.

Meister Eckhart, Teacher and Guide

Eckhart becomes a teacher and a guide, a prodder and a challenger. He himself is a mystic-warrior — or sacred activist or active contemplative — who calls humanity today to wake up before it is too late, to extend and stretch to a newer, deeper level of being and activity. With warrior courage and mystical intuition, he dares to refashion religion in deep or sacred ways, so that it fosters Deep Ecumenism, Deep Ecology, Deep Economics, and Deep Education. Are we up to the task? Only time will tell. But time is running out. We cannot say we do not have the tools. Eckhart has already offered them to us.

Eckhart's gifts to us are of such a nature that they help to articulate the mystic-warrior in us all and assist in nourishing it. In this book, we named many people who are in tune with his vision — from Rabbi Heschel to Howard Thurman, from David Korten to Adrienne Rich, from Thomas Berry to Anita Roddick, from Rumi to Black Elk — but there are countless others. In the pages of his final work, *Asian Journal*, Catholic monk Thomas Merton regularly scribbled in the margins, "Eckhart is my lifeboat, Eckhart is my lifeboat."

He is a lifeboat for many of us. Activists galore working in ecumenism, economics, ecology, and education — and these are all interconnected, aren't they? — find support, inspiration, challenge, and peace in Meister Eckhart. He is a shining example of what a prophet and mystic, a warrior and contemplative is and can be, thus helping others find their prophet and mystic within themselves. I know it. I have seen the depth of his impact on people time after time, in class after class, in circumstance upon circumstance. His presence and teachings remind us that the prophetic vocation boasts a long lineage. We are not alone. The ancestors, the communion of saints, are with us, urging us on and offering their support. Among these loud but quiet ancestors, Meister Eckhart looms within our midst.

ACKNOWLEDGMENTS

I am deeply grateful for all those who have encouraged my living with, studying, and teaching Meister Eckhart for the past forty years, with special thanks to the thousands of students who have been inspired by him and who have themselves joined the ranks of mystic-prophets as a result. A special thanks to the witness of Sister Dorothy Stang, a student of Eckhart and Hildegard, who was martyred in the Amazon for her work to defend the land and the peasants working on it. Thanks to Steven Herrmann for our many fruitful dialogues on Eckhart and Jung, Whitman, Everson, and more. To John Conger for his generously shared wisdom. To my editors, Jason Gardner and Jeff Campbell at New World Library. To Katherine L. Ziegler for her assistance with translations from the German. To Andrew Harvey for his encouragement for exploring anew the sacred activism of Eckhart. To Gianluigi Gugliermetto for his inspired work with creation spirituality in Italy. To Marvin Anderson for his love of Eckhart and study of the Beguines. And to Josef Quint for his life's work of giving us the critical editions of Eckhart's German works.

And of course gratitude to all those named in the text and footnotes who have brought depth and insight to linking Eckhart to contemporary thought and action, with a special mention of feminist poet Adrienne Rich, whose work is as timely today as it was when I first encountered her and Eckhart in the 1970s; and of M.C. Richards, whose own mystical and warrior-like soul was evidently nourished in our classes on Meister Eckhart. And to friends and associates with whom I make the journey, including Dennis Edwards, Debra Martin, Susan Coppage Evans, Phila Hoopes, Mary Plaster, Ronald Tuazon, Skylar Wilson, Adam Bucko, Pancho Ramos-Stierle, Javier Garcia Lemus, and more. And surely to Aaron Stern and the Academy of the Love of Learning, who make it possible for me to write and research my deepest passions. And finally, to my brother Meister Eckhart, whose companionship and courage teach me so much.

ENDNOTES

Following are abbreviations of primary source texts in German:

Quint Josef Quint, ed., *Meister Eckhart: Deutsche Predigten und Traktate* (Munich, Germany: Carl Hanser Verlag, 1977).
Quint2 Josef Quint, ed., *Meister Eckhart: Die deutschen Werke*, vols. I, II, III, V (Stuttgart, Germany: W. Kohlhammer Verlag, 1958–76).

All citations from Matthew Fox, *Passion for Creation: The Earth-Honoring Spirituality of Meister Eckhart* (Rochester, VT: Inner Traditions, 2000), are translated from the critical editions of Quint's work.

Introduction

Page xiii, *"it is to the mystics that"*: Jolande Jacobi and R. F. C. Hull, eds., *C. G. Jung: Psychological Reflections* (Princeton: Princeton University Press, 1978), 340, 206.
Page xiv, *"What it has taken China"*: Cited in Richard Wilhelm, trans., *The Secret of the Golden Flower: A Chinese Book of Life* (New York: Harvest/HBJ Book, 1962), 144.
Page xv, *for it was in studying Eckhart*: See Matthew Fox, ed., *Western Spirituality: Historical Roots, Ecumenical Routes* (Santa Fe, NM: Bear & Co., 1981), 215–48.
Page xv, *"Meister Eckhart and Karl Marx"* ... *"Creation-Centered Spirituality"*: Matthew Fox, *Wrestling with the Prophets* (New York: Tarcher/Putnam, 1995), 165–99, 75–104.
Page xviii, *I translated in my major work*: Matthew Fox, *Passion for Creation: The Earth-Honoring Spirituality of Meister Eckhart* (Rochester, VT: Inner Traditions, 2000), 429.
Page xix, *"Biblical compassion is not condescension"*: Matthew Fox, *A Spirituality Named Compassion* (Rochester, VT: Inner Traditions, 1999), 13, 43.
Page xix, *"Compassion is quite different from"*: Marcus J. Borg, *Meeting Jesus Again for the First Time* (San Francisco: HarperSanFrancisco, 1994), 47, 48.

Page xix, *It is a pity that Walshe ignored my work*: See Sermons 30 to 36 in Fox, *Passion for Creation*, 415–545.

Page xx, *"Where have you hidden, Beloved"*: Kieran Kavanaugh, O.C.D., and Otilio Rodriguez, O.C.D., *The Collected Works of St. John of the Cross* (Washington, DC: ICS Publications, 1973), 416, 462.

Page xxi, *"We are compassionate like the Father"*: Fox, *Passion for Creation*, 424.

Page xxii, *a new and deeper marriage of Divine Feminine and Sacred Masculine*: For more on this "Sacred Marriage," see Matthew Fox, *The Hidden Spirituality of Men: Ten Metaphors to Awaken the Sacred Masculine* (Novato, CA: New World Library, 2008), 220–76.

Page xxii, *"essentially a contemplative society"*: Steven Herrmann, *William Everson: The Shaman's Call* (New York: Eloquent Books, 2009), 51.

Page xxiii, *"The path of which I speak is"*: Fox, *Passion for Creation*, 165.

1. The God of Awe, Wonder, Radical Amazement, and Justice: Meister Eckhart Meets Rabbi Heschel

Page 1, *"Awareness of the divine"*: Abraham Joshua Heschel, *God in Search of Man: A Philosophy of Judaism* (New York: Farrar, Straus, and Cudahy, 1955), 46.

Page 1, *"All that exists rejoices"*: Fox, *Passion for Creation*, 121.

Page 1, *"beneath the dogmas and traditional"*: Fritz A. Rothschild, cited in John C. Merkle, *The Genesis of Faith: The Depth Theology of Abraham Joshua Heschel* (New York: Macmillan, 1985), xiii.

Page 1, *"the outstanding Jewish thinker...religious life in our culture"*: Ibid., xix, xvii.

Page 2, *"to almost every important Hasidic"*: Ibid., 5.

Page 2, *"Years later I realized that"*: Ibid., 5–6.

Page 3, *"how to think in a Jewish"*: Ibid., 8, 9.

Page 4, *"I speak as a person"*: Ibid., 10–11.

Page 4, *"Faith is not a stagnant pool...Christian metaphysical theology"*: Ibid., xvii, 51, 9.

Page 5, *"Everything praises God"*: Josef Quint, *Meister Eckhart: Deutsche Predigten und Traktate* (Munich, Germany: Carl Hanser Verlag, 1977), 240. Henceforth abbreviated Quint.

Page 5, *"What we lack is not"*: Heschel, *God in Search of Man*, 46.

Page 5, *"stand still and...the universe"*: Abraham Joshua Heschel, *The Insecurity of Freedom: Essays on Human Existence* (New York: Schocken Books, 1966), 47.

Page 5, *"The word 'behold' implies three"*: Quint, 376.

Page 5, *"the silent allusion of things"*: Heschel, *God in Search of Man*, 39.

Page 5, *"the world in its grandeur"*: Abraham Joshua Heschel, *Man Is Not Alone: A Philosophy of Religion* (New York: Farrar, Straus, and Young, 1951), 22.

Page 5, *"Wherever this word...silence there and stillness"*: Fox, *Passion for Creation*, 260.

Page 5, *"sense for the inexpedient"*: Abraham Joshua Heschel, *Who Is Man?* (Stanford, CA: Stanford University Press, 1965), 86.

Page 6, *"Whoever dwells in the goodness"*: Fox, *Passion for Creation*, 206–7.

Page 6, *"want to love God in the same way…are truly fully dead"*: Ibid., 207, 464.

Page 6, *"Yahweh, our Lord"*: Note that all biblical quotes are from the Jerusalem Bible.

Page 7, *"The prophet [or psalmist] marveled"*: Josef Quint, *Meister Eckharts Predigten*, vol. 1 (Stuttgart, Germany: W. Kohlhammer Verlag, 1958), 524. Henceforth abbreviated Quint2.

Page 7, *"It is an amazing thing"*: Fox, *Passion for Creation*, 65.

Page 7, *"the world is not just here"*: Heschel, *Who Is Man?*, 87.

Page 7, *"Heschel begins his depth theology…useless to himself"*: Merkle, *The Genesis of Faith*, 56, 56–57.

Page 8, *"I was once asked why"*: Quint, 311.

Page 8, *"It is impossible to be at ease"*: Heschel, *Man Is Not Alone*, 14–15.

Page 8, *"the immense preciousness of being"*: Ibid., 22; Heschel, *God's Search for Man*, 106.

Page 8, *"Just to be is a blessing"*: Abraham Joshua Heschel, "On Prayer," *Conservative Judaism* 28 (Fall 1973), 8.

Page 8, *"creation is the giving…wish not to be"*: Fox, *Passion for Creation*, 88–89.

Page 9, *"God's isness is…in its existence"*: Ibid., 90, 121.

Page 9, *"God loves all creatures"*: Ibid., 100.

Page 9, *"within our wonder we become"*: Heschel, *Man Is Not Alone*, 39. Italics mine.

Page 9, *"wonder rather than doubt"*: Ibid., 11.

Page 9, *"that begins in doubt"*: Merkle, *Genesis of Faith*, 161.

Page 9, *"the root of man's creative"*: Heschel, *Who Is Man?*, 66.

Page 9, *"to assert that the most sensitive…abyss of radical amazement"*: Heschel, *Man Is Not Alone*, 33, 13.

Page 10, *"God has formed and created"*: Fox, *Passion for Creation*, 117.

Page 10, *"when God made creatures"*: Ibid., 106.

Page 10, *"I often say, and think"*: Quint, 194.

Page 10, *"Human life is holy"*: Abraham Joshua Heschel, *Man's Quest for God: Studies in Prayer and Symbolism* (New York: Charles Scribner's Sons, 1954), 124–25.

Page 10, *"There is no sense of"*: Heschel, *The Insecurity of Freedom*, 44.

Page 10, *"The symbol of God is"*: Heschel, *Man's Quest for God*, 124.

Page 11, *"the grandeur of nature is….are only divine acts"*: Heschel, *God in Search of Man*, 97, 40, 181, 40.

Page 11, *"The roots of existence"*: Heschel, *Who Is Man?*, 31; Heschel, *God in Search of Man*, 54.

Page 11, *"the self did not originate…but a trust"*: Heschel, *Man Is Not Alone*, 48, 47, 48.

Page 11, *Eckhart concurs, saying we*: Fox, *Passion for Creation*, 507.

Page 11, *"we are witnesses rather…life a sacred thing"*: Heschel, *Man Is Not Alone*, 202–3, 226–27.

Page 11, *"God gives nothing good to creatures"*: Quint2, 5:456.

Page 11, *"I am endowed with a will"*: Heschel, *Man Is Not Alone*, 47–48.

Page 11, *"I have not brought"*: Heschel, *Who Is Man?*, 97–98.

Page 11, *"the sublime, the marvel"*: Heschel, *God in Search of Man*, 130.

Page 12, *"The whole earth is full of"*: Abraham Joshua Heschel, *Israel: An Echo of Eternity* (New York: Farrar, Straus, and Giroux, 1968), 10.

Page 12, *"Whereas ontology asks about"*: Heschel, *Who Is Man?*, 71. Italics in original.

Page 12, *"God created the world... all things new' (Ws 7.27)"*: Fox, *Passion for Creation*, 61, 111, 112.

Page 12, *"God called the world into being"*: Abraham Joshua Heschel, *The Sabbath: Its Meaning for Modern Man* (New York: Farrar, Straus, and Young, 1951), 100.

Page 12, *"There is no standing still"*: Quint2, 5:530.

Page 12, *"the transcendent care for being... hatred with love"*: Heschel, *Who Is Man?*, 91; Merkle, *Genesis of Faith*, 183.

Page 12, *"We need feel no discomfort"*: Abraham Joshua Heschel, *A Passion for Truth* (New York: Farrar, Straus, and Giroux, 1973), 159.

Page 13, *"The Torah is primarily"*: Heschel, *Man in Search of God*, 288.

Page 13, *"the just person lives... compassion means justice"*: Fox, *Passion for Creation*, 464, 465, 429.

Page 13, *"Justice is God's nature... His own nature"*: Abraham Joshua Heschel, *The Prophets* (New York: Harper and Row, 1962), 297, 220.

Page 13, *"For the just person"*: Fox, *Passion for Creation*, 472.

2. The Christ of the Cosmos: Meister Eckhart Meets Teilhard de Chardin and Thomas Berry

Page 15, *"The cosmic sense must have"*: Teilhard de Chardin, *Human Energy* (New York: Harcourt Brace Jovanovich, 1978), 82.

Page 15, *"Every being has its own"*: Thomas Berry, *The Great Work: Our Way into the Future* (New York: Bell Tower, 1999), 4.

Page 15, *"All creatures are gladly"*: Fox, *Passion for Creation*, 62.

Page 15, *"Wonder is an act... market place for you"*: Heschel, *Man's Search for God*, 98, 78. He contrasts this to the potentially narcissistic act of doubt: "Doubt is an act in which the mind inspects its own ideas."

Page 16, *"my rational scientific mind"*: personal correspondence from Arne Wyller, August 18, 1996. See Arne Wyller, *The Planetary Mind* (Aspen, CO: MacMurray & Beck, 1996).

Page 16, *"God is the mind"*: Erich Jantsch, *The Self-Organizing Universe* (New York: Pergamon Press, 1980), 308.

Page 16, *"There is no true science"*: William Hermanns, *Einstein and the Poet: In Search of the Cosmic Man* (Brookline Village, MA: Branden Press, 1983), 108, 133.

Page 17, *"storms the firmament"*: Fox, *Passion for Creation*, 120.

Page 17, *"If God had made... comparison to God"*: Quint2, 3:588, 521, 535.

Page 17, *"Humans are meant to be"*: Ibid., 511.

Page 17, *"The heavens... surround everything"*: Fox, *Passion for Creation*, 100.

Page 18, *"Our Lord does indeed"*: Quint, 414.

Page 18, *"Radical amazement is"*: Heschel, *Man in Search of God*, 30.

Page 19, *"the temple of God"*: Quint, 197.

Page 19, *"Much of the wisdom"*: Heschel, *Man Is Not Alone*, 16–17.

Page 20, *"To a mind unwarped by intellectual habit"*: Ibid., 58.

Page 21, *"A degree more of contact"*: Thomas M. King, S.J., and Mary Wood Gilbert, eds., *The Letters of Teilhard de Chardin and Lucile Swan* (Washington , DC: Georgetown University Press, 1993), 94.

Page 21, *"Ever since the first great scientific"*: Roger Garaudy, "The Meaning of Life and History in Marx and Teilhard de Chardin; Teilhard's Contribution to the Dialogue between Christians and Marxists," in *Evolution, Marxism & Christianity: Studies in the Teilhardian Synthesis* (London: The Garnstone Press, 1967), 58–59.

Page 22, *"In Colossians, Christ is the center"*: Bruce Chilton, *Rabbi Paul: An Intellectual Biography* (New York: Doubleday, 2004), 248–49.

Page 22, *"I can no longer see…have their being"*: Pierre Teilhard de Chardin, *Hymn of the Universe* (New York: Harper & Row, 1965), 26, 35.

Page 22, *"God created all things in such a way…remained in the Father"*: Fox, *Passion for Creation*, 73, 72.

Page 23, *"round-about us completely"*: Fox, Ibid., 73.

Page 23, *"God is the ground"*: Quint2, 1:483.

Page 23, *"God is in all creatures…is a book [about God]"*: Quint, 195, 120, 200.

Page 23, *"All goodness flows forth"*: Quint2, 1:488.

Page 23, *"God alone is the sole…Godself most of all"*: Quint, 105, 197.

Page 24, *"that magic word 'evolution' "*: Teilhard de Chardin, *The Heart of Matter* (New York: Harcourt Brace Jovanovich, 1978), 25.

Page 24, *"At the end of the twentieth century…out of the status quo"*: Joerg Rieger, *Christ & Empire: From Paul to Postcolonial Times* (Minneapolis: Fortress Press, 2007), 269, 269–70.

Page 24, *"the great Western discovery…form of all energy"*: King and Gilbert, *Letters*, 255, 268, 247, 218.

Page 25, *"I give the name"*: Teilhard de Chardin, *Human Energy* (New York: Harcourt Brace Jovanovich, 1978), 82.

Page 25, *"Christ is all and. . . they can to express God"*: Fox, *Passion for Creation*, 71, 61, 60, 62.

Page 26, *"That is true. God is constantly"*: Ibid., 66.

Page 26, *"People think God has…God is in all things"*: Ibid., 66, 69.

Page 26, *"God is in the soul"*: Ibid., 77.

Page 27, *"By bringing humans into…things with one another"*: Berry, *The Great Work*, 91.

Page 28, *"In some sense the human"*: Ibid., 91.

Page 28, *"This law of limits…created by humans"*: Ibid., 91–92.

Page 29, *"Our entire industrial system"*: Ibid., 93.

Page 30, *"direct assault on the various…'progress' or 'development' "*: Ibid., 122, 122–23.

Page 30, *"If anyone were to ask"*: Fox, *Passion for Creation*, 204.

Page 30, *"Why do you love"*: Ibid.

Page 31, *"love all creatures equally…is no real equality"*: Ibid., 96.

Page 31, *"The life within the animal...is life itself"*: Ibid., 99.

Page 31, *"in the realm of living beings"*: Berry, *The Great Work*, 148.

Page 31, *"An enormous base...see this universe"*: Joel R. Primack and Nancy Ellen Abrams, *The New Universe and the Human Future: How a Shared Cosmology Could Launch a Global Society* (New Haven, CT: Yale University Press, 2010), 42–43.

Page 32, *"Intelligence can burst out"*: Ibid., 43.

Page 32, *"epic of evolution...the world about us"*: Berry, *The Great Work*, 31, 49.

Page 32, *"All creatures have the capacity...is giving birth"*: Quint, 397, 208.

Page 32, *"The noblest work of God"*: Quint2, 2:754.

Page 33, *"governing principles...comprehensive bonding"*: Berry, *The Great Work*, 169.

Page 33, *"universe is composed...throughout the entire universe"*: Ibid., x–xi, 4.

Page 33, *"Every being has rights"*: Ibid., 5.

Page 34, *"The Great Work now"*: Ibid., 3, 7.

Page 34, "celebration. *It is all...into its orbit"*: Ibid., 170, 174.

Page 34, *"Life lives from its own"*: Quint, 180.

Page 34, *"God shines forth in"*: Ibid., 60.

3. The Apophatic Divinity:
Meister Eckhart Meets Buddhism via Thich Nhat Hanh

Page 35, *"If we can bring into Christianity"*: Thich Nhat Hanh, *Going Home: Jesus and Buddha as Brothers* (New York: Riverhead Books, 1999), 98.

Page 35, *"Love God as God is"*: Fox, *Passion for Creation*, 180.

Page 36, *the Dalai Lama tells us that Merton*: The Dalai Lama, *Toward a True Kinship of Faiths* (New York: Doubleday, 2010), 59.

Page 37, *"superessential darkness that...comprehend the light"*: Fox, *Passion for Creation*, 171–72, 174, 175.

Page 38, *"God is unfathomable and"*: Quint, 408.

Page 38, *"A master says of the first cause"*: Ibid., 236–37.

Page 38, *"Whatever one says...a truly hidden God"*: Fox, *Passion for Creation*, 175.

Page 38, *"God is a nothing"*: Quint, 331.

Page 39, *"Since God has transcendent being"*: Ibid., 167.

Page 39, *"we have to stammer...source of all things"*: Quint2, 2:672.

Page 39, *"The most beautiful thing"*: Fox, *Passion for Creation*, 182.

Page 39, *"Jacob the patriarch came...highest part is nowhere"*: Quint2, 2:673, 671, 673, 674, 668, 669.

Page 40, *"God is a being who always"*: Ibid., 3:538.

Page 40, *"The Word lies hidden in the soul...is to say beyond time"*: Ibid., 1:502, 512, 503.

Page 40, *"essential mind of God"*: Ibid., 3:529.

Page 41, *"All that understanding can grasp...would be present to it"*: Quint, 340, 342.

Page 41, *"must be alone as God"*: Quint2, 3:590.

Page 41, *"How then should one love God?"*: Fox, *Passion for Creation*, 180.

Page 41, *"God is not found...his nameless nothingness"*: Ibid., 183, 184.

Page 42, *"God alone sinks"*: Ibid., 184.

Page 42, *"When all the images of the soul...without likeness"*: Ibid., 185.

Page 42, *"All God wants of you"*: Quint, 180–81.

Page 42, *"True possession of God"*: Ibid., 60.

Page 42, *"the most powerful prayer"*: Ibid., 54–55.

Page 43, *"Here God's ground is my ground"*: Fox, *Passion for Creation*, 117.

Page 43, *"Indeed, if a person thinks"*: Quint, 180.

Page 43, *"The tablet is never so suitable"*: Quint2, 5:545.

Page 44, *"desires nothing at all...detached heart"*: Ibid.

Page 44, *"This cannot be learned"*: Quint, 61.

Page 44, *"It is just like learning...requires constant watchfulness"*: Ibid., 61, 62, 60, 88.

Page 45, *"You should learn to be"*: Ibid., 87.

Page 45, *"As soon as a person has...an end of growing"*: Ibid., 88, 93.

Page 45, *"accept all things...and in all things"*: M. O'C. Walshe, trans., *Meister Eckhart Sermons & Treatises*, vol. 3 (Rockport, MA: Element Inc., 1992), 147, 148. Walshe calls this "sermon" the "master's' final words." They are not found in Quint, *Meister Eckhart*, or Quint, *Meister Eckharts Predigten*, so I reproduce them here and below from Walshe.

Page 46, *"Now someone might say"*: Ibid., 148.

Page 46, *Hildegard of Bingen actually talks about Mary*: Matthew Fox, *Hildegard of Bingen: A Saint for Our Times* (Vancouver, Canada: Namaste, 2012), 111.

Page 46, *"All notions applied to the phenomenal...in using these words"*: Thich Nhat Hanh, *Living Buddha, Living Christ* (New York: Riverhead Book, 1995), 188, 144.

Page 47, *"The ultimate dimension...as a living reality directly"*: Ibid., 140, 130.

Page 47, *"I pray God to rid"*: Fox, *Passion for Creation*, 221.

Page 47, *"We cannot talk about it...touching ultimate reality"*: Thich Nhat Hanh, *Living Buddha*, 139, 151.

Page 48, *"Simple and primitive images...being, and non-being"*: Ibid., 170, 159.

Page 48, *"rid ourselves of all notions"*: Thich Nhat Hanh, *Going Home*, 101.

Page 48, *"the extinction of all...Buddha directly"*: Thich Nhat Hanh, *Living Buddha*, 142, 149.

Page 48, *"The practice of Buddhism...and of happiness"*: Thich Nhat Hanh, *Going Home*, 77.

Page 48, *"in the Buddhist tradition"*: Thich Nhat Hanh, *Living Buddha*, 158–59.

Page 49, *"In breakthrough I learn"*: Fox, *Passion for Creation*, 302.

Page 49, *"The idea of deification"*: Thich Nhat Hanh, *Living Buddha*, 123.

Page 49, *"Why did God become"*: Fox, *Passion for Creation*, 356.

Page 49, *"Mindfulness is the key...a transformational practice"*: Thich Nhat Hanh, *Living Buddha, Living Christ*, 116–17.

Page 49, *"Mindfulness is the light that shows"*: Ibid., 120–21.

Page 50, *"When you practice mindfulness"*: Ibid., 146.

Page 50, *"Concentration is the food"*: Thich Nhat Hanh, *Going Home*, 63–64.

Page 50, *"A pagan scholar was dedicated"*: Matthew Fox, *Meditations with Meister Eckhart* (Santa Fe, NM: Bear & Co., 1983), 47.

Page 50, *"In the phenomenal world"*: Thich Nhat Hanh, *Going Home*, 10.

Page 51, *"everything within the Godhead"*: Fox, *Passion for Creation*, 76–77.

Page 51, *"God is neither small nor big"*: Thich Nhat Hanh, *Going Home*, 8.

Page 51, *Eckhart uses identical language*: Fox, *Passion for Creation*, 182.

Page 51, *Meister Eckhart talks about*: See ibid., 238–50.

Page 51, *"the Buddhist teaching…and non-being"*: Thich Nhat Hanh, *Going Home*, 58–59, 27.

Page 51, *"ontological Buddha, the Buddha…always available"*: Thich Nhat Hanh, *Living Buddha*, 146, 145–46.

Page 52, *"Shakyamuni, the historical Buddha"*: Ibid., 146.

Page 52, *"Not many people…truly alive"*: Thich Nhat Hanh, *Going Home*, 106–7.

Page 53, *"When I touch a rock…that nature within you"*: Ibid., 28, 111–12.

Page 53, *"You are invited to reflect"*: Ibid., 138.

Page 53, *"What good is it to me"*: Fox, *Passion for Creation*, 336.

Page 53, *"We practice in such a way"*: Thich Nhat Hanh, *Going Home*, 92.

Page 53, *"The seed of God is in us"*: Fox, *Passion for Creation*, 118.

Page 54, *"is in your own heart"*: Thich Nhat Hanh, *Living Buddha*, 128.

Page 54, *"God is at home"*: Fox, *Passion for Creation*, 146.

Page 54, *"I like the expression"*: Thich Nhat Hanh, *Living Buddha*, 181.

Page 54, *"All things seek repose"*: Fox, *Passion for Creation*, 380–87.

Page 54, *"You do not have to abandon…in the Kingdom of God"*: Thich Nhat Hanh, *Living Buddha*, 117, 183, 152.

Page 54, *"I have often said"*: Fox, *Meditations*, 24–25.

Page 55, *"Touching the present moment"*: Thich Nhat Hanh, *Living Buddha*, 153.

Page 55, *"tickles God through and through"*: Fox, *Passion for Creation*, 464.

Page 55, *"helps the sick and the"*: Thich Nhat Hanh, *Living Buddha*, 176.

Page 55, *"For me, the Holy Spirit is…is taking refuge"*: Ibid., 177, 122–23.

Page 56, *"Relation accordingly is present"*: Fox, *Passion for Creation*, 198.

Page 56, *"Is there anything"*: Thich Nhat Hanh, *Living Buddha*, 11.

Page 56, *"there is no conflict at all"*: Thich Nhat Hanh, *Going Home*, 196.

Page 56, *"If we can bring into Christianity"*: Ibid., 98.

4. The Divine Feminine: Meister Eckhart Meets Adrienne Rich

Page 57, *"Motherhood (the powerful Goddess)"*: Adrienne Rich, *Of Woman Born: Motherhood as Experience and Institution* (New York: W. W. Norton & Co, 1976), 114–15.

Page 57, *"The maternity bed…is initiated"*: Fox, *Passion for Creation*, 357; Quint2, 3:560.

Page 57, *"Women's spiritual quest"*: Carol P. Christ, *Diving Deep and Surfacing* (Boston: Beacon Press, 1980), 13.

Page 58, *"Prepatriarchal religion…dominate the universe."* Rich, *Of Woman Born*, 107.

Page 58, *Female figurines were… "of a religious awe"*: Ibid., 115, 117.

Page 58, *"whose tides respond"*: Ibid., 108.

Page 59, *"The highest work of God...God in her' (1 Jn. 4:16)"*: Fox, *Passion for Creation*, 441.

Page 59, *"The Great Goddess is found"*: Rich, *Of Woman Born*, 108.

Page 59, *"This water is grace"*: Fox, *Passion for Creation*, 371.

Page 59, *"Sleeping, turning in turn...desecration of ourselves"*: Adrienne Rich, *The Dream of a Common Language: Poems 1974–1977* (New York: W. W. Norton, 1978), 30, 28.

Page 60, *"is the noblest part of"*: Fox, *Passion for Creation*, 367–68.

Page 60, *"The Great Mother, the female...the killer-mother Medea"*: Rich, *Of Woman Born*, 109, 116.

Page 60, *"patriarchal monotheism did not...order created by men"*: Ibid., 119, 83.

Page 61, *"We sink eternally"*: Fox, *Passion for Creation*, 180.

Page 61, *"I sink and float"*: Rich, *Dream of a Common Language*, 7.

Page 61, *"Trusting, untrusting"*: Ibid., 9.

Page 61, *"not bear fruit...trust God too much"*: Fox, *Passion for Creation*, 285–86.

Page 61, *"there is no better sign of"*: Quint, 74.

Page 62, *"The ground of the soul...shed its light"*: Fox, *Passion for Creation*, 175, 263.

Page 62, *"The more a person is sunk"*: Quint2, 2:743.

Page 62, *"We cut the wires"*: Rich, *Dream of a Common Language*, 75.

Page 63, *"and the whole chorus throbbing"*: Ibid.

Page 63, *"If we could learn to learn...with all my intelligence"*: Ibid., 10–11.

Page 63, *"The technology of silence"*: Ibid., 17.

Page 64, *"It was an old theme"*: Ibid., 19.

Page 64, *"You played heroic, necessary"*: Ibid., 55–56.

Page 64, *"an experience of* nothingness...*of power and value"*: Christ, *Diving Deep and Surfacing*, 13, 119, 13. Italics in original.

Page 65, *"The experience of nothingness"*: Ibid., 13. Italics in original.

Page 65, *"affirmation of women's...positivity valued"*: Ibid., 123, 129.

Page 65, *"the courage to see...vision into social reality"*: Ibid., 76, 81, 96.

Page 66, *"A man had a dream"*: Fox, *Passion for Creation*, 309.

Page 66, *"This is what I am"*: Rich, *Dream of a Common Language*, 64. Italics in original.

Page 66, *"extract an almost...him in a divine way"*: Fox, *Passion for Creation*, 291–413, 402, 293, 302, 301.

Page 67, *"It would mean little to me"*: Ibid., 311.

Page 67, *"The Father's speaking is...in creating the creatures"*: Ibid., 316, 322, 323, 335–37, 352.

Page 67, *"rapid river...that is, with myself"*: Ibid., 363, 364, 365.

Page 68, *"Human beings should be...emerge from within"*: Ibid., 367, 399.

Page 68, *"Words too have great"*: Quint2, 1:501.

Page 68, *"pure generation and means"*: Fox, *Passion for Creation*, 404.

Page 68, *"The maternity bed...is initiated"*: Fox, *Passion for Creation*, 357; Quint2, 3:560.

Page 68, *"the soul, too, is in no way"*: Quint, 208.

Page 68, *"God has all his joy"*: Quint2, 2:754.

Page 68, *"the soul that has God"*: Quint, 396.

Page 68, *"fearful creative power...may become 'in' "*: Fox, *Passion for Creation*, 405, 407, 408, 409.

Page 69, *"all things beget themselves"*: Quint2, 3:588.

Page 69, *"with respect to his 'staying with' "*: Ananda K. Coomaraswamy, *The Transformation of Nature in Art* (New York: Dover, 1934), 87.

Page 69, *"the maternity bed is"*: Fox, *Passion for Creation*, 357.

Page 69, *"express an attitude toward"*: Rich, *Of Woman Born*, 93–94.

Page 69, *"was invented by women...would not exist"*: Ibid., 96–97.

Page 70, *"the reception of God"*: Fox, *Passion for Creation*, 407.

Page 70, *"in primordial terms...she was a* transformer": Rich, *Of Woman Born*, 99, 98, 101.

Page 70, *"I am curious and expectant"*: Ibid., 98. Italics mine.

Page 71, *"One of the devastating effects"*: Barbara Charlesworth Gelpi and Albert Gelpi, eds., *Adrienne Rich's Poetry* (New York: W. W. Norton, 1993), 104–5.

Page 71, *"The decision to feed the world"*: Rich, *Dream of a Common Language*, 13.

Page 72, *"Bread is given to us so that"*: Fox, *Passion for Creation*, 499–500.

Page 72, *"But gentleness is active...reconstitute the world"*: Rich, *Dream of a Common Language*, 63–64, 67.

Page 73, *"By the* feminine *I mean...*new kind of human being": Erica Jong, "Visionary Anger," in Gelpi, *Adrienne Rich's Poetry*, 172, 81. Italics mine.

Page 73, *"means to change thinking, "*: Rich, *Of Woman Born*, 81. Italics mine.

Page 73, *"exists in many stages"*: Rich, *Of Woman Born*, 79. Italics mine.

Page 73, *"a natural extension of her"*: Gelpi, *Adrienne Rich's Poetry*, 171–72.

Page 73, *"I believe that feminism must imply...against the* feminine": Ibid., 172.

Page 74, *"No 'man-hater,' the poet...unmothered world"*: Ibid., 181, 187.

Page 74, *"As long as women and women only"*: Rich, *Of Woman Born*, 211–12.

Page 74, *"What do we want...exist as yet"*: Ibid., 211.

Page 75, *"If I could have one wish"*: Ibid., 215.

Page 75, *"maternal name"*: Quint2, 2:688.

5. Liberated and Liberating Sisters: Meister Eckhart Meets Dorothee Soelle, the Beguines Mechtild of Magdeburg and Marguerite Porete, and Julian of Norwich

Page 77, *"Eckhart raised a bold objection"*: Dorothee Soelle, *The Silent Cry: Mysticism and Resistance* (Minneapolis: Fortress Press, 2001), 200.

Page 77, *"The day of my spiritual awakening"*: Sue Woodruff, *Meditations with Mechtild of Magdeburg* (Santa Fe, NM: Bear & Co., 1982), 42.

Page 77, *"God feels great delight"*: Brendan Doyle, *Meditations with Julian of Norwich* (Santa Fe, NM: Bear & Co., 1983), 85.

Page 78, *"To feed the hungry means...in the life of Christ"*: Dorothee Soelle, *Theology for Skeptics: Reflections on God* (Minneapolis: Fortress Press, 1995), 92.

Page 78, *"Martin Buber said that"*: Soelle, *Silent Cry*, 230.

Page 79, *"Meister Eckhart names the three"*: Ibid., 234.

Page 79, *"comes closest to overcoming...hierarchically conceived"*: Soelle, *Theology for Skeptics*, 50, 43–44, 49–50.

Page 79, *"democratizing mysticism...drunk with God"*: Soelle, *Silent Cry*, 20.

Page 80, *"a completely free choice...because it lives for itself "*: Ibid., 25, 59–60.

Page 80, *"It is the absence of all purpose...mystical love of God"*: Ibid., 60–61.

Page 81, *"to appropriate something...the* sunder warumbe*"*: Ibid., 61.

Page 81, *"God, too, loves us without "*: Ibid., 61–62.

Page 81, *"A language free of...exclusion and persecution"*: Ibid., 62, 63.

Page 82, *"There are two ways...things you love"*: Ibid., 177.

Page 83, *Someday, Eckhart says, Mary will become*: I exegete this sermon in Fox, *Passion for Creation*, 478–94.

Page 83, *"This reversal is not only"*: Soelle, *Silent Cry*, 200–201.

Page 84, *"Coming into being at...language and ritual"*: Ibid., 165, 166.

Page 85, *"Governed by no...formalities of a group"*: Ibid., 168.

Page 85, *"a language of daring passion"*: Ibid., 65.

Page 85, *"God is not only...the pattern of myself "*: Woodruff, *Meditations with Mechtild*, 109, 93, 91, 84.

Page 86, *"The soul becomes...speechless"*: Ibid., 83, 82, 79.

Page 86, *"Love the nothing"*: Ibid., 71.

Page 86, *"There comes a time...you must leave love"*: Ibid., 60–61, 58.

Page 87, *"on fire with its long love"*: Ibid., 59.

Page 87, *"God takes the soul...richest Queen"*: Ibid., 55, 48.

Page 87, *"I who am Divine...without beginning"*: Ibid., 46, 42, 36, 33, 30.

Page 87, *"Who is the Holy Spirit?...practice it steadfastly"*: Ibid., 117, 119.

Page 88, *"Nonetheless, the work found"*: Soelle, *Silent Cry*, 120–21.

Page 88, *Soelle thinks that very likely politics*: Ibid., 122.

Page 88, *"The depth of her resistance"*: Ibid., 124.

Page 89, *"empirical and scholastic church"*: Ibid., 122.

Page 89, *"This freedom from every form of "*: Ibid., 123.

Page 89, *"It is a source of wonder...in authenticity of experience"*: Maria Lichtmann in Bernard McGinn, ed., *Meister Eckhart and the Beguine Mystics* (New York: Continuum, 1994), 69, 70.

Page 90, *"at the heart of her apparently...overflowing all boundaries"*: Ibid., 71, 73.

Page 90, *Eckhart's celebrated sermon on the Sermon*: See the sermon and my commentary in Fox, *Passion for Creation*, 213–25.

Page 90, *"pervasive concept of...with the divine will"*: Lichtmann in McGinn, *Meister Eckhart*, 75, 76, 79. The author dismisses any role for virtues in Eckhart's moral theology (note 41, page 78). I disagree strongly with this — what about the great emphasis he puts on justice and compassion?

Page 91, *"from love into...made of two One"*: Ibid., 81, 82.

Page 91, *"the paradigmatic relation...living without a why"*: Ibid., 82, 83, 84 (note 55).

Page 91, *"It is just as astonishing"*: Ibid., 84 (note 55).

Page 92, *"I heard a voice speaking to me"*: Fox, *Hildegard of Bingen*, xiii.

Page 93, *"You speak to me of"*: Woodruff, *Meditations with Mechtild*, 27.

Page 93, *"I saw that God never began"*: Doyle, *Meditations with Julian*, 88, 100.

Page 93, *"I say that beyond these two"*: Fox, *Passion for Creation*, 442.

Page 93, *"Compassion means justice"*: Ibid., 435, 419.

Page 94, *"The goodness that everything...brother and Liberator"*: Doyle, *Meditations with Julian*, 32, 103, 106, 85, 90, 104–5, 99, 101.

Page 94, *"Compassion is a kind...of as our lover"*: Ibid., 81, 80, 113.

Page 95, *"We are a small and lonely"*: Adrienne Rich, "Stepping Backward," *Adrienne Rich, Poems: Selected and New* (New York: Norton, 1975), 9.

6. The Historical Jesus: Meister Eckhart Meets Marcus Borg, Bruce Chilton, and John Dominic Crossan

Page 97, *"The parables [of Jesus]"*: Borg, *Meeting Jesus*, 73.

Page 97, *"Eckhart writes sermons"*: A talk by Dr. Helen Kenick Mainelli at ICCS, Mundelein College, Spring 1981.

Page 97, *"The Kingdom was based on"*: Bruce Chilton, *Rabbi Jesus: An Intimate Biography* (New York: Doubleday, 2000), 137.

Page 99, *"clashes fundamentally with...boots on any necks"*: John Dominic Crossan, *Jesus: A Revolutionary Biography* (San Francisco: HarperSanFrancisco, 1994), 69–70, 71.

Page 100, *"Now there exist two kinds"*: Fox, *Passion for Creation*, 213. Italics mine.

Page 100, *"rich in all things"*: Ibid., 418–19.

Page 101, *"The parables of Jesus are...understanding of life"*: Borg, *Meeting Jesus*, 73–74.

Page 102, *"Blessedness opened its mouth...since God is one"*: Fox, *Passion for Creation*, 213, 455.

Page 102, *"Jesus was known as...work with God"*: Bruce Chilton, *The Way of Jesus: To Repair and Renew the World* (Nashville, TN: Abingdon Press, 2010), 84, 85–86, 87.

Page 103, *"I want to live"*: Mary Oliver, *New and Selected Poems*, vol. 1 (Boston: Beacon Press, 1992), 93.

Page 103, *"Every totalitarian regime...which gives newness"*: Walter Brueggemann, *The Prophetic Imagination* (Minneapolis: Fortress Press, 1978), 45, 97.

Page 104, *"literalmindedness [is]...line of thinking"*: Merkle, *Genesis of Faith*, 121–22.

Page 105, *"to subvert conventional ways"*: Borg, *Meeting Jesus*, 75.

Page 105, *"a rioting mob...in the Temple"*: Chilton, *Way of Jesus*, 94.

Page 105, *"a threat to Judean"*: Chilton, *Rabbi Jesus*, 121.

Page 106, *"This temple, which God wishes"*: Fox, *Passion for Creation*, 450.

Page 106, *"so like to himself...uncreated God alone"*: Ibid., 450, 451, 453.

Page 107, *"In all Jesus' teaching...for divine justice"*: Chilton, *Way of Jesus*, 73, 74.

Page 107, *"Basileia is what kings...immediately in charge"*: Crossan, *Jesus*, 54, 55.

Page 107, *"The Kingdom was based"*: Chilton, *Rabbi Jesus*, 147, 137.

Page 107, *"alternative social vision"*: Borg, *Meeting Jesus*, 49.

Page 108, *"the open commensuality...just and equal world"*: Crossan, *Jesus*, 73, 74.

Page 108, *"bidding this very earth...I have to say"*: Fox, *Passion for Creation*, 498.

Page 108, *"Male dominance is"*: Bruce Chilton, *Mary Magdalene: A Biography* (New York: Doubleday, 2005), 107–8.

Page 108, *"manipulated and paraphrased"*: Chilton, *Rabbi Jesus*, 101.

Page 108, *"The Spirit of the Lord"*: Ibid., 100.

Page 109, *"subversive wisdom...taken-for-granted world"*: Borg, *Meeting Jesus*, 75, 81.

Page 109, *"Whatever a person willingly...abandon all things"*: Quint, 67, 53.

Page 109, *"Jesus committed himself"*: Chilton, *Rabbi Jesus*, 70.

Page 110, *"if you want the kernel"*: Fox, *Passion for Creation*, 304, 303–6.

Page 110, *"suffering was not to be...gateway to vision"*: Chilton, *Rabbi Jesus*, 277, 280, 242.

Page 110, *"Death as an image"*: Borg, *Meeting Jesus*, 86–87.

Page 110, *"As in the earlier case"*: Chilton, *Way of Jesus*, 90–91.

Page 111, *"a program to train"*: Chilton, *Mary Magdalene*, 79.

Page 111, *"Contrary to a popular fallacy...God's son"*: Chilton, *Rabbi Jesus*, 58 (note 3), 210.

Page 111, *"of festive celebration...Jesus' journeys"*: Ibid., 77, 74, 77.

Page 112, *He was announcing the new*: Chilton, *Way of Jesus*, 95–96.

Page 112, *"Banquet imagery is central"*: Borg, *Meeting Jesus*, 93 (note 47), 94.

Page 112, *"The rules of tabling and eating...into the meal"*: Crossan, *Jesus: A Revolutionary Biography*, 68, 71, 177–178.

Page 112, *"Jesus crafted his holy feasts...in the Temple"*: Chilton, *Rabbi Jesus*, 250, 253–54.

Page 113, *"The radical meaning of his words"*: Ibid., 255.

Page 113, *"Surely we have been invited...dear friends"*: Fox, *Passion for Creation*, 544.

Page 113, *"Exactly there we too"*: Quint2, 2:706.

Page 113, *"Our Lord teaches us...of God (Luke 8:11)"*: Fox, *Passion for Creation*, 510, 511.

Page 114, *"the good tree of which"*: Ibid., 511.

Page 114, *"Christ's whole nobility belongs...heart of the Father"*: Ibid., 523, 512, 514.

Page 114, *"the great Reminder...merited the anger"*: Ibid., 526.

Page 115, *"What our Lord calls a royal person"*: Ibid., 518.

7. Depth Psychology: Meister Eckhart Meets Carl Jung

Page 117, *"Only in Meister Eckhart"*: Carl Jung, *Memories, Dreams, Reflections*, A. Jaffe & R. and C. Winston, eds. (New York: Vintage, 1961), 68–69.

Page 117, *"The art of letting things happen"*: Carl Jung, commentary in Richard Wilhelm, trans., *The Secret of the Golden Flower* (New York: Harcourt Brace Jovanovich, 1962), 93.

Page 117, *"God, who is without a name"*: Quint2, 1:496.

Page 117, *"The main interest of my work"*: Gerhard Adler, ed., *C. G. Jung Letters*, vol. 1 (Princeton, NJ: Bollingen, 1953), 377.

Page 118, *"Jung was no casual reader"*: John P. Dourley, *A Strategy for a Loss of Faith: Jung's Proposal* (Toronto: Inner City Books, 1992), 116.

Page 118, *"Man is no longer a distinct"*: C. G. Jung, *Analytical Psychology: Its Theory and Practice* (New York: Vintage, 1968), 46.

Page 119, *"God, who is without a name...her highest part"*: Quint2, 1:496, 440.

Page 119, *"The soul, too, has no name...in great secrecy"*: Ibid., 2:681, 678.

Page 120, *"The Godhead alone"*: Ibid., 671.

Page 120, *Jung compares the conscious*: C. G. Jung, *Civilization in Transformation, Collected Works*, vol. 10 (London: Routledge & Kegan Paul, 1964), 454.

Page 120, *"God is a being who"*: Quint2, 3:538.

Page 120, *"There is something in the soul"*: Ibid., 1:525.

Page 120, *"Nothing so much hinders"*: Fox, *Passion for Creation*, 143.

Page 120, *"coincidence in time"*: C. G. Jung, *The Structure and Dynamics of the Psyche, Collected Works*, vol. 8 (New York: Pantheon Books, 1960), 849.

Page 120, *"The key word here is meaning"*: Steven B. Herrmann, "C. G. Jung & Teilhard de Chardin: Peacemakers in an Age of Spiritual Democracy" (unpublished manuscript, 2013), 22.

Page 121, *"if great sums of energy"*: Ira Progoff, *Jung, Synchronicity, and Human Destiny* (New York: The Julian Press, 1973), 3–4.

Page 121, *"The psychoid archetype"*: Jung, *Civilization in Transformation*, 10:450.

Page 122, *"Whatever God does...God works compassion"*: Fox, *Passion for Creation*, 441, 442.

Page 123, *"greatest thinker...the breath of life"*: Jung, *Memories, Dreams, Reflections*, 55–57, 68–69.

Page 123, *"The 'relativity of God'...by conscious effort"*: C. G. Jung, *Psychological Types, Collected Works*, ed. R. F. C. Hull, Bollingen Series XX, vol. 6 (Princeton, NJ: Princeton University Press, 1976), 243.

Page 124, *"I am as certain...we are abroad"*: Fox, *Passion for Creation*, 146–47.

Page 124, *"Today we are obliged"*: Jung, *Structure and Dynamics of the Psyche,* ¶995.

Page 124, *"I believe that, after thousands...it would never have been"*: C. G. Jung, *Archetypes and the Collective Unconscious, Collected Works*, eds. Sir Herbert Read, Michael Fordham, and Gerhard Adler, Bollingen Series XX, vol. 9 (Princeton, NJ: Princeton University Press, 1980), ¶177. Italics in original.

Page 124, *"nothing is holy"*: C. G. Jung, *The Symbolic Life, Collected Works*, eds. Gerhard Adler and R. F. C. Hull, Bollingen Series XX, vol. 18 (Princeton, NJ: Princeton University Press, 1977), 254.

Page 125, *"life itself flows from...go somewhat astray"*: Ibid., 244–45.

Page 125, *"Christ says, 'The kingdom...living in his kingdom"*: Ibid., 250.

Page 125, *"invested in objects...of intense vitality"*: Ibid., 250, 248.

Page 125, *"strongly reminiscent of that"*: Jung, *Psychological Types*, 6:249.

Page 126, *Citing Eckhart's play...in the soul now*: Steven B. Herrmann, *Walt Whitman: Shamanism, Spiritual Democracy, and the World Soul* (New York: Eloquent Books, 2010), 10, 15.

Page 126, *"The determining force...noble words"*: Jung, *Psychological Types*, 6:251. Italics in original.

Page 126, *"If anyone should ask me...renewal of life"*: Ibid., 252–53.

Page 127, *"images are to the psyche"*: John P. Conger, *Jung & Reich: The Body as Shadow* (Berkeley, CA: North Atlantic Books, 2005), 191.

Page 127, *"Saint John says that from"*: Fox, *Passion for Creation*, 363. See the entire sermon and my exegesis of it, 363–79.

Page 127, *"We read about a woman"*: Ibid., 371.

Page 127, *"How does one come...active imagination"*: Jung, *Structure and Dynamics of the Psyche*, 8:67.

Page 127, *"But the supreme meaning"*: C. G. Jung, *The Red Book* (New York: Norton, 2009), 229.

Page 128, *"the land of the mothers"*: Dourley, *Strategy for a Loss*, 94–95.

Page 128, *"With the birth you discover"*: Fox, *Passion for Creation*, 291.

Page 128, *"God is a function of the soul...the 'flood and source' "*: Jung, *Psychological Types*, 6:254, 255.

Page 129, *"The shadow is simply"*: Ibid., 85.

Page 129, *"The art of letting things happen"*: Jung, *Secret of the Golden Flower*, 93.

Page 129, *"guiding myth for his life...driven into opposition"*: Conger, *Jung & Reich*, 84, 86.

Page 130, *"imagined, unseen, primitive"*: Ibid., 87.

Page 131, *"Modern man must rediscover...sharpens our skill"*: Ibid., 88, 89, 88.

Page 131, *"Our whole being depends"*: Quint, 95.

Page 131, *"It is very silly"*: Quint2, 2:664–65.

Page 132, *"God is nothing"*: Fox, *Passion for Creation*, 194.

Page 132, *"saw nothing, and this...nameless nothingness"*: Ibid.

Page 132, *"imagined, unseen"*: Conger, *Jung & Reich*, 87.

Page 133, *"Your deep soul hides itself from...and what will be"*: Daniel C. Matt, *The Essential Kabbalah: The Heart of Jewish Mysticism* (San Francisco: HarperSanFrancisco, 1996), 124, 69, 70.

Page 134, *"If you think of yourself...and dry land"*: Ibid., 71.

Page 135, *"The development of Western philosophy"*: C. G. Jung, *Psychology and Religion: West and East, Collected Works*, eds. Sir Herbert Read and Gerhard Adler, Bollingen Series XX, vol. 11 (Princeton, NJ: Princeton University Press, 1975), ¶759.

Page 135, *"The deeper 'layers' of the psyche"*: Jung, *Archetypes and the Collective Unconscious*, 9:173.

Page 135, *Eckhart also talks about*: Fox, *Passion for Creation*, 117.

Page 136, *"Man's liberation is not"*: Conger, *Jung & Reich*, 199–200.

Page 136, *"The meeting with oneself"*: Jung, *Archetypes and the Collective Unconscious*, 9:21–22.

Page 137, *"Much of his [Jung's] psychology...numinosity of the night"*: John P. Dourley, *On Behalf of the Mystical Fool: Jung on the Religious Situation* (New York: Routledge, 2010), 196, 202, 203.

Page 137, *"The numerous analogies...creates the world anew"*: Ibid., 255, 256.

Page 138, *"the bridge from dogma...relic of the past"*: Ibid., 101, 103.

Page 138, *"Too few people have experienced"*: Murray Stein, *Jung on Christianity* (Princeton, NJ: Princeton University Press, 1999), 189.

8. Psychotherapy and the "Unio Mystica": Meister Eckhart Meets Otto Rank

Page 139, *"Human nature is...of creation itself"*: Otto Rank, *Beyond Psychology* (New York: Dover, 1941), 255, 250.

Page 139, *"If anyone were to ask life"*: Fox, *Passion for Creation*, 204.

Page 139, *"The individual is not just"*: Cited in E. James Lieberman, *Acts of Will: The Life and Work of Otto Rank* (New York: The Free Press, 1985), 396.

Page 140, *"I believe that we have"*: Otto Rank, *Psychology and the Soul: A Study of the Origin, Conceptual Evolution, and Nature of the Soul,* trans. Gregory C. Richter and E. James Lieberman (Baltimore: Johns Hopkins University Press, 1998), 113.

Page 141, *"dynamic forces governing"*: Ibid., 278.

Page 141, *"the epitome of the irrational"*: Rank, *Beyond Psychology*, 250.

Page 141, *"radical amazement...of wisdom"*: Heschel, *God in Search of Man*, 30–31, 74.

Page 142, *"Vital human values"*: Rank, *Beyond Psychology*, 14.

Page 142, *"Rationalistic psychology...more democracy"*: Ibid., 289.

Page 142, *"The only remedy is an"*: Ibid.

Page 143, *"When such a constructive"*: Ibid.

Page 143, *"human nature is...negation of life"*: Ibid., 255, 278.

Page 143, *"Joy is the human's...supremely conscious"*: Matthew Fox, *Sheer Joy: Conversations with Thomas Aquinas on Creation Spirituality* (San Francisco: HarperSanFrancisco, 1991), 119, 120.

Page 143, *"The individual is not just"*: Lieberman, *Acts of Will*, 396.

Page 144, *"Man is born beyond"*: Rank, *Beyond Psychology*, 16.

Page 144, *"power of rebirth"*: Otto Rank, *Art and Artist* (New York: Knopf, 1932), 128.

Page 144, *Eckhart says the first*: Fox, *Passion for Creation*, 111–13.

Page 145, *"in the jointly created"*: Robert Kramer, "The Birth of Client-Centered Therapy: Carl Rogers, Otto Rank, and 'The Beyond,'" *Journal of Humanistic Psychology* 35, no. 4 (Fall 1995), 95.

Page 145, *"beyond experiences...a greater whole"*: Rank, *Art and Artist*, 110.

Page 145, *"cries out in beloved"*: Otto Rank, *The Trauma of Birth* (New York: Dover, 1924), 177.

Page 145, *"potential restoration of a union"*: Rank, *Art and Artist*, 113.

Page 146, *"This identification is the echo"*: Otto Rank, *Modern Education* (New York: Agathon Press, 1968), 376.

Page 146, *"Psychology is searching"*: Rank, *Beyond Psychology*, 37.

Page 146, *"Immensity is within ourselves...of his own being"*: Gaston Bachelard, *The Poetics of Space* (Boston: Beacon Press, 1994), 184, 193, 195.

Page 147, *"God is voluptuous and delicious"*: Fox, *Meditations with Meister Eckhart*, 33.

Page 147, *"In the psychic realm...corresponding Now"*: Rank, *Psychology and the Soul*, 127. Italics in original.

Page 147, *"from the past to the* present": Otto Rank, *A Psychology of Difference: The*

American Lectures, trans. Robert Kramer (Princeton, NJ: Princeton University Press, 1996), 268. Italics in original.

Page 147, *"God is in this power"*: Fox, *Passion for Creation*, 113.

Page 148, *"unborn self"*: Ibid., 217.

Page 148, *"We sink eternally from"*: Fox, *Meditations with Meister Eckhart*, 49.

Page 148, *"I have learned that"*: Rank, *Psychology of Difference*, 270.

Page 148, *"is unable to accomplish"*: Ibid.

Page 149, *Mysticism is our "yes"*: See Matthew Fox, *Prayer: A Radical Response to Life* (New York: Jeremy Tarcher, 2001).

Page 149, *"All neurotic reactions"*: Rank, *Psychology of Difference*, 258. Caps and italics in original.

Page 149, *"Neither Freud, nor Jung…create externally"*: E. James Lieberman and Robert Kramer, eds., *The Letters of Sigmund Freud & Otto Rank: Inside Psychoanalysis* (Baltimore: Johns Hopkins University Press, 2012), 276, 277.

Page 150, *"United with God"*: Fox, *Passion for Creation*, 494.

Page 150, *"We do not possess…into the child"*: Rank, *Psychology of Difference*, 271.

Page 150, *"The child lives mentally…with cosmic life"*: Ibid., 272, 273. Italics in original.

Page 151, *"Instead of psychologizing the child"*: Ibid., 273.

Page 152, *"beyond Freud"*: Rank, ibid., 116, 242.

Page 152, *"In The Trauma of Birth"*: Rank, *Psychology and the Soul*, 113.

Page 153, *"Psychology has less to do…facts are interpretations"*: Ibid., 127–28, 95, 270–71, 277.

Page 153, *"Relation is present"*: Fox, *Passion for Creation*, 198.

Page 153, *"The new hero, still"*: Lieberman, *Acts of Will*, 335.

Page 154, *"he is unable to accept this"*: Rank, *Psychology of Difference*, 268.

Page 154, *"The individual is both"*: Ibid., 103.

Page 154, *"you will discover all"*: Fox, *Passion for Creation*, 291.

Page 154, *"a much more active role"*: Rank, *Psychology of Difference*, 268. I have written in greater length about Rank's contribution to a spirituality of creativity in my essay "Otto Rank on the Artistic Journey as a Spiritual Journey, the Spiritual Journey as an Artistic Journey," in Matthew Fox, *Wrestling with the Prophets* (New York: Jeremy Tarcher, 1995), 199–214. See also Matthew Fox, *Creativity: Where the Divine and the Human Meet* (New York: Jeremy Tarcher, 2002), passim.

Page 154, *"I meant by artist the creative"*: Lieberman and Kramer, *Letters of Sigmund Freud*, 276.

Page 155, *"Whatever can be truly"*: Fox, *Passion for Creation*, 399.

Page 155, *"Correct understanding is one of…one's own ego"*: Rank, *Psychology of Difference*, 209, 95.

Page 155, *"more about research than…creature to creator"*: Lieberman and Kramer, *Letters of Sigmund Freud*, 287, 277.

Page 155, *"the post-Freudian challenge"*: Ibid., 287.

9. Wisdom of Hinduism: Meister Eckhart Meets
Ananda Coomaraswamy and Father Bede Griffiths

Page 157, *"Eckhart's* Sermons *might well"*: Coomaraswamy, *The Transformation of Nature in Art*, 61, 201 (note 55).

Page 157, *"In Hinduism, everything turns to"*: Bede Griffiths, *The Cosmic Revelation: The Hindu Way to God* (Springfield, IL: Templegate Publishers, 1983), 17.

Page 157, *"The divine nature is"*: Fox, *Passion for Creation*, 380, 381.

Page 158, *"unique fusion of...universal language"*: Robert Strom, ed., *Guardians of the Sun-Door: Late Iconographic Essays & Drawings of Ananda K. Coomaraswamy* (Louisville, KY: Fons Vitae, 2004), back cover.

Page 159, *"There was a time when...and at all times"*: Coomaraswamy, *Transformation of Nature*, 3, 201 (note 55), 201–2 (note 56). He adds: "See from this point of view R. Otto, *Mysticism East and West* (New York, 1931), and my *New Approach to the Vedas* (London, 1934)."

Page 159, *"there is nevertheless a...the gift of God"*: Ibid., 61.

Page 160, *"The real analogy between"*: Ibid., 61–62.

Page 160, *"Eckhart's nearest and natural"*: Ibid., 202 (note 57).

Page 160, *"Eckhart's whole conception"*: Ibid., 62.

Page 161, *"recollection, contemplation, illumination"*: Ibid., 93–94. I have removed Coomaraswamy's references to these phrases found in Eckhart's sermons, since they are taken from the Evans translations.

Page 162, *"sharing one another's...and to share"*: Griffiths, *Cosmic Revelation*, 7, 16, 17, 25.

Page 162, *"translate the mystery of Christ...tend to betray it"*: Bede Griffiths, *Return to the Center* (Springfield, IL: Templegate Publishers, 1977), 114, 108.

Page 163, *"a divine revelation...the divine Mystery"*: Ibid., 109, 110.

Page 163, *"The fact that Rome became"*: Griffiths, *The Marriage of East and West* (Springfield, IL: Templegate Publishers, 1982), 202.

Page 163, *"We have to go beyond...Confucianism and Shintoism"*: Ibid.

Page 164, *"It would seem that Hinduism"*: Ibid., 175.

Page 164, *"it is not sufficient to return...surpasses knowledge"*: Griffiths, *Return to the Center*, 111–12.

Page 164, *"the 'house of the womb'"*: Griffiths, *Cosmic Revelation*, 37.

Page 165, *"It is a mystery which cannot...this, not this"*: Ibid., 49, 54.

Page 165, *"The Father is* nirguna...abyss of nothingness"*: Griffiths, *Return to the Center*, 126, 128.

Page 165, *"the essential truth of Hinduism...being is revealed"*: Ibid., 120.

Page 166, *"We reduce everything to atoms...animals, in people"*: Ibid., 52.

Page 166, *"Where is God?...present in everything"*: Ibid., 24, 43.

Page 167, *"is the source of all"*: Griffiths, *Marriage of East and West*, 60.

Page 167, *"the cosmic man...transcendent consciousness"*: Ibid., 66–67.

Page 168, *"Shiva Nataraja, the Dancing"*: Ibid., 41–42.

Page 168, *"In the center of the castle"*: Juan Mascaro, trans., *The Upanishads* (New York: Penguin, 1965), 120, 121.

Page 168, *"a little thing round as"*: Doyle, *Meditations with Julian*, 25.

Page 168, *"The wise man...to self knowledge"*: Griffiths, *Marriage of East and West*, 66.

Page 169, *"If you want to reach your true"*: Ibid., 62.

Page 170, *"What is this kingdom of God?...kingdom of heaven, within"*: Griffiths, *Return to the Center*, 107–8.

Page 170, *"All external religion...transform men's lives"*: Ibid., 108, 116–17, 118.

Page 171, *"The Western world...form of religion"*: Griffiths, *Marriage of East and West*, 153.

Page 171, *"Intuition is a knowledge...rational consciousness"*: Ibid., 154, 155.

Page 171, *"receives the impressions of...original ground"*: Ibid., 156. Italics mine.

Page 172, *"Intuition, then, is the knowledge...we have to learn"*: Ibid., 157.

Page 172, *"the intuitive which grasps...the rational mind"*: Ibid., 47.

Page 173, *"Attain to the utmost emptiness"*: Ibid., 158.

Page 173, *"as if the eternal wisdom...efforts and motions"*: Fox, *Passion for Creation*, 380–81, 382, 380.

Page 174, *"not by intellect, or by reason"*: Griffiths, *Return to the Center*, 120–21.

Page 174, *"living word of God...still remains unspoken"*: Fox, *Passion for Creation*, 57–59.

Page 174, *"which means to swell...Brahman, one only"*: Griffiths, *Marriage of East and West*, 59–60.

Page 175, *"The arising of the image"*: Coomaraswamy, *Transformation of Nature*, 76. Italics mine.

Page 175, *"All the evidence of history...of integral wholeness"*: Griffiths, *Marriage of East and West*, 45.

Page 176, *"For most people the way"*: Griffiths, *Return to the Center*, 140.

Page 176, *"among things and not in things...he or she does"*: Fox, *Passion for Creation*, 481, 483, 485, 489, 493.

Page 177, *"be done with detachment"*: Griffiths, *Return to the Center*, 140–41.

Page 177, *"God 'must do, willy-nilly' "*: Coomaraswamy, *Transformation of Nature*, 88–89.

Page 177, *" 'Working for work's sake' sounds"*: Ibid., 89.

10. Eckhart as Sufi: Meister Eckhart Meets Rumi, Hafiz, Ibn El-Arabi, and Avicenna

Page 179, *"Ah, one spark flew"*: Jonathan Star and Shahram Shiva, trans., *A Garden beyond Paradise: The Mystical Poetry of Rumi* (New York: Bantam Books, 1992), 112.

Page 179, *"In the spark of the soul"*: Fox, *Passion for Creation*, 373–74.

Page 179, *"Love is the creed"*: Idries Shah, *The Sufis* (New York: Doubleday, 1964), 153.

Page 179, *"I have made the journey"*: Daniel Ladinsky, trans., *The Gift: Poems by Hafiz the Great Sufi Master* (New York: Arkana, 1999), 148.

Page 180, *"Love is nothing other than"*: Fox, *Passion for Creation*, 76.

Page 180, *"Exactly how old is...a necessary adventure"*: Shah, *Sufis*, 54, 56.

Page 181, *"Destroy your house"*: Ibid., 447–48.

Page 182, *"Within mankind is a 'treasure'"*: Ibid., 447.

Page 182, *"He who tastes not...by external means"*: Ibid., 62, 47.

Page 182, *"I say that beyond these two...works compassion. Amen."* Fox, *Passion for Creation*, 442.

Page 183, *"Writing often under threat...through divine love"*: Shah, *Sufis*, 48, x.

Page 184, *"This is not a religion"*: Ibid., 49.

Page 184, *"the greatest Master...reasoning powers"*: Ibid., 161–62.

Page 185, *"whereas Christian mystics"*: Ibid., xv–xvi.

Page 185, *"so strongly resembles...'we must go,' said Francis"*: Ibid., 258.

Page 186, *"very much penetrated...looking for his roots"*: Ibid., 261–62.

Page 186, *"dervish organization...an Arab salutation"*: Ibid., 263.

Page 186, Shah makes the point... *"still my creed and faith"*: Ibid., 62, 55, 165.

Page 187, *"Cross and Christians"*: Ibid., 153.

Page 187, *"You claim skill in every"*: Star and Shiva, *Garden beyond Paradise*, 31.

Page 188, *"poetry was only...Rumi was practicing"*: Shah, *Sufis*, 151, 152.

Page 188, *"Secretly we spoke"*: Star and Shiva, *Garden beyond Paradise*, 35.

Page 188, *"Noise is a cruel...most want to say"*: Ladinsky, *Gift*, 51, 143.

Page 189, *"We search for him"*: Star and Shiva, *Garden beyond Paradise*, 101.

Page 190, *"There is something in the soul"*: Quint2, 1:525.

Page 190, *"the apex of the soul...is He the Father"*: Quint, 385.

Page 190, *"What we have to do"*: Shah, *Sufis*, 351.

Page 191, *"You cannot just...an inner organ"*: Ibid., 352, 354.

Page 191, *"God has not bound...take Him equally"*: Quint2, 5:522.

Page 191, *"People know in the now...eternal now."* Ibid., 3:566.

Page 191, *"spirit is the highest"*: Quint, 396.

Page 192, *"In every way the spark"*: Quint2, 1:510.

Page 192, *"hidden something like...recognizes God"*: Fox, *Passion for Creation*, 373, 374.

Page 192, *"This spark...wants nothing"*: Quint, 316.

Page 192, Eckhart scholar Reiner Schurmann... *"I possess everything"*: See Fox, *Passion for Creation*, 374, 108, 109–10, 113.

Page 193, *"radiance, splendor, brilliance...the point of Wisdom"*: Matt, *Essential Kabbalah*, 175.

Page 193, *"from which evolved...varieties of existence"*: Ibid., 97, 52.

Page 194, *"In the Beginning...and sparkled as one"*: Daniel Matt, trans., *Zohar: The Book of Enlightenment* (New York: Paulist Press, 1983), 119.

Page 194, *"raise those sparks...food and drink"*: Matt, *Essential Kabbalah*, 97, 144, 149–50.

Page 194, *"there is no greater path...you serve God"*: Ibid., 151.

Page 195, *"new realization of love"*: Shah, *Sufis*, 361.

Page 195, *"The sun's eyes are painting"*: Ladinsky, *Gift*, 189–90.

Page 196, *"I have made the journey"*: Ibid., 148.

Page 197, *"All creatures are God's children...he loves for himself"*: Ana Matt, *Islam* (Berkeley, CA: n.d.), 115, 105, 106, 115.

Page 198, *"the Earth is a mosque...of those signs"*: Ibrahim Abdul-Matin, *GreenDeen: What Islam Teaches about Protecting the Planet* (San Francisco: Berrett-Koehler, 2010), 1, 7.

Page 198, *"Ah, one spark flew"*: Star and Shiva, *Garden beyond Paradise*, 112.

11. Indigenous Wisdom and Shamanism: Meister Eckhart Meets Eddie Kneebone, Black Elk, and Bill Everson

Page 201, *"The round form of the drum"*: Joseph Epes Brown, ed., *The Sacred Pipe* (New York: Penguin Books, 1972), 69.

Page 201, *"The aspect of being at one with"*: Eddie Kneebone, "An Aboriginal Response," in Catherine Hammond, *Creation Spirituality and the Dreamtime* (Newtown NSW, Australia: Millennium Books, 1991), 93–94.

Page 201, *"God loves all creatures"*: Fox, *Passion for Creation*, 92.

Page 202, *"The cave painters were concerned"*: Thomas Merton, *Conjectures of a Guilty Bystander* (Garden City, NY: Doubleday & Company, 1966), 307.

Page 203, One shamanistic scholar believes: Herrmann, *Walt Whitman*, 14.

Page 203, *"In moments of confusion"*: Thomas Berry, *The Dream of the Earth* (San Francisco: Sierra Club Books, 1988), 211.

Page 203, *"God dwells in the innermost"*: Fox, *Passion for Creation*, 65.

Page 204, *"Poetry is more primitive"*: Tim Hunt, ed., *The Collected Poetry of Robinson Jeffers* (Stanford, CA: Stanford University Press, 2000), 4:374–75.

Page 204, *"every creature is a word...the entire cosmos"*: Fox, *Passion for Creation*, 65.

Page 204, *"We should understand that"*: Brown, *Sacred Pipe*, xx.

Page 205, *"are persons who stand out"*: Mircea Eliade, *Shamanism: Archaic Techniques of Ecstasy* (Princeton, NJ: Princeton University Press, 1964), 8.

Page 205, *"fundamental in the human condition...and in beauty"*: Ibid., 504, 507, 4, 5, 12.

Page 205, *"The shamans have played...'powers of evil'"*: Ibid., 508, 509.

Page 206, *"This is the Dreamtime"*: Hammond, *Creation Spirituality*, 12.

Page 206, *"Aboriginal spirituality is the belief...from the Dreamtime"*: Ibid., 89.

Page 206, *"God poured his being"*: Fox, *Passion for Creation*, 92.

Page 207, *"I give you a new commandment...strength in all things"*: Ibid., 98, 99.

Page 207, *"I have found peace of heart"*: Hammond, *Creation Spirituality*, 93.

Page 207, *"The aspect of being at one...a part of it"*: Ibid., 93–94.

Page 208, *"If mysticism is found...read its signs"*: Ibid., 47, 46.

Page 209, *"state of silence...people is sealed"*: Ibid., 48, 42.

Page 209, *"The ordinary man sees God...transformation the poet celebrates"*: William Everson, *The Excesses of God: Robinson Jeffers as a Religious Figure* (Stanford, CA: Stanford University Press, 1968), 12, 13.

Page 210, *"the totem of the shaman"*: Lee Bartlett, ed., *Earth Poetry: Selected Essays & Interviews of William Everson* (Berkeley, CA: Oyez, 1980), 187.

Page 210, *"dancing yet...who ever lived"*: Herrmann, *Walt Whitman*, 30, 255, 1.

Page 210, *"primacy of the Word"*: Bartlett, *Earth Poetry*, 187.

Page 210, *"The whole function of"*: Ibid., 189.

Page 210, *"searches inwards...which they can reveal"*: Fox, *Passion for Creation*, 65, 60, 65, 63, 62, 57, 58–59.

Page 211, *"Jesus clearly exercises shamanic...for their disciples"*: Bruce Chilton, *Rabbi Paul: An Intellectual Biography* (New York: Doubleday, 2004), 204.

Page 211, *"Christ was perhaps...very humbling thing"*: Herrmann, *William Everson*, 94, 98.

Page 212, *"very ancient shamanistic...suffering redeemer"*: Ibid., 103, 104.

Page 212, *Jesus addressed the...of poetic shamanism*: Ibid., 104, 105.

Page 212, *"The connection between Christ...shamanizing will cease"*: Ibid., 106, 107, 111, 115.

Page 213, *"can access alternative...otherwise are not met"*: Ruth-Inge Heinze, *Shamans of the 20th Century* (New York: Irvington, 1991), 13.

Page 213, *"abolishes the present human condition"*: Eliade, *Shamanism*, 99.

Page 213, *"Just as every created thing...speak about 'God'"*: Fox, *Passion for Creation*, 62, 77.

Page 214, *"Every real shaman has"*: A. Lommel, *The World of the Early Hunters* (London: Evelyn, Adams & Mackay, 1967), 60.

Page 214, *Herrmann speaks of the "lightning"*: Herrmann, *William Everson*, 121; Fox, *Passion for Creation*, 243.

Page 214, *"hidden something like"*: Fox, *Passion for Creation*, 373–74.

Page 214, *"to bring to life...much suffering"*: Brown, *Sacred Pipe*, xv.

Page 215, *"people will live for"*: Ibid., xvii.

Page 215, *"I saw that the sacred...form a great circle"*: John G. Neihardt, *Black Elk Speaks* (New York: Washington Square Press, 1959), 43, 164–65.

Page 215, *"being is a circle...spirit of the Lord"*: Fox, *Passion for Creation*, 84; Quint2, 2:711.

Page 215, *"Heaven runs constantly...placed in the heart."* Fox, *Passion for Creation*, 367, 368.

Page 216, *"understanding must be of the"*: Brown, *Sacred Pipe*, xx.

Page 216, *"The first peace, which is the most"*: Ibid., 115.

Page 216, *"Creator's aim when he created...repose in them"*: Fox, *Passion for Creation*, 380.

Page 216, *"The whole universe...our voice to* Wakan-Tanka*"*: Brown, *Sacred Pipe*, 25, 24, 25.

Page 217, *"Running through the stem"*: Ibid., 73.

Page 217, *"Long ago* Wakan-Tanka*"*: Ibid., 68.

Page 218, *"One of the standing people"*: Ibid., 69.

Page 218, *"brave dancer...people may live"*: Ibid., 94.

Page 218, *"As you know, the moon"*: Ibid., 71.

Page 219, *"especially sacred and important"*: Ibid., 69.

Page 219, *"The fire which is used...to Your powers"*: Ibid., 32, 33.

Page 219, *"The most sacred rite"*: Ibid., 43.

Page 220, *"one of the first symbols"*: Herrmann, *Walt Whitman*, 1.

Page 220, *"At that moment when"*: Joan Halifax, *Shamanic Voices: A Survey of Visionary Narratives* (New York: Arkana, 1979), 30.

12. Warriors for Ecological and Economic Justice: Meister Eckhart Meets Dorothy Stang, Karl Marx, David Korten, Serge Latouche, Anita Roddick, and Howard Thurman

Page 221, *"The person who understands"*: Quint2, 1:453.

Page 221, *"The old economy of greed"*: David Korten, Living Economies Forum Website: The Online Home of David Korten, http://livingeconomiesforum.org.

Page 221, *"Why not improve life"*: Anita Roddick, *Business as Unusual* (London: Thorsons, 2000), 117.

Page 221, *"Christianity as it was born"*: Howard Thurman, *Jesus and the Disinherited* (Richmond, IN: Friends United Press, 1981), 28.

Page 221, *"The person who understands…the same as justice"*: Quint2, 1:453, 3:588.

Page 222, *"We found 715 other planets"*: Tom Toles, cartoon, "Opinions," *Washington Post*, March 3, 2014.

Page 223, *a long and substantive Latin treatise…"to be compassionate"*: Fox, *Passion for Creation*, 420; for his treatise and my commentary, see 416–39.

Page 223, *"What is compassion is also…peace have kissed"*: Ibid., 435, 436.

Page 223, *"We read in Proverbs 21…own body and soul"*: Ibid., 421, 422, 423.

Page 224, *"We therefore are compassionate…'horse and mule' "*: Ibid., 424.

Page 224, *"Is that the sort of fast…in desert places"*: Ibid., 432.

Page 225, *"God's peace prompts…involved in one another"*: Ibid., 446.

Page 225, *"The just person is one who"*: Ibid., 464.

Page 226, *"For the just person as such"*: Ibid., 472.

Page 226, *"For all works are surely…and his works live"*: Ibid., 465, 464–65.

Page 226, *"The Father gives birth…alone you live"*: Ibid., 465, 466.

Page 227, *"God and justice are one"*: Quint, 104.

Page 227, *"In relation to the earth…international community"*: Berry, *Dream of the Earth*, 215, 218–19.

Page 228, *"the earth must not be injured"*: See Matthew Fox, "Hildegard as Eco-Warrior," in *Hildegard of Bingen: A Saint for Our Times* (Vancouver: Namaste Press, 2012), 33–44.

Page 228, *"are keeping her memory alive"*: Binka Le Breton, *The Greatest Gift: The Courageous Life and Martyrdom of Sister Dorothy Stang* (New York: Doubleday, 2007), 229.

Page 229, *a news story was published*: Jon Bowermaster, "Chilling Report: Earth Loses 300 Billion Tons of Ice Each Year," Take Part.com, July 16, 2013, http://www.takepart.com/article/2013/07/16/satellite-study-reports-greenland-and-antarctica-losing-300-billion-tons-ice-each.

Page 230, *"God is the denial"*: Quint, 160.

Page 230, *"It is time for the spiritual"*: Adam Bucko and Matthew Fox, *Occupy Spirituality: A Radical Vision for a New Generation* (Berkeley, CA: North Atlantic Books, 2013), xviii.

Page 230, *A 2013 bipartisan study conducted*: Salvatore Cardoni, "Young Voters on Climate Deniers: 'Ignorant, Out of Touch, Crazy,'" *Yahoo News*, July 26, 2013, http://news.yahoo.com/young-voters-climate-deniers-ignorant-touch-crazy-184303009.html.

Page 233, *"Jesus then went into the temple…out of the temples"*: Fox, *Passion for Creation*, 450–51.

Page 233, *"give them something…in the same way"*: Ibid., 451.

Page 233, *"God places himself with…with the same wisdom"*: Ibid., 453, 454, 455.

Page 234, *"boasts two kinds of slaves…need a new system"*: Bucko and Fox, *Occupy Spirituality*, xxvii.

Page 234, *"In the rupture of the ordinary…way anyone expects"*: Nathan Schneider, *Thank*

You, Anarchy: Notes from the Occupy Apocalypse (Berkeley, CA: University of California Press, 2013), 31, 42, 184.

Page 235, *"in Eckhart the heretical…apart from me"*: Matthew Fox, "Meister Eckhart and Karl Marx: The Mystic as Political Theologian," in Fox, *Wrestling with the Prophets,* 167, 176, 177, 178.

Page 236, *"How nobly humans are…ground of blessedness"*: Ibid., 179, 180, 181.

Page 237, *"One thing is certain"*: Ibid., 181. Italics mine.

Page 238, *"In the Wall Street economy…of the New Economy"*: David Korten, *Agenda for a New Economy: From Phantom Wealth to Real Wealth* (San Francisco: Berrett-Koehler, 2009), 32, 34.

Page 239, *"How is it that our nation"*: David Korten, "How to Liberate America," *Yes Magazine,* July 19, 2011, http://www.yesmagazine.org/blogs/david-korten/liberate -america. Unless otherwise noted, all quotes by David Korten in this section are from this article.

Page 240, *"global suicide economy…by a love of life"*: David Korten, "Economics for Life," *Yes Magazine,* September 30, 2002.

Page 241, *"The old economy of greed"*: Korten, Living Economics Forum Website.

Page 242, *"fundamentalist belief…and sustainable contraction"*: Serge Latouche, *Farewell to Growth* (Malden, MA: Polity Press, 2009), vii (note 1).

Page 242, *"Where are we going?…progressive totalitarianism"*: Ibid., 2, 3, 5, 9.

Page 243, *"anyone who believes that"*: Ibid., 16.

Page 243, *"Advertising makes us want…road to hell"*: Ibid., 17, 19, 22.

Page 243, Latouche endorses the *"slow food"*: Ibid., 45f.

Page 243, *Like David Korten, he endorses…"measures that are needed"*: Ibid., 49, 55, 56.

Page 244, *"resulted in corruption…them about development"*: Ibid., 60.

Page 244, *"Capitalist civilization is moving"*: Ibid., 65.

Page 245, *"Why does business have…in the majority world"*: Roddick, *Business as Unusual,* 117.

Page 246, *"Read the Universal Declaration of…around the world"*: Ibid., 116, 114.

Page 246, *"My vision, my hope…not private greed"*: Ibid., 26, 24, 25.

Page 247, *How like Eckhart this is*: I lay out a theology of work, based heavily on Eckhart's teaching, in my book *The Reinvention of Work: A New Vision of Livelihood for Our Time* (San Francisco: HarperSanFrancisco, 1994).

Page 247, *"Leaders in world business…but on family farms"*: Roddick, *Business as Unusual,* 14, 12.

Page 247, *"have no intention or desire…significant than money"*: Anita Roddick, *Body and Soul* (London: Vermillion, 1992), 255, 256.

Page 248, *"when they become…going green"*: Ibid., 253, 248.

Page 248, *"What Eckhart calls the 'uncreated'…is love"*: Howard Thurman, *Deep River and the Negro Spiritual Speaks of Life and Death* (Richmond, IN: Friends United Press, 1996), 52, 94.

Page 248, *"more importantly, God is the Creator"*: Howard Thurman, *The Creative Encounter* (Richmond, IN: Friends United Press, 1954), 29.

Page 249, *"The basic fact is that"*: Thurman, *Jesus and the Disinherited*, 28–29.

Page 249, *"became, through the intervening...the life-process itself"*: Ibid., 29, 50, 49.

Page 249, *"The individual must have a sense"*: Howard Thurman, *The Luminous Darkness* (Richmond, IN: Friends United Press, 1989), 94.

Page 249, *"human spirit [is] stripped to"*: Thurman, *Creative Encounter*, 152.

Page 249, *"the last barriers between"*: Fox, *Wrestling with the Prophets*, 153.

Page 250, *"is justice itself"*: Fox, *Passion for Creation*, 467.

Page 250, *"the closer one is to"*: Quint, 300.

13. Warriors for a Deeper Education: Meister Eckhart Meets YELLAWE, Theodore Richards, M.C. Richards, and Lily Yeh

Page 251, *"The schooling that we seek"*: M.C. Richards, *Imagine Inventing Yellow: New and Selected Poems* (Barrytown, NY: Station Hill, 1991), 129.

Page 251, *"People called inner-city North Philadelphia"*: Lily Yeh, *Awakening Creativity: Dandelion School Blossoms* (Oakland, CA: New Village Press, 2011), 21.

Page 251, *"Living offers the most noble"*: Fox, *Passion for Creation*, 479.

Page 251, *"not a theoretical doctrine"*: Ibid., 50.

Page 252, *"What is life?"*: Quint, 184.

Page 252, *more and more boys are getting*: Peg Tyre, *The Trouble with Boys: A Surprising Report Card on Our Sons, Their Problems at School, and What Parents and Educators Must Do* (New York: Three Rivers Press, 2008).

Page 253, *"If the idea of the universe be"*: Maria Montessori, *To Educate the Human Potential* (Oxford, England: Clio Press, 1989), 6.

Page 253, *Pulitzer Prize–winning author Ernest Becker*: Ernest Becker, *Beyond Alienation: A Philosophy of Education for the Crisis of Democracy* (New York: George Braziller, 1967), 62–86.

Page 254, *"raise those sparks hidden"*: Matt, *Essential Kabbalah*, 97.

Page 254, *"draw out the holy spark"*: Ibid., 151.

Page 254, *angels learn only by intuition*: Matthew Fox and Rupert Sheldrake, *The Physics of Angels: Exploring the Realm Where Science and Spirit Meet* (San Francisco, CA: HarperSanFrancisco, 1996), 82–85.

Page 255, *it also equates to the seventh chakra*: Matthew Fox, *Sins of the Spirit, Blessings of the Flesh: Lessons for Transforming Evil in Soul and Society* (New York: Harmony Books, 1999), 315–27.

Page 255, *"At the center of our being"*: Merton, *Conjectures of a Guilty Bystander*, 142.

Page 256, *A rebirth of ritual and ceremony is essential*: For a fine and practical guide to making ceremony from the Native American tradition, see Linda Neale, *The Power of Ceremony: Restoring the Sacred in Our Selves, Our Families, Our Communities* (Portland, OR: Eagle Spirit Press, 2011).

Page 257, *I also wrote a book describing*: Matthew Fox, *The A.W.E. Project: Reinventing Education, Reinventing the Human* (Kelowna, BC, Canada: CopperHouse, 2006).

Page 259, *With the Eastern categories*: I discuss using the chakras to develop an alternative language for ethics in Fox, *Sins of the Spirit*, 161–328.

Page 260, *"Human salvation lies...a destructive, force"*: Theodore Richards, *Creatively Maladjusted: The Wisdom Education Movement Manifesto* (Danvers, MA: Hiraeth Press, 2013), xx.

Page 260, *"Our school system, like pretty...are maladjusted"*: Ibid., xxi.

Page 260, *"first what is wrong...mere reform"*: Ibid., xxiv, xxv–xxvii, 1.

Page 261, *"the first and most important...labor and attention"*: Ibid., 19–20, 18.

Page 262, *"Because I was bright and had"*: M.C. Richards, *The Crossing Point: Selected Talks and Writings* (Middletown, CT: Wesleyan University Press, 1966), 140.

Page 262, *"duplicity, sneers, sarcasm, oneupmanship"*: Ibid., 156.

Page 263, *"They put the student through"*: Ibid., 104.

Page 263, *"I am interested in...as well as outwardly"*: M.C. Richards, *Toward Wholeness: Rudolf Steiner Education in America* (Middletown, CT: Wesleyan University Press, 1980), ix, x, xi, xii.

Page 264, *"Myths were regarded as fictions"*: Richards, *Crossing Point*, 143.

Page 265, *I published an essay on her book*: See "Deep Ecumenism, Ecojustice, and Art as Meditation," in Fox, *Wrestling with the Prophets*, 215–42.

Page 265, *"How does transformation...in an even grain"*: M.C. Richards, *Crossing Point*, 55.

Page 266, *"The purest example I know"*: Ibid., 207.

Page 266, *"when we are children...seasons and their festivals"*: Ibid., 63–64.

Page 267, *"to help the students"*: Richards, *Imagine Inventing Yellow*, xiv.

Page 267, *"The schooling that we seek"*: Ibid., 129.

Page 268, *"When I see brokenness, poverty, and"*: Yeh, *Awakening Creativity*, inside cover.

Page 269, *"They all began running...the will to start over"*: Ibid., 7.

Page 269, *"William Sloane Coffin said"*: Ibid.

Page 269, *"vital, joyful community...inspire learning"*: Ibid., 8.

Page 270, *"a strong urge to go home...my path of return"*: Ibid., 15, 18.

Page 270, *"People called inner-city North Philadelphia"*: Ibid., 21.

Page 271, *"Living offers the most noble"*: Fox, *Passion for Creation*, 479.

Page 271, *"The fallen / The criminal"*: Richards, *Crossing Point*, 205.

Page 271, *Many of the principles for*: See Acadamy for the Love of Learning, www.alove oflearning.org.

Conclusion: Where Might Eckhart Take Us?

Page 274, *"the danger...is that the logical"*: Griffiths, *Return to the Center*, 105.

Page 276, *"Even though you are designated"*: Matthew Fox, *The Coming of the Cosmic Christ* (San Francisco: HarperSanFrancisco, 1988), 241.

Page 277, *"God is on all paths"*: Walshe, *Meister Eckhart Sermons*, 3:147. I have altered the word from Walshe's "modes" to "paths" in the first phrase.

Page 279, *"justice is one's being...soup he needs"*: Fox, *Passion for Creation*, 472.

Page 281, *"There is no true science"*: William Hermanns, *Einstein and the Poet*, 108.

ABOUT THE AUTHOR

Matthew Fox was a member of the Dominican order for thirty-four years. He holds a doctorate (received summa cum laude) in the History and Theology of Spirituality from the Institut Catholique de Paris. Seeking to establish a pedagogy that was friendly to learning spirituality, he established the Institute in Culture and Creation Spirituality, which operated for seven years at Mundelein College in Chicago and twelve years at Holy Names College in Oakland, California. For ten of those years at Holy Names College, Cardinal Ratzinger (later Pope Benedict XVI), as the Catholic Church's chief inquisitor and head of the Congregation of Doctrine and Faith, tried to shut the program down. Ratzinger silenced Fox for one year in 1988 and forced him to step down as director. Three years later he expelled Fox from the order and the program was aborted. Rather than disband his amazing ecumenical faculty, Fox started the University of Creation Spirituality in Oakland, where he was president for nine years.

He is currently a visiting scholar with the Academy for the Love of Learning in Santa Fe, New Mexico. He is working with others to create a new educational experience for inner-city youth called YELLAWE (Youth and Elder Learning Laboratory for Ancestral Wisdom Education) and new ritual experiences through the Cosmic Mass (www.thecosmicmass.com). He lectures, teaches, writes, and serves as president of the nonprofit he created in 1984, Friends of Creation Spirituality. He is the author of thirty books and lives in Oakland, California. His website is www.matthewfox.org.